Feminine Feminists

Feminine Feminists

Cultural Practices in Italy

Giovanna Miceli Jeffries, editor

University of Minnesota Press
Minneapolis
London

Copyright 1994 by the Regents of the University of Minnesota

Grateful acknowledgment is made for permission to quote from the following publications: Rachel Guido de Vries, "Litany on the Equinox," *Sinister Wisdom* 41, *Il viaggio delle donne* (Summer/Fall 1990); Diane di Prima, "We are not alone . . . ," "You are the hills . . . ," and "that she is black . . . ," all published most recently in di Prima, *Pieces of a Song: Selected Poems* (San Francisco: City Lights, 1990); Marcia Falk, *The Song of Songs: A New Translation and Interpretation* (San Francisco: Harper, 1990); Maria Gillan, "Public School No. 18: Paterson, New Jersey," *Sinister Wisdom* 41, *Il viaggio delle donne* (Summer/Fall 1990); Diana Gravenites, "Shadow Sister," *Sinister Wisdom* 41, *Il viaggio delle donne* (Summer/Fall 1990); Carol Lazzaro-Weis, portions of chapters 1 and 6 of *From Margins to Mainstream: Feminism and Fictional Modes in Italian Women's Writing, 1968–1990* (Philadelphia: University of Pennsylvania Press, 1993); Denise Leto, "We Do the Best I Can," *Sinister Wisdom* 41, *Il viaggio delle donne* (Summer/Fall 1990); Rose Romano, "Vendetta," from *La Bella Figura: A Choice* (San Francisco: malafemmina press, 1993).

Every effort has been made to obtain permission to reproduce copyright material in this book. The publishers ask copyright holders to contact them if permission has inadvertently not been sought or if proper acknowledgment has not been made.

All rights reserved. No part of this publication may be reproduced, stored in a retrieval system, or transmitted, in any form or by any means, electronic, mechanical, photocopying, recording, or otherwise, without the prior written permission of the publisher.

Published by the University of Minnesota Press
111 Third Avenue South, Suite 290, Minneapolis, MN 55401
Printed in the United States of America on acid-free paper

Library of Congress Cataloging-in-Publication Data

Feminine feminists : cultural practices in Italy / Giovanna Miceli Jeffries, editor.
    p. cm.
Includes bibliographical references and index.
ISBN 0-8166-2477-1 (hc)
ISBN 0-8166-2479-8 (pb)
    1. Feminism–Italy. 2. Feminist theory–Italy. 3. Femininity (Philosophy) I. Miceli Jeffries, Giovanna.
HQ1642.F445   1994
305.42'0945–dc20   94-14631

The University of Minnesota is an
equal-opportunity educator and employer.

To Angelica, Carla, Francesca, and Tom

Contents

Acknowledgments   ix

Introduction   *Giovanna Miceli Jeffries*   xi

I. Registers of History

white and black madonnas: historical origins of femininity and feminism
Lucia Chiavola Birnbaum   3

Unseduced Mothers: Configurations of a Different Female Subject Transgressing Fascistized Femininity   *Robin Pickering-Iazzi*   16

The Transparent Woman: Reading Femininity within a Futurist Context
Graziella Parati   43

II. Reading Cultural Texts

Filial Discourses: Feminism and Femininity in Italian Women's Autobiography   *Maria Marotti*   65

Caring and Nurturing in Italian Women's Theory and Fiction: A Reappraisal   *Giovanna Miceli Jeffries*   87

"Cherchez la femme": The Case of Feminism and the "*Giallo*" in Italy
Carol Lazzaro-Weis   109

Contents

III. Fashion, Cinema, and Other Orders

Feminism in High Culture, Femininity in Popular Culture: Italy in the Nineties?   *Maurizio Viano*   135

The Novel, the Body, and Giorgio Armani: Rethinking National "Identity" in a Postnational World   *Beverly Allen*   153

Fashion as a Text: Talking about Femininity and Feminism
Eugenia Paulicelli   171

Filming Female "Autobiography": Maraini, Ferreri, and Piera's Own Story
Áine O'Healy   190

IV. Toward a Transcultural Dialogue

I Don't Know What You Mean by "Italian Feminist Thought." Is Anything Like That Possible?   *Serena Anderlini-D'Onofrio*   209

Between the United States and Italy: Critical Reflections on Diotima's Feminist/Feminine Ethics   *Renate Holub*   233

Contributors   261

Index   265

Acknowledgments

I wish to thank first of all the contributors to this volume who worked with patience, understanding, and faith and gave generously of their time and advice. Janaki Bakhle and Robert Mosimann of the University of Minnesota Press deserve our gratitude for their unsurpassed professionalism and competence. People and institutions helped with time and financial support. I am grateful to Dr. Anna Maria Lelli, director of the Istituto Italiano di Cultura in Chicago for making possible a grant to help meet costs. Paige Byam read and polished the manuscript in its first stage and gave guidance and expertise. My husband, Tom Jeffries, gave me unrelenting support throughout with his suggestions and his enthusiasm.

Giovanna Miceli Jeffries

Introduction

In the last few years, several book-length studies and collections of critical essays have introduced the American public to Italian women's voices: they are very valuable contributions to Italian women's literature and to the Italian women's movement and theoretical feminism.[1] The present collection differs from others to date in that it is neither primarily historical nor literary-critical, but rather ranges over a variety of discursive and theoretical topics and modes. It centers on how feminism and femininity are embedded in a broad spectrum of Italian cultural practices. By cultural practices we mean not only the practices of everyday life—which are sometimes understood as popular culture or material culture—but also the disciplines and forms of knowledge that order information, analyze it, reflect on social potentials, and delimit specific practices. In this broader sense, cultural practices constitute the arena in which theories are produced and tested against the multiple ways in which people organize their lives and endow them with meaning.

This volume contains essays exploring the dynamics of relations between feminism and femininity within the context of Italian studies and situated in Italian culture. The contributors to this volume all do research in Italian studies here in the United States. All are interested in the trajectories of Italian feminism; the essays reflect their involvement with various aspects of the extraordinarily heterogeneous Italian feminist movement. The essays also reflect the authors' specific critical interests in cinema, fashion, and cultural history, both past and present. Some essays address the issue of feminism and femininity in the popular culture of everyday life, while others examine the problem in the context of philosophical cul-

Introduction

ture, of ethics, or of national identity within a global culture. Some explore the issues with the conviction that performing "femininity," whether actualized in a woman's appearance or in her caring and nurturing practices, can be a culturally liberating project. Others problematize the liberatory aspect of such a performance, and still others call into question the presumed liberatory potential of ascribing to feminine rather than to feminist values.

I share Rita Felski's use of the term "feminine" or "femininity" as referring to "a set of ideological configurations, a cluster of nineteenth-century symbolic associations between the female gender and a specific, though often contradictory, range of psychological and cultural attributes" (1104). But in a descriptive and not pejorative or evaluative sense, femininity is cultural productions, and for this reason it is both women's culture and women's history. These categories are governed by socialization and biology, and they encompass a large range of expressions: an aesthetic of appearance and demeanor; a distinctive ethic of caring for and nurturing the physical and human environment; a defined configuration of the organization of the family. Feminism, by critically deconstructing women's history, enables women to valorize feminine cultural practices.

While feminist thought and feminine practices seem to share some basic attributes in all societies, they acquire their specificity in individual cultures. In Italy today, "femininity" is called *il femminile*, both a noun and an adjective, meaning what pertains to or is characteristic of the female gender. Italian feminism demystifies and regenerates a feminine culture in its theorization and praxis of the concept of difference. Feminist theoretical approaches in the late 1980s in Italy have mainly emphasized the politics and practices of "difference," specifically differences between women, rather than equality between women and men. One can take that also to mean that women's external appearance, with its emphasis on differentiating oneself from the other, might be understood as a strong endorsement of another kind of differentiation: as a "pleasurable assertion" (as Viano sees it in his essay in this volume), one that consists in a refusal to be like men. Such a refusal might express itself in a reappropriation of fashion and sex appeal in which women turn themselves into subjects rather than objects. Yet in a closer look at many contemporary Italian feminist theorists, many of whom are proponents of the most radical interpretations of sexual difference, it becomes clear that they are currently addressing feminism and femininity not in relation to daily cultural manifestations or practices, but rather in relation to larger philosophical, legal, and political questions.[2] It is possible today in Italy to see "feminine feminists," politically conscious women who explore ways of enhancing their femininity through an ironic distance that was not present in the past. That is, they act with a consciousness of being feminine for their own pleasure and out of a personal, subjective choice.[3] It is possible that the complex programs of sexualizing social relations and of promoting a radical alterity of and for women that have been expounded by Italian feminist theorists may be paralleled by the practitioners of "feminine feminists," of those who externalize or popularize, by way of their choice in fashion, their political and ethical belief in the need for differentiation. The subtext of all the essays included here—whether acknowledged or not—is the authors' perception of the complexity of the current state of Italian feminist thought and practice.

It should not surprise the readers that, given this understanding of cultural practices, Lucia Birnbaum and Renate Holub are among the contributors to this book. Birnbaum's research focuses on popular culture, what she calls "vernacular" culture, and Holub's research focuses on the most theoretical construction Italian feminism to this day has produced. Yet what both have in common are socially and sociologically informed research programs that seek to identify some of the structures—visible and invisible alike—underlying Italy's remarkably heterogeneous feminist culture.

As we know from the pioneering work on Italian feminism in English by Lucia Birnbaum and Renate Holub,[4] Italian feminists traditionally have operated by organizing themselves into collectives in various communities in some of the major Italian cities, around universities and women's bookstores, but also in small towns, where they are engaged in consciousness raising and activism. In what Holub has called the "third wave" of Italian feminism, starting in the middle 1980s, communities evolved out of the former collectives, with an agenda committed mainly to the elaboration of a rigorous feminist discourse that is expressed through a critique of Western philosophical traditions.[5] Of these communities, the most prominent and outspoken is Diotima, in Verona, which is composed of women philosophers. They have articulated and continue to elaborate and promote a philosophy of liberational practices based on the concept of sexual difference and a concomitant program of feminist/feminine ethics. Inspired by Luce Irigaray's positions, these Italian women philosophers postulate the establishment of a feminine order on symbolic and ethical levels. But they depart from their mentor in that they propose a feminist pragmatics based on a new, revolutionary, and yet traditional practice of *affidamento*, or entrust-

Introduction

ment, in which younger and inexperienced women entrust themselves to other, older, more powerful and influential women. These women mentors become the younger women's mediators to the outside world, thus allowing the establishment of a feminine order of thought and practice. By consciously and deliberately taking on what Teresa de Lauretis calls the "risk of essentialism," Diotima not only promotes a theory of sexual differentiation and separation (if not segregation) but, most important, activates a vertical hierarchy within the women's community. In this way, they produce a setting of double alterity (other from man and other from the other woman) where the potentiality of the feminine subject can express itself with its own language, culture, and ethical standards. Having achieved as a judicial principle a relative equality with men, Italian feminists are now striving for "difference," as an "existential principle" (N*on credere di avere dei diritti*, 30) where true social freedom can be won, for women's social freedom is determined by the degree to which the source and measure of women's social worth are defined within the context of their own sexed/gendered nature and therefore independently from their relationships with men (146).

It is not hard to imagine the array of reactions and subsequent reflections that the Diotima's positions have elicited among Italian feminists and the larger intellectual community. Teresa de Lauretis and Renate Holub are among the first in North America to elaborate meaningful critiques of the challenging paradoxes and radical views of Diotima's claims for social freedom.[6] Those claims, argues de Lauretis, "demand not vindication of the rights of women, no equal rights under the law, but only a full, political and personal accountability to women" ("The Essence of the Triangle," 26). This has to be seen, however, in the light of the same paradoxes and contradictions that reside in a woman and define her as "captive and absent in discourse, asserted and denied, negated and controlled" (26). In de Lauretis's reading of the Italian feminists' theory and practices of sexual difference, the difference they talk about "is not one culturally constructed from biology and imposed as gender," but rather "a difference in symbolization, a different production of reference and meaning out of a particular embodied knowledge" (27). More than an essentialist view of woman's difference, this concept of sexual difference appears to be a historically specific analysis of "the state of emergency in which feminists live" (27).

In order to understand the vivid reaction of many Italian feminists to Diotima's program, one must keep in mind some of the structures that sustain Italian feminism. Traditionally, feminists in Italy have operated under the umbrella of the former Italian Communist party (now called Partito Democratico di Sinistra). Today's raging debates on the politics of sexual difference are taking place among women activists, members of the party; between those such as Miriam Mafai and Rosanna Rossanda who are more concerned with a practical level and who work toward an emancipatory politics of equal rights and opportunities for women, and others such as Livia Turco who support the separatist philosophy of Diotima and go as far as to propose practices like keeping separate voting booths (blue and pink), and sexually segregated classrooms in school. To the old Communist guard such as Mafai and Rossanda (author of a "Carta delle donne"), the proponents of sexual difference are proof of practical failure resulting from an excess of theory (*Non credere di avere dei diritti*, 160). They argue that the practice of *affidamento*, with its diadic relationship pattern, is an operation that is limited and restricted to social relations, and therefore is elitist as well as potentially hierarchical, not really dealing with the masses, the economic and institutional issues. In addition, Diotima's theory and practices of sexual differences do not appeal to feminists who do not see in a separatist, self-fulfilling politics an ethical advantage for humanity at large. This attitude is at the basis of a feminist politics whose project is to change the social order by way of privileging and revalorizing typical traditional feminine practices, such as caring for and nurturing of the weaker and needier, selfless giving, and fighting against the use of violence. To this admittedly noble and morally desirable political project, Diotima's answer is that it is politically ineffectual and humanly mean, for it assumes that feminine difference depends on ethical contents and concerns. The political project embedded in the discourse of Diotima claims a different liberational goal and outlines a different ethical system: for women to recognize first of all that it is only in a visibly social and public rapport of disparity among women that they will acquire a clear sense of individual and social valorization. From this recognition, women will establish and operate in a symbolic order of social justice (164).

Italian women, and especially the leftists, are still far from being satisfied with economic and political gains; if some of them, like Livia Turco, propose a sexualization of the voting process itself through pink and blue voting booths, others are engaged in proposing legislation that will allow women more free time from work for the family, up to a maximum of seven years, with paid contributions and work security. Others ring an alarm bell at this last initiative, fearing the "danger of devaluating women's work outside the home," of reemphasizing the reproductive aspect of motherhood and therefore "abdicating the possibility of acceding to high-

Introduction

er social and political positions of power."[7] Parallel to these issues is the more personal one for women of how to (re)establish a tender relation with a man. Some feminists in Italy realize the necessity of enacting a calculated dependency in order to allow men to feel virile and to reassure them. These women know that beneath the perhaps authentic recognition and admiration the Italian man has for the independent and emancipated woman, he is in crisis, confused, still oscillating between the persistent illusion of being irresistible and the difficult adaptation to a new partnership role within the couple or the family. Rather than being contrary to feminist emancipation, this role-playing results from a recognition of sexual difference. Whereas women are now aware of their role and can actively choose it, before they were unconsciously playing it, out of fear or in order to conform to atavistic, unmediated behavioral roles. Now they recognize their strength and their impact in relationships with men and consciously choose to use their resources. Far from being politically innocent, these "neofeminine arts" are a conscious operation with strong political implications of nurturing and caring for the other's psychological well-being.[8]

It seems to me that the current divisions and debates among engaged Italian feminists provide a condition ripe for a revamped commitment to discourse and action. While Diotima's theorists insist on the necessity and obligation for women to reflect on their intellectual and philosophical potential and on the generation and practice of feminine discursive subjectivity, at the same time—as shocking and as paradoxical as it may seem—the critique of these positions from politically operative women's groups is bound to produce a stronger positionality, a more sustained input into social issues related to women, and a clearer sense of the necessity of keeping an informed, variable, and critical perspective.

In Part I, entitled "Registers of History," Chiavola Birnbaum's contribution deals with the ways in which "historical femininity"—namely, women's church-sanctioned inequality and submission—has been supplanted by a "feminist femininity." This difference, she argues, has been "carried into politics by autonomous women." Her position derives from the experience and exhaustive study that culminated in the writing of her book *Liberazione della donna*, in which is assiduously and enthusiastically analyzed and documented the centrality of woman's presence in Italian culture from pre-women's liberation to liberation and post-liberation. In her essay, Chiavola Birnbaum discusses this centrality through the sociology of religion and folkloristic traditions centered on the presence and worship of Madonnas, especially Black Madonnas. Her contribution to the understanding of the position and expression of Italian feminism is the fruit of her second large project—*Black Madonnas: feminism, religion, and politics*—from which her essay is drawn. She interprets the message of the Black Madonna as one of "difference," in that it attracts the unprivileged and marginalized and heightens their awareness of racism, sexism, inequality, instilling in them a resistance to patriarchal domination. Examining a vast range of historical materials, from ancient women's cultures to contemporary social symbols and issues, the author sees the Black Madonna as the key to a woman-centered moral power stirring the consciousness of Italians who strive for change and react with empathy to the unseen and unrepresented.

In the other two essays of Part I, feminist and feminine experiences in women's cultural production are viewed against the background of Fascism by one scholar (Robin Pickering-Iazzi) and against the background of Futurism by another (Graziella Parati). By sifting through a rich variety of women's productions under the Fascist regime, cultural productions such as writings and fashion, Pickering-Iazzi points to subtle ways in which women negotiated their opposition to dominant codes of femininity by soliciting, through fashion, a different female subject. According to her, this new female subject demanded new terms of identification subversive of Fascist ideology. In this sense, this author challenges the accepted view of female "consent" to the Fascist ideology of femininity. While recognizing the issue of women's consent to Fascist dictatorship, she also criticizes analyses that fail to consider "the complex processes of discursive address and reception" of women's literary and cultural productions of the time.

Graziella Parati, on the other hand, examines the seduction of women through images of femininity proposed in intellectual discourse. By transposing Gianni Vattimo's philosophical concept of "transparency" onto the Italian Futurist movement, the author detects the Futurists' attempts to construct a "transparent woman," one who would be totally penetrable and dominatable. Parati understands this Futurist practice as a way to order and unproblematize the condition of women and to solve the destabilizing "woman's problem." Parati documents how, within the "literary seduction and conversion of women" practiced by the anarchic agenda of Futurist men, Futurist women writers subvert, oppose (although within inner contradictions), and construct a more "opaque," complex model of femininity. These models claim physical and intellectual independence from Marinetti's "seduced" woman and aspire to a more abstract and symbolic presence for women in society, only to be eventually trapped in the contradictions of

Introduction

simultaneously negating male values and accepting men as models of virility and power.

In the second part of the volume, entitled "Reading Cultural Texts," Maria Marotti, Giovanna Miceli Jeffries, and Carol Lazzaro-Weis examine literary culture. Autobiographical texts of matrilineal and patrilineal discourse are selectively examined in Maria Marotti's essay. She maintains that the autobiographer's view of her relationship to both parents "shapes her position in society," as well as her own claims, negotiations, and culture of feminism and femininity. In Marotti's view, women's autobiographies display noncanonical forms, and she therefore situates such writings on an axis intersected by both fiction and autobiography, giving the genre a more liberating aspect and subversive potential. Because of this, Marotti considers the genre an "ideal locus" for the study of feminist discourse as it unfolds with the idea of femininity in the Italian culture. She observes that while in the Italian context of this century discourses of female emancipation look patrilineal—marked by desire to do and write like men, to escape maternal roles of female subordination—more contemporary female autobiographies tend toward a reappropriation of the female body and culture through matrilineal discourse. Essentialist positions and processes are explored in these autobiographies as women's ways of managing resistance and assertion in male-defined cultures. In the writings of some authors, femininity is seen as the opposite pole of feminism and is practiced as a way of surviving in certain sociopolitical and familial contexts.

My own essay in Part II explores representational modes of nurturing and caring in two Italian women writers. Keeping in perspective the works of Carol Gilligan in the field of women's psychology and ethics, I consider how contemporary Italian women writers establish a discourse of care and nurturing within a liberated, emancipated consciousness. Homemaking, "domestic science," are no longer passive feminine pursuits, contested or resisted, but rather active threads of the narrative fabric itself, in which the personal blends with the political and historical in such a way that the relationships with food and with the house become keys to understanding and repositioning oneself and others. On the theoretical level, the elaboration by Italian feminists of a practice of "entrustment," where a younger, inexperienced woman entrusts herself to an older, more influential one, revalidates the concept of care within a distinctive feminine ethics. Whether they are practicing motherhood or "entrustment" or providing food, women seem to reach out for empowerment while registering the contradictions and the ideological constructions of those same practices.

Introduction

A desire for justice and moral fairness together with an opportunity for narrative authority seems to be at the base of the growing interest among women writers in detective novels, contends Carol Lazzaro-Weis. A feminization of the genre, in the portrait of a more "tolerant, fallible detective," could radically change the form, as well as fulfill society's expectations of women as morally weak and emotional. In observing that Italian detective novels by women include feminist themes and ideas, exploiting generic conventions rather than reflecting femininization of the genre, the author aptly integrates in her discussion contemporary debates in Italy concerning the relationship of theories of sexual difference to social justice. Feminists' appropriation of the detective novel for the purpose of exposing injustice is, maintains Lazzaro-Weis, another "system of thought," which the genre seems to absorb into its tradition, thus allowing "more women writers to write their vision and criticism" while asking the questions that gender poses.

In Part III, "Fashion, Cinema, and Other Orders," Maurizio Viano, Beverly Allen, Eugenia Paulicelli, and Áine O'Healy examine feminist/feminine practices in women's private and public lives. Maurizio Viano's essay is written, as several of the other essays are, from a strong subject position that leads to a relentless process of inquiry into the manifestations and operative modes of femininity and feminism as they are consumed and reflected in popular culture productions and in theoretical productions, respectively, in today's Italy. His polarization of "high culture" and "popular culture" is symptomatic of the impasse and ambiguity that a cultural, political, and "gendered" reading is bound to provoke. Maurizio Viano's is the only male contribution to this volume, and his "male-gendered" critical reading of femininity and feminism is explicitly announced in his essay. Viano raises the issue of whether femininity and feminism are complementary and nondisassociable wherever women are actively operating and producing in society. He points to the risk of woman's objectification in her investment in appearance, while arguing as well against wholly negative feminist appraisals of neofemininity as too simplistic. In support of neofemininity, Viano notes that from a more popular point of view, and on the commonsense level, women are indeed making choices about their appearance and are therefore initiating a subjective public discourse through the manipulation of their femininity.

Beverly Allen's essay challenges clichéd readings of Armani's fashion (or fashion in general) in relation to women from a cultural studies perspective. That is, she suggests that the discourse of fashion be contextual-

Introduction

ized within its national setting, and in particular within the specificity of national identity. Her analysis of Armani's fashion goes along with that of the postnational novel as the author thinks about the contemporary valence of national "identity" and its relation to notions of femininity. A reading of Armani's cultural production of the 1970s, for instance, "bears a political valence based on a construction of femininity which is mostly legible when the national 'identity' of that production is kept in mind." In Allen's argument, fashion becomes a potential feminist discourse in that it encompasses and demystifies its reading as a gendered, feminine practice by grounding its discourse politically and ideologically. Women can then at least claim its bodily reality, enclosed in a parabolic movement between ideology, rhetoric, and referent.

On the other hand, the semiotic reading of fashion as language and image suggested by Eugenia Paulicelli focuses on the discourse of fashion as a rather broad and pervasive system operating in contemporary Italian society and society in general. In her analysis of fashion both as *factio* and *mode*, the author explores the communicative game we establish with reality and the complex and subtle interactions between images and text that we, as consumers and readers, process. Feminism as a political movement has empowered women to take control of their "looks," to politicize them by reacting to male-inspired and male-directed fashion. Paulicelli warns, however, that as information becomes more and more a spectacle through the manipulative operations of media, new modes and political slogans become clichés; therefore, transgressive fashion, appropriated by the fashion industry, becomes a dictate, a manifestation of unquestioned, uncritical social attitudes.

Áine O'Healy's essay is a feminist analysis of Mario Ferreri's film *Storia di Piera*, which O'Healy calls the first Italian film to interrogate and problematize issues of feminine identity and subjectivity. The singling out of this movie as the most challenging and problematic film rendition of women's issues is justified by the fact that its script is a collaboration between the feminist writer Dacia Maraini, the stage actress Piera degli Espositi, and the director Mario Ferreri, who is "variously perceived as a misogynist and as a male feminist." At the center of O'Healy's analysis is the complex interplay of feminine identity and subjectivity, represented in the movie through the gaze of a young girl who is coming of age within a triangular, Oedipal family scenario. The attraction and repulsion of her mother's femininity and active sexuality constitute the daughter's critique of the gendered construction of femininity. This critique culminates in the sacrifice of the mother's sexuality; it is pathologized and therefore punished (a process in which the daughter is accomplice). The daughter then acquires a displaced, specular identity through her theatrical career.

In the last part, "Toward a Transcultural Dialogue," Serena Anderlini-D'Onofrio's and Renate Holub's essays engage, from different positions and agendas, in a dialogue and critique of the encounter of Italian and American feminisms and theories. Anderlini-D'Onofrio's essay draws from her personal experience as an Italian feminist expatriate in the United States. She introduces a unique position, and an analysis of what "re-acculturation" means in a postmodern, multicultural society where a feminist, and especially an Italian feminist, still has to prove herself and act quickly to resist "commodification of action, learning, and position." Her argument is based on the reception and preconception of Italian feminist thought and practices in Anglo-American culture, including feminist culture. As a protagonist of active Italian feminism, the author details the situatedness of Italian feminism since its postwar inception, its dialectical relation with the former Italian Communist party, and its historical rejection of Fascist univocal identities. With one eye on American feminist discourse and the other on various articulations of Italian feminism, she suggests that Italian feminism has been able to indicate, in its "strategic essentialism," a possible "third way" in the oppositional logic on which dichotomies of culturalism and essentialism, multiculturalism and Eurocentrism, and liberalism and socialism are based.

Renate Holub's concluding essay enacts a transcultural feminist bridge between Italy and the United States. Her writing is informed by a strong penchant—almost a resolution—to position both the lack of and the sites of a feminist ethics. She centers her "reflections" on concepts of liberational practices and of a feminist/feminine ethics based on the notion of sexual differences espoused by the Italian community of women philosophers called Diotima. While introducing Diotima's practices, she develops a critical-comparative analysis of contemporary feminist theory and practice in the United States. Starting with a generous introductory discourse, she floods her essay with questions on the validity and feasibility of women's positions vis-à-vis a complex array of issues that are currently being debated among feminists and theorists of different currents of thought. In the debates and polarization of essentialists, antiessentialists, postmodernists, and proponents of sexual difference, Holub depicts the paradoxical absence of ethics, "in practices originally constructed upon a nonnegotiable discourse on ethics." She argues that, although Irigaray's inspiration

Introduction

informs the positions and politics of the Diotima community, a new problematic has been raised by the pragmatic urgency of realizing an ethical order in "concrete steps"—a set of new categories based on the concept of double alterity among women and the principle of *affidamento* (entrustment). The enactment of these two practices may lead women to the true acquisition of higher stages of liberation and freedom—that is, to an operating, not just a rhetorical, feminine symbolic.

As each essay of this volume attempts to analyze the interplay of both feminism and femininity within the Italian cultural context, the specific focus of the discussion and the area of analysis necessarily shifts the weight of the two. The fact that this volume brings forth the problematic of femininity in the discussion of feminism reflects the larger problem existing in feminism in general in dealing with the issue. It still takes courage, confidence, and a degree of risk for women and scholars to examine the component of femininity in a specific cultural context of women's experiences. Ironically, feminism is, in a way, a comfortable passport introducing women as agencies capable and ready to deconstruct femininity. This volume wishes to be a step ahead on the road to an enlightening and fruitful critique of women's cultural productions.

Notes

1. These volumes are *Liberazione della donna: Feminism in Italy*, by Lucia Chiavola Birnbaum; *Donna: Women in Italian Culture*, ed. Ada Testaferri; *Contemporary Italian Women Writers in Italy: A New Renaissance*, ed. Santo Aricò; "Women's Voices in Italian Literature," a special issue of *Annali d'Italianistica* 6 (1989), ed. Dino Cervigni and Rebecca West; Teresa de Lauretis, *Sexual Difference: A Theory of Social-Symbolic Practice*; *Italian Feminist Thought: A Reader*, ed. Paola Bono and Sandra Kemp; *Women and Italy: Essays on Gender, Culture and History*, ed. Zygmunt G. Baranski and Shirley W. Vinall.

2. In the works of the Diotima group of Verona—which are widely discussed in this volume—we find exemplified the extent, thoroughness, and engagement of Italian feminist thought with respect to every major discourse as it redefines and reexamines femininity in the making and interprets social reality. Of these works I wish to mention in particular Adriana Cavarero's *Nonostante Platone*, Luisa Muraro's *L'ordine simbolico della madre*, and DIOTIMA *Il pensiero della differenza sessuale*, now also in English translation.

3. Apropos here are the remarks of Susan Bassnett that the sight of "beautifully dressed Italian women, accompanied by men, sitting and discussing high-level theories of female consciousness" may look a bit suspicious, or "a betrayal of the earlier cries for alliance between women and workers as mutually oppressed social groups" (130). But, she argues, one also learns that "the image of the 'active feminist' is as much a male construct as any other image of women" (130). The point here, it seems to me, is that emancipated Italian women are expressing and living their feminist "core" along with the outer shell, and if one senses apparent contradictions and oscillations, these come with the territory. Women's femininity consciously played out or unconsciously released is bound to produce or diffuse erratic messages, regardless of how convinced we are of its social constructedness. It is part of the full

picture to see or perceive women both acting "feminine" and being feminists, living their femininity and regularly deconstructing it. It is perhaps, as Nancy Chodorow puts it, still unexplained "tenacious" behavior (in need of sound theoretical and psychological explanation) in a liberated social and personal environment that accounts for the interest and attraction liberated women feel for masculine (macho) men, and men for feminine, sexy women. Recent books such as Naomi Wolf's *The Beauty Myth* and *Fire with Fire*, Susan Faludi's *Backlash*, and Camille Paglia's *Sex, Art, and American Culture* are a further indication of how the discussions on feminism and femininity are in our present times at the center of many advanced cultural debates.

4. Lucia Chiavola Birnbaum is well known for the first book in English on current Italian feminism, which was nominated for many prizes. Renate Holub's feminist work in the context of Italian studies dates back to the late 1970s. While still a graduate student, she organized the first feminist Italian sessions at the MLA (1979/82). In the early 1980s she attempted to organize "Women in Italian," a group similar to organizations that already existed in French, Spanish, German, philosophy, and countless other disciplines. Her efforts failed, perhaps due to the indifference, disinterest, fear, or opportunism of established scholars and not-so-established scholars alike. Her essay "Towards a New Rationality? Notes on Feminism and Current Discursive Practices in Italy" appeared in 1982 in *Discourse: Berkeley Journal for Theoretical Studies in Media and Culture* (*Discourse* 4 [1982]: 89–107). As an associate editor of *Differentia: Review of Italian Thought*, she has consistently pursued a feminist course, which for her appears to be never only theoretical but also practical.

5. I am drawing here from Holub's article "Italian 'Difference Theory': A New Canon?" (forthcoming in *Re-writing the Canon*, ed. Maria Marotti).

6. De Lauretis's important essays on Italian feminist theory are "The Essence of the Triangle" and the introductory essay to her English translation of the book *Non credere di avere dei diritti* (Don't believe you have any rights). Holub's work on the Diotima group is "For the Record: The Non-language of Italian Feminist Philosophy" (*Romance Language Annual* 1 [1990]: 133–40). Her forthcoming work in book form is *The Feminist Challenge in Italy*.

7. These positions are reported in Maria Antonietta Macciocchi's new book, *La forza degli italiani* (The Italians' strength), in her interviews with many Italian women throughout the peninsula (p. 75).

8. This issue is well developed also in Macciocchi's chapter "Anna e le sue compagne. Ho visto le italiane tutte nuove" (pp. 69–79).

Works Cited

Aricò, Santo, ed. *Contemporary Italian Women Writers in Italy: A New Renaissance*. Amherst: University of Massachusetts Press, 1990.

Baransky, Zygmunt G., and Shirley W. Vinall, eds. *Women and Italy: Essays on Gender, Culture, and History*. New York: St. Martin's Press, 1991.

Bassnett, Susan. *Feminist Experiences: The Women's Movement in Four Cities*. London: Allen & Unwin, 1986.

Birnbaum, Lucia Chiavola. *Liberatione della donna: Feminism in Italy*. Middletown, Conn.: Wesleyan University Press, 1986.

Bono, Paola, and Sandra Kemp, eds. *Italian Feminist Thought: A Reader*. London: Basil Blackwell, 1991.

Cavarero, Adriana. *Nonostante Platone: Figure femminili nella filosofia antica*. Rome: Editori Uniti, 1990.

Collettivo della libreria delle donne di Milano. *Non credere di avere dei diritti: la generazione della libertà femminile nell'idea e nelle vicende di un gruppo di donne*. Turin: Rosenberg & Sellier, 1987.

DIOTIMA *Il Pensiero della differenza sessuale*. Milan: Tartaruga, 1987.

Introduction

de Lauretis, Teresa. "The Essence of the Triangle or Taking the Risk of Essentialism Seriously: Feminist Theory in Italy, the U.S., and Britain." *Differences* 1, 2 (1990): 3–37.
———, and Patricia Cicogna. "The Practice of Sexual Difference and Feminist Thought in Italy: An Introductory Essay." *Sexual Difference: A Theory of Social-Symbolic Practice*. Bloomington: Indiana University Press, 1990.
Faludi, Susan. *Backlash: The Undeclared War against American Women*. New York: Crown, 1991.
Felski, Rita. "The Counterdiscourse of the Feminine in Three Texts by Wilde, Huysmans, and Sacher-Masoch." PMLA 5 (1991): 1094–1105.
Holub, Renate. "The Politics of Diotima." *Differentia* 6 (1990): 161–72.
———. "Towards a New Rationality: Notes on Feminism and Current Discursive Practices in Italy." *Discourse* 4 (1981–82): 89–107.
———. "Weak Thought and Strong Ethics: The 'Postmodern' and Feminist Theory in Italy." *Annali d'Italianistica* 9 (1991): 124–41.
Macciocchi, Maria Antonietta. *La forza degli italiani*. Milan: Mondadori, 1990.
Muraro, Luisa. *L'Ordine simbolico della madre*. Rome: Editori Riuniti, 1991.
Paglia, Camille. *Sex, Art, and American Culture*. New York: Vintage, 1992.
Testaferri, Ada, ed. *Donna: Women in Italian Culture*. Toronto: University of Toronto Press, 1989.
Wolf, Naomi. *The Beauty Myth: How Images of Beauty Are Used against Women*. New York: William Morrow, 1991.
———. *Fire with Fire: The New Female Power and How It Will Change the 21st Century*. New York: Random House, 1993.

Part I
Registers of History

Lucia Chiavola Birnbaum

white and black madonnas
historical origins of femininity and feminism

Antecedents of femininity, for Italian and Italian American women, may be Eve and white madonnas of the Roman catholic church. Antecedents of feminism may be *la gran dea Mediterranea* and black madonnas of Italian vernacular culture. My working definition of feminism is women who express the values of the goddess and black madonnas: justice, equality with difference, nurturance of all life, and transformation (Birnbaum, B*lack Madonnas*).

Eve and the obedient, sorrowful, white madonnas of papal catholicism are major symbols sustaining patriarchy. Upholding church doctrine that defines women as sinful and subordinate to men, the negative implications of these symbols, and their influence on subsequent conservative political theory, have been analyzed, notably by Marina Warner and Elaine Pagels (Warner, A*lone of All Her Sex*; Pagels, A*dam, Eve, and the Serpent*). My task in this essay is to suggest primordial and vernacular sources of feminist values.

Indisputable archeological evidence of the existence of the civilization of the goddess of Old Europe has been uncovered by Marija Gimbutas, who states, "The goddess-centered religion existed for a very long time, much longer than the Indo-European and the Christian . . . leaving an indelible imprint on the Western psyche" (*Language of the Goddess*, p. xvii). The ancient goddess who personified the earth and stages of life (birth to maturity to death and regeneration) and the implacable justice of the sequence of

---

Note: *This essay follows contemporary Italian usage in removing capitals from words connoting hegemony.*

Lucia Chiavola Birnbaum

seasons had different names and images, but her civilization, when men, women, and all creatures lived in harmony with each other and with the earth, is verified in Italy by archeological evidence all along the Ligurian, Tyrrhenian, Aegean, Adriatic, and Mediterranean seacoasts, pervasively in the Mezzogiorno south of Rome and dramatically on the Mediterranean islands of Sicily, Sardinia, and Malta (Gimbutas, *Language of the Goddess*).

Although subsequent male-dominant cultures attempted to suppress the belief, traces of the goddess may be found in Hebrew and christian scriptures: in the black woman of the Song of Songs, in Sophia of the Wisdom literature, and in the apocryphal gospels (Elisabeth S. Fiorenza, *In Memory of* Her; Elaine Pagels, *Gnostic Gospels*). In the christian era the worship of the goddess, as I have documented in B*lack Madonnas*, persevered in veneration of black madonnas of vernacular cultures.

Varying in shades of dark earth, what all black madonnas of Italy share is location on or near evidence of the civilization of the goddess, the popular perception that they are black, and the belief that black madonnas side with the poor and the miserable—beliefs suggesting a unique liberation theology (Birnbaum, B*lack Madonnas*, chaps. 7–9).

The memory of the prechristian goddess has persisted in everyday rituals of peasant women, folklore, and festivals, as well as in pilgrimages to black madonnas. The goddess, whom Apuleius in the second century C.E. described as a nurturing mother who saw to food, fostered love between the sexes and the continuance of life, warded off evil, gladdened the earth, and succored those in need (Apuleius, *Golden Ass*), was remembered in long centuries of Italian peasant culture in the figures of *comari, mammane, sante, streghe, fattuchieri, riputatrici*, and *sibille* (Birnbaum, B*lack Madonnas*, chap. 3). *Comari*, or godmothers, were women bonded together in Maria to help one another. *Mammane*, or midwives, presided over birth and abortion. *Sante*, or saints (of whom the first was Maria), were protectors and helpers. *Streghe*, or witches, were integral to village society. In the modern age males in authority feared and murdered them, but in millennia of peasant history, witches were considered similar to healers, women in magical touch with nature. *Riputatrici*, or *prefiche*, were mourners who presided over death and regeneration. *Sibille*, or sibyls, according to a contemporary Italian feminist, were "all our grandmothers," transmitting in their lives, songs, rituals, and stories the remembrance and vision of a peaceful communal society (Birnbaum, B*lack Madonnas*, chap. 10).

In Italy, paleolithic and neolithic sites of the goddess are located on or near sanctuaries of black madonnas in areas that historically resonated

white and black madonnas

in heresy and that today are characterized by radically democratic cultural and political beliefs. In Apulia, for example, evidence of the communal culture of the goddess can be viewed near a sanctuary of L'Incoronata, "black madonna of the poor," in an area of peasant communism. Here, after each world war of the twentieth century, Italian women with babies, statues of their madonnas, and communist banners occupied the land. Here, the last week of April, people go in pilgrimage to the black madonna and then participate on May first in communist celebrations. Today, *comunità di base* of Apulia, looking to their black madonnas, work for nonviolent transformation of Italy and extend a hand to poor countries of the east and the south of the globe (Birnbaum, B*lack Madonnas*, chap. 8).

The new democratic communist party of Italy, Partito democratico della sinistra, grounded in vernacular beliefs (Birnbaum, B*lack Madonnas*, chaps. 1 and 10), has chosen for its logo the international socialist hammer and sickle, placed on the roots of a leafy oak tree—evoking the image of the black madonna of the poor, L'Incoronata, near Foggia, depicted for a thousand years in an oak tree (Birnbaum, B*lack Madonnas*, chap. 7).

A subterranean tradition with a woman at the center seems to run like a deep stream throughout Italian history and culture (Birnbaum, L*iberazione della donna*). The stream sometimes rises; after 1968 it became the flood of Italian feminism that placed impressive women's legislation into the Italian code. The centrality of a woman in Italian culture has been suggested by Robert Bellah, an American sociologist of religion, who considers this woman "only uncertainly articulated" with the church image of Mary of Nazareth (90–94).

In 1880 Verga described in L*a lupa* traits of the goddess as they appeared in autonomous peasant women who controlled their own sexuality: "As in a remembrance from long ago, he stopped cultivating the vines in fertile green fields and went to remove the axe from the elm tree." La Lupa, "pale and staring," not lowering her eyes, went to meet him "with her hands full of red poppies, her black eyes seeming to devour him. Nanni gasped, 'Oh cursed be your soul!'" (9).

Carlo Levi, confined in the south of Italy during world war II, and not blinkered by christianity, suggested the continuum from the goddess to black madonnas: "The black madonna among the grain and the animals was not the passive Mother of God, but a subterranean divinity, black as the shadows of the womb of the earth, a peasant Persephone, an infernal goddess of the harvest."

Leonard Moss, a U.S. soldier wandering around Apulia at the end of world war II, found a black madonna at Lucera and was reminded of the black woman of the Song of Songs of Hebrew scriptures. He verified the connection in the inscription at the bottom of the black madonna of Tindari, and spent the rest of his life studying her.

Marcia Falk's translation of the Song of Songs captures the connection:

> Yes, I am black! and radiant—
> O city women watching me—-
> As black as Kedar's goathair tents
> Or Solomon's fine tapestries.
> The Song of Songs, poem 2

For some contemporary feminists, the black woman of the Song of Songs suggests Lilith, the disobedient first wife of Adam, who would not be beneath him physically or spiritually. For others the Song recalls the primordial mother who sustained all life; Falk has pointed out that the Song is the only book of love poetry in the bible (Falk, Song of Songs, p. xiii).

The centrality of a woman in the unconscious of Italians is suggested in the favorite exclamation of southerners: Bedda Matri!, beautiful mother, whom they contrast, in their stories, with the *"egoista"* mother of Saint Peter. The dark earth colors of black madonnas recall the goddess worshiped as the earth; the pubic triangle of paleolithic and neolithic scratchings became in the christian era the triangular figure of black madonnas fusing mother and child. The identification of the primordial mother with the "other" is suggested in the triangle the nazis forced Jews to wear, and in the pubic triangle feminists of the late twentieth century used to identify themselves with witches.

The goddess is remembered in Italian folk stories, sometimes lightly disguised as the female figure of Giustizia (justice) who considerably resembles the *"forti"* mothers of Italy. In Giufà stories, perhaps a metaphor for the vernacular theology of Italians, the mother has a clown son with a Moslem name, a son whose life the mother "almost completely determines." She sends her child to do her errands in the world, subverting patriarchy (Birnbaum, Black Madonnas, chaps. 3, 4).

Radically egalitarian and as different as sisters, black madonnas of Italy are believed to have the power to effect miracles, a belief the church has often tried to dispel by "retouching" black madonnas to make them white. Even when she is painted white, however, people refer to her as the "madonna nera."

The dark madonna in the church of Santa Maria in Trastevere, built in the Jewish community of Rome in the first centuries of christianity, has been identified with the black woman of the Song of Songs. The very "black madonna of the staring eyes," in a sanctuary built in the fifth century C.E. at Siponto, reminds the observer of the sharp decline in the role of women in the early christian era: the many dimensions of the goddess were reduced to those of the obedient mother of Jesus, whom church fathers left out of the trinity. The grim face of La Sipontina suggests a woman spurned (Birnbaum, Black Madonnas, chaps. 2, 8, 9).

At her national shrine at Loreto, the black madonna and her son are enclosed in a *casa* that suggests the indwelling feminine presence of god, the shekhina of vernacular Jewish tradition. On the facade of the *casa* are ten sibyl prophetesses standing before ten Jewish prophets. The art of this significant marian sanctuary suggests that the prophetic tradition of justice originated in prechristian prophetesses who were succeeded by Judeo-christian prophets. In this prophetic tradition, Mary and Jesus are enclosed in the house of her "everyday life." It was this house of Mary's everyday life that, according to legend, was carried by angels in the thirteenth century from Nazareth to Loreto (Birnbaum, Black Madonnas, chap. 7). And it is these peaceful values of women's everyday life that are looked to today by Italy's large nonviolence movement (Azione Nonviolenta) to transform Italy.

In southern Italy, the black madonna of the poor of Seminara is near Crotone, where prechristian women Pythagorean philosophers taught the value of "harmonia," and near the place that San Giovanni in Fiore in the thirteenth century preached the heresy that the ages of the father and of the son would be succeeded by the age of the holy ghost (Crocco, *Gioacchino da Fiore*). Subsequently, women heretics identified the holy ghost with a woman (Muraro, *Guglielma e Maifreda*).

In the north, the black madonna of Oropa is situated in an area where Waldensian heretics (several centuries before the protestant reformation) suggested that the salvation of the people did not require the intercession of the church, believed women could preach, and founded a sanctuary for the poor on this site of a black madonna (Birnbaum, Black Madonnas, p. 134).

Outside Naples, the sanctuary of the grey madonna dell'Arco is in a region with abundant evidence of the civilization of the goddess. Historically this region abounded with stories of witches and with heresies. After the Council of Trent the church may have thought to control this volatile environment by establishing a marian sanctuary that attracts passionate pilgrims (Birnbaum, B*lack* M*adonnas*, chap. 8).

Vernacular beliefs cannot easily be extirpated by the church; one ex-voto drawing in the sanctuary of the madonna dell'Arco has a black madonna watching church inquisitors torture a woman heretic. In the nearby sanctuary of Montevergine at Avellino, the church-retouched Mamma Schiavona, great black slave mother, is adjoined by a folk art exhibit depicting the story of mother and child in its many cultural interpretations, including prechristian images (Birnbaum, B*lack* M*adonnas*, chap. 8).

At Trapani, the easter week procession of the beautiful black madonna of the workers takes place at the foot of Mount Erice, where sailors from time immemorial brought wine and offerings to Isis (goddess of the Egyptians in Africa), Cybele (goddess of Asians of Anatolia), Diana of Ephesus (also of Anatolia), Astarte (goddess of the Phoenician/Canaanites who settled in Africa), Aphrodite (goddess of the Greeks), and Venus (goddess of the Romans). Every summer Italians set doves in flight for Africa from there. The ritual may enact a genetic memory of the first major migrations of humans—out of Africa and Asia (Louise Levathes, "A Geneticist Maps").

At Livorno, the church-retouched black madonna of Montenero is located outside the city where the Italian communist party was founded, and where base communities today work in liberation politics in solidarity with decolonization movements throught the world. At Foggia and elsewhere, a hidden black madonna in the *duomo* suggests the invisible church.

Black madonnas of Italy may embody women's perennial resistance to the subordinate role of women in the catholic church and other patriarchal institutions. For the snake *festa* in May at Cocullo, women bake *ciambelle*, bread in the form of a snake in a circle, remembering the primordial goddess as regeneratrix and Circe, a siren whose site is nearby. Before men bring the snakes into the church and before saint Domenic (to whom the church gave the power to sedate snakes and to heal snakebite) emerges, a procession of women in folk costume takes the lead in the ritual. With an ancient sense of self, women of Cocullo put large triangles (pubic symbol of the goddess) on their heads, to which they have attached circle breads (recalling Demeter and Circe), and precede the men going into, and out of, the church (Birnbaum, B*lack* M*adonnas*, 56–57).

The pagan woman divinity symbolized the earth's nurturance of all life. As the Roman goddess Diana who originated in Anatolia, she can be viewed today at Tivoli outside Rome, her many breasts nurturing human babies, small animals, bees, and pomegranates. As the precursor of black madonnas, she may be seen in the seven-foot black Diana in the Museo Nazionale at Naples. As the folk figure Giustizia in Italian stories, she led, in a seventeenth-century procession, twelve equal human tribes.

The values of the goddess were historically transmitted in pilgrimages to black madonnas and by peasant mothers singing domestic ballads whose messages were subversive of patriarchy. The lives, stories, and songs of "all our grandmothers," for Joyce Lussu, "remembered a future" of a world "without bosses and without wars" (Lussu, "La sibilla appenninica," 221–39).

The laughter of the goddess infiltrated all peasant holidays. In carnival satire of the pretensions of patriarchy, Sicilian peasants of the nineteenth century shouted, "A carnilivari, tutti semu aguali!" (at carnival, we are all equal!) (Birnbaum, Black Madonnas. chap. 6).

Italy today is a culture and nation in rapid spiral to the third millennium. Since 1968 Italian women have been taking their moral power, transmitted for two thousand years in rituals and folk stories, into the political arena. The strength of Italian feminists is apparent not only in the impressive legislation they have placed in the Italian code (Birnbaum, Liberazione) but in their transformation of Italian communism in the 1980s into a party aligned with nonviolence, in which religious beliefs take priority over politics. In the l990s the Partito democratico della sinistra rings with notes of the women's movement, and with the secession from patriarchy of men of the new left into movements for nonviolence and protection of the earth.

In 1990, transition has been accelerated by a nonviolent revolutionary movement of Italian university students. Students of *novanta* (the nineties) differ from their antecedents of 1968, whose revolutionary hope turned, in the 1970s, into violence. The uprising of the students of *novanta* has been nurtured by stories of grandmothers, activities of feminist mothers, and the model of fathers seceding from patriarchy.

Choosing the black panther as a symbol for resistance throughout Italy, students declare "La pantera siamo noi," recalling the feline that walked alongside Cybele, the feline that was the familiar of Isis, and the feline that is the symbol of the Black Panther movement of the United States. Aiming for the transformation of Italy, students have occupied all major universities, demonstrated against U.S. imperialist killing in the Persian Gulf, and settled into a long siege of resistance. The resistance is marked in l993 by the use of the symbol *Bocca della verità* (the mouth of truth), located on a site occupied by a prechristian woman divinity and later by a black madonna, to inspire what appears to be a nonviolent revolution. The Italian peaceful revolution has proceeded by uncovering corruption in high places and by indictment not only of right-wing and centrist political leaders but also of socialist leaders (such as Bettino Craxi) whose socialism is considered equivocal (Birnbaum, B*lack Madonnas*, chap. 11).

Students of *novanta*, said Stefania (a protesting student), want "a free and democratic university, a critical and wise culture, a society without manipulative managers, corrupters, exploiters," a genuinely democratic university open to everybody and dedicated to authentic culture, as well as a university in solidarity with the suppressed of the world. Describing themselves as antifascist, democratic, and nonviolent, students of *novanta* want to reach "the collective unconscious of millions of persons who do not recognize themselves in this democracy" (*La Pantera Siamo Noi*).

In the enterprise of reaching the collective unconscious of Italians, students are joining the feminist effort to recover women's history and culture and to deconstruct the patriarchate. Franca Bimbi, closely studying the transformation of Italian women's identity since 1945, recently found that in Italy patriarchy founded on religion has become "a privilege without legitimation" (Birnbaum, B*lack Madonnas*, 180).

In the glimpse of the third millennium offered by contemporary Italy, women's historical difference may be the significant shard of light, a difference defined and carried into politics by autonomous women and marking the difference of feminism from historic femininity. Historically, popes and bishops have defined the meaning of Maria, and of women's femininity, as *pazienza*, or patience in the face of suffering. *Pazienza*, or inactivity, is what the patriarchate enjoins not only on women but on all of the poor peoples of the earth.

Italian feminists have been engaged in furthering a nonviolent revolution aiming for cultural and political transformation, whose signs are visible in politics (where women are strategically placed in all Italian political parties) as well as in women's art and literature. The sculpture of Alba Gonzales uses African marble in recreating earth mothers of Asia Minor and Etruscan harmonious couples. Dacia Maraini has been rescuing the values of the ancient goddess, and of black madonnas, in drama and stories tracking the hidden history and culture of everyday, deviant, and mute women (Dacia Maraini, *La lunga vita*).

Signs of transformation are also apparent in men's writings. The central figure of the implicit theology of the novelist Gesualdo Bufalino (who lives in Sicily on the slopes of the Iblaean mountains named for the goddess, and near the sanctuary of the miracle-working madonna of Chiaramonte Gulfi) is a crucified pagan/Jewish woman (Gesualdo Bufalino, *The Plague Sower*).

Translating cultural revolution into political power, contemporary Italian women are determining Italian politics with networks that cross parties. In positions of leadership in the new Partito della sinistra they aim for the "democracy of socialism." For Livia Turco, major leader of the PDS, communism in a postmodern age means transformation, with recognition of the value of each of the seasons of life (Birnbaum, *Black Madonnas*, 192).

The values of the goddess and of black madonnas were carried by grandmothers to the United States where the legacy is visible in the contemporary blossoming of creativity among Italian American women writers. Cultural and political implications of this literature for a multicultural United States are conveyed by Maria Gillan, who addresses her WASP teachers:

> Remember me, ladies
> the silent one? I have found my voice
> and my rage will blow
> your house down.
> ("Public School No. 18")

Denise Leto remembers

> these matriarchs [who] could throw
> power into words with staggering aim
> though we never knew who won
> next day grandma
> would make peanut butter & jelly sandwiches
> gripping the knife with a fierceness
> that belied the task
> she would pull the sliced bread apart
> with distaste
> Bread, this?
> ("We Do the Best I Can")

Frances Tramontana Patchett remembers that her "grandma was a woman of faith, but she was not religious. The Catholic rituals were important to her, but I never had the impression that she paid much attention to

Lucia Chiavola Birnbaum

priests" (Frances T. Patchett, "Francesca Ranieri Tramontana"). Lorraine Macchello recovers women's values of everyday life in "The Dowry" and "Peppina." Rose Romano,

> Whose grandmother had a statue of
> the Virgin Mary, Blessed Mother, Madonna,
> Goddess on her dresser, a votive candle
> before it and a crocheted scarf
> under its feet?
> . . . whose grandmother worshipped
> before an altar to honor the Goddess,
> looking into the mirror at her own
> reflection, herself an aspect
> of the Goddess, as she tied her hair
> tight at the back of her neck?
> ("Vendetta")

Rachel Guido de Vries writes a "Litany on the Equinox":

> The Earth is my mother
> she maketh me in her image
> I shall always want
> her voice wind thru trees
> in fall rush of waves
> at midnight or dawn
> the earth dark as the lover
> I dream of on the eye
> of the equinox big breasted
> woman, mountains rosy tipped
> as sunrise above the hills . . .
> ("Litany on the Equinox")

Diana Gravenites celebrates

> Shadow Sister . . . that disowned part of myself:
> the dark side,
> the earth,
> the snake,
> the female,

> the unbound female
> ("Shadow Sister")

Perhaps the spiral of the goddess/black madonnas/Italian/Italian American women is most dramatically visible in the poetry and politics of Diane di Prima. In the 1960s student revolutionaries read her poetry:

> we are not alone: we have brothers in all the hills
> we have sisters in the jungles and in the ozarks
> we even have brothers on the frozen tundra
> they sit by their fires, they sing, they gather arms
> they multiply: they will reclaim the earth.
> (*Pieces of a Song*)

In her Loba series, di Prima invokes "lost moon sisters" on Bleeker and Fillmore streets:

> you are the hills, the shape and color of mesa
> you are the tent, the lodge of skins, the hogan
> the buffalo robes, the quilt, the knitted afghan
> you are the cauldron and the evening star
> you rise over the sea, you ride the dark.

Di Prima deepens the *chiaroscuri* of this essay. She considers it a "lie" to say of la Loba

> that she is black, that she is white
> that you always know who she is
> when she appears.

And

> that there is anything to say of her
> which is not truth.
> (*Pieces of a Song*)

I think of my Italian American mother's fierce love of her children and her rage against injustice, my sister's nurturance of animals and humans. I remember that the festa of Santa Lucia, for whom I was named, marks the winter solstice (December 13 in the Julian calendar). Traces of the goddess, as Pamela Berger has documented, persisted in traits of saints (*The Goddess*

Lucia Chiavola Birnbaum

14 Obscured). In christian hagiography, the stark incised eyes of the paleolithic and neolithic goddess were reduced to the eyes of Lucia, the virgin martyr of Syracuse who plucked out her eyes, in the church version of the story, to keep her virginity. In vernacular culture, witches remembered Lucia as the pagan Sabine mother goddess of light, Juno Lucina, who protected against *mal'occhio*, and opened the eyes of newborn babies.

Today uncounted numbers of Italian and Italian American women are carriers, not always consciously, of the values of the goddess and the meaning of black madonnas—feminists challenging injustice, beginning with gender injustice, working to save the earth and all life.

Works Cited

Azione Nonviolenta: Satyagraha. rivista mensile del Movimento Nonviolento. Perugia.

Bellah, Robert. "The Five Religions of Modern Italy." In Robert Bellah and Philip E. Hammond, *Varieties of Civil Religion*. San Francisco: Harper & Row, 1980.

Berger, Pamela. *The Goddess Obscured: The Transformation of the Grain Protectress from Goddess to Saint*. Boston: Beacon Press, 1985.

Birnbaum, Lucia Chiavola. *Black Madonnas: Feminism, Religion & Politics in Italy*. Boston: Northeastern University Press, 1993.

———. *Liberazione della donna: Feminism in Italy*. Middletown, Conn.: Wesleyan University Press, 1986, 1988.

Bufalino, Gesualdo. *The Plague Sower*. Hygiene, Colo.: Eridanos Press, 1988.

Crocco, Antonio. *Gioacchino da Fiore e il gioachismo*. 2d ed. Naples: Liguori Editore, 1976.

de Vries, Rachel Guido. "Litany on the Equinox (poem)," in *Sinister Wisdom* 41, *Il viaggio delle donne* (Summer/Fall 1990).

di Prima, Diane. *Pieces of a Song*. San Francisco: City Lights Books, 1990.

Falk, Marcia. *The Song of Songs: A New Translation and Interpretation*. San Francisco: Harper, 1990.

Fiorenza, Elisabeth Schussler. *In Memory of Her: A Feminist Theological Reconstruction of Christian Origins*. New York: Crossroad, 1983.

Gillan, Maria. "Public School No. 18: Paterson, New Jersey," in *Sinister wisdom* 41, *Il viaggio delle donne* (Summer/Fall 1990).

Gimbutas, Marija. *The Language of the Goddess*. San Francisco: Harper & Row, 1989.

Gravenites, Diana. "Shadow Sister (poem)," in *Sinister Wisdom* 41, *Il viaggio della donne* (Summer/Fall 1990).

Leto, Denise. "We Do the Best I Can: A Series of Portraits (poem)," in *Sinister Wisdom* 41, *Il viaggio della donne* (Summer/Fall 1990).

Levathes, Louise. "A Geneticist Maps Ancient Migrations," in the section Science Times, *New York Times* (July 27, 1993).

Levi, Carlo. *Cristo si è fermato a Eboli*. Milan: Mondadori, 1945.

Macchello, Lorraine. "The Dowry," in *Journal of the Institute for Research on Women and Gender* 16. 1.

———. "Peppina," unpublished.

Lussu, Joyce. "La sibilla appenninica." In STORIE. Bologna: Il lavoro editoriale, 1986. 221–39.

Maraini, Dacia. *La Lunga Vita di Marianna Ucria*. Milan: Rizzoli, 1990, Premio Campiello, 1990.

———. *Viaggiando con passo di volpe: Poesie 1983–1991*. Milan: Rizzoli, 1991.

La Pantera Siamo Noi: I Cronache, immagini, documenti e storie dell'occupazione universitarie del '90, ed. Marco Capitello. Rome: Instant Books, C.I.D.S., 1990.

Pagels, Elaine. *Adam, Eve, and the Serpent*. New York: Random House, 1988.
Patchett, Frances Tramontana. "Francesca Ranieri Tramontana: 1887–1963 (narrative)." *Sinister Wisdom* 41, *Il viaggio delle donne* (Summer/Fall 1990).
Romano, Rose. *La Bella Figura: A Choice*. San Francisco: malafemmina press, 1993.
Verga, Giuseppe. "La Lupa," *Tutte le novelle*. Milan: Arnaldo Mondadori, 1942, 1975.
Warner, Marina. *Alone of All Her Sex: The Myth and the Cult of the Virgin Mary*. New York: Wallaby Pocket Books, 1976.

Robin Pickering-Iazzi

Unseduced Mothers
Configurations of a Different Female Subject Transgressing Fascistized Femininity

> A *given socio-historical moment is never homogeneous; on the contrary, it is rich in contradictions. It acquires a "personality" and is a "moment" of development in that a certain fundamental activity of life prevails over others and represents a historical "peak": but this presupposes a hierarchy, a contrast, a struggle. The person who represents this prevailing activity, this historical "peak", should represent the given moment; but how should one who represents the other activities and elements be judged? Are not these also representative?*
> Antonio Gramsci, Cultural Writings (93–94)

Recent historiographic studies on the forms of culture and society in the Fascist state have broadened the parameters of debate beyond the terms of "consent" and "resistance"—with corollary revisions in the areas and methods of inquiry—thus formulating a more complex notion of gendered social subjects and their relations to discourse. Such works as *Fascism in Popular Memory* by Luisa Passerini, *Rethinking Italian Fascism* edited by David Forgacs, *La nuova italiana* (The new Italian woman) by Elisabetta Mondello, and *How Fascism Ruled Women* by Victoria De Grazia have contributed to this direction in critical thought, and enabled more diversified analyses of subjectivities and discursive mechanisms designed to construct the sites and means of their engagement in society during Fascism. With few exceptions, however, literary scholarship, particularly when speaking of women's writing produced in the years of Fascism, has tended to rely upon traditional cultural studies, which worked through "consent" as the primary interpretative category.[1] Thus conventional representations of this period within the tradition of

Italian women's literature generally conceive of women as objects of repression forced into resigned silence, or as objects of ideological seduction coerced into reproducing the patriarchal ideology of femininity emblematized by the image of the Woman-Mother. I propose that this notion derives more from the interpretative framework used than from women's discourses and how they may have figured in the broader dynamic of culture and society. My concern in the opening section of this essay is therefore to work through some of the problems a critical model developed to interrogate female "consent" poses for examining women as speaking subjects in the Fascist regime. At the same time, I posit methods of inquiry that enable us to see different discourses on femininity by mapping the interchanges and contradictions between women's cultural production in life and literature and Fascist discourses intended to reconstruct female self-concept in the image of the supreme Wife and Mother. By delineating the configurations of a different female subject, transgressing the dominant ideology of femininity, I intend to make possible more articulated readings of the modes of self-representation, narrative practices, and systems of address women writers elaborated during Fascism, and how they may have engaged women among the reading public.

Though recent scholarship in the United States and abroad has made significant progress in the reconstruction of the tradition of Italian women's writing, thereby inviting revisionary readings, relatively few studies have endeavored to examine women in the Fascist regime as writing and reading subjects. Recent years have seen growing critical interest in Italian romance literature, which experienced a boom among women readers in the 1920s and 1930s, but a book-length study examining the broad range of women's literary achievements during this period in poetry, the novel, and the short story has yet to be written. The reasons this subject has been marginalized in literary commentary stem from complex problems—periodization, canon formation, and unfamiliarity with both the rich variety of women's literature produced during the dictatorship and its modes of publication—not the least of which is an ongoing reliance on historical accounts concentrating on issues of female "consent" to the regime. This trend has forestalled a consideration of women as producers of social meaning through their own practices of writing and reading. Maria Antonietta Macciocchi's study *La donna "nera": "Consenso" femminile e fascismo* (The woman in "black": Female "consent" and Fascism) represents the most authoritative historical analysis of women elaborated upon the critical model of "consent." Though published in 1976, Macciocchi's work continues to exert substantial influence on how literary commentators think about women writing during the dictatorship and their relation to the ideology of femininity disseminated by the Fascist regime.[2] Macciocchi's analysis does merit attention for what it reveals about the construction of Woman in Fascist ideology and the systems of address used in attempts to reinstitute the traditionally defined female gender role. I wish to argue, however, that the method of examination used in *La donna "nera"* prevents us from seeing the different, if not oppositional, discourses articulated by women in Italian culture and society during Fascism.

Macciocchi's project is admittedly ambitious: "I finally relocate women in collective society," she states, "making them revolutionary agent subjects whom everyone, the right and left complicitous, has ended up negating. Only by starting from the negation and by studying it, I negate the negation of the negation and arrive at the dialectic: *women are the ones who make history*" (22). The intent of this undertaking and the interpretative model stand at cross-purposes, however; Macciocchi proposes to make Italian women subjects in the history of the dictatorship by examining discursive and material mechanisms through which Mussolini "seduced" women into investing their desire in Fascism. Such an articulation of the problem, along with the method of analysis—using a psychoanalytic model relying upon Freud's notion of the death impulse—locks women into a symbolic system of meaning in which they are representable only in relation to man as object of desire.

Though never fully theorized by Freud, the notion of the death impulse, along with the related themes of sexual repression, self-sacrifice, passivity, and masochism—components frequently identified with culturally constructed femininity—provide the vocabulary with which Macciocchi intends to clarify how Fascism was ostensibly able to deflate female opposition, and to coerce women into submission. Thus she argues:

> From its inception, Fascism aimed at an acceptance, which I have defined as masochistic, on the part of women: an acceptance of every "torture," and of a kind of "death impulse" (Freud) celebrated with the everlasting rite of those killed in battle and widows exalting their chastity-sacrifice. . . . From this renunciation of life is born woman's self-negating joy: it is the "joy" of the relation between woman and power: renunciation, subordination, domestic slavery, in exchange for the abstract, verbose, demagogic love of the Leader, the Duce, the greatly virile Fascist clown. (38)

As accurate as Macciocchi's reading of the process designed to fascistize femininity may be, it does not elucidate how this ideology may have been transformed by female subjects, who had achieved increasing degrees of socioeconomic mobility, into daily practices and behaviors. Rather, the author's essentialist theorization of a mass female psychology, aligned with the work of Helene Deutsch and Marie Bonaparte, reproduces the notion that masochistic tendencies constitute a determinant element structuring the female relation to self, sexuality, and social interaction, an idea that had lost currency in psychoanalytic thought by the late 1960s. Anticipating female masochism as a means to solicit the female subject, Fascist discourses addressing a female audience operated according to the formula "power-joy-sacrifice = joy in sacrifice," and shaped, Macciocchi tells us, women's relation to power in the state. Thus, she concludes, Mussolini's appeals for female self-sacrifice elicited women's voluntary surrender, performed with "masochistic joy," enabling the Duce to "'enchant,' 'mystify' and 'possess' millions of women," seducing them into the prescribed role of Wife and Mother (34). Within this phallic economy, the compensation for female self-effacement consisted of the symbolic love conferred by Mussolini, "the Male par excellence, the Husband of all women, or the lover of each woman," as well as the Father of the children they would give for their country (41).

Yet I question whether this is an account of female subjectivity, or an instance of the Fascist body politic's self-representation. One could hardly dispute the claim that Mussolini displayed himself as the model for all Italian males, virile in love and war, or that the notion of self-sacrificial motherhood occupied a central position in Fascist ideology. Perhaps in no other period has Woman been so politicized, institutionalized, and publicized. For some twenty years state discourses constructed images of the Woman-Mother, the stock-in-trade of the regime's communications apparatuses, a highly self-conscious "technology of gender" whose business was to reconstitute gender roles along the patriarchal model, in order to strengthen a sex-gender system undermined by the sociocultural and economic changes of modernity. Inextricably equating femininity with motherhood, the figure of the Woman-Mother dominates prescriptive discourses as a trope meant to align women with a politics of demographics, claiming for the maternal institution the fulfillment of female desire, nature, and social mission. But it would be unwise to assume that the image of Woman in prescriptive documents describes the aspirations, pursuits, and notion of self of historical women in the Fascist state.

Here, what concerns me about Macciocchi's study, and others that work through the category of consent, is the tendency to give insufficient attention to the complex processes of discursive address and reception, and thus the other responses the monochromatic representation of Woman may have elicited in modern Italian women representing a broad spectrum of class, ideological, and geographic differences. In other words, she collapses the distinction between discursive mechanisms—here, seeking to engineer conformity with the Woman-Mother ideal—and female subjectivity. In her essay "Semiotics and Experience," Teresa de Lauretis elaborates a conceptual framework for examining the potential functions of externally produced representations and experience in the construction of subjectivity, demonstrating how this ongoing process is "the effect of that interaction—which I call experience; and thus is produced not by external ideas, values, or material causes, but by one's personal, subjective, engagement in the practices, discourses, and institutions that lend significance (value, meaning, and affect) to the events of the world" (*Alice Doesn't*, 159). Privileging the power of language over experience in the process of constituting subjectivity, Macciocchi excludes from her examination the components of experience, which de Lauretis defines as a "complex of meaning, effects, habits, dispositions, associations, and perceptions resulting from the semiotic interaction of self and outer world" (*Technologies of Gender*, 18). Thus, if we are to examine the positions women assumed in relation to the model of femininity publicized by the regime as well as to other cultural images of the feminine, it is necessary to expand the field of inquiry to the practices and discourses that engaged female subjects.

I do not intend to diminish the ongoing importance of questions about why women, or other marginalized social groups, may accommodate (tacitly or otherwise) political powers that operate against their interests. Because historical accounts interrogating "consent" to Fascism in Italy generally focus on dominant sociopolitical systems of address and representation while construing social subjects as passively constructed consumers, they have produced limitations in our perception of the discursive field and how women figured in it as not only objects but also subjects of discourse. This critical approach tells much about repressive official structures, but it tells little about how women perceived, thought, or spoke themselves during Fascism. As argued by Michel de Certeau, such "elucidation of the apparatus by itself has the disadvantage of *not seeing* practices which are heterogeneous to it and which it represses or thinks it represses" (*The Practice of Everyday Life*, 41). The theoretical framework developed by de Certeau to examine the sites and means of "oppositional" activities that normative forces seek to suppress or redirect toward their own interests has promising applications for examining the complex subject of women's authorship of the 1920s and 1930s. Three premises elaborated by de Certeau have particular pertinence for the present study, enabling the reconstruction of a different female subject, resisting the Fascistization of femininity in Italian life and culture of the interwar years. First, de Certeau restores the fundamental distinction between the originary production/dissemination of representations (performed by institutions of power) and "secondary" or "consumer production" (consisting of the ways "cultural users" utilize those representations in daily life). Second, he conceives of social subjects as agents whose everyday practices (of work, study, reading, and self-presentation in Italy of the 1920s and 1930s, for instance) constitute means of social activity and cultural production. Finally, de Certeau valorizes instances of popular cultural production as potential sites of resistance to dominant ideas, values, or ideals. The resultant critical paradigm has significant implications for examining women as producers of social meaning during Fascism, when official political structures and discourses negated them as such. Broadening the area of investigation to encompass the different imbricating spheres of cultural production (official, high, and popular) enables us to consider how women may have appropriated their femininity through practices, behaviors, and attitudes marked "masculine" in the Fascist division of culture and society, thus articulating different forms of female subjectivity. Such a project makes possible a more complex notion of the shifting locations of female subjects within the discursive field. It also provides an overdue critical framework for reassessing the context and terms of female address, self-representation, and identification in women's literary production of the 1920s and 1930s.

By way of foregrounding the arguments I advance in the following sections of this essay, I would like to refer briefly to Elisabetta Mondello's recent study *La nuova italiana* (The new Italian woman), a history of the women's press during Fascism that offers a suggestive profile of practices of reading and writing in this area of cultural production. Though Mondello's project is primarily one of documenting contradictions between the official model of Woman prescribed in Fascist discourses and different social and cultural female models delineated in the women's press, the critical importance of this work for literary studies should not be underestimated. For one thing, Mondello's archival research dispels the notion of women as passive consumers reproducing the dominant ideology of femininity, and thus creates a space for a different perspective. Assessing the significance

Robin Pickering-Iazzi

of her study for the process of reconstituting women in the regime as historical subjects, Mondello maintains:

> In years like those of the Fascist regime when the socialization of the private, elevated as the keystone for the construction of the Fascist state, represented the most powerful instrument used in addressing women, mapping a gap between cultural models supported by women's periodicals and the Fascist stereotype of the "exemplary wife and mother" must dispel the most commonly held vision of the role women actually filled in that period. (9)

Even more important, as Patrice Petro has persuasively argued, the women's press—through its explicit solicitation of female readers—lends itself to the critical examination of the terms of female address, identity, and sexuality.

Mondello excludes from examination clandestine women's publications affiliated with parties of opposition, as well as magazines published in Paris for Italian female readers in the 1930s (*Voce della donna*—Woman's voice—and *Noi donne*—We women). She concentrates instead on women's publications that, as part of media institutions, would come under the scrutiny of government authorities "regulating" cultural production, and thus would be expected to reproduce the staples of Fascist propaganda and promote such "female" virtues as motherhood, self-sacrifice, and obedience. What Mondello finds, however, is a multichromatic female mass culture rich with ideological autonomy, innovation, and alternative models valorizing women's intellectual, social, and creative production.

For the purpose of reconstituting women as reading subjects, the prefatory statements in women's publications, delineating the audiences they address and their intent, form a noteworthy reference. They testify to different terms of female identity—evinced by women's practices, concerns, interests, and tastes—that conventional postwar commentary has repressed by concentrating on prescriptive representations of femininity in Fascist discourses. Thus in 1922, the magazine *Almanacco della donna* (Women's almanac, published in Florence) stated that it would address progressive housewives, professionals, and "women who have neither the time nor means to dedicate themselves to their homes" (in Mondello, 58). Its purpose was to inform and educate its readers about women's organizations, cultural, social, and political achievements, as well as specific professional pursuits of women journalists, writers, playwrights, painters, and sculptors. Sharing many similar topical concerns was *Rassegna femminile italiana* (Women's Italian review, published in Rome), directed by Elisa Majer

Rizzioli, a recognized supporter of Mussolini. Though *Rassegna femminile italiana* was originally founded as a publication for members of the Fascist women's organization, it represents a means of women's cultural production whose self-management (the staff was made up almost exclusively of female editors, journalists, critics, and contributors) stands in striking contrast to the image of female identity manufactured by the regime. This may have contributed to Mussolini's decision to suspend production of the magazine, which did later resume, albeit with a more subdued tone. The weekly *Il Giornale della donna* (The woman's magazine, published in Rome) addressed women working in small industry. Though this publication became an organ of the *Fasci femminili* in 1929, it publicized a suggestive program in 1930—and reconfirmed it in 1934 and 1935—promising its readers "very interesting columns on professional schools and schools for home economics, on small industry and handcrafted goods production, articles on literature and the arts, on the home, work, and fashion. It treats all issues that concern women and their work, social services, child welfare, women's spiritual and cultural elevation" (in Mondello, 209 n.9). Finally, the changing publishing policies of the Catholic magazine *Fiamma viva* (The bright flame) merit attention for what they say about the tastes of women readers and their power to influence dominant channels of discourse in the directions of their own interests. This magazine maintained a longstanding opposition to romance literature (a position shared by Fascist exponents) on the premise that such fiction instilled a hedonistic notion of love divested of maternal ideals. Such literature thus provided visions of female sexuality and desire negated by the Fascist model of femininity. Yet *Fiamma viva* changed its policy, and began publishing stories of love and adventure in response to the requests of Catholic women readers. As stated in a letter one woman wrote to the magazine in 1921, "The greatest error we Catholics and our publications make is to be afraid of speaking about love.... Why, for example, couldn't a periodical be published with the title '*Love*'?" (in Mondello, 123).[3]

Mondello's historical account of the women's press reveals much about a different female subject in Italian culture and society, raising complex issues concerning the extent to which women belonging to the middle classes and social elite, and assumed to be supportive of Fascist endeavors, responded to the attempted institutionalization of female thought, emotion, and action. Where gender identity is concerned, women's practices of reading would suggest a sustained engagement in representations of women's modernity that address women's social, economic, and cultural issues. In response to the female readership's tastes and interests, women's magazines dedicated substantial space to women's literary production, which relentlessly encroached upon this male preserve of intellectual and creative synthesis; they published bibliographical information, book reviews, and fiction by such writers as Grazia Deledda, winner of the Nobel Prize for literature in 1926, Ada Negri, Gianna Manzini, Maria Luisa Astaldi, and Clarice Tartufari, regardless of their political orientation. A survey conducted in 1923 by *Almanacco della donna* asking readers to choose the ten most illustrious Italian women of their times gives an indication of the immense popularity and admiration women writers generated (*La nuova italiana*, 180). Despite scant reader participation (perhaps the reluctance to respond to surveys is not culture-bound), the results, reflecting answers submitted by some 200 of the magazine's 17,000 readers, are significant for the kinds of women who were chosen and the order in which they were ranked: Ada Negri, Grazia Deledda, Eleonora Duse, Matilde Serao, Annie Vivanti, Queen Elena, Térésah, the Duchess Elena of Aosta, Francesca Bertini, Teresa Labriola. Barring members of the royal family, these female figures (as well as others who did not make the final listing, for example the lawyer Lydia Pöet and Sibilla Aleramo, author of the first Italian feminist novel, A *Woman*, published in 1906) were recognized as much for their progressive, emancipated thinking as for their cultural achievements. The scope of Mondello's study does not permit an extensive analysis of the fiction renowned and popular women writers contributed to the women's press. Yet, as I intend to demonstrate in the final section of this essay, the thematics and textual practices elaborated in women's fiction, which had unprecedented popularity among readers of the 1920s and 1930s, solicit a different female subject by creating new terms of identification in their representations of nontraditional gender roles.

> *Let's not digress into a discussion of whether woman is perhaps superior or inferior; let's affirm that she is different.*
> Benito Mussolini (1925)

In order to avoid reproducing the binary opposition between female and male culture that Fascist ideologues wished to impose upon Italian cultural production prior to and during the Fascist dictatorship, this section of my essay maps contradictions between women's practices in everyday life and the prescriptive and descriptive drifts in hegemonic discourses of the 1920s and 1930s. These contradictions articulate the configurations of a female subject whose difference has been repressed. First, however, I would like to make a different but related point that establishes a new perspective from which to assess the function of gender politics during the dictatorship. It must be stressed that in Italy the institutionalization of gender difference in anthropology, sociology, and medicine does not represent an innovation attributable to Fascist ideologues, though its politicization in mass media possibly does. As demonstrated by Piero Meldini in *Sposa e madre esemplare* (The exemplary wife and mother), the notion of femininity in Fascist ideology owes a profound debt to the positivist anthropology of the 1800s, whose formulation of a "scientific" justification for female oppression roughly coincides with the participation of increasing numbers of women in the economic, social, political, and cultural dimensions of Italian life.[4] In such texts as *La donna delinquente, la prostituta e la donna normale* (The criminal woman, the prostitute and the normal woman, 1893) by Lombroso and Ferrero, biologistic theory, structuring discourses on the female organism in the sciences, privileges reproductive organs as *the* determining component of the female; they compromise woman's development, as demonstrated by her inferiority in all valences: intellectual, moral, emotional, physical, psychological, and sexual (because nonphallic). Postulating a causal relationship between female biology and development, Enrico Ferri, an expert in criminal sociology, states:

> I have Darwinistically explained that (inferior sexual sensitivity) in woman is due to the great, miraculous maternal function which, in order to sustain the life of the species, depletes so much of woman's strength, and condemns her to a lower level of biological evolution, between that of a young boy and an adult with regard to physiognomy, voice, and muscular strength, as in psychology. (Meldini, 30)

Extending the scientific definition of Woman, inclusive of "natural" and thus normative behaviors, to the sociocultural scene, turn-of-the-century social commentators in Italy supported a politics of gender designed to contain female desires exceeding the boundaries established to maintain patriarchal relations of power.

At the same time, however, women's practices in Italian life and culture suggest ways women appropriated their femininity. In her article "Aridità sentimentale" (Emotional aridity), published in the Turin daily *La Stampa* (July 11, 1911), Amalia Guglielminetti strongly critiques the scientific method for the assumption that it can articulate a woman's subjectivity simply by analyzing her material body: "Gynecologists and psychiatrists who have dissected women's bodies, listened to their heartbeat, and measured their craniums can not reveal their intimate essence." Rather, she argues, women, particularly writing women, have the right and responsibility to strip away any falsity, any male-designed trappings of femininity, and to write their experience of femaleness in the first person, producing "a document of extraordinary truth." Correspondingly, at the level of everyday life, women deflected the restraints on their socioeconomic activity advanced by the culturally constructed notion of Woman as only Mother. Numbers of women from impoverished rural areas moved to find work in rice or tobacco fields, or in machine, woolen, and cotton factories (the expanding clothing industry, as Lucia Birnbaum notes, provided many forms of employment for women), while women of the middle class occupied positions in the business sector as bookkeepers, typists, and secretaries. Women increasingly broke into the fields of teaching, journalism, and literary production. Within the broader Italian socioeconomic context, demographic shifts, as well as the intensifying militancy among proletarian, lower-middle-class, and intellectual working women, changed the dynamics of sexual relations, undermining male authority in the interrelated domestic and social spheres.

Not surprisingly, political discourses produced prior to Mussolini's establishment of the regime indicate the different ways women and men experienced this process of change (accelerated by World War I), the overriding male response being discontent with the ambiguity of gender identities. The writings of Filippo Tommaso Marinetti, founder of the Italian Futurist movement, help to explicate the complex intersection of cultural, economic, political, psychological, and gender issues. Cinzia Blum's rereading of Marinetti reveals the contradictions inherent in his representations of woman:[5] while he ostensibly calls for a cultural revolution that would radically change the institutions of marriage and family, gaps in his discourse inscribe deepening anxiety over already destabilized gender identities. In Marinetti's piece "Contro il matrimonio" (Against marriage, 1919), the ideological and psychological drifts of his argument collide while creating a vivid picture of female social mobility and male identity in crisis. The extensive participation of women in the work market, according to Marinetti, has created a "matrimonial grotesque":

> Due to her job, the wife necessarily leads a life that has little to do with running the household, whereas the husband, since he's out of a job, devotes all of his energies to an absurd preoccupation with keeping the house in order.

A complete family reversal in which the husband has become a useless woman with overbearing male manners and the wife has doubled her human and social value.

An inevitable clash between two partners, conflict, and male defeat. (368, translation mine)

This passage highlights the connection between a male position marked by a jealous defense of traditional gender roles and the presence of a different female subject who transgresses these roles and thus escapes male control. Hence the predominance of the Woman-Mother image in hegemonic discourses of the 1920s and 1930s, implemented to reestablish gender boundaries in the Fascist state, may be ascribed at the psychological level not to female masochistic tendencies but to male anxiety manifested in the absence of the object of desire. Thus the persistent adoption in the male discourse on Woman of such terms as re-institute, re-construct, re-establish, re-animate, re-instate, and re-valorize must be considered responses to the experience of loss and/or unfulfilled desire and the anxiety generated by this experience: only in discourse can the male subject conjure the reappearance of the Woman-Mother.

Meldini's collection of articles, published primarily in Fascist journals, to which I referred at the beginning of this section, demonstrates that throughout the years of the dictatorship the representations of the female constructed in sociology, medicine, history, theology, and economics equate the feminine with motherhood. In this context it is important to emphasize that the term motherhood refers to biological reproduction (giving birth to a child, preferably a son) as well as to the symbolic "mothering" of husbands, sons, fathers, and brothers. In an uncanny way, the Fascist discourse on the Woman-Mother thus coincides with Freud's story of femininity, in which "a marriage is not made secure until the wife has succeeded in making her husband her child as well and in acting as a mother to him" ("Femininity," 112–35). While these male-authored discourses tell the contemporary reader much about male desire, they also inscribe the presence of a female subject whose resistance to the ideal of the Woman-Mother generates male anxiety. The correlation between male desire and anxiety is exemplified in the 1930 article "Donne e culle" (Women and cradles), by the Fascist writer and social critic Manlio Pompei. Mapping the trajectory of male desire, Pompei claims:

Nothing ties us men more and nothing pleases us more than the woman-mother, the woman statuesquely personifying that need for intimacy, attentiveness, and peace which is the inevitable object of our every battle and our every labour, she who in her acting goodness reminds us of our mother's face, she who thus makes an inseparable union of our past and future, where memories of yesterday and hopes for tomorrow meet, uniting in the warmth of a single devoted caress.[6]

But the desired object is lost. As Pompei apprehensively observes, this kind of woman, a deeply religious woman, has disappeared, thereby disrupting his vision of historical continuity. In contrast, the modern woman

> is in a hurry to live and therefore heedlessly guards the treasures of her femininity; she makes man fearful of taking the step to unite himself with her for the rest of his life . . . and due to her extraordinary needs she constitutes an element of disorder and disorientation in families. (182–83)

Though Pompei's article, among others written for journals and newspapers by such diverse Fascist ideologues as Ferdinando Loffredo, Giuseppe Bottai, and Giuseppe De Libero, has the intent of gendering female experience, it registers modern women's opposition to the male ideal of "absolute femininity," which woman may achieve, according to Julius Evola, writing in 1934, only by "giving herself entirely to another . . . whether he is the man she loves or her child . . . thereby finding the meaning of her own life, her joy, her reason for being" (231). As hegemonic discourses inscribe the contradictory relation of Italian women to Woman, in an endeavor to redirect women to their "natural" function, so they paradoxically circulate representations of a new culturally articulated femininity, creating different possibilities for female identification with practices that the mechanisms of control seek to repress.

Among the most frequently censured expressions of modern female identity that transgress the Fascist ideology of the feminine are women's pursuit of education, employment, and such leisure activities as moviegoing, reading romance novels, and dancing, as well as their tastes in fashion. The author of the 1933 article "Compiti della donna" (Woman's duties), while arguing that the Fascist woman must undergo a spiritual evolution to develop a sense of self-sacrifice in order to fulfill her social and political mission as mother, supports his position with an account describing how education figures in modern women's aspirations:

> In the space of little more than thirty years, women have invaded middle schools, then high schools and universities, and today they form a clear majori-

ty in some majors; they have a monopoly in some programs of professional study; correspondingly, they are working, the majority of them obtain employment, and they practice a profession. (214)

Now, it is true that females outnumbered males in elementary and middle schools; only limited numbers of women, however, had gained access to higher education. In fact women accounted for only 13 percent of university students in the 1926–27 academic year, and 15 percent in that of 1935–36.[7] By 1942, female enrollments in Italian universities had undergone a notable increase, reaching 29.9 percent according to Alexander De Grand in "Women under Italian Fascism" (960).

Perhaps more important are women's own ways of speaking about their educational ambitions. In a 1930 article published in the *Giornale della donna*, a female student—countering the argument that feminism was responsible for Italy's declining birthrate—states:

> According to us feminism does not even enter into the desire of women to educate themselves, to better themselves, to act independently. If possibly it is a consequence, it is not a cause of such desires. It is born when the necessity arises to defend and further women's work which has been discouraged and denigrated only because it is done by women. (De Grand, 963)

Testimonies from female adolescents raise further doubts regarding the effectiveness of Fascist discursive and material apparatuses intended to reconstruct women's self-concept on the model of patriarchal femininity. Professor Spolverini, the director of an Italian pediatric clinic, reports in 1938 that the foremost desire of young girls, as expressed to their doctors, is not to have a husband and children, but to get an education and practice an intellectual profession (teaching at a high school, college, or university), or to have a well-paying position, so that "they can be self-sufficient . . . and lead an intellectually and economically independent life" (Meldini, 263). Similarly, the attitudes of one thousand Roman schoolgirls between the ages of sixteen and eighteen expressed in interviews conducted by Maria Gasca Diez in 1938 tell us that young women in urban areas may have aspired to something other than being the guardian angel of hearth and family. Though these adolescents had grown up during Fascism, only 10 percent had any interest in domestic tasks and responsibilities, while 27 percent hated them; very few wanted a large family, the clear preference being one child, or two at the most. Finally, the majority of young women expressed the wish to command rather than obey. In an article about these findings, published in the woman's magazine *Almanacco della donna italiana*

(1938), Luigi Gozzini urgently advocates a new educational program that would guide woman back "to her natural function in social and national life, a work of education which would reconstruct *ab imis fundamentis* the pillars of family conscience" (263–64).

The majority of articles arguing against women's presence in institutions of learning and the workplace are couched in the politics of demographics, conferring sociopolitical legitimacy solely upon the female reproductive function. "Have children, have children," Mussolini would say. "There is power in numbers!" But beneath the facile exterior typical of Mussolini's slogans, complex economic, political, psychological, and gender issues compete; male authority, levied by economic means, is truly at stake. Pompei, in his 1933 analysis of the crisis of family, the smallest unit reflecting the condition of the Fascist state, creates a thought-provoking description of the changing significance employment outside the home has for women, as well as its "dangerous" implications for men. Though supporting oneself was once an economic necessity for some women, the desire to join the work force eventually became a trend. Modern women, however, conceive of employment as a right, enabling their autonomy, which strips the title *pater familias* of meaning.[8] De Libero, a clerical Fascist, confirms this observation in 1938, though he attributes women's desire for economic independence to the feminist movement, stating that "woman no longer wants to be economically dependent on man in order to form the most perfect of societies, the family, rather, she wants to break away and support herself" (249). In 1933, Mario Palazzi perceives a more tragic scenario: "Since the contribution of earnings is what potentially and concretely determines man's supremacy in the family, and since woman is escaping this supremacy to the detriment of other men, producing obvious tension, and a progressive loosening of family bonds and male authority in the bosom of the family, at the rate things are going there will be a matriarchy" (209).

Echoing the apprehensive tonality of Marinetti's matrimonial grotesque, the voices of Palazzi, Pompei, and Evola in the 1930s do not speak of female submission. They articulate male defeat in their representations of sexual relations where the male sex, which was supposed to win the "battle of the sexes," "has been ignominiously defeated by masses of strong-willed masculine women"; instead of keeping their women in line, men have become "entirely dominated" feminized "puppets" (211, 116).

One could hardly argue that Italian society was on the verge of matriarchy in the late 1930s, or that male-authored representations of different female desires constitute merely specters of male anxiety. A growing body of historical material, however, documents women's pursuit of economic and intellectual autonomy in Italian society during Fascism. A complex variety of factors—among them age, sexual orientation, class, and geographic location—clearly influenced women's choices regarding education, employment, and childbearing. Yet the oral testimonies examined by Luisa Passerini in *Fascism and Popular Memory*, for instance, materialize female self-perceptions among the Turin working class as active social subjects whose decisions to be employed in the factories and to have fewer children represent (in social, political, and symbolic dimensions) the progress these women had made since their mothers' generation. Employment figures more centrally in identity formation in the self-descriptions provided by women of the middle classes working as typists, secretaries, and teachers. For these women, Passerini maintains, "work seemed to offer not only material independence but also the primary basis for a psychological and social identity, despite relative indifference, especially among clerical workers, toward the content of the job" (50). This different model of female subjectivity, inscribed in women's practices and in social commentary, forces us to reconsider the traditional notion of the ideological system and the discourses, institutions, and practices that constitute it.

Within a broader framework of ideology—which encompasses the quotidian as a site for the production of social meaning—we can also read modern women's employment of their bodies in public self-presentation, carriage, gestures, and dress as appropriations of femininity and as an attack on male authority in what Iain Chambers (via Umberto Eco) refers to as "sign warfare." Postulating a concept of the social subject as one who, through choices and tastes, constructs a "public identity" interacting with the larger system of signs where ideology is "inscribed in our clothes, our homes, hair styles, reading and viewing habits; in our gestures, our sexuality, our selves," Chambers reformulates the notion of resistance, as well as its means and significance in daily living. Objects of fashion, for instance, may be employed to assert oneself in public spaces, threatening identities imposed by dominant institutions if not creating new ones (Chambers, 212, 54).[9] In an interesting way, Chambers's argument here echoes Paolo Araldi, a clerical exponent of Fascism, who drew a similar conclusion in 1929. He clearly perceives the ways women's fashion may disrupt social conventions, though he does not take into account the female consumer's agency or tastes: "As soon as fashion headquarters gives the order to take yet another veil off the shrine of her modesty, woman obeys without examining the importance fashion exerts on customs, which is incommensurable" (161).

A comparison of the ways male social critics write the maternal body and read the modern female body (a body consciously produced through dieting and exercise) explicates the psychic relation between male psychopolitical *desire*, with the Woman-Mother as its object, and male *anxiety*, attached to a female social subject unseduced by the maternal ideal. The maternal body personifies robust shapeliness, physical and sexual health, and solidity. "Woman," Pompei reminds his readers in 1930, is "home," which is to say, the Woman-Mother houses, protects, and nourishes all but herself. Instead, the new female body accommodates only herself. Modern women's bodies are "flat, skinny ... perpetually adolescent" (182). The new feminine body insinuates itself onto the dominant ideological system as a sign challenging fascistized femininity, and signaling the failure of the regime's demographic politics. Moreover, this gender indeterminacy marks the absence of the object of male desire. Though Mussolini's pronatalist campaign aimed to double the declining birth rate, the number of births per thousand obstinately fell from 23.4 to 22.2 between 1934 and 1936; social analysts reported "frightening numbers" of abortions, estimated to be "as high as 30 per cent of all conceptions" in 1929 (Mack Smith, 160). It would be unwise to read the fluctuations in population growth solely as a manifestation of women's oppositional consciousness.[10] Yet working-class women in Turin speak of how their self-management of reproductive activity signified personal and social agency. And in some cases women do conceive of their decision to limit family size in terms of political resistance to the demographic campaign, as we see from what Fiora has to say:

INTERVIEWER: How many children did you have?

FIORA: I had three.

INTERVIEWER: Are they alive?

FIORA: Yes, Yes. They're all alive. I would have had more, but you didn't to spite Mussolini, you see. (Passerini, 150)

Though Fiora's testimony does not provide the basis for a general assessment of how women received Fascist discourses prescribing motherhood as a sociopolitical value, it is suggestive.

Unable to conceive of forms of female identity other than Mother, in a defensive gesture male critics label women's practices of work, education, leisure, and self-presentation symptoms of aberrant masculinized sexuality, or bisexuality, the Freudian theory most feared by cultural commentators in the Fascist party. In 1938, well after Fascist authorities had disbanded women's organizations with an oppositional political agenda, De Libero writes that the "feminist movement" or "movement of masculinization" would like "to make a man out of woman, and since their sex prevents this, they do it through expressions, fashion, and gestures in life" (249). I would propose that the ways women appropriated social practices, spaces, fashions, and attitudes marked "masculine" in Fascist ideology articulate different configurations of female subjectivity. By so doing, they provide a new perspective on women as reading subjects and the sites and means of their engagement in literary discourses produced by women writers during Fascism.

> *No one has ever known anything about us women.*
> Ada Negri (1926)

A correlative to the male distress provoked by the changing social identities of women which I analyzed in the preceding section can be found in the anxiety over gender ambiguity among male critics of literature elicited by the claims to authority Italian writing women made in the area of literary production. In the following representation of women's writing in the twenties and its relationship to the male canon, the prominent literary critic Giuseppe Ravegnani reveals his expectations as reader and the distress caused by women writers who fail to reproduce the traditional image of femininity:

> Is there, in Italy, a female literature in the traditional sense, that is to say, something lively, well-nourished, spontaneous, that has definite and clear ties with our own literate climates? Or, is there at least an exceptional temperament, an intellectual shrew, a woman-monster? Now, there are some women writers, five or six excellent at that: but we do not believe there is a real and well-defined female literature. What such literature there is, by and large lives and nourishes itself on the margins of another greater, greatly more sober and conclusive literature. It seems to us . . . that female literature, particularly the recent one, has the habit of putting on trousers, and has the mania of putting on its face an unprejudiced and even cynic mask. . . . As for us, we would like a woman, especially if overflowing with ink, to be old-fashioned, maybe romantic, homey, and a little exhausted by housework. (*Contemporanei*, 55–56)[11]

In his attempt to demonstrate that a tradition of female writing does not exist—a topic of heated debate during the 1920s—Ravegnani outlines the different terms of women's literary discourses. Despite his wish to displace women's literature onto the fringes of the Italian literary tradition, the vampirish image he creates of such writing, nourishing itself on the margins of the "greater," that is, male literature, conveys the potential danger it poses by eating away the boundaries between masculine and feminine, a kind of textual "cross-dressing," to modify Showalter's term. Since women's literary production of the twenties does not embody Ravegnani's ideal of femininity, he can perceive their claim to the authority of authorship only in terms of masquerade. This critical perspective is symptomatic of Irigaray's notion of the "blind spot" limiting the male visual field to an Oedipal trajectory that cannot see forms of female identity, sexuality, and desire differing from that of the Woman-Mother.

In the 1920s and 1930s, however, women's writing in various genres enjoyed an unprecedented boom, heightened by the short fiction such critically acclaimed and popular authors as Grazia Deledda, Ada Negri, Gianna Manzini, Maria Luisa Astaldi, and Clarice Tartufari contributed to the cultural page (*la terza pagina* or the third page) of Italian newspapers.[12] This means of publication has inestimable value for critical looks at gender and genre, modes of textual production, circulation, reception, the mutually informing dimensions (high and popular) of cultural composition, and the theorization of a different female social subject. By publishing their short narratives on the cultural page (its fiction was largely uncensored during the Fascist dictatorship), these writers, among such others as Luigi Pirandello, Eugenio Montale, and Alberto Moravia, could perform a direct intervention in the formation of ideas among a mass popular audience for whom the price of books was still prohibitive. For instance, by 1943 Sibilla Aleramo's internationally acclaimed novel A *Woman* (1906) had sold fifty thousand copies. Yet by the mid-1930s fiction published in the *Corriere della Sera*, a Milanese newspaper, reached over 600,000 readers a day. Antonio Gramsci, a key figure in European Marxist theory who gives concentrated attention to literary production and its relation to the broader historical and social process, has underscored the formative influence fiction published in the daily press may have on subjectivity by articulating the desires, emotions, aesthetic needs, and aspirations of people in everyday walks of life.

More important, while examining the problematic of an Italian "national-popular" literature, Gramsci details the tastes, interests, and reading habits of women among the mass newspaper readership, a subject that literary commentary has repressed by concentrating on the appeal romance fiction had among women readers. Gramsci maintains that in decisions regarding which newspaper to buy "women have a large say in the choice and insist on the 'nice interesting novel.' (This does not mean that the men do not read the novel too, but it is the women who are particularly interested in it and in items of local news.)" Taking generational and economic differences into account, Gramsci goes on to note that political papers were bought by young "men and women, without too many family worries, who were keenly interested in the fortunes of their political opinions" (Gramsci, *Cultural Writings*, 207). One may safely speculate that these factors remained constant in the 1920s and 1930s when the cultural pages of such major newspapers as the *Corriere della Sera* (Milan), *Il Giornale d'Italia* (Rome), and *La Stampa* (Turin) showcased primarily self-contained short stories rather than serialized novels. Newspaper advertisements for food, clothing, and vitamins addressed apparently to female consumers testify to sufficiently large numbers of women readers to make such campaigns profitable. Furthermore, as demonstrated by the comprehensive publicity campaign launched by *Proton* (a product claiming to remedy that "run-down feeling" in everyone from pre-adolescents to menopausal women), the marketplace solicited women through representations of modern female practices—studying, working in offices, doing sports—that convey different terms of modern female identity. The 1929 ad for the Fiat convertible, though not necessarily addressed solely to women, emblematizes female mobility at the material and symbolic levels in particularly powerful terms. Here the fashionable modern woman, now able to go wherever she desires, sits alone at the wheel of her convertible, which looms large as it is superimposed on a map of the Italian peninsula.

To be sure, the availability, minimal cost, and brevity of short fiction published in the Italian daily press appealed to sectors of the popular female readership who may have had neither the time nor the financial means to dedicate to novels. To my mind, however, the factors accounting specifically for the explosive popularity of women's fiction largely concern the narrative systems of address, self-representation, and female subjectivity elaborated by such critically recognized and popular writers as Deledda, Negri, Carola Prosperi, and Marinella Lodi. These authors thematize such gender issues as the ways women in patriarchal society may experience childhood, adolescence, sexuality, marital union, motherhood, and aging, and examine their different relations to self, to other women, and to Woman. Their short stories solicit women as reading subjects through distinct textual practices. These include direct address to the female reader, first-person female narrators, and narrative representations of women's conversations, intimate dialogues, and monologues, which convey the experience's subjectivity, delegitimating the "objective" male authorial stance. Moreover, the discursive systems produced by women writers contributing to the cultural page generally draw upon everyday vocabulary and speech patterns, making the fiction accessible to a broad audience.[13] This rejection of the "high" Italian literary style, which Gramsci critiques as an exclusionary address to the social elite, sets women's writing practices against the literary canon, creating a space for cultural, social, and political opposition to patriarchy, a position shared by such contemporary Italian feminist writers as Dacia Maraini, Patrizia Cavalli, and Jolanda Insana.[14]

The body of short fiction contributed by women writers to the cultural page exhibits a broad spectrum of subject matter and textual practices. A recurrent component in their forms of textuality, however, is the recontextualization, through secondary usage, of dominant notions of Woman, achieved by reproducing such notions in opposition to alternative representations of female identity, sexuality, and desire. This strategy, which self-consciously writes possibilities for diverse gendered negotiations of meaning into the text, may account for the widespread popularity of women's fiction among male and female readers. This form of textuality furthermore elucidates how fiction of dissent may have eluded apparatuses in the media industry attempting to shut down the circulation of ideas.[15] The writers' gender likely helped them elude censorship, since creative genius with persuasive power supposedly belonged to the male domain. And who would have suspected sociopolitical dissent in stories published in the daily press with such innocuous titles as "Woman with a Little Girl" by Negri (*Corriere della Sera*, 1926), "A Boy" by Pia Rimini (*Il Giornale d'Italia*, 1933), or "Portrait of a Country Woman" by Deledda (*Corriere della Sera*, 1926)? Yet these narratives set different visions of female identity against the official cultural image of femininity in much the same way that women's practices of daily living challenged the ideology of the Woman-Mother. They thus create different possibilities for female identification. I would speculate that in some cases the author's choice of title manipulates the dominant political discursive code for her own interests. For instance, as the regime attempted to deploy a totalitarian rhetoric of "virility," the title "Man and Death" (*Giornale d'Italia*, 1925) might suggest a thematic of virility, honor, and war, when in fact Marinella Lodi tells a story of female adolescence, attempted sexual abuse, and the girl's successful rebellion against patriarchal power in an act of self-assertion.[16] Similarly, the title "Sensitivity" (*Giornale d'Italia*, 1936) would probably lead the reader to expect a story glorifying a female character for her embodiment of this quality—but Guglielminetti attributes this capacity to respond emotionally, traditionally associated with the feminine, to a male character as well, figuring male sensitivity, not virility, as the quality eliciting female desire.

Nowhere is the circumvention of repressive apparatuses designed to neutralize, if not erase, a different female subject more apparent than in the ways women writers decenter the image of the Woman-Mother in fiction published on the cultural page. They do so in part by representing ways other than mothering for women to know themselves, as well as their relation to mechanisms of material and psychological oppression. As in Marinella Lodi's story "Man and Death," which valorizes autonomy as a productive component of female self-concept, in "The Captain" (*Corriere della Sera* 1931) Ada Negri elaborates the notion of "a dominating femininity and an intelligent, rash energy" in the figure of a young girl. Though these particularizing traits of female difference are ultimately repressed by socialization in Negri's piece, Amalia Guglielminetti's retelling of the Ariadne myth in "Sensitivity" offers a scathing critique of the objectification of Woman in patriarchy while creating a revisionary image of femininity. In fact, much of the narrative concerns problems of male vision and the representation of female desire. Thus Arianna, whose notion of self is constituted by her intelligence, spiritual qualities, and intellectual curiosity, breaks three engagements to men whose vision is limited to her physical beauty—"a varnish destined to decompose and disappear with time." Though Arianna's different desire is fulfilled, her subversive power is not contained within the narrative economy. Rather, Guglielminetti's sardonic closing line, which reveals that Arianna's husband is blind, censures the normative male vision and representation of Woman.

The critical rewriting of motherhood as institution and potential experience constitutes another displacement of the Woman-Mother as a desirable ideal for women or society. Far from glorifying the culturally constructed image of the Mother, the many visions of motherhood authored by women throughout the 1920s and 1930s articulate a consciousness resistant to the essentialist ideology of the maternal as they refashion the terms and context of mothering. In view of the importance the traditional nuclear family assumed in Fascist ideology, a preponderant number of short stories explore the conditions of women's mothering in a nontraditional family nucleus. Abandoned lovers and wives, surrogate mothers, prostitutes, and widows occupy maternal narratives, with no reference to the fathers, dramatizing the subjective and social experience of motherhood and the changing material realities of the nuclear family. Within this context, such writers as Grazia Deledda, Pia Rimini, Maddalena Crispolti, and Maria Luisa Astaldi give particular authorial attention to the ties that bind mothers in a nonproductive scheme of relationship operating upon the societal value of maternal self-sacrifice. As these writers transform domestic space, furnishings, and clothing into symbols of confinement and social marginalization, they narrate intimate dramas of entrapment wherein attributes of women's difference have been repressed, and desire figures as a wish for autonomy.

The problems concerning the unrepresentability of mothers as sexual subjects in life, society, and culture constitute the thematic and representational concerns in Crispolti's "A Drama in Silence" (1934). Crispolti recontextualizes the dominant notion of motherhood as the sole function of femininity by dramatizing how this cultural ideal merely blinds men to female sexuality. Though women's critical rewritings of motherhood form a predominantly dismal composite, some short stories evidence a different ethic of mothering. "The Pomegranate" (1936) by Gianna Manzini, for instance, posits autonomy as a property of productive nurturing. With the image of a pomegranate, symbolizing the "reconciliation of the multiple and diverse within apparent unity," the author creates a telling metaphor for a new relation between mother and child that makes both autonomy and connectedness possible. This ideal challenges the patriarchal values of dominance and control.

Conceived as a critical intervention, this study endeavors to shift our field of vision to the sites where women speak as subjects of discourse in Italian life and literature during Fascism. By examining the different accomplishments, ideals, and desires inscribed in practices of everyday living among urban women of the middle and popular classes, we may better question the possible investments of female subjects in representations intended to fascistize femininity—a process to distil differences among and within women in the image of the Woman-Mother and in competing representations depicting female endeavors to think, act, know, and imagine themselves independently. I expect this exploratory inquiry and the materials it makes available in English to enable more differentiated studies of communities of women writing and reading in the years of Fascism, by taking into consideration the varied sites of female cultural production, and hence the different ways in which women negotiate their opposition to dominant codes. For this to happen, however, we must first begin to read the broad spectrum of literature produced by women who, though fashioning different phases in their life courses, continued their "search for self" during Fascism.[17]

Notes

I extend grateful acknowledgment to the Center for Twentieth Century Studies of the University of Wisconsin-Milwaukee for the 1989–90 Fellowship that enabled the research for and writing of this study through financial and critical support. I also thank Kathleen Woodward and Lynn Worsham for their reading of this essay and for their critical insights.

1. Among the most important works adopting "consent" as the primary interpretative category are *Mussolini il duce: Gli anni del consenso, 1929–1936* (Mussolini the Duce: The years of consent, 1929–1936) by Renzo De Felice; *La fabbrica del consenso* (The manufacturing of consent) by Philip V. Cannistraro; *The Culture of Consent* by Victoria De Grazia; and *La donna "nera"* (The woman in black) by Maria Antonietta Macciocchi. De Grazia's contributions to "Alle origini della cultura di massa" and "Culture popolari negli anni del fascismo" clearly signal the shift from the consent paradigm to critical methods enabling analyses of contradictions between and within female subjectivities. Since the writing of this essay, the publication in 1992 of De Grazia's *How Fascism Ruled Women*, which documents many female models with extensive archival research while analyzing the shifting positions women adopted in relation to the regime's sexual politics, stands as a landmark for as yet unexplored directions in the study of women as writing and reading subjects during the dictatorship.

2. Macciocchi's analysis of women's relation to Italian Fascism, from which she draws conclusions regarding women's complicity with current forms of fascist ideology, continues to be cited by scholars from Italy and elsewhere, and thus merits a critical rereading. See, for example, *New French Feminisms*, ed. Elaine Marks and Isabelle de Courtivron, and an important earlier article by Jane Caplan, "Introduction to Female Sexuality in Fascist Ideology," which contextualizes Macciocchi's theoretical concerns in the article "Female Sexuality in Fascist Ideology," appearing in the same volume. (I thank Thomas Piontek for referring me to Caplan's article.) What concerns me here, however, is how Macciocchi's interrogation of female "consent" to the Fascist ideology of femininity has structured the thinking of literary critics who equate the inferior political status of women with inferior literary production, and as a consequence represent this twenty-year period as a gap in the tradition of Italian women's writing. See Augustus Pallotta, "Dacia Maraini," Paola Blelloch, *Quel mondo dei guanti e delle stoffe* (That world of gloves and fabrics), and Maryse Jeuland-Meynaud, "Le identificazioni della donna nella narrativa di Elsa Morante" (Forms of woman's identification in Elsa Morante's narrative). Unless otherwise noted, all translations from Italian to English are mine. For an examination of other problems contributing to the marginalization of women's writing produced during Fascism see the introduction and critical afterword to *Unspeakable Women* by Robin Pickering-Iazzi.

3. It is beyond the scope of this essay to examine either the convergence of Fascist and Catholic ideologies of woman and the family or the regional, socioeconomic, and political differences shaping both the popular reconstitution of Catholicism in different areas of Italy and women's different relations to Catholic systems of belief. For a salient analysis of this topic and a rich bibliography see Stefania Portaccio "La donna nella stampa popolare cattolica" (Woman in the Catholic popular press); and De Grazia, *How Fascism Ruled Women*.

4. In *La voce che è in Lei* (The voice within her), Giuliana Morandini states that in the 1870s "besides opposing their oppression, Italian women, and therefore women writers, request work and autonomy, they want to participate in public life, and to have a political voice. Precisely in the 1870s, the request for women's suffrage is presented several times in parliament, and is strongly opposed. The same irritations and fears over 'the dissolution of the family and morality' cause the first battles for divorce" (15).

Robin Pickering-Iazzi

5. Cinzia Blum, "'L'uomo metallizzato e il cuore a compartimenti stagni': Defense Strategies in Marinetti's Discourse on Love." F. T. Marinetti's writings and the relations between Futurism, Italian Fascism, and modernity have recently become a hot topic of debate, as seen, for example, in Russell A. Berman, "The Aestheticization of Politics," Jeffrey Schnapp, "Forwarding Address" and "Epic Demonstrations," and Andrew Hewitt, *Fascist Modernism*.

6. Meldini's study of how Woman figures in Italian Fascist ideology includes an extensive collection of articles written by Fascist exponents and ideologues, published primarily in Fascist journals. Unless otherwise noted, my examples in this section are taken from this collection of individually authored articles.

7. Meldini notes that in the 1934–35 academic year females made up 88 percent of the students in elementary school, 69 percent of those in middle school, and only 16 percent of those in high school.

8. According to the statistics provided by Meldini (73), the numbers of women employed in several sectors (domestic services, commerce, finance, administration, teaching, and health care) increased, sometimes markedly, between 1921 and 1931, while female employment in agriculture, the sector Mussolini attempted to strengthen, sustained a notable decline. Increased mechanization in farming and population shifts from rural to urban areas may in part explain the decline in agriculture.

9. For a detailed examination of fashion as an expression of identity, desires, and ideas see also Elizabeth Wilson, *Adorned in Dreams*.

10. See Leslie Caldwell, "Reproducers of the Nation"; Luisa Passerini, *Fascism in Popular Memory*; and De Grazia, *How Fascism Ruled Women* for studies of women's mediations of Fascist demographic policies.

11. This translation is drawn from Sergio Pacifici's *The Modern Italian Novel from Capuana to Tozzi* (49). I have revised some antiquated terminology and restored some images to a more accurate form.

12. Alberto Bergamini founded the cultural page (*la terza pagina*) in 1901, when he designated the third page as a vehicle for cultural dissemination. Conceived as a means to diffuse the ideas of Italian intellectuals among an educated public, Bergamini's program actually enjoyed widespread popularity among a demographically diverse audience, due in great part to the collaboration of critically acclaimed and popular writers. The program became a prototype for the journalistic and literary institution of the cultural page, which remains unique to Italian journalism. For a more detailed account of the cultural page and its literary component see my analysis of the short story genre and the daily press in "Pirandello and Buzzati" and of women's practices of storytelling on the third page in "The Poetics of Discovery."

13. For a comprehensive analysis of linguistic practices elaborated in popular literature by women writers, see Daniela Curti, "Il linguaggio del racconto rosa."

14. See Beverly Allen's introduction to *The Defiant Muse*.

15. Tania Modleski in "Feminism and the Power of Interpretation" examines this strategy, stating that through mimicry a single text seems to conform with the oppressor's ideas, yet provides "a dissenting and empowering view for those in the know" (129).

16. The short stories to which I refer appear in the collection *Unspeakable Women*, ed. Robin Pickering-Iazzi.

17. In her dedication for the 1926 prose collection *Le strade* (Streets), Ada Negri describes her stories as "the poor, troubled pages of a woman who never found peace in any land, and is still searching for herself."

Works Cited

Allen, Beverly. "Introduction." *The Defiant Muse: Italian Feminist Poems from the Middle Ages to the Present*, ed. Beverly Allen, Muriel Kittel, and Keala Jane Jewel. New York: The Feminist Press at the City University of New York, 1986. xv-xx.

Berman, Russell A. "The Aestheticization of Politics: Walter Benjamin on Fascism and the Avant-Garde." *Stanford Italian Review* 8 (1990): 35–52.
Birnbaum, Lucia Chiavola. *Liberazione della donna: Feminism in Italy*. Middletown, Conn.: Wesleyan University Press, 1986.
Blelloch, Paola. *Quel mondo dei guanti e delle stoffe: . . . Profili di scrittrici italiane del 1900*. Verona: Essedue, 1987.
Blum, Cinzia. "'L'uomo metallizzato e il cuore a compartimenti stagni': Defense Strategies in Marinetti's Discourse on Love." Paper presented at the Annual Conference of the American Association of Teachers of Italian. Boston, Mass., Nov. 17–19, 1989.
Caldwell, Leslie. "Reproducers of the Nation: Women and the Family in Fascist Policy." *Rethinking Italian Fascism*, ed. David Forgacs. 110–41.
Cannistraro, Philip V. *La fabbrica del consenso: Fascismo e mass media*. Roma: Laterza, 1975.
Caplan, Jane. "Introduction to Female Sexuality in Fascist Ideology." *Feminist Review* 1 (1979): 59–66.
Chambers, Iain. *Popular Culture: The Metropolitan Experience*. New York: Methuen, 1986.
Curti, Daniela. "Il linguaggio del racconto rosa: Gli anni 20 ed oggi." *Lingua letteraria e lingua dei media nell'italiano contemporaneo*. Florence: Felice Le Monnier, 1987.
de Certeau, Michel. *The Practice of Everyday Life*, trans. Steven Rendall. Berkeley: University of California Press, 1984.
De Felice, Renzo. *Mussolini il duce*. I. *Gli anni del consenso, 1929–1936*. Turin: Einaudi, 1974.
De Grand, Alexander. "Women Under Italian Fascism." *Historical Journal* 19.4 (1976): 947–68.
De Grazia, Victoria. *The Culture of Consent: Mass Organization of Leisure in Fascist Italy*. Cambridge: Cambridge University Press, 1981.
———. "Culture popolari negli anni del Fascismo." *Italia contemporanea* 157 (1984): 63–90.
———. *How Fascism Ruled Women: Italy 1920–1945*. Berkeley: University of California Press, 1992.
———, et al. "Alle origini della cultura di massa: Cultura popolare e fascismo in Italia." *Ricerca folklorica* 7 (1983): 19–25.
de Lauretis, Teresa. *Alice Doesn't: Feminism, Semiotics, Cinema*. Bloomington: Indiana University Press, 1984.
———. *Technologies of Gender: Essays on Theory, Film, and Fiction*. Bloomington: Indiana University Press, 1987.
Forgacs, David, ed. *Rethinking Italian Fascism: Capitalism, Populism, and Culture*. London: Lawrence and Wishart, 1986.
Freud, Sigmund. "Femininity." New Introductory Lectures in *The Standard Edition*, vol. 22, 112–35.
Galoppini, Annamaria. *Il lungo viaggio verso la parità: I diritti civili e politici delle donne dall'unità ad oggi*. Bologna: Zanichelli, 1980.
Gramsci, Antonio. *Selections from Cultural Writings*, trans. William Boelhower, ed. David Forgacs and Geoffrey Nowell-Smith. London: Lawrence and Wishart, 1985.
———. *Selections from the Prison Notebooks of Antonio Gramsci*, trans. and ed. Quintin Hoare and Geoffrey Nowell-Smith. New York: International Publishers, 1971.
Guglielminetti, Amalia. "Aridità sentimentale." *La Stampa*. July 11, 1911.
Hewitt, Andrew. *Fascist Modernism. Aesthetics, Politics, and the Avant-Garde*. Stanford: Stanford University Press, 1993.
Jeuland-Meynaud, Maryse. "Le identificazioni della donna nella narrativa di Elsa Morante." *Annali D'Italianistica* 7 (1989): 301–24.
Macciocchi, Maria Antonietta. *La donna "nera": "Consenso" femminile e fascismo*. Milan: Feltrinelli, 1976.
Mack Smith, Denis. *Mussolini: A Biography*. New York: Vintage, 1983.
Marinetti, Filippo Tommaso. "Contro il Matrimonio." *Teoria e invenzione futurista*, ed. Luciano De Maria. Milan: Mondadori, 1983. 368.

Marks, Elaine, and Isabelle de Courtivron, eds. *New French Feminisms: An Anthology*. Amherst: University of Massachusetts Press, 1980.

Meldini, Piero. *Sposa e madre esemplare: Ideologia e politica della donna e della famiglia durante il fascismo*. Florence: Guaraldi, 1975.

Modleski, Tania. "Feminism and the Power of Interpretation: Some Critical Readings." *Feminist Studies/Critical Studies*, ed. Teresa de Lauretis. Theories of Contemporary Culture 8. Bloomington: Indiana University Press, 1986. 121–38.

Mondello, Elisabetta. *La nuova italiana: La donna nella stampa e nella cultura del ventennio*. Rome: Riuniti, 1987.

Morandini, Giuliana. *La voce che è in lei: Antologia della narrativa femminile italiana tra 1800 e 1900*. Milan: Bompiani, 1980.

Negri, Ada. *Le strade* in *Tutte le opere di Ada Negri*, vol. 2. Turin: Mondadori, 1966.

Pacifici, Sergio. *The Modern Italian Novel from Capuana to Tozzi*. Carbondale: Southern Illinois University Press, 1973.

Pallotta, Augustus. "Dacia Maraini: From Alienation to Feminism." *World Literature Today* 58.3 (1984): 359–62.

Passerini, Luisa. *Fascism in Popular Memory: The Cultural Experience of the Turin Working Class*. Cambridge: Cambridge University Press, 1987.

Petro, Patrice. *Joyless Streets: Women and Melodramatic Representation in Weimar Germany*. Princeton: Princeton University Press, 1989.

Pickering-Iazzi, Robin. "Pirandello and Buzzati: A Profile of the Short Story *Elzeviro*." *Quaderni d'Italianistica* 8.2 (1987): 194–215.

———. "The Poetics of Discovery: Female Storytelling and the *Terza Pagina* in Early Twentieth Century Literature." *Italiana* 1 (1988): 291–306.

———. *Unspeakable Women: Selected Short Stories Written by Italian Women during Fascism*. New York: The Feminist Press at the City University of New York, 1993.

Portaccio, Stefania. "La donna nella stampa popolare cattolica: *Famiglia cristiana* 1931–1945." *Italia contemporanea* 143 (1981): 45–68.

Ravegnani, Giuseppe. *Contemporanei: Dal tramonto dell'Ottocento all'alba del Novecento*. Turin: Fratelli Bocca, 1930.

Schnapp, Jeffrey. "Forwarding Address." *Stanford Italian Review* 8 (1990): 53–80.

———. "Epic Demonstrations: Fascist Modernity and the 1932 Exhibition of the Fascist Revolution." *Fascism, Aesthetics, and Culture*, ed. Richard J. Golsan. Hanover: University Presses of New England, 1992. 1–37.

Wilson, Elizabeth. *Adorned in Dreams: Fashion and Modernity*. London: Virago Press, 1985.

Graziella Parati

The Transparent Woman
Reading Femininity within a Futurist Context

In Futurist manifestoes Woman appears variously as a symbol, a metaphor, or a flexible entity. She is negated and rejected as the decadent heroine of D'Annunzio's and Fogazzaro's works; as symbol of the past, she is the victim of a nihilistic approach to femininity, to gender identity, on the part of the Futurist man. Deprived of these old signifieds, woman is absorbed within Marinetti's movement (and in works by Corra, Settimelli, and Fillia) as an empty signifier that can be manipulated by the Futurist man.[1]

The separation between *femmina* and *donna* is the starting point for Marinetti as well as for Fillia, who declares "the death of Woman" in a 1925 collection of short stories. While the "female" is the acceptable sexual entity for man's natural needs and for reproductive purposes, "woman" is "a degeneration of man, a spiritual weakness, a passivity."[2] Woman is, therefore, an invented entity that needs to be eliminated since she is "an exploitation of feminine material imagined by the male in periods of deep moral decadence" (Fillia, 178). The binary opposition between the gendered woman and the biological female—which appears to be clearly defined from a theoretical point of view—is complicated by futurist practice. Marinetti negates this theoretical separation in *Mafarka*, a novel in which the goal of the Uebermensch is to appropriate woman's reproductive abilities and therefore become the father of a Futurist son: the airplane. In Vasari's play, L'A*ngoscia delle macchine* (The anguish of machines, 1925), one character defines woman as a "useless gender" which must be "relegated to the old continent."[3] The contradictory elements in this masculine construction of femininity transform the entity "woman" into a *problema femminile* that needs to be resolved.

The metaphor of woman as "tunnel" is the key to reconciling some of the contradictory statements of Marinetti and his followers.[4] The oversimplified *reductio ad unum* of woman to a symbolical "tunnel" provides Futurist writers with the opportunity to consider woman as a receptacle for essentialist definitions. This metaphorically and physically penetrable tunnel, as presented by Marinetti in *Come si seducono le donne* (How to seduce women, 1916), awaits the signification necessary to create a Futurist woman complementary to and controllable by man. This one-way tunnel of femininity is the locus of absolutes regarding women, of "strong truths" that are expected to resolve the male construction of the *problema femminile*.

Gianni Vattimo, in his recent book *La società trasparente* (The transparent society, 1989), defines transparent society as "self-conscious [and] enlightened," an entity that can be known.[5] Vattimo's interest in "weak" as opposed to "strong" truths and "opaque" as opposed to "transparent" society is useful in my argument to differentiate the role of male and female discussions in the creation of problematic concepts of femininity within Futurism. A transparent, modern society is intended by Vattimo to be the opposite of his idea of a postmodern contemporary society. The idea of transparency is connected with the inherent possibility, within modernity, of constructing a "unitary concept of history" and, through a unitary weltanschauung, to reach "strong truths" that belong to the realm of metaphysics. A postmodern society, on the other end, is intended as "opaque." In *La società trasparente* Vattimo writes that "the liberation of many cultures and many weltanschauungen, made possible by the mass media, has denied, rather, the very ideal of transparent society." This fragmented society is the realm of "weak truths."[6] I am freely adopting Vattimo's terminology to a Futurist context where the male agenda is to construct "strong truths" in order to create a "transparent woman" that is not only known but completely mastered. She is an entity complementary to Marinetti's Futurism and instrumental to the Futurist agenda. The idea of transparency in Marinetti's construction of femininity explains the way in which the gendered identity of woman must be completely legible to the Futurist man. Marinetti writes: "There are women who are exceptionally intelligent, loyal, generous, self-denying, sensitive, heroic, but all these virtues are profoundly sexual" (1920, 40). As sexual beings, women are penetrable and controllable through the tunnel of femininity, states Marinetti's manual of seduction. The result is a "self-transparent" creature whose lack of signified is easily remedied by male intervention.

The presence of Futurist women within the movement transforms the "self-transparent" and overcodified woman into an "opaque" entity, which is not as easily readable as Marinetti had desired in his *Come si seducono le donne*. These female-gendered contexts, which appear en masse as part of a literary movement, play the role of fragmenting elements in Futurism (the role of mass media in Vattimo's opaque society). Supplying a separate weltanschauung, Futurist women writers disrupt the male attempt to create an instrumental "transparent woman." In this process of negation Futurist women are soon trapped in the order they negate and they paradoxically reaccept fragments of the male discourse (for instance, the idea of seduction) which they had previously rejected. What needs to be underlined, however, is the attempt by women writers to present a separate discourse (to which very little critical attention has been paid) within a male-dominated movement and to publicly figure in a literary movement. The often contradictory female fringe created literary acts of resistance to the gendered identity constructed by Marinetti and his followers. Of course, it would be a mistake to overestimate the influence of women's writings within Futurism. Nevertheless, it is vital to bring to the surface the importance of "minor" writers such as the Futurist women in order to analyze the relationship between separate constructions of gender, of femininity. This relationship, as explored here, is intended as a dialogue between texts written by the male and the female members of this avant-garde movement.[7]

The journal *Italia futurista* (Futurist Italy), directed by Maria Ginanni, is the arena for a discussion on the representation of woman in Marinetti's *Come si seducono le donne*. The advertisement for the book announces Marinetti's work as "a war book which gives a solution for the *problema femminile*."[8] Corra and Settimelli's article of October 7, 1917 presents and summarizes Marinetti's opus of seduction. They state that *Come si seducono le donne* is a manual created "out of practice and not of theory" and that it is a book in which the author attempts to destroy "woman not as she really is, but as a product of the selfish passions of the oriental man and of romantic literature."[9] What is not defined here is "what woman really is." The core of the book delivers the idea of seduction as a means to transform woman into the perfect Futurist "mate," untouchable by romantic love. This game of seduction is a displaced reflection of the war, and woman becomes the enemy. Seduction is, therefore, the weapon to control woman, who can always reveal her castrating potential and prevent man from becoming the

Uebermensch. During the war period, Marinetti, faced with changing female roles in the public sphere, reveals his preoccupation. The hidden threat for men in the sociohistorical context of the time is the "effeminization" of the soldier, the Ardito (shock troops). Indeed, Marinetti writes: "the massive participation of women in the national labor caused by the war has created a characteristically grotesque matrimonial situation." Thus the unemployed veteran "concentrates his activity in an absurd preoccupation with housewifely concerns" (Marinetti, 1920, 60).

In an issue of Italia futurista dated October 7, 1917, female voices also appear to comment on Marinetti's manual of seduction. Some of these writings reappear in the 1918 edition of Come si seducono le donne. Enif Robert proposes a new construction of femininity that contrasts the two prevailing conceptions of woman within Futurism: woman as a decadent heroine or as an intellectual feminist, openly despised by Futurist men. The alternative is a woman characterized by "balance, harmony and cohesion of heart, spirit, mind and senses."[10] This vague portrait of a female identity is enriched by Robert's addendum in her letter to Marinetti:

> The verb "to seduce" has for some time lost any meaning . . . let's forcefully devalue this obsession with weakness, fragility, with predator and prey, which is so willingly accepted by a "smaller and smaller" number of women who are not yet oriented towards the victorious possession of their precise and confident personalities.[11]

Seduction, which is for Marinetti a male-activated process of converting decadent women into active *Futuriste*, is rejected by Robert, who creates a feminine rite of passage from languid women to active participants in the avant-garde. Woman is portrayed by Robert as the opposite of the simple formula "they all have a soul which depends, however, on the length of their hair" (Marinetti, 1920, 166), enunciated by the male leader of the movement. In her construction of femininity, Robert's woman reveals a latent desire for independence from the limitations imposed by dominant male Futurism. Marinetti's transparent woman, whom he physically and intellectually seduces in the Futurist alcove, reappears in Robert's writing in order to reveal her "opaqueness," that is, her complexity in relation to the gendered identity created by the literary movement. Robert states:

> There are women who are rendered precious by a very happy correspondence, a perfect cohesion, of soul and senses, when they give of themselves in a room "filled with parfumes and shadows," but they know then, at the right time, how to be also alive, brave, strong, VIRILE, INTELLIGENT, beside their men.[12]

Woman as heir of the past and the present is a gendered identity that deviates from Marinetti's seduced and converted women. These transformed women's voices appear in *Come si seducono le donne*. One of the women proclaims that "today women become attatched to men's ideas" and thus are tied to the men who incarnate those ideas.[13] Accepting this messianic idea of man, woman acquires her *raison d'être* as a disciple of the Futurist man. On the contrary, Robert's conclusion, in both her article in *Italia futurista* (1917) and in the appendix to Marinetti's manual (under the title "Sedurre o essere sedotto," "To seduce or to be seduced"), proclaims independence for Futurist women's creativity. She writes: "but women, smiling, in a pregnant silence, sharpen their minds more and more in order to contend in myopic men—who knows?—maybe even . . . the monopoly of intelligence!" (Marinetti, 1918, 210).

Enif Robert's utopian project is contradicted by other statements even within the context of her own work. In the same article the writer aggressively rejects the idea of seduction and conversion only to reaccept it later, since she recognizes the superiority of man, the Futurist, who has "the VERY RARE gift of an equal power of perception and thought" (Marinetti, 1918, 208). Futurist men, "who know how to give a feeling of vertigo in the mind and the thrill of seduction," are at the top of a hierachical structure in which women occupy an inferior position (Marinetti, 1918, 208). Futurist women are, however, by men's concession, superior to the male crowd of bourgeois *"passatisti,"* "vulgar men," and "eunuchs" (Marinetti, 1918, 208). In this new social-intellectual-political structure, "woman" is in a position controlled by Marinetti, who sees the Futurist woman—because of her "spiteful claws"—as the instrumental object for the destruction of the parliamentary order (what Marinetti calls the "animalization of politics") and consequently, the destruction of "rationality."[14]

Enif Robert's reacceptance of male superiority is not unique among Futurist women writers. Rosa Rosà's article, published along with Robert's in *Italia futurista*, presents the same contradictory elements. In her article "Le donne del posdomani" (The women of "after-tomorrow," 1917), Rosa Rosà analyzes the change in the concept of femininity among women and attempts to explore the future evolution of women's roles in private and public spheres. Yet she states:

> Our contemporary life lacks the means to manifest these transformations of female instincts, which are slowly changing into superior ones: (I confirm through this the *superiority* of man!). Women are going to become men.[15]

To become like a man is the agenda of Rosà's construction of femininity. The writer creates a connecting line between the private (female) sphere and the public (male) sphere. The role of the mother is the center of Rosa Rosà's attention. Her aim is to destroy the traditional maternal role which separates women from the outside world and excludes them from an active participation in an hermeneutical approach to events in the public sphere. In order to reconcile the identities of "mother" and of "free personality," women must be subjects of a metamorphosis in which mothers can create a new dialogue with children. Rosa Rosà writes:

> One might object that then, in effect, if this female metamorphosis is to take place, every young boy will not have a father and a mother any more, the former to give him a strong and virile education, and the latter to accompany him with her sweetness, which does not dispute him, but only loves; he will have, rather, TWO FATHERS and no mother.

One of the goals of the regendered woman as father is the construction of an independent "I" who can acquire an active role in the public sphere. The result is the elimination of "traditional love" because "love means the abolition of one's ego, it means subtracting the essence of life from another individual's substance and not from one's own roots." Rosà's portrayal of "love" partly coincides with Marinetti's condemnation of "horrible and heavy Love" which, just like woman, prevents men from becoming "the multiplied man," the U*ebermensch*.[16] Rosà is, however, attempting to deconstruct the idea of love as "the only content," the sole signified, of woman. The article succeeds in problematizing even further the relationship between the two spheres in proclaiming women's right to partake of both. She struggles against fixed roles for women and against an essentialistic definition of female gender: "All women are the same." Such a reductive statement, says Rosà, is formulated by men "as soon as one can see that a strong and emancipated woman fulfills her duties as wife and mother like all the others, finding in it a great or small amount of happiness, like any woman."

What Rosa Rosà intends for emancipated woman is further developed in her contribution to the appendix of Marinetti's *Come si seducono le donne*. Her impatient rhetorical question "So, who can tell me what women should be like?" marks the beginning of her creation of an emancipated woman who declares her physical and intellectual independence from Marinetti's movement. Rosà writes:

Women warn men that in addition to their ability to love, and to be sweet and sometimes stupid mates, who are subservient, sometimes illogical, candid, unselfish and in love, and sometimes false and immoral, they are going to acquire a novelty: a "meta-center" which is ABSTRACT, unconquerable, and inaccessible to the most expert seductions. . . . They are acquiring the awareness of an immortal and free "I," which does not give itself to anybody or anything.

Rosà disrupts Marinetti's metaphor of woman as a "tunnel," as a totally controllable physical entity that has no secrets for the Futurist man. Robert's and Rosà's texts succeed in translating *il problema femminile* into a *mise en abyme* where the construction of femininity is not teleological, but is repeatedly problematized by each individual female author. The dialogue between texts by Futurist writers reveals the complexity of the construction of femininity in a social-historical period when women's roles in the public sphere are quickly changing due to the impact of the world conflict on Italian society. The "strong truths" about woman sought by Marinetti are fragmented into "weak truths" that belong only to an isolated context in Futurist writings. Rosa Rosà substitutes the self-transparent woman with the opaque and unknowable creature who can escape men's direct control only to end up internalizing the patriarchal structure she is attempting to oppose. Her construction of femininity is trapped in the circular structure that simultaneously negates male values and accepts them as models that enable women to become "as men" and to occupy visible roles in the public sphere.

Rosa Rosà's contributions to Marinetti's *Come si seducono le donne* appear only in the 1918 edition of the book; they disappear in the 1920 edition of the manual. Her controversial discussion of Marinetti's construction of a controllable gender is sacrificed together with a letter by Shara Marini, another Futurist writer. Only Enif Robert's letters are kept in the reprint of Marinetti's work. In fact Marinetti and Robert later collaborated on a book, *Un ventre di donna: Romanzo chirurgico* (A woman's womb: A surgical novel), which is paradoxically a female autobiographical act completed by a male writing hand. In the 1918 edition of *Come si seducono le donne*, however, another letter by Rosà is included, and carries the title "Risposta a Jean-Jacques" (Reply to Jean-Jacques). It contains a further elaboration of the term "emancipated woman." Rosà's ideas this time can be included in the agenda of "humanist feminism" as originating in Simone de Beauvoir's theories. The equality of judgment for men's and women's intellectual abilities is the core of Rosà's statements in which the emancipated woman is represented as an androgynous being. The writer states:

How much I hope that one day people will not say any more: yes, very well, but she is a woman, or yes, very good, but he is a man. And people will not judge a person this way: "He is a moron" or "He is intelligent." You see. I am not a feminist, I am an "ist" for whom the first part of the word has not been found, yet.[17]

In her failure to create a neologism capable of expressing her position as a hybrid feminist, Rosa Rosà has a follower. Shara Marini is a little-known Futurist writer whose letter to Corrado Morosello is published in the 1918 edition of Marinetti's manual of seduction. She aims to construct a separation between male and female creativity and stresses the independence of female work from the dominant artistic creations of the Futurist movement. Commenting upon Marinetti's idea of seduction, Marini argues: "Female intuition, which always successfully reaches shores unknown to man's intelligence, tells me that you have made a gross mistake."[18] In her statement it becomes evident, however, that women's intuition and men's intelligence are placed on two different levels. Woman is brought back to instinctuality, to an intellectual *naiveté*.

Shara Marini's letter offers another member of the Futurist movement, "VOLT il Futurista," the opportunity for a critical letter addressed to Maria Ginanni and published in *Come si seducono le donne* (1918).[19] VOLT develops the thematic of "female intuition" and "instinctuality" to restate Marinetti's theories of women as a menace to men's constructed superiority. VOLT declares:

> In the end their instinct demands only one thing: to subjugate Man, keeping him in a state of perpetual unsatisfaction by denying him the right and natural fulfillment of his amorous passion. And women act that way because "they cannot act in any other way." (1918, xv-xvi)

If women are already "instinctively" a threat to men, they appear even more menacing in their public discussion on femininity, in their constant presence in the literary life of the movement, in the proclamation of their desire to become like men, and in their presence in the work force during the war years. Men's uneasiness with this attempted female independence in the construction of new sex roles is verbalized in an article by Emilio Settimelli. In "Maria Ginanni prima grande scrittrice italiana" (Maria Ginanni first great Italian woman writer), Settimelli reviews the latest poetry book published by the woman writer who is also the director of *Italia futurista*.[20] He underlines the poet's "full, couragious and impetuous strength without losing the enchantment of her very subtle femininity," but, at the same time, he must approach the topic of the independence of Maria Ginanni's poetic creativity from the Futurist movement. Settimelli writes that Ginanni is "hopelessly far from some of our [Futurist] convictions" and proceeds with a revealing statement: "Her criticism is so sharp and so profoundly sincere that we cannot but respect and accept it so that it will not succeed in modifying us."

This fear of contamination is also latent in Marinetti's work, in his attempt to control the changes in women's roles. The result is a number of statements in which Marinetti tries to create a compromise between the "new" and the "old" woman. In "Donne, preferite i gloriosi mutilati" (Women, choose our glorious mutilated soldiers), the leader of the Futurist movement invites women to fight in the trenches with men (Marinetti, 1920, 175). His invitation is aimed only at those women who are not mothers or workers in the fields: "Let's balance this way the strength of both sexes! All the responsibilities to you as well Italian women, if you want to be worthy of loving the glorious mutilated soldiers" (145). Marinetti's statement is revealing: women are allowed to become like men, so that they can qualify to love mutilated soldiers. This contradictory woman is created as a temporary solution to the *problema femminile* that *Come si seducono le donne* promises to resolve.

The double threat of castration, coming from the contaminating presence of women in the public sphere and from the war, compels Marinetti to create a new kind of U*ebermensch* whose physical deficiency is transformed into an increased virility. The new superman is the personification of the Futurist war and is paradoxically enriched by a loss. He succeeds in acquiring a new "member" from the mutilation of a metaphorical "arm." According to Marinetti, "nothing [is] more beautiful than an empty and flapping sleeve on one's chest because the gesture that orders the charge ideally leaps out of it" (173). Woman is therefore brought back to a position of inferiority because of her incompleteness in comparison with the soldier who acquires rank in "virility" through a lack, the empty sleeve, which is transformed into a Futurist "erection." Female castration becomes more evident. Only the new Futurist U*ebermensch* can transform women into "deserving" Futurists. Marinetti writes, "you do not understand me because you are incomplete," and he proceeds in creating an equation that puts woman and nature on the same level (60). They are both "hungry for war" and can both be modified by the Futurist man thanks to the "hygenic" war, the Futurist ideal violent cure (60). In *Come si seducono le donne*, Marinetti argues:

A woman without a war is an unloaded pistol. War gives its true taste to a woman's body just like it gives true beauty to mountains, rivers, woods. . . . A beautiful woman cannot have any other lover than a soldier armed in every way, who came from the front and is about to leave for it. (63)

In Marinetti's preoccupation of supplying both woman and nature with their lacking signifier, the deliberate shift in the literary context from male to female castration becomes evident. Threatened by the war and the social and political changes, the Futurist man concentrates his attention on woman as a sexual threat. *Come si seducono le donne* proposes too explicitly a male control of women and easily obtains a large response from women who, even if in a contradictory way, criticized it.[21]

Enif Robert's critical voice gradually disappears when in 1919 she collaborates with Marinetti in writing a woman's construction of self in a pseudo-female autobiographical act, controlled by the male intervention in the text. U*n ventre di donna: Romanzo chirurgico* is introduced by the manifesto of Futurist women, in which Robert's desire to put an official distance between female and male Futurist writings becomes evident. The formula "COURAGE + TRUTH" represents the base for the rules of a female Futurist-*verista* avant-garde which attempts to create the theoretical background for the autobiographical novel.[22] The manifesto is not an independent document, however. It is countersigned by Marinetti, who writes: "I unconditionally approve" (Marinetti and Robert, xiv). Robert becomes, therefore, the heroine of a tautology, a literary "transgression" controlled and approved by the "Master." The novel begins with the description of Robert's desire to break away from the suffocating oppression of society's rules. She is a widow who refuses to remarry and is determined to construct a self that is independent from the gendered identity created by society. She states: "Love is not enough for me. I really feel very little like a woman right now" (4). Once again, the quest for a female self is restated. The novelty in this autobiographical context lies in the presence of the active male writing hand within a woman's work.

The woman's search is complicated by physical illness, by disturbances of the womb that are preceded by moments of "terrible boredom," of melancholia (16). She is partly awakened from her sleepy, still decadent life by the irresistible Futurist man, Biego Fortis, who loves her "ferociously." The main thematic core of the novel is therefore displaced to the new relationship of the woman with the Futurist *Uebermensch*. Fortis leaves for the war and consequently the woman's body slowly loses its individuality to become a reflection of the violent experience men are facing on the front. Her diseased womb soon needs surgical intervention and Robert "becomes" her womb, the open wound of femininity. This relationship between woman and disease introduces a new component: the intervention of the male doctor in the female body, which represents the only way for the woman to become "whole" again. If the protagonist becomes her disease, the separation between physical and mental illness is destroyed. The newly created woman-womb is in need of a cure that can go beyond the practical intervention of the surgical knife. Only psychoanalysis can supply such a cure. In fact, melancholia, disease, and wound are three symbolic steps upon which Freud comments:

> The complex of melancholia behaves like an open wound, drawing to itself cathetic energy—which in the transferance neuroses we have called anti-cathexes—from all directions, and emptying the ego until it is totally impoverished.[23]

The female quest for an independent self is deviated into the representation of a female empty ego, woman as open wound, and the attention is displaced to the female diseased body and its sterility. The book becomes a report of a troubled voyage from one hospital to another, from a doctor to a surgeon. Woman is reduced to "impotence" by the disease and the attempted cures. She is gradually transformed into the "transparent woman" and becomes the constructed representation of the castration of the already lacking woman whose now empty ego is the appropriate receptacle for male Futurist signifieds. Robert exclaims: "How disgusting to be a suffering uterus while men are fighting" (25). Robert's work offers an example of a failed solution aiming to create a literary space where woman can overcome the limitations imposed on a middle-class widow and mother in order to enter the public sphere by becoming a member of a literary movement. Marinetti directly intervenes in her writing in order to control her "disease" and her search for an independent identity, which represent latent threats to male virility and power. The leader of the Futurist movement proves himself a dutiful disciple of Nietzsche; he appears to share the German philosopher's opinion of sickness and "female disease":

> Is there any place today where the sick do not wish to exhibit some form of superiority and to exercise their tyranny over the strong? Especially the sick females, who have unrivaled resources for dominating, oppressing, tyrannizing. The sick woman spares nothing dead or alive: she digs up long buried things.[24]

The image of the sick woman as hyena becomes for Marinetti the image of woman as a potentially castrating presence; she must therefore be controlled and dominated. In fact, Robert's translation of her struggle against her sick core hides the signified of a completely different struggle, which is the search for a role in the movement. Marinetti gains control of the narrative by translating Robert's experience; he moves it into the public sphere by linking the scars on the womb to the lines of the trenches on the earth. One of the final chapters, entitled "Dialogo fra Due Trincee" (Dialogue between two trenches), contains revealing statements in which trenches, enemies, wounds, and woman and her diseased womb are connected as objects to be controlled by the Futurist man:

> Now to conclude, you dirty pigs, I will make you listen to a piece of music by Anastasi! . . . Very Original! . . . A surgical music! My own work! In fact, it is my musical operation! . . . My light hand is not painful for the patient, at all! . . . Our line is an irregular line . . . a tumor: your colonel's shelter! (79)

Illness and the female body are for Marinetti texts to be read and interpreted in the search for a hidden signified, which, in fact, he constructs. Robert describes the symptoms of her disease, but they are interpreted by Marinetti, who formulates the equation between womb and earth, wound and trenches.

The text written by the woman writer does not succeed in constructing a female identity through the troubled experience of the "diseased womb." She only succeeds in creating a separation between herself and "other" women by inventing a "hybrid woman" who struggles to become as the Futurist man.[25] The link with ideas expressed by Rosa Rosà in "Le Donne del Posdomani" is manifest. In this autobiographical context, however, Robert's inner "manliness" is read and made evident by a man, a doctor, who intepretshercomplex personality: "Here it is: even though it is hard to define you, I would say that you seem to me to have an overly virile mind in an overly feminine body" (97).

This divided woman with her quickly changing moods can easily be defined as hysteric. Hysteria, from the Greek word for womb, justifies in the narration the shifting of attention from the female identity of the woman protagonist to the symptomatic womb. On this subject Mary Ann Doane writes: "The nineteenth century defined this disease [hysteria] quite specifically as a disturbance of the womb—the woman's betrayal by her own reproductive organs."[26] Marinetti acquires the role of doctor and psychoanalyst who can cure—that is, transform—the female body. In fact,

The Transparent Woman

in the introduction of *Come si seducono le donne*, Settimelli writes: "Marinetti is a great orator with a cutting voice and with energetic and chiselling gestures." In the second part of U*n ventre di donna*—which begins with a chapter bearing the revealing title of "Jack lo sventratore" (Jack the womb-ripper)— Marinetti's epistolary contribution to the text supplies a psychoanalytic cure that becomes effective together with a parallel surgical intervention on the womb. The Futurist cure is therefore a verbal treatment and a surgical operation which resembles the hygienic operation, of the war that can cure the body of the earth in Marinetti's manifestos. "Il manuale terapeutico del desiderio-immaginazione" (The therapeutic manual of desire/imagination) is the title of one of the chapters in the autobiographical novel; it contains the detailed Futurist cure dictated by Marinetti, which also includes the "order" to Enif Robert to read Futurist books.[27]

Seduction is not mentioned any more, but U*n ventre di donna* is indeed the new manual of seduction created by Marinetti. It is again the narration of male appropriation of the female body through the attempted cure of the "diseased tunnel of femininity." *Come si seducono le donne* is, in fact, specular to Enif Robert's autobiographical act. Marinetti begins writing his manual in a war hospital where he is recovering after several wounds *"all'inguine"* (in the groin).[28] The book of seduction is a therapeutic text. It represents Marinetti's self-made verbal cure in which language plays the role of controlling the body and of safeguarding man's virility so that he, after recovering, can return to exceptional sexual exploits, the main subject of the manual of seduction. Marinetti then turns to the female body and becomes a new hermeneutical hero who transforms the woman's decision to have an operation performed on her womb into a metaphor that invites Italians to take part in the war, the only means to extirpate what is rotting, what is decadent. The only hope of recovery for the womb lies in the Futurist cure, which is able through language to supply signifieds that can modify reality, the female body.

In U*n ventre di donna* a woman's construction of an independent identity fades into Marinetti's dominating discourse, which Robert gradually adopts. Her attempt to write in "parole in libertá" is promoted by the letters sent her by the leader of the movement. While commenting on Freud's theories Luce Irigaray writes, in her book *Speculum of the Other Woman*:

> She [the girl] borrows signifiers but cannot make her mark, or re-mark upon them, which all surely keeps her deficient, empty, lacking, in a way that could

be labelled "psychotic": a *latent* but not actual psychosis, for want of a practical signifying system.[29]

Enif Robert borrows in toto the male discourse. Her active role in searching and discovering, which begins the narration, turns into the passive role of adopting the male signifying system. Even male fear of castration appears in her writing as female fear: "God! What horror! Here is a beautiful A*lpino* indecently castrated! I think that women in Vienna rival the Ethiopian women and devour the genitals of Italian prisoners" (169).

Robert's recovery is not recorded in the narration, which in the last chapter shifts to a different story in which the characters remain, if not the same, similar to the ones in the main plot. A princess, with yet another diseased womb, invokes the intervention of a surgical knife on her body (i.e., Marinetti's cure). The Futurist man answers with an act of violence, killing the princess's husband and therefore erasing the rotting decadence of the institutions that the prince represents. Charged by the strength and violence of the Futurist act, the woman is cured of her "toilettite," her romantic (and rotting) core. She is now ready for the "Lotta dei Ventri Femminili" (The struggle of the female wombs)—the title of one of the final chapters of U*n ventre di donna*. Pulled by that "supermannish" strength the princess rises from bed and, in order to "celebrate" her husband's death, offers herself naked at the window. She is ecstatic in this moment of *jouissance* that only the Futurist man can give. Marinetti succeeds here in creating the epitome of the "transparent woman," the penetrable and empty shell of signifiers that also appears in his manifesto "Contro il lusso femminile" (Against feminine luxury) (March 11, 1920):

> *Toilettite* typically favours the development of homosexuality and we will soon have to adopt the hygienic remedy used by a Venetian D*oge* who made beautiful Venetian women expose themselves with naked breasts, standing between two candles at a window, in order to put men back on the right road.[30]

The female voice in U*n ventre di donna* gradually is silenced by Marinetti's literary voice. The weaker voice of Futurist women writers is suffocated on the one hand by their acceptance of male discourse and on the other by Futurist men's active construction of a self-transparent woman. In borrowing from male discourse, woman has, however, made "her mark, or re-mark" on the movement. Irigaray's statement concerning the "deficient, empty, lacking" woman, unable to "mark" male discourse, is valid for Enif Robert as protagonist of the autobiographical act, but it cannot encompass all Futurist women's creative efforts. By reclaiming male-dominated Futurist aesthetics, women writers in the movement succeeded in bringing to the surface, from the private to the public sphere, woman's desire to construct an independent female identity. Responses to *Come si seducono le donne*, such as Rosa Rosà's letters to Marinetti or Shara Marini's appendix to the manual of seduction, have "marked" the Futurist movement itself by provoking a dialogue, even if an unbalanced one, between Futurist texts.

Marinetti's construction of a Futurist "self-transparent" woman has certainly been helped a posteriori by many critics' approaches to Futurism. They have too often privileged the dominating voice of the male component of the movement, ignoring the parallel female voices. Defining women writers' role within Futurism as only mimetic is, however, erroneous; the proof of their importance and their "opaqueness"—in short, their visibility—lies in Marinetti's repeated negation of women's mark on "his" movement. This "negative mark" reveals itself in Marinetti's role within the autobiographical narration of U*n ventre di donna* and in his evident need to control the threat of the construction of a female independent self.

Silencing woman by engendering her can summarize the Futurist agenda, but this turns into a self-defeating project. In 1925 Fillia declares "la morte della donna" (the death of woman) in the eponymous collection of short stories. In the same year, he also publishes *Sensualitá* in which the U*ebermensch* is stabbed to death by the same "decadent" woman in love previously negated by Futurist writings.[31] Fillia's play is followed in 1932 by Vasari's R*aun*, in which the Futurist man himself destroys his mechanical modernist world to embrace once again the old myth of "Mother Earth."[32] This "self-silencing" by Futurist male voices announces the death not of woman (this time) but of the possibility of constructing a "transparent femininity."

Notes

1. In her book T*abù e coscienza* (Taboo and conscience), Anna Nozzoli dedicates a chapter to Futurist women where she analyzes the relationship between women writers and avant-garde by looking at texts by Enif Robert, Rosa Rosà, Valentine de Saint Point, and Maria Ginanni, and discusses the relationship between women's Futurist works and Marinetti's literary production. Anna Nozzoli stresses the problematic entrapment of female creativity within the dominating male ideology of the movement. She concludes by creating a triangular structure in which the link between Futurism and Fascism is represented by the work of a Futurist woman, who wrote predominantly in the late 1940s. Maria Goretti's creative effort is a pillar in the construction of what Nozzoli calls "the new aesthetics of the 'Mussolinian' war" (63) and it also concludes Nozzoli's panorama of women writers in Marinetti's movement.

Cinzia Blum in her article "The Scarred Womb of the Futurist Woman" concentrates her critical attention on Enif Robert's novel U*n ventre di donna*. Her intention is to reject the com-

Graziella Parati

mon assumption that "the women in the movement [Futurism] [had] a simply mimetic, entirely subordinated relation to the male Futurists" (15). Blum instead stresses that "the Futurist experience is a significant episode in women's activity on the Italian cultural and literary scene at the beginning of the twentieth century" (15). Through her analysis of Robert's autobiography, however, Blum must recognize what she calls "the limits of the strategy adopted by the Futurist women: to follow an avant-garde practice prescribed by a male-centered movement which does not seriously threaten the social organization of gender" (26).

This thematic—entrapment of female creativity within a male movement—seems to be the common denominator of both Anna Nozzoli's and Cinzia Blum's articles. Lucia Re, in her essay "Futurism and Feminism," instead focuses her attention on the "feminist" potential of Futurist women's writings. In regard to the *questione femminile* within the Futurist movement, Lucia Re describes the often contradictory, but always prescriptive definitions of Woman in Futurist works by men and women writers. Her article, like Anna Nozzoli's essay, ends with Maria Goretti's literary homage to Fascist ideology. Re's reading of this female "involution" offers a solution to the problematic of "female creative entrapment" in Marinetti's literary movement. Lucia Re argues: "Maria Goretti's book—along with some of the other works by futurist women written in the period of the fascist 'involution' of the movement—could be read as the locus where, in the face of the fascist regimentation of the female subject and of her discourse, a new 'ventriloquized' form of expression developed whose 'secret' resistance-function is precisely that of carrying out a poetic deconstruction of the fascist myth of femininity" (271). In my discussion concerning the construction of a concept of "femininity" within Futurism, I adopt, as starting point, Lucia Re's idea of "resistance-function." I dispense with the adjective "secret," however, and investigate the existence of a "female Futurist agenda" parallel to Marinetti's. I also argue that the female agenda succeeds—even in a contradictory way through progress and involutions—in influencing the Futurist male construction of a feminine ideal, intended as a complementary and inferior being to the "Futurist Superman." Futurist women create literary "acts of resistance" that oppose an exclusively male definition of gender. Their contradictory but alternative description of Woman as member of the Futurist movement provokes the failure of Marinetti's creation of woman as a completely known and mastered being. No longer identified as the products of weaker voices, female texts can be seen as active participants in a male movement, which does not succeed in avoiding the feared "contamination" of women's creativity.

2. Fillìa, *La morte della donna* (The death of woman), in *Prosa e critica futurista* (Futurist prose and critical works), ed. Mario Verdone, 177.

3. Ruggero Vasari, *L'angoscia delle macchine: Teatro italiano d'avanguardia* (Italian drama of the avant-garde), 180.

4. F. T. Marinetti, *Come si seducono le donne e si tradiscono gli uomini* (1920), 21.

5. Gianni Vattimo, *La società trasparente*, 11.

6. Vattimo, *La società*, 14. In "Dialettica, differenza, pensiero debole" (Dialectic, difference and the weak thought), in *Il pensiero debole* (ed. Gianni Vattimo and Pier Aldo Rovatti), Vattimo articulates his concept of a "weak ontology of the notion of truth": "Wishing to sum up what a weak ontology of the notion of truth supposes, one could start by saying that: a) truth is not an object of noetic prehension like evidence, but it is the result of a verification process, which produces it in respect to certain procedures which are always already given for each time (the world-project which constitutes us in as much as it is us); in other words, it does not have a metaphysical or logical nature, but a rhetorical one . . . ; b) truth is the fruit of interpretation, not because a direct grasping of truth is reached by way of the interpretative process . . . , but because it is only within the interpretative process, understood, above all, in reference to the Aristotelian sense of *hermeneia*, an expression or formulation, that the truth is established" (26).

The Transparent Woman

7. I am here borrowing the idea of a "dialogue between texts" from Gianni Vattimo's *La società trasparente*: "The possible 'truth' of the world of mass-media communication is a 'hermeneutic' logic which looks for the truth in a continuity, a 'correspondence,' a dialogue between texts, and not in a proposition's conformity to a mythical state of things" (40).
8. Bruno Corra and Emilio Settimelli, "Come si seducono le donne."
9. *Italia Futurista* has no page numbers.
10. Enif Robert, "Una parola serena."
11. Enif Robert, "Sedurre o essere sedotto," in Marinetti, *Come si seducono le donne e si tradiscono gli uomini* (1920), 204.
12. Ibid., 207.
13. F. T. Marinetti, *Come si seducono le donne*, ed. Maria Ginanni and Settimelli (1918), xiv.
14. F. T. Marinetti, "Contro l'amore e il parlamentarismo" (Against love and parliamentarism), in *Teoria e invenzione futurista*, 253.

Lucia Re in "Futurism and Feminism" comments upon the apparent feminist overtones in Marinetti's "Contro l'amore e il parlamentarismo." In fact, antifeminism and feminism coexist in Marinetti's text as inseparable elements in those manifestos that present his construction of the relation between public and private spheres. Lucia Re writes: "Marinetti, with the radical irreverence typical of the first phase of futurism, vilifies woman but at the same time paradoxically defends the women's movement and the call to extend suffrage to women in order to launch an attack against the basic structures of Italian society and its democracy under premier Giovanni Giolitti's notoriously opportunistic and corrupt leadership" (257).

15. Rosa Rosà, "Le donne del posdomani," n.p.
16. Marinetti, "Contro l'amore," 250.
17. Rosa Rosà, "Risposta a Jean-Jacques," in Marinetti, *Come si seducono le donne* (1918), xi.
18. Shara Marini, "Lettera a Corrado Morosello," in Marinetti, *Come si seducono le donne* (1918), xiv.
19. VOLT, "Lettera a Maria Ginanni," in Marinetti, *Come si seducono le donne* (1918), xiv-xvi.
20. Emilio Settimelli, "Maria Ginanni prima grande scrittrice italiana," n.p.
21. A parody of Marinetti's book was written at the time by Mari Annetta, who entitled her manual *Come si seducono gli uomini* (How to seduce men) (Rocca di San Casciano: Cappelli, 1918).
22. F. T. Marinetti and Enif Robert, *Un ventre di donna: Romanzo chirurgico*, xiv.
23. Sigmund Freud, "Mourning and Melancholia," 253.
24. Friedrich Nietzsche, *The Genealogy of Morals*, 260.
25. Other women are defined (in *Un ventre di donna*) as "deformed mothers": "I have nothing in common with those huge, flabby, Neapolitan matrons in bathing-suits; they are black, slimy, and spread out like seals on the sand, with their wriggling and boiling offspring dished out around them" (4). Seeing through the male gaze, Enif Robert also describes the nurse who is "a poor deformed being" (43) and reminds her of a "head of boiled veal" (154). She despises Woman as intellectual, and mimetically condemns learned women to ridicule, as Marinetti has done before: "Here is a case which makes one think. An ugly woman, made even uglier by barbarous clothing, her mind encumbered by erudite solemnity, and thus the least suitable person for asserting the most modern simplifiers of life and art. She holds them instead, with an entertaining mastery, fastened at least two ['erudite solemnities'] at a time to the clownish pompon of her ridiculous little hat" (202).
26. Mary Ann Doane, *The Desire to Desire: Women's Film of the 1940's*, 38.
27. Marinetti's cure (from *Un ventre di donna*) is divided into "Theory" and "Practice":

"'Theory':
Health is the sum of all the desires/strengths which keep us attached to life. In all serious illnesses, the rending or softening of these ties can be found.

Graziella Parati

"One lives in as much as one has many reasons for living. One dies in as much as one loses the reasons for living, little by little.

"Therefore, in order to get better, one must form new attachments to life by means of strong ties.

'Practice': Every day think about something pleasing which you have seen or dreamed, or which you would like to see, touch, eat, drink, hold, or possess . . .

"Dream about multiplying hundredfold, with a gesture of love, the activity or artistic talent of a man you love . . .

"Dream up the ideal ornament for your charm." (124)

Under Marinetti's control even the "toilettite" can lose its negative connotation in order to become "curative." What Marinetti guarantees is that "after a month of this regime you will feel an enormous strength tumultuously rise in you in order to break, at all cost, the foul snare of the illness" (124).

28. Marinetti writes: "The first part of this book was drafted by me in a bed of the military hospital in Udine, where the eleven wounds in my groin and my legs forced me to remain immobile" (1918, 26).

29. Luce Irigaray, *Speculum of the Other Woman*, 71.

30. F. T. Marinetti, "Contro il Lusso Femminile," in *Teoria e invenzione futurista*, 476.

31. Fillia (Luigi Colombo), *Sensualità* (Sensuality), 120–47.

32. Roberto Tessari, in a chapter of *Il mito della macchina* entitled "Esperimenti teatrali di un'avanguardia al tramonto: morte del superuomo e del dio-macchina e ritorno al culto della Grande Madre" (The theatrical experimentation of an avant-garde in decline: the death of the superman and the machine-god, and the return of the cult of the Great Mother), extensively analyzes how Futurist myths change in literary creations in the final years of Futurism.

Works Cited

Blum, Cinzia. "The Scarred Womb of the Futurist Woman." *Carte Italiane* 8 (1986–87).
Corra, Bruno, and Emilio Settimelli. "Come si seducono le donne." *Italia futurista* (Oct. 7, 1917): n.p.
Doane, Mary Ann. *The Desire to Desire: Women's Film of the 1940's*. Bloomington: Indiana University Press. 1987.
Fillia (Colombo, Luigi). *Sensualità*. Turin: Sindacati artistici, 1925.
Freud, Sigmund. "Mourning and Melancholia." In vol. 14, *The Complete Psychological Works of Sigmund Freud* (1914–1916). London: Hogarth Press and Institute of Psycho-Analysis, 1964.
Gherarducci, Isabella. *Il futurismo italiano*. Rome: Editori Riuniti, 1984.
Irigaray, Luce. *Speculum of the Other Woman*. Ithaca: Cornell University Press, 1985.
Marinetti, Filippo Tommaso. *Come si seducono le donne*. Florence: Edizioni da Centomila, 1916.
———. *Come si seducono le donne*. Ed. Maria Ginanni and Emilio Settimelli. Rocca di San Casciano: Tipografia L. Cappelli, 1918.
———. *Come si seducono le donne e si tradiscono gli uomini*. Milan: Sonzogno, 1920.
———. *Teoria e invenzione futurista*. Ed. Luciano de Maria. Milan: Mondadori, 1983.
Marinetti, Filippo Tommaso, and Enif Robert. *Un ventre di donna: Romanzo chirurgico*. Milan: Facchi, 1919.
Nietzsche, Friedrich. *The Genealogy of Morals*. New York: Doubleday, 1956.
Nozzoli, Anna. *Tabù e coscienza: La condizione femminile nella letteratura italiana del novecento*. Florence: La Nuova Italia, 1978.
Re, Lucia. "Futurism and Feminism." *Annali d'Italianistica* 7 (1989).
Robert, Enif. "Una parola serena." *Italia futurista* (Oct. 7, 1917): n.p.
———. "Sedurre o essere sedotto." In Marinetti, *Come si seducono le donne e si tradiscono gli uomini*.

Rosà, Rosa. "Le donne del posdomani." *Italia futurista* (Oct. 7, 1917): n.p.
Salaris, Claudia. *Storia del futurismo*. Rome: Editori Riuniti, 1985.
Settimelli, Emilio. "Maria Ginanni prima grande scrittrice italiana," *Italia futurista* (March 4, 1917): n.p.
Tessari, Roberto. *Il mito della macchina: Letteratura e industria nel primo nevecento italiano*. Milan: Mursia, 1973.
Vasari, Ruggero. *L'angoscia delle macchine: Teatro italiano d'avanguardia* (Italian drama of the avant-garde). Ed. Mario Verdone. Rome: Officina, 1970.
Vattimo, Gianni. "Dialettica, differenza, pensiero debole." In *Il pensiero debole*, ed. Gianni Vattimo and Pier Aldo Rovatti. 7th ed. Milan: Feltrinelli, 1990.
———. *La società trasparente*. Milan: Garzanti, 1989.
Verdone, Mario. *Teatro italiano d'avanguardia*. Rome: Officina, 1970.
———, ed. *Prosa e critica futurista*. Milan: Feltrinelli, 1973.

Part II
Reading Cultural Texts

Maria Marotti

Filial Discourses
Feminism and Femininity in Italian Women's Autobiography

Italian criticism of women's writings often uses the word "novel" to refer to texts that should instead be considered autobiographies. This misclassification may be due in part to the tendency of Italian criticism to be less interested in the theory of genre than in other theoretical trends. The application of the word "novel" by women writers to their own work, however, also points to their marginal position in the Italian critical and literary world.[1] Until a few decades ago, autobiography was considered a minor genre by Italian literary critics. It is then understandable that an already marginalized group of writers (and their publishers as well) would prefer to avoid such labeling of their serious works—a labeling that could only further their marginalization.[2]

Like women's autobiography from other cultures, Italian women's autobiography displays noncanonical forms at the borderline between genres—especially between fiction and family biography. This noncanonical position, which is yet another sign of the marginalization of women's writings, has nonetheless the potential to free women's autobiographical texts from some of the strictures of male autobiographical discourse. Free from a linear method and design, the female autobiographer is less bound by a writing/reading pact with the reader concerning the verifiable factual content of her text.[3]

It is obvious that an autobiographer who has labeled her text a "novel"—as is the case for several Italian female autobiographers—has an even greater freedom to expand the possibilities of her method of composition, freely crossing the boundaries of fiction and nonfiction. Even the identity of the writing subject in such autobiographical texts does not completely coincide throughout the narrative with that of the protagonist of the story, thus allowing another crossing of generic boundaries—that between biography and autobiography.

The liberating aspect implicit in women's autobiographies is paralleled by the subversive potential of the genre for women. Female autobiographers, unlike writers of diaries and letters, take a public stance and address an audience, thus asserting that the personal is public.[4] They break the silence to which patriarchy has relegated women by inscribing female identity, traditionally the object of male description and definition. By doing so, they question and challenge patriarchal values and views pertaining to womanhood. All this makes women's autobiography the ideal locus for the study of a feminist discourse and its interplay with the idea of femininity in Italian culture.

Yet such a study is only possible if one considers feminism to be "the site of difference," in Teresa de Lauretis's words, and a point of resistance to patriarchal values, rather than a monolithic ideology.[5] To this purpose, Nancy K. Miller's emphasis on the writers' self-consciousness about women's identity and on their resistance to and revision of socially constructed plots and conventions concerning female lives, as forms of feminist strategy, is particularly helpful (Miller, 8). These aspects of feminist strategy surface in the text that I have chosen to discuss.

One must note, however, that these autobiographers' resistance to patriarchy is always loaded with ambiguity. It is often interwoven with complex and contrasting attitudes: the idea of woman shaped by patriarchy often surfaces in the texts. Indeed, the definition of female identity that is offered in these autobiographies encompasses aspects of women's lives that have already been described by patriarchy as inherently "feminine." In contrast, many trends of feminist thought view such aspects of women's lives through a completely different optic, either as means of female survival in a repressive male society or as expressions of women's difference. (I am referring in particular to trends present in French and Italian feminism as well as in North American feminist thought.)[6] In particular, French feminism's insistence on difference based in women's sexuality and Italian feminism's emphasis on cultural gender difference tend toward a revision of western male-centered definitions of femininity.

Defining femininity is an even more troublesome task than defining feminism. Is femininity what pertains to the female body and the female experience? Or is it "the accepted view of woman as the possessor of an ahistorical, eternal feminine essence, a closeness to nature that served to

Filial Discourses

keep women in 'their place'"?[7] In the context of this discussion I refer to both these concepts when I point to the emergence of the "feminine" in the texts.

In her study of British women writers, Elaine Showalter uses the terms "feminine," "feminist," and "female" to describe the historical development of women writing in England. "Feminine" refers to nineteenth-century women writers who "wrote in an effort to equal the intellectual achievements of the male culture, and internalized its assumptions about female nature." The term "feminist" refers to writings at the turn of the century that, while rejecting accepted views about femininity, described "the ordeals of wronged womanhood." Finally, during the "female phase," which covers the modernist and contemporary periods, writers turn from "both imitation and protest . . . to female experience as the source of an autonomous art" (Showalter, 137–39). Proceeding in the discussion, one finds Showalter's definitions helpful. Yet one notices that a purely diachronic scheme would not fit the autobiographies examined here. Even though a formidable evolution of thought concerning womanhood has occurred in Italy throughout the decades of our century, and it is reflected in these texts, earlier "feminine" attitudes persist in later "female" texts, while "feminist" writings already contain some "female" ideas. Moreover, for the purposes of this study and for clarity's sake, I use the term "prefeminist" when Showalter would use "feminine," and "neofeminist" instead of "female."

I have chosen for discussion autobiographies centering on a filial discourse.[8] These autobiographers place an emphasis on their relations to matrilineage and patrilineage. It has become apparent to me in my reading of Italian women's autobiography that the way in which autobiographers view their relationships to both parents, and the parents' relationships to each other, shapes their approaches to patriarchy. In a discussion of the interplay of feminism and femininity in autobiographies, an exploration of such relationships is therefore seminal. These autobiographies include Sibilla Aleramo's A Woman (1906), Gianna Manzini's Ritratto in piedi (1971) and Sulla soglia (1973), Natalia Ginzburg's Family Sayings (1963), Fausta Cialente's Le quattro Ragazze Wieselberger (1976), and Fabrizia Ramondino's Althenopis (1981).

A classic of Italian feminism, Sibilla Aleramo's autobiography, A Woman, displays in embryo many of the issues that were debated then and later by the feminist movement: women's right to sexual expression and control over their bodies; the need for women to acquire an autonomous voice and be able to define themselves rather than letting patriarchy define them; and the need for women to live up to their own expectations rather than to those of society. Aleramo dismisses the myth of the necessity of mothers' sacrifices for the ultimate good of their children. She also links feminism to other issues of social and economic justice.

A *Woman*, as is the case with most autobiographical writings, is written from the perspective of the present—the moment of writing. That explains the ideological orientation of the text. Besides being the explanation to her son of her choice to break off her marriage and leave (as the final pages profess to be), the memoir is also a complex and often contradictory search by the author for the origin of feminism in her life.

Aleramo traces the source of her feminism back to her childhood—to her relationship with her parents and her early development. She rejects early the maternal model that she perceives to be charged with a self-destructive potential, and embraces the paternal model with all its potential for liberating and self-affirming choices. Later, disappointed by her father, she temporarily falls back on the path traced by her mother, only to discover that in doing so she has violated essential demands of her nature. For the young Rina it is almost natural to cross over to the paternal side because of the debilitating options presented by the maternal model, and because of the constant devaluation to which her mother is subjected by her father. Instead, the paternal model appears particularly attractive to her because, despite his authoritarian behavior, her father is a free thinker who allows her freedom and the possibility of self-expression. In describing herself as an adolescent Aleramo traces an androgynous ideal:

> I remember a photograph of myself taken a year later when I started to work regularly in the factory office. I was wearing an odd assortment of clothes—a straight-cut jacket with lots of small pockets for my watch, pencil, and notebook, over a short skirt. My hair fell in curls over my forehead but had been cut short at the back, making me look like a young boy—at my father's suggestion I had sacrificed my glossy pigtails with their golden gleams. My odd appearance reflected clearly the way I thought of myself: no longer a girl, but as yet with no proper sense that I was a woman. (15–16)

The device of the photograph—another topos of autobiography—allows Aleramo to describe herself, with some detached objectivity, at a transitional age when, due to her exceptional position as a worker in her father's factory, she was able to delay her entrance into a state of being that could only mean enslavement. She can thus linger in the foreign territory of the father in a position that allows temporary relief from gender.

A few chapters later, an image of conventional femininity counteracts that of the androgynous adolescent. It is the image in the mirror of herself as a mother. "I saw my rosy cheeks, my radiant eyes and open face: I seemed the very image of maternity" (62). The androgynous image of the photograph is described through memory ("I remember . . .") and followed by an interpretation of its meaning from the perspective of the moment of writing; the mirror image is, instead, viewed through the eyes of the protagonist as it appeared to her at the time of the events, with no further explanation or comment by the autobiographer. The images in both the photograph and the mirror are charged with cultural meaning. The photograph reflects the dream of a life outside gender, while the mirror gives back a totally gendered image.

Motherhood gains Rina a temporary acceptance by family and society as well as joy and vitality for herself. Yet she soon discovers that that acceptance is at the cost of denying her feelings and repressing her sexual and intellectual needs. Moreover, her mother's mental illness keeps haunting her as a reminder of a persistent threat for women who renounce the self. The more her life follows in the traditional path of a bourgeois marriage, the more strongly Rina rejects her mother, whom she starts to perceive as a negative mirror image of herself. Later, depression and suicidal tendencies surface in her own life as a response to her husband's repression and violence.

Aleramo structures her autobiography as a bildungsroman in which the protagonist, through initiation into the reality of a male-dominated society, gains insight, strength, and self-discovery. The victory consists partly in retrieving her essence, which had surfaced without restraint during childhood but had been repressed later by social conventions surrounding femininity. The various phases of the initiation are marked by images and episodes reminiscent of death-rebirth rituals. The protagonist's suicide attempt, and later the deaths of her guides and mentors (the town doctor and her Scandinavian friend), are followed by periods of insight and moral advancement. Death creates a sense of tragic urgency in the text, an allusion to themes of the death and survival of the self. Both of these themes are in turn also linked in the text with the image of the insane mother and of motherhood itself.

Aleramo distinguishes quite lucidly between motherhood as experience—a possible source of vitality and creativity in a woman's life—and motherhood as institution—a set of repressive expectations created by society demanding from mothers the sacrifice of the self.[9] Such a sacrifice can lead to madness (her mother's case) or to suicide (nearly her case). Yet women are responsible for the persistence of this debilitating self-sacrificial notion from generation to generation. She argues that mothers perpetuate women's self-sacrifice through their daughters:

> Why do we idealise sacrifice in Mothers? Who gave us this inhuman idea that mothers should negate their own wishes and desires? The acceptance of servitude has been handed down from mother to daughter for so many centuries that it is now a monstrous chain which fetters them. . . . Yet what would happen if this dreadful cycle was broken, once and for all? What if mothers refused to deny their womanhood and gave their children instead an example of a life lived according to the needs of self-respect? (193–94)

In writing her autobiography, Aleramo rereads her own life, and through the process of writing acquires a new view of her relation with her parents.[10] At the beginning of the autobiography she traces the source of her psychological independence back to the paternal model; later, her mother's madness seems to play an even deeper role in her recognition of women's predicament in a patriarchal society. In the last part of the text, Aleramo tells of her discovery of one of her mother's letters to her own parents. The letter reveals that the mother had contemplated the possibility of leaving her husband in order to preserve her sanity. Thanks to the letter, the previously rejected mother becomes almost a mentor for Rina; the discovery of the letter plays an important role in her final decision to leave her marriage. The episode is crucial for two reasons. It shows that the writing of the memoir has fostered an evolution in Aleramo's interpretation of her own life. It also marks the autobiographer's recognition of the mother as her mirror image, both in its shadowy connotation of the insane mother and in the more positive one of the potentially rebellious mother. The acceptance of such an image shows the evolution from the conventional and narcissistic initial image of maternity as bliss to more complex and unconventional reflections on the reality and institution of motherhood.

A *Woman* is also a historical document for Italian feminism. Despite fictionalization, it effectively recreates the scene of Italian feminism at the turn of the century. While tracing the network of connections that she establishes among Italian feminists, Aleramo points out the main shortcomings of Italian feminism: the lack of a central organization and its foundation in the bourgeoisie. She also thinks that women need to develop their own artistic forms and autonomous voice—a kind of écriture feminine avant la lettre. Yet her own feminism suffers from her feminization of the individualistic male myth of the exceptional individual who soars high over the rest of humankind and who is not bound by common rules—a myth made particularly fashionable in those years by D'Annunzio. This is especially noticeable when she expounds her essentialist view of feminism as "female genius which had always existed but had only been communicated by exceptional individuals." Aleramo shows also a clear understanding of social conditioning, however, when she finishes this statement by explaining that this is true only "since women had always needed so much strength to overcome the restrictions of law and convention" (139). The autobiography is less tainted by the individualistic myth than her subsequent works.[11]

Aleramo's early internalization of the paternal image as a model of independence and courage might account for her almost prefeminist individualism and for her everlasting admiration for male models. Nonetheless, one of her most important contributions to Italian feminism is her clear recognition of female desire and the link between desire and liberation: "It was to my body that I owed my liberation" (210).

A strong paternal image also characterizes Gianna Manzini's autobiographical *Ritratto in Piedi* (1971, Standing portrait) and *Sulla soglia* (1973, On the threshold), which are devoted to her father and her mother, respectively. Manzini's lack of explicit involvement with feminist issues in these works does not prevent the unfolding of a discourse on femininity and on the social constraints placed upon women.

The daughter of separated parents, Gianna is the "diaphragm" that links them and their opposite worlds—that of the anarchist movement and that of the bourgeoisie. She partakes of both environments. Her sympathies, however, are with the marginalized and rebellious world of the father. In *Ritratto in piedi* the father is always characterized by images of light; throughout the text his luminosity never abates.[12] In the text the mother is characterized by silence:

> However, at home they had commented: "All postures"; and mamma had bowed the head, yes; but she had not defended him. I myself alone, what tears, in another room. She could have rebelled and, instead, not a word. I hated her! (37)[13]

Maria Marotti

The silent and silenced mother is the prisoner, and the object of barter in the bourgeois family. Gianna's mother has been compelled by her own family to accept separation from her husband, who is an anarchist and therefore almost an outlaw in early twentieth-century Italy. The mother's captivity is a function of her femininity, which makes her the object of both patriarchal repression and aesthetic pleasure.

The young Gianna perceives the connection between her mother's captive role in the family and her femininity, signified by elegant clothing. In a poignant scene, during childhood, Gianna, while half asleep, urges her mother—or she imagines she does—to leave her patriarchal family and join her husband. She feels that by doing so she is moving into a sphere of clarity and luminosity where all conflicts will be solved—the sphere of the father, who is the source of luminosity. Suddenly, while talking to her mother (almost on the threshold of sleep), the child visualizes one of her mother's wonderful dresses, and realizes the hold that clothing has on both her mother and herself. She feels that the dress has "bewitched" them both. She whispers: "Dress . . . prison." Only years later does the autobiographer decode the confusing words: "I wanted to say: 'Mamma, we are prisoners of that dress of yours'" (129).

Clothing is not only an aspect of the mother's captivity, however; it is also a mode of artistic expression and a silent language that the mother addresses to her separated husband. Gianna often becomes the text in this language. By giving painstaking care to her daughter's clothing, her mother makes Gianna into the personification of the emotional link that exists between herself and her husband ("How else could I show you that I keep our daughter like a reliquary"; 166). At other times, the mother herself becomes such nonverbal text.

The mother's silence contrasts with the father's loquacity. *Ritratto in piedi* is structured around a series of dialogues between father and daughter, which are prolonged even beyond death. Her father is a mentor for Gianna. The daughter identifies with his perspective, and admires his integrity and courage. It is indeed a heroic portrait of a martyr. The mother's world—clothing, bourgeois conventions, hesitation—is belittled by contrast.[14] In one episode, mother and father face each other at a distance. He is below in the street while she is on the balcony of her paternal house. They stare at each other silently. The father sends a mental message to the mother inviting her to join him in an uncertain, although heroic life. After an initial moment when it seems that she will be able to free herself from her bondage, the mother loses strength. In her daughter's perception, the railing of the balcony, the small wall that separates the couple, becomes higher and higher while the mother shrinks.

Although in many dramatic episodes in the book the mother's silence is expressive, its ability to communicate relies on other languages and it remains debilitating. The nonverbal mother, who is silenced by the daughter-writer, is a topos in late nineteenth- and early twentieth-century fiction.[15] This character type survives that period; its trace can still be found in modern literature. The mother's silence allows the daughter to detach herself from her, and cross over to the world of the father, a verbal world in which the daughter can gain freedom of expression, and thus refuse to follow in her mother's footsteps. Manzini dismisses the option of silence—her mother's debilitating choice—by writing; yet in her writing she does not leave her mother behind, because through her own imagination she reconstructs her mother's submerged discourse.

In *Sulla soglia*, her final autobiographical novella, Manzini interprets her mother's point of view. The encounter with the mother occurs in a surrealistic space at the border between life and death, between sleep and consciousness. The dialogue, led by the autobiographer, is often interrupted by extraneous characters, signifying the incapacity of a materialistic and male-dominated society to understand the mother/daughter bond. While evoking memories of their lives together, Manzini explains her mother's actions and reconstructs her hidden desires and forbidden fantasies.

Here again the mother is often denoted by nonverbal language based on clothing, glances, and gestures; it is a language of apparent impotence and frustration. Yet, in some episodes, she explicitly reveals her desire. In one instance, the young Gianna overhears her mother talk to another woman in the next room:

> From the next room, every sob of yours exploded in my chest, tearing me apart. All of a sudden, you, with a choked voice: "I am twenty-eight. Alone. Alone for ever: I can't stand it." (121)[16]

Thanks to the mediation of a friend, the mother has tried to arrange a clandestine encounter with her husband, but he has refused to see her. Gianna, obeying the command to stay in the next room, overhears her mother's bitter remarks and violent sobs. She is appalled and petrified. The episode reveals the mother's sexual and emotional frustration and victimization, caused in this case not only by social conventions but also by the father's demanding integrity and extreme heroism. In the episode, Gianna's position as the child who overhears her mother's violent outburst in the next room parallels that of the older autobiographer, Manzini, who interprets her mother's actions and reads them as expressions of desire ("your love letter," 123).

While *Ritratto in piedi*, written from the perspective of a child enamored of her father, depicts the mother's silence as lack of courage, *Sulla soglia* charges silence with deeper meanings that the child can already perceive. A greater understanding is gained through the child's identification with her mother ("every sob of yours exploded in my chest, tearing me apart"), an identification with even deeper roots than that experienced with the father, its source being the pre-Oedipal stage.[17] Here, the job of the adult autobiographer is to unveil hidden meanings and retrieve buried childhood perceptions.

In both autobiographical works, femininity appears both as a form of language and as a social constraint imposed upon women. It is the only language allowed to women in a repressive patriarchal society, and therefore their only form of power; it is also, at the same time, the means by which they are made passive objects of trade and male desire. By adopting her father's radical perspective Manzini discloses women's oppression in terms that we can define as feminist.

In *Family Sayings* (1963) femininity appears instead with more positive connotations of expression of female culture, and as a means of psychological survival. The book is defined by its author, Natalia Ginzburg, as "a record of [her] family" that "should be read as though it were a novel, that is, read without demanding of it either more or less than what a novel can offer" (7). By placing her work at a crossroads of genres—fiction and biography—Ginzburg shows in her preface a concern with readers' expectations that reminds one of Philippe Lejeune's later definition of the autobiographical pact.[18] On the one hand, Ginzburg confirms this pact by declaring: "The places, events and people in this book are all real. I have invented nothing" (7). On the other hand, she avoids the pact by stating her unwillingness to be the protagonist of her text; she tries instead to establish a different agreement with the reader, based on the expectations usually associated with the reading of novels. She shows a concern with the limits of her own memory, warning us that "memory is treacherous and books founded on reality are so often only faint reflections and sketches of all that we have seen and heard" (7). In doing so she seems to aspire to a total objectivity, an impossible ideal.

Ginzburg's concern with the reader's expectations reveals a polarity in her approach that shapes the entire text. She implicitly recognizes the

Filial Discourses

existence of a critical establishment whose presence she evokes through her acknowledgment of its expectations. As we read the text we notice that this establishment is possibly male-dominated, since male readers are indeed inscribed in the text itself. In the final pages of *Family Sayings*, male readership and expectations are represented by Natalia's friends and colleagues at the publishing house. Despite her awareness of the literary conventions set up by such a group of readers, Ginzburg points out her difference in placing her work outside conventions whose right to exist she does not challenge, although she manages to avoid them. In a similar way, in her text the female world manages to survive male despotism by circumvention rather than subversion.

Family Sayings yields itself to a feminist reading that overcomes a strict genre categorization.[19] Despite Ginzburg's admitted unwillingness "to speak of [herself]," the text partakes of some recurrent traits of women's autobiography and could very well be called a "relational" memoir, in which the author defines her identity in terms of her relationship to other people. Unlike male autobiographers, whose sense of selfhood is often based on individualism and separation, female autobiographers explore the relations surrounding them and view themselves as the result of connections.[20] Such relations are here family and friends, and the political and historical context of Fascist and post-Fascist Italy. Natalia's presence, both as observer and character, surfaces in the text through the evolution of the other characters' relations to each other and to herself. She is equally fascinated by the artistic and the scientific personalities compounded in her family, and even though she eventually absorbs her mother's artistic temperament she inherits her father's scientific linearity as well, both of which are expressed in her writing.

The relational aspect of the text illuminates the textual play between male dominance and female survival. In the Levi household (Natalia's original family), Lidia, the mother, personifies an unconventional femininity that is both eccentric and artistic. She expresses her femininity through her storytelling, her songs and poems, her acute interest in fashion and clothing, and the friendship of other women. Using her artistic and personal interests both as means of psychological survival and expressions of female desire, she resists her husband's bullying. Rather than challenging or opposing her husband's irascible despotism, Lidia makes herself somewhat autonomous by ignoring his commands:

Maria Marotti

> My Mother on the other hand enjoyed telling stories—storytelling made her happy. Turning to one or another of us at table she would begin a story. Whether it was about my father's family or her own, she became radiant with pleasure, and it always seemed as if she were telling that story for the first time to ears that had never heard it. "I had an uncle," she would begin, "whom everyone called Whiskers." If one of us said, "I know that story, I have heard it heaps of times," she would turn to another of us and go on with the story in a low voice. "I have heard this story so many times," my father would bellow if he caught what she was saying. My mother would continue under her breath ... (23)

Through the dynamics of the parental relationship, in which the mother whispers rather than accepting silence and the father bellows in an ineffective attempt to repress her, Ginzburg establishes the tenets of her "heretical" feminism.[21] This kind of feminism is resistance based both on indifference to power and on the expression of female desire. On this specific issue, Ginzburg's position could be compared to that of Julia Kristeva, who "sees certain liberatory potentials in [women's] marginal position."[22] Femininity is not the opposite pole of feminism in Ginzburg's narrative, but rather a way in which, given sociohistorical circumstances and political context, women have managed to survive as people.

In *Family Sayings* Ginzburg creates a discursive form that captures the oral communication of domestic life. The narrative develops through dialogues and sayings, which reveal, with objective realism, the personal obsessions and ethnocentric prejudice of a privileged class. Through the unsentimental and often impersonal mode of narration, the autobiographical self surfaces with reserve and stoicism. Ginzburg positions herself at the margins of her own text, more often as an observer of family dynamics than as a participant. Omissions, as the preface warns us, play an important role in the text. Instead of placing the text outside the genre of biography, however, omissions are the trace of deeply personal events, of emotions that are subjective. This is the case of all events that concern Natalia personally. Particularly meaningful are the omissions of emotional reactions to Leone Ginzburg's (the author's husband) death. The event is first referred to and then mentioned briefly through another character's perspective, and the autobiographer's emotional participation is always omitted.

Ginzburg's own resistance to assuming a definitively autobiographical voice reminds one of the hesitation that many early women autobiographers displayed in dealing with their lives.[23] Just as the apologetic tone of these early autobiographies reveals the difficulty of female writers writing for a male-dominated readership, Ginzburg's omission of her most personal feelings and the repression of deeper aspects of her female experience signal her self-consciousness before a male-dominated audience.

Ginzburg's resistance to the subjective mode persists in most chapters of her semi-autobiographical collection, *The Little Virtues*. Yet in one story entitled "He and I," Ginzburg narrates in a light, humorous way her own relationship to her second husband. Here again the mode is that of a "relational" autobiography, where the subject exists only in relation and often in opposition to the other. Another story, entitled "My Vocation," also bears the marks of female difference. In describing her apprenticeship in writing, Ginzburg acknowledges the importance of female experience in the process:

> Now I no longer wanted to write like a man, because I had had children and I thought I knew a great many things about tomato sauce and even if I did not put them into my story it helped my vocation that I knew them; in a strange, remote way these things also helped my vocation. (63)

Throughout the essay, however, Ginzburg argues that although writing is affected by the personal life of the writer, the material of writing is never the life of the writer. Ginzburg is thus aligning her work with more canonical and less personal aspects of Italian letters. Even though her valorization of femininity as expression of female culture anticipates some threads of neofeminist (female) thought, her attitude toward her own work and its place in the canon reveals a prefeminist (feminine, in Showalter's terms) thought inspired by a desire to equal the achievements of male authors.

A much more straightforward attempt to create an autobiography and a family biography is *Le quattro Ragazze Wieselberger* (1976) by Fausta Cialente. Here the author shows an explicit concern with the history of women in her family. Before starting her own autobiography, Cialente traces the biography of the maternal side of her family. The unfolding of their lives is interwoven with the history of Trieste's *irredentismo*, with the events of World War I, and with the subsequent annexation of Trieste by Italy. The daughter of a former lyrical singer from Trieste and a career military officer from Southern Italy, Cialente identifies with her mother and her cultural background, even though she is critical of her political choices.

The city of Trieste and the region of Istria acquire for the autobiographer the connotations of "motherland." Cialente remembers the yearly childhood visits to Trieste and Istria as returns to the only place that held some kind of continuity and familiarity for her. Yet the motherland also plays the role of the "other" land. Trieste is for the autobiographer the land of a fallacious dream, a dangerous delusion (*irredentismo*) which her mother (and her entire family) supports. The world of the mother is therefore a place from which she chooses to remove herself. *Irredentismo*—the patriotic movement that led to Trieste's independence from Austria and annexation to Italy—is a dream of belonging to a land and a culture. Through an alternative historical reconstruction, Cialente argues that the dream was fallacious and that her maternal family was under a delusion. An equally dangerous delusion is, for her, the female dream of belonging to a man—a desire that leads women to marry and have families. Throughout the first part of the autobiography Cialente's concern is to set the record straight—the historical record as well as the family record. She traces a parallel between the impending demise of the city and that of the female members of the Wieselberger family as a consequence of their yearning for annexation to Italy and marriage to Italians.

Cialente's memoir is a conscious attempt to create a women's history, a matrilineal history based on female ascendancy and on a rereading of official history. The first part of the memoir devoted to the Wieselbergers' family and their entanglement with *irredentismo* serves the dual purpose of creating a historical background and also an alternative rereading of the region's history. Such rereading shows Trieste as a culturally and ethnically autonomous and prosperous community under Austrian rule. Cialente also argues that *irredentismo* was based on middle- and upper-class delusions, as well as on racism against the Slovenian ethnic minority. An alternative historical reconstruction sets up the tone for a matrilineal history. The errors of official history concerning Trieste—and probably Italy and Europe in general—serve as a paradigm for similar methodological errors in the patriarchal handling of women's place in history. Part I of the book also shows women's participation in the delusions and prejudices of the patriarchal system; this participation is the main cause of their subsequent victimization.

In Parts II and III, Cialente's emphasis on her bond with her mother and rejection of her father further stresses the matrilineal theme of the text. The link with the mother includes her family (described as well educated, very musical, and refined), her language (the Triestino dialect, the only dialect that Fausta ever learned), and her place of origin (Trieste, depicted as a place of high civilization).

Her rejection of the father is extended also to his family (viewed as petty and ignorant), his language (a Southern Italian dialect that the young Fausta and her brother never learn), and his place of origin (Central and Southern Italy, constantly described negatively as a primitive land). Because of the strong polarization in the text, the place of the mother, Trieste, and that of the father, Italy, acquire opposite connotations. The mother's psychological and economic victimization by the father is paralleled by Trieste's cultural and economic victimization by Italy.

Cialente's memoir could be viewed both as a feminist and a neofeminist text whose main merit lies in advocating the separation of women from patriotic and militaristic projects leading to wars. As intriguing as Cialente's project is, however, it has some limitations that undermine its potentially feminist message. In Part IV of the book—the only part devoted to Cialente's life as an adult—it clearly appears that her position as autobiographer is that of an outsider, both to Italian culture and the feminine world. Cialente writes that her early rejection of the rural and provincial world of Central and Southern Italy, as well as her yearning for the "civilized" world of Trieste, might now appear a snobbish, infantile response (86). Yet nothing in the subsequent parts of the memoir indicate any substantial change in this attitude. Indeed, Cialente shares her much-hated father's global and spiteful condemnations of Italian culture: "Siamo un gran popolo di cialtroni" (We are a good-for-nothing people; 208). This reveals Cialente's unacknowledged shift to the world of the father: a world of separatism, spiteful distance, and disconnection. Moreover, her identification of the concept of "culture" with bourgeois culture greatly hinders her understanding of sociohistorical phenomena and power relations.

Cialente's obsession with setting the historical record straight surfaces to the very end. In the final scene of the autobiography, she is walking at sunset on a beach on the Persian Gulf; she is accompanied by her daughter and her granddaughter. In a glimpse she feels the strong matrilineal thread uniting them, while at the same time she has the mystical perception of the presence of her dead mother. She then imagines her mother saying:

> I still love you, but leave me alone, now, and try and live making as few mistakes as you can. We made so many mistakes. (257)[24]

In the final scene the matrilineal theme of the text is overt. The mother is granted acceptance in the daughter's matrilineal scheme, however, only at the price of disowning the choices (errors) of her life. At the same time that she gives her mother a voice the writer deprives her of her own language, and condemns her to silence. Unlike Manzini who, through her own poetic interpretation, tries to give expression to her mother's silenced speech, Cialente silences her mother by subverting her politically incorrect intentions.

In Cialente's case, the matrilineal theme of her autobiography leads to the construction of a hypothetical women's separatism, as the result of a rejection of any patriarchal project—be it a patriotic movement or a marriage contract. Her condemnation of women's participation in patriarchy is done with the same outsider's perspective that taints her cultural and historical views. Her crossing over to the world of the father—unacknowledged as it is—is much more than a purely ideological move: it is a disowning of the ambiguous complexity of femininity; it is the assumption of a male discourse.

Despite their recognition of female culture, both Cialente and Ginzburg share the absence of female physical life in their autobiographical texts. The entire world of birth, parturition, menstruation, and sexual impulse is absent from their autobiographical texts. These are aspects that are instead deeply probed by more contemporary writers. In her unusual autobiographical text, *Althenopis* (1981), Fabrizia Ramondino takes a deep plunge into the ethnic cultures of the Neapolitan areas and the female world of her family. Her book is a fresco of an area and an era (the war, and the postwar coastal Campania). As a child she spent a few years in a small town near Naples; after her father's death, she settled in Naples. Her vivid and detailed memories of the life, the places, the traditions, and the food create a realistic background to which the characters are inextricably connected. With vivid, yet unsentimental descriptions, she delineates family dynamics. In an overall patriarchal society, the family is the domain of women—a form of enclosed matriarchy in the larger context of patriarchy. Hence the importance of the country houses and Neapolitan apartments in which women leave their imprint. Ramondino organizes her narrative around these spaces and the people who are closely connected to them. In her descriptions she retrieves the clear, almost defamiliarized point of view of her own childhood. It is only in the third part of the memoir that a relational focus surfaces in the narration. As an adult, returning from the North, she comes back to the maternal home to encounter the central relationship of her life—that with her mother. In an attempt to achieve a realistic objectivity and to extract an almost universal value from her experience while dealing with extremely sensitive material, Ramondino narrates this part in the third person. She also omits names of people. Here again, as in the first two sections of the book, matriarchy operates somewhat autonomously from the larger context of the society that contains it. The mother who appears defeated in other life circumstances exerts emotional control over her daughters.

The matrilineal theme surfaces in a subtle way in the narrative, yet it is solidly based in the female body, where the connection between sexuality and death is unequivocal. The young protagonist recalls, at the occurrence of her first menstrual period, her recently deceased grandmother, and feels her connection to her.

In the final episode of the book, her own dying mother's last (although unaware) message to her daughter is a gesture—touching her vagina—which evokes the repression of female sexuality and, at the same time, a finally liberated desire.

> That gesture, which for so many years had remained buried, alighted in her lap, to reclaim her rights and assert them, to peel away from the old dying body and enter the soul of her who grasped it, to lift the ban and make her fertile, that others born of woman might see the light. (261)

Ramondino's evocation of the matriarchal world of the Neapolitan family highlights the constrictive rules for women endorsed by a matriarchy existing in the context of patriarchal society.[25] The older female cousins try to forbid the dying woman to repeat what appears to them to be an obscene gesture: "You don't do that, you don't do that." To which she answers: "I'm a baby girl, I'm a baby girl," thus retrieving the nongendered freedom of childhood.

As much as the relationship with the mother is intense and disturbing, that with the father is almost nonexistent. His lack—his frequent absences and then early death—is not significantly filled by any other surrogate paternal image. Yet in Ramondino's observations of Neapolitan society men are those who retain the greater power—be it financial or social. Their power exists, however, through some diplomatic balance with matriarchy.

The perspectives on feminism and femininity displayed by the autobiographers that I have discussed in this by no means all-inclusive study are disparate. Yet we can find some unifying tendencies. Even though a historical development can be traced, prefeminist, feminist, and neofeminist threads of thought intertwine in all texts. Despite the fact that not all the autobiographers seem to be interested in a feminist project, all of them express a more or less conscious resistance to patriarchy (which I have earlier identified as the most general feature of feminism), while they also reject the idea of woman shaped by their male-dominated society. The writers challenge this idea through either a reappropriation of an exclusively female space or the creation of an alternative ideological construct for femininity.

Maternal and paternal models play important roles in shaping these writers' responses to patriarchy. While they resist identification with the debilitating maternal model, they develop an early and keen awareness of female oppression in patriarchal society through the examples of their mothers' lives. In the process of writing their memoirs, they discover, through hindsight, their matrilineal links, and some of them acquire a deeper perspective on their own lives as females. The paternal model changes as we move from text to text. While in Aleramo's and Manzini's autobiographies fathers inspire rebellious attitudes in their daughters, in Ginzburg's and Cialente's texts fathers personify some aspects of patriarchal oppression; in Ramondino's book the father stands instead for an absent and hidden power—the power of patriarchy coexisting with domestic matriarchy.

The wavering of the filial discourse between matrilineage and patrilineage parallels the oscillation of the feminist discourse throughout the decades of our century. While it resists patriarchy, Italian feminist thought also entertains a relation with a long-standing tradition of liberal, radical, and socialist thought. Through the daughters' relationships with the paternal figures in Aleramo's, Manzini's, Ginzburg's, and Cialente's texts, this dialectical relation is apparent. Yet even liberal, socialist, and anarchist fathers internalize patriarchy at least to some extent; thus the father appears at the same time as model of rebellion and patriarch to be resisted.

The interplay between feminism and femininity illuminates some other cultural and historical aspects of the texts. If one looks at all the texts in a diachronic perspective, one can be tempted to conclude that the more recent autobiography by Ramondino (1981) is the only one that tends toward a reappropriation of the female body through matrilineage, and is in this way consistent with some contemporary trends in feminist theory, literature, and society.[26] Although this is true, we should also acknowledge that such attitudes are already in embryo in Aleramo's groundbreaking work at the beginning of the century. Moreover, although devoid of any overt feminist project, Manzini's two memoirs display insights into the condition of women (especially through her identification with the maternal body) which could only result from awareness of female oppression by patriarchy. In their autobiographies the three writers have "returned to the origins in the mother and the silent silenced 'culture' she shares with all women" (Smith, 58). The absence of the female body in the autobiographies by Ginzburg and Cialente might instead signal their separation from the most complex aspects of the female experience, a separation that may be linked to a general aspiration for equality with the male world. This aspiration takes diverse forms: the meeting of the literary expectations of a male-dominated critical establishment, and hence the resistance to personal forms of writing; the ideological identification with the father through the assumption of a male discourse; and the distancing of one's self from female "limitations." This aspiration is in tune with the post-World War II period—a time of some (conditional) opening to women's emancipation. In some of the aspects of their memoirs, Cialente and Ginzburg illuminate the double bind in which female writers are caught. In order to overcome the danger of being silenced like their mothers, Italian women writers of their generation had to step over to the paternal side; they often had to "speak and write as men."[27] Yet, as with all the autobiographers that we have discussed, they too have been able to integrate female difference into their writings, and therefore write with a double voice that bears the traces of both paternal and maternal discourses.

Notes

1. Santo L. Aricó, "Introduction," in *Contemporary Women Writers in Italy*, 3–8.

2. The use of the word "novel" to define autobiographies creates, at first, some problems for a scholar of autobiography. It is a problem that can be overcome only by discounting such labeling and by considering, instead, those structural aspects of texts that make them autobiographies. One such aspect is the pact that the author-narrator-protagonist consist of the same person; another is that the content of the text is made of verifiable facts. See Philippe Lejeune, "The Autobiographical Pact," in *On Autobiography*, 3–30. I find Lejeune's categorization helpful in establishing the basic structures of autobiography.

3. Lejeune, *On Autobiography*, 28–30.

4. Sidonie Smith, *A Poetics of Women's Autobiography: Marginality and the Fictions of Self-Representation*, 44.

5. Teresa de Lauretis, *Feminist Studies/Critical Studies*, 14–15. De Lauretis argues that the "image . . . of a homogeneous, monolithic Feminism is something that must be resisted."

6. Carol Gilligan, *In a Different Voice*. Gilligan proposes in her study a different female ethic stemming from a different perception of problems. An Italian feminist work I am referring to is Diotima, *Il pensiero della differenza sessuale* (Milan: la Tartaruga, 1987). I am also referring to Hélène Cixous's "The Laugh of the Medusa," 245–64.

7. Teresa de Lauretis, *Alice Doesn't*, 4.

8. My study has been inspired in particular by Marianne Hirsch, *The Mother/Daughter Plot: Narrative, Psychoanalysis, Feminism*. Hirsch traces a historical development of female plots shaped around the mother/daughter relationship. In some of my observations I am also

influenced by Nancy Chodorow's theories of female development. Luisa Muraro's L'ordine simbolico della madre has also played a role in shaping my thinking. Muraro's utopian work proposes a new symbolic order as a foundation for women's culture—the symbolic order of the mother. She traces some threads of this symbolic order in the mother/daughter relationship that surfaces in some women's texts.

9. It is interesting to note that Aleramo's views about motherhood as institution are similar to those of several contemporary feminist theorists. See Coppelia Kahn, "The Hand That Rocks the Cradle: Recent Gender Theories and Their Implications," 73–75. See also Adrienne Rich, Of Woman Born: Motherhood as Experience and Institution; Nancy Chodorow, The Reproduction of Mothering: Psychoanalysis and the Sociology of Gender; and Dorothy Dinnerstein, The Mermaid and the Minotaur: Sexual Arrangements and Human Malaise.

10. Paul John Eakin, Fictions in Autobiography: Studies in the Art of Self-Invention. Eakin argues that in the process of writing their autobiographies, autobiographers acquire a new perspective on their lives which is in turn reflected in their texts.

11. See Richard Drake, "Introduction" to A Woman, xxix-xxx.

12. Giovanna Miceli Jeffries, "Gianna Manzini's Poetics of Verbal Visualization," 100.

13. The translations of quotations from Ritratto in piedi are mine.

14. Anna Nozzoli, "Gianna Manzini: Metafora e realtá del personaggio femminile," 67–68.

15. Marianne Hirsch argues that "to speak for the mother . . . is at once to give voice to her discourse and to silence and marginalize her" (16). She deals more specifically with maternal silence in nineteenth-century fiction at pp. 44–45.

16. Translations of quotations from Sulla soglia are mine.

17. Chodorow, Reproduction of Mothering, 126–27, 169.

18. Lejeune, On Autobiography, 28–30. Lejeune defines the autobiographical pact as a writing/reading pact with the reader according to which autobiographers deal with verifiable facts of their lives.

19. Elaine Showalter, "Feminist Criticism in the Wilderness," 243–47; and Annette Kolodny, "Dancing Through the Minefield: Some Observations on the Theory, Practice, and Politics of a Literary Criticism," in The New Feminist Criticism: Essays on Women, Literature, Theory, ed. Elaine Showalter, 151.

20. Smith, A Poetics of Women's Autobiography, 12. See also Chodorow, Reproduction of Mothering, 126–27.

21. Cesare Garboli, "Prefazione," Opere di Natalia Ginzburg, xxv-xxx.

22. Ann Rosalind Jones, "Writing the Body: Toward an Understanding of L'Ecriture feminine," in New Feminist Criticism, ed. Showalter, 363. Julia Kristeva emphasizes the role of resistance to social, cultural, and linguistic conventions that "woman" represents. See "Oscillation between Power and Denial," in New French Feminisms, 165–67. See also Alessandra Bocchetti, "The Indecent Difference," in Italian Feminist Thought, ed. Paola Bono and Sandra Kemp, 148–62. Bocchetti argues that difference can be used "as a path of self-knowledge for women" (159).

23. Mary G. Mason, "The Other Voice: Autobiographies of Women Writers," in Life/Lines: Theorizing Women's Autobiography, ed. Bella Brodzki and Celeste Schenck, 19–44.

24. Translations of quotations from Le quattro Ragazze Wieselberger are mine.

25. Carol M. Lazzaro-Weis, "From Margins to Mainstream: Some Perspectives on Women and Literature in Italy in the 1980s" in Contemporary Women Writers in Italy, ed. Aricó, 209–10.

26. See in particular the reappropriation of the female body fostered by Hélène Cixous in connections with her concept of écriture feminine in "The Laugh of the Medusa," in New French Feminisms, ed. Marks and de Courtivron.

Filial Discourses

27. Xavière Gauthier writes: "As long as women remain silent, they will be outside the historical process. But, if they begin to speak and write as men do, they will enter history subdued and alienated." "Is There Such a Thing as Women's Writing?" trans. Marilyn A. August, in *New French Feminisms*, ed. Marks and de Courtivron, 162–63.

Works Cited

Aleramo, Sibilla. *A Woman*. Intro. Richard Drake, trans. Rosalind Delmar. Berkeley: University of California Press, 1980.
Aricó, Santo, ed. *Contemporary Women Writers in Italy*. Amherst: University of Massachusetts Press, 1990.
Bocchetti, Alessandra. "The Indecent Difference." In *Italian Feminist Thought*. Cambridge, Mass.: Blackwell, 1991.
Brodzki, Bella, and Celeste Schenck, eds. *Life/Lines: Theorizing Women's Autobiography*. Ithaca: Cornell University Press, 1988.
Chodorow, Nancy. *The Reproduction of Mothering: Psychoanalysis and the Sociology of Gender*. Berkeley: University of California Press, 1979.
Cialente, Fausta. *Le quattro Ragazze Wieselberger*. Milan: Mondadori, 1976.
Cixous, Hélène. "The Laugh of the Medusa." In *New French Feminisms: an Anthology*, ed. Elaine Marks and Isabelle de Courtivron. Amherst: University of Massachusetts Press, 1980.
de Lauretis, Teresa, *Alice Doesn't: Feminism, Semiotics, Cinema*. Bloomington: Indiana University Press, 1984.
———, ed. *Feminist Studies/Critical Studies*. Bloomington: Indiana University Press, 1986.
Dinnerstein, Dorothy. *The Mermaid and the Minotaur: Sexual Arrangements and Human Malaise*. New York: Harper & Row, 1976.
Drake, Richard. "Introduction." In *A Woman*, by Sibilla Aleramo. Berkeley: University of California Press, 1980.
Eakin, Paul John. *Fictions in Autobiography: Studies in the Art of Self-Invention*. Princeton: Princeton University Press, 1985.
Garboli, Cesare. "Prefazione." In *Opere di Natalia Ginzburg*. Milan: Mondadori, 1986.
Gilligan, Carol. *In a Different Voice*. Cambridge, Mass.: Harvard University Press, 1982.
Ginzburg, Natalia. *Family Sayings*, trans. D. M. Low. New York: Arcade, 1989.
———. *The Little Virtues*. Manchester, Eng.: Carcanet Press, 1985.
———. *Opere di Natalia Ginzburg*. Milan: Mondadori, 1986.
Hirsch, Marianne. *The Mother/Daughter Plot: Narrative, Psychoanalysis, Feminism*. Bloomington: Indiana University Press, 1989.
Jeffries, Giovanna Miceli. "Gianna Manzini's Poetics of Verbal Visualization." In *Contemporary Women Writers in Italy*, ed. Santo L. Aricó. Amherst: University of Massachusetts Press, 1990.
Kahn, Coppelia. "The Hand That Rocks the Cradle: Recent Gender Theories and Their Implications." In *The (M)other Tongue*, ed. Shirley Nelson Garner, Claire Kahane, and Madelon Sprengnether. Ithaca: Cornell University Press, 1985.
Kristeva, Julia. "Oscillation between Power and Denial." In *New French Feminisms*, ed. Elaine Marks and Isabelle de Courtivron. Amherst: University of Massachusetts Press, 1980.
Lejeune, Philippe. *On Autobiography*. Intro. Paul John Eakin, trans. Katherine Leary. Minneapolis: University of Minnesota Press, 1989.
Manzini, Gianna. *Ritratto in piedi*. Milan: Mondadori, 1971.
———. *Sulla Soglia*. Milan: Mondadori, 1973.
Miller, Nancy K. *Subject to Change: Reading Feminist Writing*. New York: Columbia University Press, 1988.
Muraro, Luisa. *L'Ordine simbolico della madre*. Rome: Editori Riuniti, 1991.

Maria Marotti

Nozzoli, Anna. "Gianna Manzini: Metafora e realtá del personaggio femminile." In *Tabú e coscienza: La condizione femminile nella letteratura italiana del Novecento*. Florence: La Nuova Italia, 1978.
Ramondino, Fabrizia. *Althenopis*. Trans. Michael Sullivan. Manchester: Carcanet Press, 1988.
Rich, Adrienne. *Of Woman Born: Motherhood as Experience and Institution*. New York: Harper & Row, 1976.
Showalter, Elaine, ed. *New Feminist Criticism: Essays on Women, Literature and Theory*. New York: Pantheon, 1985.
Smith, Sidonie. *A Poetics of Women's Autobiography: Marginality and the Fictions of Self-Representation*. Bloomington: Indiana University Press, 1987.

Giovanna Miceli Jeffries

Caring and Nurturing in Italian Women's Theory and Fiction
A Reappraisal

In recent years, the work conducted by communities of Italian women philosophers—the most active and prominent being Diotima[1]—has familiarized American scholars with contemporary Italian feminism and feminist theory produced in Italy. Diotima's aim is to elaborate and construct a distinct women's system of thought, which is actualized in the practice of *affidamento* (entrustment), a relationship established between a younger, less experienced woman who entrusts herself to an older, more experienced and influential one. This is a practice of care and empowerment that leads to the establishment of a female symbolic order paralleling, if not balancing, male hegemonic systems.[2] In this essay I will discuss some important works of fiction and nonfiction by contemporary Italian women writers whose representations of women's self-reflectivity and the practice of care affirm a distinctive women's ethics, and articulate a singular interplay of feminism and femininity. The work of psychologist Carol Gilligan is also of special importance in my arguments; she defines a different women's ethics and "thinking" determined by women's practices of care, nurturing, and connecting to others, which constitutes our mode of operating in and effecting our social and natural environment. The theoretical framework substantiating my analysis derives from Nancy Chodorow's theorization of gender and sexual difference and her suggestion of a relational notion of difference.

It might seem at first surprising that a work bearing the title of *La forza degli Italiani* (The Italians' strength), by Maria Antonietta Macciocchi, reflects aspects of caring and nurturing within a feminist agenda. The seemingly boasting title—conjuring a Fascist manifesto—could not be more remote

87

from Macciocchi's political and literary orientation. Her 1976 book, *La donna "nera": "Consenso" femminile e fascismo* (The woman in black: Female "consent" and Fascism), was the first resolute inquiry into the silence around the role Italian women played in Fascist ideology. In that book, Macciocchi disclaimed the mechanisms of Fascist persuasion that made Italian women masochistically accept renunciation and regression through a propaganda of mystified power in motherhood. In *La forza degli Italiani*, however, we notice a shift in Macciocchi's earlier position; she observes that women's maternal and caring practices are also part of their "strength." The book chronicles the author's journey throughout Italy, a journey she embarked upon in order to meet and talk to people, especially to women.[3] From these encounters Macciocchi portrays a spectrum of "differences" in the way Italian women conduct their lives, live their feminism, and problematize their relationship with men. Not surprisingly, given her background, Macciocchi rediscovers the power of Italian women's work. "The evolution of Italian women is based on the economic independence they achieve" (83), she writes. In every part of Italy she sees women engaged in all kinds of professional activities, both new and traditional. In Macciocchi's view, Italian women have been particularly instrumental in their country's noted "economic miracle." The strength of Italian women is evident both at work and at home, where they have discovered the pleasure of being both "grasshoppers and ants" (fun-loving and hard-working) without seeing opposition between the two. These neofeminists, as Macciocchi calls them, are engaged in a "thinking of being a woman in its own difference"; it is an autonomous difference, by which "a friendly relation with men who are decisive interlocutors" (77–78) is also possible.

Though the maternal feminine has the potential trappings of stereotyped glamour, this model represents many aspects of the *forza delle italiane*. The features of Piero della Francesca's *Madonna di Senigallia* inform the author's visions and representations of contemporary Italian women throughout her journey around the peninsula. In the lofty pride of the Woman-Mother, Macciocchi sees a mixture "of hieratic strength, austere responsibility, and loving gesture toward her child" (80). Contemporary women have a "different" philosophy of the maternal: they have discovered, writes Macciocchi, "the creative role of motherhood"—its potential to enrich the "sensual and thinking aspect of womanhood" (80). And she gives a highly publicized example of this maternal strength by referring to the vicissitudes of a literal *madre coraggio* (mother courage), Angela Casella, an Italian mother from Northern Italy who persevered for years in a cam-

Caring and Nurturing: A Reappraisal

paign for the release of her kidnapped son. Her strength and inviolability resided in her status as mother. For all Italians, this woman exemplified a combination of the stereotyped Italian mother and the effectiveness of a woman's resolution: her actions, determination, and calculated visibility paid off in the end. When the collective efforts of the police and offerings of ransoms had failed, her son was freed alive. Her face is familiar to every Italian household, having appeared on TV daily as she carried on her crusade throughout Italy, and her constant vigil in the mountainous villages of the South, where the young man was presumably being held. Yet the solemn containment in Casella's face as she embraces her son upon his release neutralizes every cliché: "She lifted her aquiline profile toward her son, her hair pulled in the ordered bun, the smile of a Gothic virgin" (229). She has the victorious, modest smile of a Woman-Mother.

Over and over, the mixture of inner gendered political strength is revealed in Macciocchi's women, most palpably and impressively in their faces. The author seems to be determined to unveil the obvious: that is, that Italian mothers have a great deal of power within and outside their families. What she wants her readers to know is that these mothers are first of all women. Most of them are doing what they have always done: keeping a neat home and an elegant and well-kept personal appearance in addition to holding down three jobs: the office or the school, or the factory, the family business, and the family. Many Italian women know their rights, since a huge volume, *Codice Donna* (Woman's legal code), was published a few years ago under the auspices of the government commission for equal rights. This reference book contains everything that is pertinent to know in terms of women's civil rights. As Macciocchi warns at the beginning of her book, we are not left with a simple "description" of what she sees. Instead, the author examines the expressions of neofeminism within the larger problems of contemporary Italy: its apparent ungovernability, the conspiracy of the media, the dependency on TV, and so on. All that she relates about the "strength of the Italians" is open to confirmation or critique, according to the reader's own experiences. Her timely reexamination of the basic ground reveals an extraordinary—because unexpected—position on Macciocchi's part that is revisionist and progressive at the same time, a sort of seasoned touch willed by a committed mind. For Macciocchi, women derive their strength from the values and specificities of their personal identities and histories, which eventually, and quite necessarily, are characterized by specific cultural traits.

It is, however, the caring practices of contemporary Italian women that Macciocchi depicts with noticeable interest, whether seen in the commitment of a young feminist braving stormy weather to keep a political festival alive, or in Angela Casella's determination, or in the uneasy and troubled caring for the "masculinity" of one's partner. What prompts the author's interest? What do these practices mean to the "new," emancipated Italian women Macciocchi discovers on her journey?[4] What does "caring" represent exactly for women, and how has it evolved into a conscious choice?

In Nancy Chodorow's 1978 book *The Reproduction of Mothering*, we learn about the wide-ranging reproductive functions of women in society. According to Chodorow, women "reproduce people—physically in their housework and child care, psychologically in their emotional support of husbands, in their maternal relation to sons and daughters" (36). This function could be seen as another generational, reproduced strength of women. But, as Chodorow remarks, there is an imbalance in family and society in that "no one supports and reconstitutes women affectively and emotionally" (36). This asymmetry accounts for the belated, reduced presence of the feminine in the political order of society. In Chodorow's view, mothering capacities and commitments are built developmentally into the feminine personality: "biology and instinct alone do not provide adequate explanations for how women come to mother" (205). Ten years later, in her book *Feminism and Psychoanalytic Theory*, she reelaborates some of her positions from a rather anti-essentialist stand by stressing that gender difference is not "absolute, abstract, or irreducible" (100). Differences and gender don't come into existence by themselves; instead, they are produced in an ongoing process "developmentally and in our daily social and cultural lives" (112).[5] Through the social sciences and developmental psychology women understand "the perpetuation of ideology about gender roles" (205). Once they understand the process of gender formation, their relationships with their mothers, their own offspring, and their partners are bound to be expressed in a consciously different ethical mode.

These premises form the framework for the following analysis of how an ethics of care and responsible nurturing informs the narrative of a new Italian woman writer, Clara Sereni, whose insistent representation of women nurturing provides a clear picture of the interactionality and self-reflectivity of women operating in and within the domestic sphere. At the same time, ironically, the specificity of these representations allows a very subtle deconstructive critique of a gendered identity, where mothering and caring are also unmistakably oppressive social and psychological forces. In Sereni's work, we see the subtle play of deconstructive discourse within the legitimacy of the representation of caring. The female characters reutilize the same objects of feminine passivity as they are brought into the narrative, often incongruously, in their ephemerality and anachronism, functioning momentarily as symbols of "normalcy" and certainty in abnormal, exasperating situations.

Like Macciocchi, Sereni has a background of political activism within the former Italian Communist party, and belongs to that characteristic *borghesia rossa romana* where a strong leftist orientation, membership in the intelligentsia, and economic affluence mix together in an original and specifically Italian cocktail. Sereni's maturation takes place during the years of social unrest and protests from every component of Italian society, but she does not call herself a feminist. In her last two successful novels, *Casalinghitudine* (Homemakerness) and *Manicomio primavera* (Bedlam spring —the title is excerpted from Sylvia Plath's poem *Spinster*, which is a preface to the book), she privileges cooking and mothering.[6] Both books infuse these gendered roles with a new spirit of self-exploration, performance, and ethical reflection. Her women characters come to both of these practices with few preconceptions and embark thereafter on a self-teaching process. In each of these areas women operate in a traditional domestic environment, but with a heightened, critical consciousness that always aims at a balance between the care of the other and that of the self. Yet these are not just stories of self-sacrifice, struggles, and self-discovery, although all these experiences are cautiously filtered through the fabric of the narrative (how can they not be?). Instead, Sereni represents the substance and the tenacity of being a self-reflective, informed woman, neither omnipotent nor constantly complaining, a woman who makes the ordinariness and repetitions of domestic life, as well as the contradictions of motherhood, functional and creative. A style of life neither heroic nor insipid discreetly but firmly unfolds a deep awareness of the protagonist's own limits—yet she never loses her desire to overcome these limits. In an emblematic story, *Tutto s'impara* (Everything has to be learned), which sets the tone for the rest of the situations and reveals the protagonist's heightened awareness of the gendered role of motherhood, a mother who has just delivered her first child chronicles her confused feelings after the birth. Exhausted by an emergency cesarean section, she has not seen her child, and neither does she long for it. When the infant is finally brought to her, she readily registers her apathy, her lack of enthusiasm for the unattractive little creature for whom she should show affection and joy. As she honestly recognizes and deals with her "unnatural" feelings, she finally turns her baby toward her and determines that she is going to learn to love him: "Tutto s'impara" (27), even to be a mother, she tells herself. In other words, nobody is born a mother—it is an acquired capacity, as Chodorow has shown.

The subtle, unglamorous, yet deeply felt sense of caring present in Sereni's women seems to stem from a moral configuration that has been at the center of Carol Gilligan's work. Gilligan's investigations—mostly conducted in private and predominantly white all-girls middle and high schools—have developed a definition of women's morality that is differentiated from man's morality in its structure and effects, because the categories of caretaker and nurturer have a central position in woman's moral development. The knowledge and practice of care is something that has historically and across the cultures always defined women. Gilligan argues in her book In a Different Voice, "Because that knowledge in women has been considered 'intuitive, instinctive,' a function of anatomy coupled with destiny, psychologists have neglected to describe its development"(17). According to Gilligan, "Women's moral development centers on the elaboration of that knowledge and thus delineates a critical line of psychological development in the lives of both sexes" (17). Because in women, Gilligan maintains, moral problems arise from "conflicting responsibilities rather than from competing rights," resolving these problems requires a mode of thinking that is contextual and narrative rather than formal and abstract. Contemporary feminist theory might not be at all comfortable with this privileging of gendered nurturing and caring in the process of determining women's moral standards, since such a definition could represent a setback, an invitation to keep biting at our tails.[7] But I would argue that viewing this as a setback, as a sedimentation of femininity in traditional women's roles and practices, is too simplistic: a definition of woman's morality constructed on the practice of care and nurturing is in itself a practice of differentiation. Regardless of the argument that women have passively accepted and performed the role (of caretaker and nurturer) in a patriarchally ordered society, we need to focus on and valorize the outcome and products of such practice, for its significance in human history was not and still is not negligible or inconsequential. We must evaluate the representations of these practices—especially their most contemporary representations—in the voices of women who are aware of ambivalent and often contradictory ways of looking at their own femininity.

In her article "The Generalized and the Concrete Other: The Kohlberg-Gilligan Controversy and Feminist Theory," Seyla Benhabib argues against contemporary universalist moral theory that addresses the "generalized" other. In her view, this theory excludes from its consideration an entire "domain of human activity, namely nurture, reproduction, love and care, which becomes the woman's lot in the course of the development of modern, bourgeois society" and therefore "is relegated to the realm of 'nature'" (83). In arguing that the contextuality and specificity of woman's moral judgment is not a sign of weakness or deficiency (as in Freud) but a manifestation of a vision of moral maturity that sees the self in a continuous relational network, Benhabib advances an "anticipatory" critique of universalistic moral theory from a feminist perspective. She points to the "epistemic incoherences" of universalistic moral theory restricted to the standpoint of the "generalized other" as the repository of an ideal, desirable moral autonomy (81). Benhabib believes that it is the task of feminist critical theory to reevaluate woman's moral history in its characteristic manifestations of contextuality and interactionality in the public and historical realms, from its traditional, gendered, and "natural" level, thus recognizing its complementary operative function in the formulation of a comprehensive universalistic moral theory.

In Sereni's books we find a solid contribution to women's morality, to the process of woman's understanding, demystification, and empowerment. In Sereni's novels, "women's thinking" is particularly directed to the values of care and the connections of individuals and the self. She expresses one such new, different, and unconditioned voice in the representation of a conscious and intelligent femininity in its late-1980s version. Her books make a new claim in a territory that has been too often overlooked, if not repudiated, by women writers and theorists, or at least not sufficiently enlightened—the domestic, including simple home economics, the care and nurturing of others, and especially the care of the self. Observing the evolution of women's thinking from a preliberation movement reaching into the 1980s, Gilligan notices a shift that makes the concept of relationship change from a bond of continuing dependence to a dynamic of interdependence. Furthermore, "the notion of care expands from a paralyzing injunction not to hurt others to an injunction to act responsively toward self and others. Women's rights change women's moral judgments, seasoning mercy with justice by enabling women to consider it moral to care not only for others but for themselves" (*Different Voice*, 149).[8] In Clara Sereni's narrative, caring and nurturing are also extended to the self, with the understanding that caring for oneself also means better caring for others. At times the author's tools are traditional feminine ones, which are now revitalized by the mediating power of her crystalline language, bringing a profound self-consciousness to the surface. Sereni's maternal voices develop strategies of caring in which there is no self-effacement, but a mirroring, specular process, and the mother relates to her child while examining herself in the process. Self-reflectivity is heightened, resulting in a desentimentalization of motherhood, or rather a restoration of motherhood to a moral imperative, the conscious recognition of a nondeferable responsibility, and moreover a unique relationship and experience of caring that also elicits self-caring. Sereni's poetic manipulation of the details that make up daily living prevent this representation of motherhood from becoming too self-conscious and controlled. She describes small rituals, habits of necessity or of comfort, as amulets that protect her women characters and keep the horrors of defeat momentarily at bay—the desperation, helplessness, and most of all, the unconscious self-wounding that traditionally come with motherhood and womanhood. Paradoxically, by acting on and through the very objects and symbols of a gendered femininity, Sereni's mothers become subject[s] "of discourse, rather than [only] the source of life and the object[s] of desire and anger."[9]

The two basic arenas of Sereni's women are mothering and the preparation of food. While the preparation of food and the formulation of recipes chronicle the protagonist's life in *Casalinghitudine*, the maternal voice informs every story except one of *Manicomio Primavera*. The situations in these stories are not common; in most of the cases these women/mothers are dealing with autistic and severely handicapped children. Here the temptation to play omnipotent and to reinforce the protective role is stronger, and therefore it becomes a constant challenge for the mother to seek a balance in her mothering: to let go of that child, to give him (since it is always a male child) some responsibility, the mother has to take a larger portion of it in her own life. According to Sereni, in an interview at her home in Rome, a woman needs roots of her own in order to know how to give them to her child, and these roots must be strong enough to enable her, finally, to let go of her child.

A day in the life of a mother and her autistic child is an experience of maddening difficulty. As we follow one mother in her long day of anticipated actions and small events, looking forward to an evening out with her husband to celebrate their anniversary, we almost unconsciously feel a familiar refrain in her rite of preparations for a different time, the sense of a déjà vu of common, normal expectations. Yet the mother feels each hour of her day goes so slowly, and each hour is so full of premonitions, that one can anticipate how tiring the organization of a day around abnormal circumstances can be. This mother-child relation, seen from the mother's point of view, can easily result in an overwhelming sense of the mother's victimization and unrecognized heroism. Honesty with herself, however, and her recognition of life as a larger "project," prevail and we see her femininity harboring this mother within its gratifying clichés: a bubble bath, some makeup, perfume or a silk dress, an elegant table at the restaurant. All are small tokens of a gendered heritage—amulets, rituals—sought out despite their own ephemerality, but indispensable to a temporary and temperate happiness. These amulets of femininity, or domesticity, are defined in Clara Sereni's basic, irrevocable lexicon: they are "morbidezze perdute, lievità inutili e basilari [lost softness, a useless and yet basic lightness of life]" (*Manicomio*, 111); they are atmospheres, not tangible, yet as real as the pain of the woman's awareness and nightmares, and as real as the scent of the detergent emanating from the laundry that "gives her respite" (99).

As Gilligan observes, it is traditionally difficult for women "to include themselves among the people they consider it moral to care for. The inclusion of the self is genuinely problematic not only for women but also for society in general. Self-inclusion on the part of women challenges the conventional understanding of feminine goodness by severing the link between care and self-sacrifice" (*Mapping*, xxx). In Sereni's representation of the mother-child relationship, we seldom see guilt but rather a contained pain and a diffuse sense of wisdom that allow the woman to clean up only the worst part of the mess and to try not to see the rest. From this experience she realizes and practices a necessary resistance to the tendency of her fatigue to become sickness: "Arginare, farsi trincea: e intanto ricordarsi di non rinunciare a vivere [We need to burrow ourselves in, dig a trench, and at the same time never forget that we cannot renounce living]" (*Manicomio*, 104).

Remarkably enough, the survival mechanism that allows this mother to enjoy life and to love and care for her child is not the product of subliminal tapes or support groups; it is composed of her operations on the ordinary and unpoetic level that allow her to bump into small epiphanies. Amid her son's intermittent, autistic questioning, the stack of freshly ironed laundry appears to her "uno spazio di disciplina e di certezze [a space of discipline and certainty]" (99). Along the same line, calmly sorting out the laundry, "the gestures of the homemaker," done in solitude, could be comforting. But at the same time, she is aware of the risks of homemaking: she sees the traps that exist even as they offer temporary solace, and she tells herself that she should read a book or the newspaper. She saves herself from the burgeoning, asphyxiating warmth of the home—and its illusory power—with her ability to reinvent her environment and thus avoid simple reproduction. Therefore, reinventing new flavors in old recipes, creating a new pattern in her knitted sweaters, reorganizing and rationalizing her spaces, are modifications in her self and her home. Sereni's women clearly realize that the only roots they can hold on to are their own, since they also depend, often heavily, on the "outside," which cannot grant certainty and self-assurance. The home—its habits, loneliness, and work—while allowing the woman to deepen in her roots, is itself a conspicuous, expanding root demanding constant care. The thousand daily gestures to keep at bay the inexorable decay of life are a form of control, and are survival tactics the woman exercises over passive operativity. Sereni represents the symbiotic relation of the woman and the home as a choreography of objects and places defining and at the same time expanding the common place of homemaking: "così le mie radici aeree affondano nei barattoli, nei liquori, nelle piante del terrazzo, nei maglioni e coperte con i quali vorrei irretire il mondo . . . perché nella mia vita costruita a tessere mal tagliate . . . la casalinghitudine è *anche* un angolino caldo [and thus my aerial roots spread in the jars, in the syrups, in the plant of my terrace, in my sweaters and blankets with which I wish to entice the world . . . because in my life, put together with badly cut mosaic pieces, homemakerness is *also* a little warm corner" (*Casalinghitudine*, 165). The passage is exemplary of Sereni's extraordinary ability with her medium—language and images—as she empowers ordinary, unpoetic, domestic objects and places to unfold the woman's conflictual rapport with the home. The oxymoron "aerial roots"—a clear deterrent to the facile sublimation one may surmise from the passage—illustrates the protagonist's awareness of her unsettling condition while the highlighted "also" (homemakerness is *in addition to and despite* its traps) conjures up a yearning to find, in her practices of homemaking, comfort and stability.

The writer's full awareness that the home is a potentially risky place—self-indulgent and self-serving—is easily inferred in her further elaboration of the "little warm corner": "Un angolino da modificare ogni momento, se fosse fisso sarebbe morire, le ricette solo una base per costruire ogni volta nuovi sapori, combinazioni diverse [a cozy little corner to vary each time: if it were the same, fixed, it would mean death; the recipes are only the base for building new flavors, different combinations each time]" (165). The home could also function as a gateway, a place from which to reinvent a dimension that makes it possible to overcome the limits of homemaking and gendered identity.[10] This possibility reaches the tone of a more historical and impersonal injunction in the protagonist's caustic and finalizing comment at the end of the same passage: "Tutto è già detto, tutto è già stato scritto. Reinventare unico sconfinamento possibile, reinventare per non rimasticare, reinventare per non mangiarsi il cuore [Everything has already been said, everything has already been written. You need to reinvent, to go beyond your own limits, to avoid chewing over and over again or eating your heart out]." It is an admonition for her, and for her readers: in other words, literature is made of literature, experiences repeat and reproduce themselves as recipes, and above all, the history of mankind has been written, canonized outside the home. What is then this home, the "cozy corner," if not the only uninterrupted thread of women's history? The home then becomes a place where women, in their daily living, "stake the borders of their separateness and make it both radication and home; it is staying with oneself in an absolute belonging to oneself that comes before—and actually it makes possible—the doing of other things and taking off from there."[11] Therefore, the time and the space of the home—negative categories of inaction if measured in terms of patriarchal productive output—constitute categories of empowerment and entirety, symbolizing birthing and new life. Thus the risk of reading the "little warm corner" as self-serving and self-indulgent is neutralized by the hyperconsciousness of the protagonist, and the deconstructive process of writing itself.

The care of the self, whether actualized in small gestures and habits or by consciously self-monitoring, is never totally divorced from other forms of care. It functions as an energizing practice to enable better care for others. In the story "Primavera," the mother of another "special child" is empowering herself by focusing on her looks. A beautiful early spring day is all she needs to convince herself to dress nicely and attractively to go and pick up her handicapped son from school. Makeup and colors, and a few touches such as a sprig of flowers on the collar of her blazer, are her rite of appeasing her son in the new season. For once she wants to play at being like normal people. She lets her son have an ice cream cone with another schoolmate, knowing all too well the difficulties he will have in handling that, and she puts herself to a test as she watches his awkward and mostly unsuccessful attempts to contain and salvage the leaking cone as it melts into a mess. She does not intervene, for fear of embarrassing him in front of his classmate, but she cannot leave him totally alone. Although she does not physically move, her energy and emotions reach toward him in her growing anxiety to help him: "tutto il corpo è proteso nell'aiuto che sa di non dovergli dare, lo sostiene con tutto quello che ha dentro, qualcosa che forse può definirsi anima [all her body is bent to give help, which she knows she is not supposed to give him; she supports him with all that she has inside, something that maybe can be defined as soul]" (120). As she notices the melting pistachio ice cream running through one of her blazer's sleeves, she does not have a word of resentment. She picks up a bunch of paper napkins and, in her rehearsed wisdom, wipes out "the most evident traces" of the mess. Back in her car, her son at her side, she tries to restore some order to her clothes. The temptation to feel sorry for herself, to see herself in a comic strip and to capitulate, is palpable. Now more than ever she needs to see some order to recompose her previous plan of a beautifully common spring day. The sight of her nylons still tight and perfect against her legs gives her an instantaneous, subtle pleasure, a serendipity, enough to make her keep going for that time: "Sedendosi lei stira con la mano la seta gualcita della camicetta, raddrizza il mazzolino sul bavero. Le calze sono rimaste ben tese [As she takes her seat inside the car, she tries to flatten with her hand the wrinkles of her silk shirt, she straightens the sprig of flowers on her blazer. Her nylons were still straight and tight on her legs]" (120). In her awareness of order she even finds courage to promise her son that he can have another ice cream sometime. This is a poignant, economic image of condensed psychological drama. This woman is enacting in the most unglamorous way what Carol Gilligan calls an ethic of care and encouragement. A woman who remembers to refuel herself from the larger project of life as well as from its smallest accessories may be struggling constantly for balance, but she is also drawing a new maternal figure in teaching herself each time how to mother and how to live, having left the presumption of universal motherhood to others.

Significantly, Sereni's first successful book, *Casalinghitudine*, is about preparation of food, nurturing, and the relationship established between life experiences and food. This relationship produces recipes, for, as Susan J. Leonardi remarks, "Like a story, a recipe needs a recommendation, a context, a point, a reason to be" (340). Structured into chapters corresponding to courses and other specific uses of food, *Casalinghitudine*'s first section is devoted to baby food, while its last section concerns canning and preserves. There are 105 recipes in the whole book, some in small groups, others interspersed singly within the narrative. The homemade baby food opens the book in its startling simplicity and basicness: various grains are first browned, then cooked in liquid, to feed a difficult, crying baby. Once in awhile, a touch of love, which is not included in the list of ingredients, makes its way into the text, heightening the emotional connotation of food: "Per tenerezza, aggiungo talvolta un po' di miele [Sometimes, out of tenderness, I add a little honey]" (5).

The recipes are graphically separated from the narrative: the list of ingredients is followed by a very simple, first-person narration of the preparation. The narrative following or preceding is more or less connected to the recipes and is in a way an extension of the recipe itself, and vice versa. The reader is not told how to prepare a dish in a prescriptive tone, as we normally see in cookbooks or even on TV food preparation narratives. Instead, we witness or listen to the author telling in first person how she does it. In the process, she lets surface personal reflections, advice, and brief recommendations, which are almost gestures, as in this baby's vegetable soup: "Della verdura scelgo le parti più verdi, non importa se dure: attenzione agli spinaci perché sono molto amari, le foglie di cavolo macchiano duramente di verde perfino il vetro. Sciolgo la farina con il liquido, intiepidisco rapidamente e condisco con il parmigiano, al piú un goccio d'olio d'oliva [I choose the greenest part of the greens, whether they are harder or not. Must pay attention to the spinach because it is very bitter, cabbage leaves heavy stains even on glass. I dilute the flour in the liquid, warm it rapidly and sprinkle with Parmesan cheese, or at most with a drop of olive oil]" (6). The nonprescriptive, colloquial style of the recipe clearly evokes the orality of traditional practices among women sharing recipes: it suggests that there is no one way of doing a dish, and it discloses the narrator's personal imprint in her cooking. She does not address an audience, but gathers her readers around her: they are the recipients of her recipes, and she introduces them to her own idiosyncrasies, her manias and habits. Her recipes are the *literal* products (for we are free to copy and reproduce them) of Clara Sereni's book, which itself is a *literary* production.[12]

When I asked Clara Sereni what cooking and the preparation of food represented in the past and still represent for her, she commented that her interest in cooking and food is a form of caring. She didn't feel cared for in her own life, and therefore she realized she needed to provide for herself, to take care of herself in her cooking, in her food.[13] While cooking she reinvents flavors for her lovers and herself. Her recipes in the text, although grouped in categories, form intersections of ingredients, people, time. The pasta and minestra dishes are food for growing up, for the first taste of independence, irregular meals in the middle of active, searching experiences. "Pasta e fagioli" (bean soup with noodles) becomes her flag of independence as she reproduces a much better version of her father's rather insipid dish. The need to find herself, to reroot, is revealed not only in her renewed interest in food but also in "the woman's insistence on the ritualism of the past, always played down, but at the same time always recognized, expanded" (A. Bianchini, 35). This is a nontraditional awareness of the quotidian, something like her recipes that "look like" traditional recipes, but have changed and are now "promoted with a new heart, a new spirit" (35).

Food in the novel in general, remarks Gian-Paolo Biasin, "is a cognitive tool used to outline the problematic relations among subject, nature, and history" ("Italo Calvino in Mexico: Food and Lovers, Tourists and Cannibals," 74). Across cultures, recipes and food appear in women's novels to recreate personal histories, to reconnect, as Mexican author Laura Esquivel observes, "the self with the elements of the universe" and thus "come to understand our past and ourselves."[14] For the African American author Ntozake Shange, the recipes in her novel *Sassafras, Cypress & Indigo* reveal and differentiate the personalities of the three sister protagonists, their lifestyles and common background. At the same time she sees recipes as a valorization of women's traditional role of caretakers, of all the time they spend cooking for and feeding others.[15] Still, to the educated female Ph.D. in William Least Heat-Moon's *PrairyErth*, who chooses to run a small-town café and cook for a living, the provision of food becomes the opportunity to see her femaleness differently; her feminism is "connected with other people, not just with feminists" (130). Food for thought, indeed.

Likewise, the simplicity of certain home recipes proposed in *Casalinghitudine* indicates a preoccupation with a *substance* of life, with an almost ideal goodness discovered in the 1960s, and revalorized. Unlike the first feminist wave of the 1960s and 1970s, here the daily repetitions, the care of children, the preparation of food, and the tending of the house are not flatly refused, or passively accepted as in prefeminist days; they become active experiences, "metabolized in a desire for totality, of rejoining of the body to the heart and mind" (M. Rusconi, 22). This we notice especially in the last chapter of *Casalinghitudine*, devoted to the canning and preservation of food, a topic that is perfectly rendered in the Italian infinitive title "Conservare" (Preserving). The narrator, in between preserves, marmalades, and vegetables canned in oil, reflects on her relationship with her house and "homemakerness" as a means of finding and preserving her roots. For Sereni, these roots are a woman's imprints on her domesticity, her "marchio di origine controllata [trademark]." At the same time, they represent rituals that sometimes become necessary for self-preservation. They consist of an exercise of power and control over the immediate environment: picking up toys from the floor, or ironing a pile of clothes and seeing them in a clean stack. They are exercises to help oneself survive. Still, *casalinghitudine* could be a trap. That sense of control and power could turn into a tendency to blackmail others and to nag oneself unbearably. Therefore, the simply functional house becomes lethal; there is also need for a touch of refined care, a scent of frivolity, luxury, and beauty in this woman's life, even though she is aware that neither order and care of the home nor comfort and wealth will grant her clear understanding and security ("chiarezza definitiva, né tantomeno sicurezza," 140).

Casalinghitudine (the practice of homemaking), as represented by Clara Sereni, shows at least three ways of operating in a woman's life: (1) a redefinition and reappropriation of a filtered, bourgeois conscience (less interested in the economic value than in the beauty and aesthetic of the object or practice); (2) the consciousness of a specific (species) socioanthropological gendered operativity that is essentially womanly and thus valorizes an informed, feminine conscience's involvement in attention, care, and responsibility for daily homemaking; (3) the necessary retrenchment of a politically disillusioned conscience that no longer believes in radical changes and needs to withdraw from pointless attempts at radicalization ("Everything has already been said, everything has already been written," 165).

The space that food as "metonymy of the world" occupies in literature cannot be underestimated. According to Gian-Paolo Biasin, author of the very pertinent study I *sapori della modernità: Cibo e romanzo* (The flavors of modernity), the representation of food in fiction brings into play various dimensions, all interacting and explicating different functions: anthropological, sociological, political, and cultural (2). Food and self-care in *Casalinghitudine* are also signs of educated awareness, of social status: a privilege of the informed and advantaged woman. Sereni represents this connection in an ambiguous mixture of subtle irony and self-determination in a critical moment of a woman's life. When the narrator is hospitalized during her pregnancy because of a diabetic condition, she finds herself sharing a large hospital room with several other diabetic women, mostly from small towns in southern Italy. Since she keeps a very close eye on her condition, judiciously following her doctor's instructions, fully aware of the possible complications to herself and her child, she notices the other women's attitudes toward her, and especially their eating habits. She senses the group's unaccepting stance toward her stemming from the objects that reveal her social status: her books, her diligent diet, the antistretch cream that she daily applies on her stomach. But the protagonist is tenacious. She knows that she needs to survive in that environment and she searches for a common ground, which she finds easily once she starts concentrating on the "inside" of the institution. Her strictly followed diet is, however, viewed with suspicion. To make up for the insipid food of the hospital, the southern women produce clandestine supplies of homemade, robust food, "the real meals" (128). This food is to be shared, and its acceptance by the narrator means, on the one hand, the ratification of her complete inclusion and, on the other hand, the possibility of impairing her health and that of the baby she's carrying. A clandestine container with steaming cabbage and onions swimming in olive oil seems too hard to resist, but feeling "stupid and brave at the same time," the narrator continues eating her own insipid food. By this time the narrator and the other women have shared not only the room, but their knitting skills, their "cabala of amniocenteses, glycemic curves, test results, and fears" (128). Yet self-caring, represented also by their diet, their food choices, stays as a mark of difference between them. It is the gulf between two social classes that years of economic miracles have not filled: the narrator's informed self-care versus the uninformed, suspicious-minded self-care practices of the unprivileged. Her final sense of wonder—"Would it have been so serious if I had eaten that food?" (129)—from her writing perspective, shows her critique of and personal irresolution toward the (scientific) establishment that her diet represents, with its inherent homologizing, uncritical discourse.

While the operation of Sereni's characters in the personal/feminine sphere could be considered a successful valorizing of sexual difference—of a sense of feminine entirety and historicity—Sereni's operation on the symbolic order is far from creating the impact that Italian theorists of sexual difference envisage and project. Cooking and taking care of children, viewed as traditional gendered roles, seem a far cry from sexual freedom. We need to keep in mind, however, that in the practice of *affidamento* (entrustment) postulated by the women philosophers of Diotima, we may discern an exercise of care: the caretaker/provider is the mediator to the world—to the dangerous, often inhospitable world—for the younger, inexperienced woman.[16] Moreover, shouldn't the first practice of entrustment start primarily at home, between mother and child? What better opportunity for testing its effectiveness! Therefore, the question that comes next is this: How do Italian theorists of sexual difference (Diotima philosophers and radical Italian feminists) read Clara Sereni? How do they place an ethics of caring and nurturing within the potential "irresponsibility" that women need to carry on in order to free themselves from justifying their femininity?

A feminist political project, according to Italian feminists, is not one of "making the world better" (Non credere d'avere dei diritti, 152) but rather of freeing women and making them subjects of free choices. Women, due to the unavoidable fact of being born women (and not men), live in a condition of irresponsibility in a world thought and ordered by men. Women don't owe anything to men, and there is no "social pact" between women and men, because men have not allowed such a pact. The politics of victimization justify a sense of irresponsibility that women should feel toward society. Women owe nothing to anybody; they don't need to justify their femininity, their gender. A politics of a different, feminine ethics, on the other hand, has as its primary project changing the social order through the practice of strong, gendered, feminine values: pacifism, nurturing, care, self-giving. It is a question of theoretical or ideological priority. In the first case women cannot be bothered about acting in or affecting society until they first create and develop a society ordered by women and for women.

The relationship of *affidamento*, however, reproposes the issue of responsibility inasmuch as women are in a relation of disparity, trading authority for gratitude and therefore establishing a symbolic, ethical, social order to create a new genealogy of women.[17] The shortcomings of these positions are that they do not address the mundane, the ethics of everyday life—still made up of oppositions and dialectical practices among the sexes and the generations—or "the tenacity of people's commitment to our social organization of gender and sex," all of which literature by men and women represents and keeps representing.[18]

Since Diotima has not produced a critique of Sereni's works, I will attempt my own in the form of conclusions. Sereni's women don't ask themselves too often why they are mothers or women; neither do they problematize these issues, which, of course, by themselves become representational issues. Women keep practicing good mothering, feeding, caring, and nurturing not because they are necessarily essentially fit and predisposed to these functions. Many of today's informed women, as represented in Sereni's narrative, keep performing these functions because they know how, because they are good at it (Chodorow), and because they thereby make a difference—because, willingly or unwillingly, it is their history, their culture. Women who choose these practices—and that act of choosing is infused with power and projection—do so with an understanding that a nurturing woman is in a historical continuum, enacting a decisive, different ethical operation in society. In so doing, women—feminist and neofeminist—seem to propose a renewed relationship to these roles. They show an intelligent, self-reflective ethical imperative that is directed toward the entire environment: the human and the nonhuman, the critical and the accessory. Moreover, Sereni represents a woman's ability to make her environment hers, to reevaluate the home, the obvious, and make it consequential and important to her existence as a woman.[19]

That food and care are operations on the "real" rather than theoretical debates of feminist thought does not have to prompt us to dismiss these representations as reductive aspects of essentialist plots, of an unmediated, feminine "nature." I share at this point Rita Felski's concern that postmodern attempts to "dematerialize the natural by insisting on the totalizing claims of the textual may echo rather than challenge a long-standing aesthetic tradition that has sought transcendence through a denial and repression of the (female) body" (1104).[20] Phyllis Grosskurth voices a similar discomfort as she reviews some recent works by feminist psychoanalysts and theorists, and what she sees as Freudian-dependent feminist theorists. She argues that some feminist theorists are too polarized and too "enamored of complicated explanations of theory and evasive on practical questions of equality within the working place, violence in family life." She sees the possibility that "feminism could become as divorced from reality as poststructuralism" (32).

It is to my mind politically and socially naive, in a society that registers a steady growth of single-mother households, to dismiss women's practices of nurturing and caring as essentialist and politically ineffective. Granted that women need as much, and maybe more, infrastructural support than cooking skills and nurturing attitudes to go about their daily lives as mothers and productive individuals, what is one to do with these private, gendered operations? Are they always going to be domestic issues? It is time for us to give political legitimacy to these feminine practices and make them integral in a feminist agenda, for, in the final analysis, the choice to be nurturing, caring individuals is a truly political and consequential issue in women's lives.

Caring and Nurturing: A Reappraisal

Notes

All quotations in English from the books of Macciocchi and Sereni, unless otherwise stated, are my translations from Italian. The same is true of quotations from *Non credere d'avere dei diritti* (Don't believe you have any rights) and *Diotima: Il pensiero della differenza sessuale* (A thinking of sexual difference).

1. While women's "groups" were prevalent in the 1970s, they had a tendency to homologize individual programs in order to produce a more uniform voice. Communities such as Diotima, based in Verona, Transizione, based in Naples, and Ipazia, based in Milan, better represent the trend of the 1990s, since they tend to valorize the individual itineraries and contributions of their members.

2. As already annotated by other contributors, the positions of the Diotima group are presented in detail in their *Diotima: Il pensiero della differenza sessuale*.

3. Maria Antonietta Macciocchi is a well-known Italian writer and feminist, previously a representative of the former Italian Communist party, a fierce anti-Fascist, and a protagonist of emancipatory battles during the years of the so-called hard feminism.

4. Made stronger in their "difference," Italian women live what Macciocchi calls a "third type of feminism" (77), where they can see man no longer as their enemy but as someone who in turn needs support. In this third stage of feminism, Italian women can also revalorize their own gendered practices. "In my long journey, I saw the Italian women all new, 'smile of the universe' (as Dante said). Looking for oneself is better than reading polls. And to look around while crossing ten thousand kilometers is even better than taking a peek from a window, as certain reporters do. Italian women have changed physically in addition to psychologically: theirs is the largest cultural mutation in Italy. They defend a new value previously dismissed: *difference*, not as inferiority, but as strength" (81–83).

5. It is to Chodorow's credit that, as a feminist theorist and psychoanalyst, she maintains a clear and pragmatic perspective on the social organization of gender within her personal Freudian parameters of female development and her anti-essentialist stand. In her view, people as sexed and gendered are "an inextricable totality or unity: the social organization of gender is built right into our heads. . . . We live our past in the present and people cannot change easily: we do not just react to our contemporary situation and conscious wishes" (168). The point is that feminine personality comes to define itself "in relation and connection to other people more than masculine personality does" (45). And because girls' lives are always involved in deep, primary relationships (mother, children, other women), they internalize an object-relation mode of perceiving and operating, where values of caring and nurturing are expressed.

6. "Homemakerness" as well as "homemaking" are my best attempt to translate the Italian title *Casalinghitudine*, which is Sereni's very suggestive combination of two words: *casalinga*, that is, homemaker or housewife (noun) or homely, domestic (adjective), plus the suffix *-tudine*, which means habit, practice (i.e., *abitudine* = habit). Since the publication of the book, the word *casalinghitudine* has become a new favorite expression used in casual conversation (it is now included in the Italian *Dictionary of New Words*) as well as in popular magazines and literary journals to indicate women's rapport with the domestic condition. A show, of the same title and inspired by the book, was staged in a theater in Rome December 8–20, 1992. In Italy there are between 8 and 12 million women registered as homemakers or working at home in the national Federcasalinghe association. About half a million of these women are seeking employment outside the house (*Panorama*, Sept. 27, 1992).

7. The political usefulness of Gilligan's positions on woman's morality could appear questionable within contemporary debates about the notions of feminist essentialism, cultural feminism, and so-called poststructuralist feminism where cross-preoccupations of radicalization, universalism, and revisionism keep surfacing in the attempt to produce a viable,

sustainable feminist critical theory. One can surmise that Gilligan's position has been categorized as essentialist for its claim of woman's difference with respect to ethical behavior. A fruitful, engaging debate can be found in Teresa de Lauretis's articles "The Essence of the Triangle" and "Technology of Gender."

8. It is interesting to note how one commentary on the aftermath of the Clarence Thomas and Anita Hill hearings draws from Gilligan's theory of women's connectedness to advance the possibility that Anita Hill's controversial behavior could have been motivated by an ethics of justice and care. "Caught between conflicting loyalties to race and gender, Anita Hill faced a predicament that has tormented black women for more than a century" (56), writes Rosemary L. Bray in the New York Times Magazine. Bray says in her article that Gilligan did not find it implausible that Anita Hill might have experienced the events she described, yet continued to work with Judge Thomas. She quotes Gilligan as saying that "her basic assumption was that you live in connection with others, in relationship with others . . . she was trying to resolve conflict without breaking connection" (101).

9. This model of analyzing the figure of the mother is proposed by Barbara Johnson in her essay "Mallarmé as Mother," as she considers developmental narratives that show pre-Oedipal structures of maturation and gender. Echoing Carol Gilligan's findings on the gender bias of existing models of ethical development, Johnson points out the desirability of studying "mothering's" representations and narrative functions (e.g., in Mallarmé) as "one of several maturational models for people of both sexes," rather than "simply regressive" structures (42–43).

10. Sereni herself cautions against the equivocation to which her now widely used term *casalinghitudine* can easily lead. She always finds her own relationship with the house "insidious" and "suspect," and cautions us that "there is always a risk of becoming absorbed, consumed by the rapport with floor!" (*Panorama*, Sept. 27, 1992).

11. Cf. Adriana Cavarero, *Nonostante Platone* (18). It is Cavarero's intent in this book to "steal" some women figures from the context of classical western philosophy and literature in an attempt to read their history in their own separate and different place of signification, removed from a context that traditionally denies them meaning and recognition. Cavarero's terse interpretation of Penelope, who, she says, "keeps herself in the present and through her work of weaving and unweaving marks a separate place where she belongs to herself" (14), advances a reevaluation of the relationship between women and the home. As the repetitive gestures of Penelope's weaving and unweaving allude to an intelligence that cannot be separated from the body, the similar rhythm of women's daily home practices points to an intelligence of the daily experience that "day after day keeps itself awake in order to let existence take its roots and mark a place of belonging" (16). The terms of this belonging in Cavarero's analyses are birth and radication as opposed to men's terms of action and death. Since death in Plato's philosophy is the detachment and liberation of the soul from the limitedness and constriction of the body, the experience of men—seeking action and newness—at least in the western cultural tradition, is underscored by a constant theme of death. In death one acquires the immortality of the legend and the immortality of the soul. The experience and the rhythms of women's lives are exactly the opposite, for in the defined and apparently finite space of her home, woman secures the entirety of her body and thought from splitting Platonic categories, in an "interweaving of intelligence and sensibility" that gives and protects life.

12. Aspects of the reproducibility and sharing of recipes are examined by Susan J. Leonardi in her essay "Recipes for Reading," as she points out, "Like a narrative, a recipe is reproducible, and, further, its hearers-readers-receivers are encouraged to reproduce it and, in reproducing it, to revise it and make it their own. . . . Unlike the repetition of a narrative (folktales, ghost stories), however, a recipe's reproducibility can have a literal result, the dish it-

self. This kinship to the literality of human reproducibility, along with the social context of the recipe, contributes to the gendered nature of this form of embedded discourse" (344).

13. I am drawing here from an interview with Clara Sereni, recorded at her home in Rome, July 1990.

14. See Marialisa Calta's article "Take a Novel, Add a Recipe, and Season to Taste," in the February 17, 1993, New York Times.

15. Ibid.

16. For other discussions in this volume of the concept of *affidamento* (entrustment) developed by Italian feminist theorists, see the Introduction and the essay by Renate Holub, "Between the United States and Italy: Critical Reflections on Diotima's Feminine/Feminist Ethics."

17. Elvia Franco of the Diotima community makes this clear in her pedagogical proposal of *affidamento* when she says that "if entrustment is being in the world through the mediation of another woman, then it can have an immediate and real practice. Entrustment demands respect, affection and recognition of a relation of disparity" (153).

18. In her argument on the necessity of a feminist psychoanalytic theory, Nancy Chodorow points to the practical need for women, and men as well, to explain the "tenacity" of people's behavior in a liberated climate: "Why people often cannot change even when they want to; why a 'liberated' man still has difficulty parenting equally . . . ; why a feminist woman might find it hard to be attracted to a non-macho, non-traditionally masculine man, or to be unambivalent about choosing not to have children" (171). These questions and representations, I think, ought to be a priority in the ethical commitment of feminist writing and thinking. That is, we should not understate or dismiss the full range of our ongoing experiences as they are lived, while seeking the support of theory to understand and evaluate the underlying elements of our unconscious and conscious choices.

19. The importance of women's historical experiences for the recovery of a feminine collective unconscious has long been emphasized by feminists. In a recent interview, Italian feminist writer Dacia Maraini reaffirms the extent of gender-historical experience. "Historical experience is what counts," she says, and drawing from a Jungian metaphor, she appropriates the strong symbolism of the home as the custodian of women's history and women's identity: "The layers of history belong to our internal house, our soul" (Serena Anderlini, "Prolegomena," 150).

20. In her analysis of texts of late-nineteenth-century European male avant-garde writers, Felski draws a parallel between fin-de-siècle misogynist parodization of the feminine as subversive and contemporary feminist anti-essentialism, both seen as "long-standing aesthetic traditions" that privilege transcendence (textual theory) through denial and repression of the organic (female) body, seen as unmediated nature.

Works Cited

Anderlini, Serena. "Prolegomena for a Feminist Dramaturgy of the Feminine": (Interview: Dacia Maraini with Serena Anderlini). *Diacritics* 2–3 (1991): 148–60.
Benhabib, Seyla. "The Generalized and the Concrete Other." In *Feminism as Critique*. Minneapolis: University of Minnesota Press, 1988. 77–95.
Bianchini, Angela. "Il vivere quotidiano." In *Scritture, Scrittrici*. Milan: Longanesi, 1988. 27–36.
Biasin, Gian-Paolo. *I sapori della modernità: Cibo e romanzo*. Bologna: Il Mulino, 1991. The English translation, *The Flavors of Modernity*, is published by Princeton University Press (1993).
———. "Italo Calvino in Mexico: Food and Lovers, Tourists and Cannibals." *PMLA* 108.1 (1993): 72–88.
Bray, Rosemary L. *The New York Times Magazine*, Sunday, November 17, 1991.

Calta, Marialisa. "Take a Novel, Add a Recipe, and Season to Taste." *The New York Times*, February 7, 1993.

Cavarero, Adriana, et al. *Diotima: Il pensiero della differenza sessuale*. Milan: La Tartaruga, 1987, 1990.

———. *Nonostante Platone: Figure femminili nella filosofia antica*. Rome: Editori Uniti, 1990.

Chodorow, Nancy. *The Reproduction of Mothering: psychoanalysis and the Sociology of Gender*. Berkeley: University of California Press, 1978.

———. *Feminism and Psychoanalytic Theory*. New Haven: Yale University Press, 1989.

Collettivo della Libreria delle donne di Milano. *Non credere di avere dei diritti: La generazione della libertà femminile nell'idea e nelle vicende di un gruppo di donne*. Turin: Rosenberg & Sellier, 1987.

de Lauretis, Teresa. "Technology of Gender." In *Technologies of Gender: Essays on Theory, Film, and Fiction*. Bloomington: Indiana University Press, 1987. 1–30.

———. "The Essence of the Triangle or Taking the Risk of Essentialism Seriously: Feminist Theory in Italy, the U.S., and Britain." *Differences* 1.2 (1990): 3–37.

———. "The Practice of Difference: An Introductory Essay." In *Sexual Differences: A Theory of Social Symbolic Practice*. Bloomington: Indiana University Press, 1990.

Esquivel, Laura. *Like Water for Chocolate*. New York: Doubleday, 1992.

Felski, Rita. "The Counterdiscourse of the Feminine in Three Texts by Wilde, Huysmans, and Sacher-Masoch." PMLA 5 (1991): 1090–1105.

Gilligan, Carol. *In a Different Voice*. Cambridge, Mass.: Harvard University Press, 1982.

———, ed. *Mapping the Moral Domain*. Cambridge, Mass.: Harvard University Press, 1988.

Grosskurth, Phyllis. "The New Psychology of Women." *New York Review of Books*, Oct. 24, 1991.

Heat-Moon, William Least. *PrairyErth*. Boston: Houghton Mifflin, 1991.

Johnson, Barbara. "Mallarmé as Mother." In *A World of Difference*. Baltimore: Johns Hopkins University Press, 1988. 137–43.

Leonardi, Susan J. "Recipes for Reading." PMLA 3 (1989): 340–47.

Macciocchi, Maria Antonietta. *La forza degli italiani*. Milan: Mondadori, 1990.

———. *La donna "nera": "Consenso" femminile e fascismo*. Milan: Feltrinelli, 1976.

Miceli Jeffries, Giovanna. Interview with Clara Sereni. Rome, July 1990.

Rusconi, Marisa. "Nuovi percorsi tra esperienza e scrittura." In *Scritture, Scrittrici*. Milan: Longanesi, 1988. 11–26.

Sereni, Clara. *Casalinghitudine*. Turin: Einaudi, 1987.

———. *Manicomio primavera*. Florence: Giunti, 1989.

Shange, Ntozake. *Sassafras, Cypress & Indigo*. New York: St. Martin's Press, 1982.

Carol Lazarro-Weis

"Cherchez la femme"
The Case of Feminism and the "Giallo" in Italy

Sherri Paris begins her book review of two recent critical works on women and the crime novel (Kathleen Klein, *The Women Detective: Gender and Genre*; Maureen Reddy, *Sisters in Crime: Feminism and the Crime Novel*) by answering an implicit question: "Why should women read and write detective novels?" Besides the obvious answer that these novels are popular and sell well, a reason that women writers searching to create their own space in the publishing world cannot afford to ignore, Paris suggests that this emerging and powerful interest in the genre on the part of women is motivated by a desire for justice, which is as "persistent, irrational and romanticized a human need as the search for Perfect Love" (9). The detective novel in all its variations from the cerebral types to the "politically correct lesbian" mode can be used to reflect radically diverse moral outlooks of particular social groups. Thus, according to Paris, detective novels, including feminist ones, bring us to contemplate the following questions: "Is moral fairness achievable? Can it be attained within, or only by dodging or subverting, the sanctioned judicial system?" (9).

As Paris does not fail to point out, however, how successful women writers are in answering the above questions varies greatly according to what questions feminist critics of such fiction ask. Kathleen Klein restricts herself to studying only those works in which a professional woman detective is portrayed, since these women rather than amateur sleuths are in a position to threaten the established social order. She finds that the genre (which is inherently male and conservative) and feminism do not mix. Klein reads women's detective novels expecting to find representations of emancipated women enjoying equal rights and finds that women are still victimized by a patriarchal society. Ultimately, a competent woman detective has to reinforce the establishment and concede to the patriarchy, whereas a truly feminist detective novel, such as M. F. Beal's *Angel Dance*, destroys the genre by showing that there is no justice: "Knowing the truth does not lead to justice or action; and radical feminism cannot work within the system" (Klein, 220). Hence, Klein concludes that perhaps the two ideologies can never mesh without producing "an unsatisfactory version of both which has compromised all of their greatest attractions" (221).

In contrast to Klein, Maureen Reddy sees in the detective novel an opportunity for women to "play around with the issue of narrative authority" (10), and to use feminist viewpoints to point out the many patriarchal convictions and myths that shape our society. This perspective allows Reddy to view the hesitation and compromising actions of women sleuths in these novels as signs of empowerment rather than capitulation.

Both readings, while affording important insights, attest to the power of the reader/critic to determine her own results by virtue of the methodology she chooses and the questions she asks. Although both Reddy and Klein could be faulted for reading literature as if it could and should directly reflect real-life situations, Maureen Reddy's book appears more sympathetic to feminist achievements in the genre than Klein's because her orientation is more in keeping with what the genre can do as opposed to what it cannot. Reddy's theory that feminist writers use the genre to play with the issue of narrative authority indicates that many women writers are exploiting the capability of the form to trick the reader with a plethora of possible, probable, but untrue *récits*. Therefore, although Reddy may be amenable to thinking that the portrayal of a more "tolerant and fallible detective" has feminist overtones that radically change the form, Klein would tend to condemn this representation as one showing women fulfilling society's expectations of them as emotional and scatterbrained beings incapable of the ratiocinative deductions of the truly unfeeling detective. As Klein demonstrates on numerous occasions, however, the elimination of such "feminine" features does not solve the problem, since strong women detective figures do not herald the creation of new stereotypes but rather, in most cases, evoke in the reader the image of another established negative female stereotype, the frustrated shrew who denies her femininity in order to defeat and claim male power.

The resistance of the detective novel to feminist interpretation and goals has been noted by male critics of the genre. Both the detective novel and the crime variant presume upon two female stereotypes: the *femme fa-*

tale whom the hero must conquer if he is not to become the dupe of his own culturally constructed fears, or the angel he must rescue to prove his masculinity (Hilfer, 72–73). Although the unmasking of male incompetence or hypocrisy affords more sympathy to the women in the text, it only marginally improves a female image that is, according to Martin Priestman, strongly influenced by the Oedipal pattern that locks women into the role of the strong mother figure whose main goal is to conserve her socially determined maternal role and powers (107). Thus, contemporary women writers of detective novels face the main problematic of this collection of essays in a (here strongly overdetermined) generic framework: Is it necessary to destroy femininity to use the detective form to campaign for change or can "compromise" and "cooperation" with the traditional images of the form be read in another, more subversive key? And the differences in the readings of Klein and Reddy are due to an unresolved issue that neither critic specifically addresses: to what extent should feminist literary theory base its evaluation of a work on criteria such as political correctness or the work's ability to express a certain feminist theme?

This question frames Helen Vendler's review article entitled "Feminism and Literature." Vendler writes that the most conspicuous successes of feminist critics have been in the realms of history and sociology, since the information they make known to the public has "explanatory power" concerning the changing positions of women in different societies (19). The informative and explanatory power of feminist literary theory, however, is considerably less impressive, charges Vendler, and all too often bases its study and judgment of women's writings on their political and social value rather than on their literary properties. In many cases, these theories tend to reinforce prejudices that the texts under analysis are indeed inferior as literature, although Vendler blames this more on theory than on the works themselves.

The failures of American feminist criticism and French deconstructionist theories when applied to women's writings are treated in depth in Rita Felski's *Beyond Feminist Aesthetics: Feminist Literature and Social Change*, one of the books Vendler reviews. Felski argues that a feminist textual theory must be able to account for "the levels of mediation between literary form and social domains" (8). According to Vendler, however, despite Felski's attention to literary form in this work, she engages primarily in what used to be called the "sociology of literature," and in so doing again demonstrates the inability of feminist criticism to evaluate women's writing without reducing it to a propaganda tool. Vendler then points out that some feminist critics are beginning to question the primacy of the category of gender in the production of literature and its evaluation. She concludes with a quote from Mary Gordon's interview of the Italian writer Natalia Ginzburg, who flatly denies the influence of gender and even of nationality on her writing: "You sit down, you write, you are not a woman, or an Italian. You are a writer."[1]

Rather than tolling the death knell for relationships between feminism and literature, Vendler's evocation of the image of the writers as an androgyne participating in a universal enterprise in which ideology, feminist or otherwise, plays no part primarily reflects her uneasiness with certain pronouncements of feminist literary theory concerning what women's literature should be and do. Feminist deconstructionists such as Julia Kristeva and Luce Irigaray dismissed a large part of women's literary endeavors, especially those written in a more traditional and representational vein, as being inherently conservative and conciliatory. Theories concerning difference in women's writing based in gender start out to defend woman's right to express herself differently from men but often end up prescribing limits and emphasizing sameness; they can also paradoxically reinforce arguments for writers as androgynes.[2] Theories of the innate oppositionality of women's literature, whether they privilege experimental or traditional forms, risk ignoring differences between women writers and their individual innovations since the critic searches for general, communal types of oppositional strategies that fight the same, often undifferentiated enemy.

Italian feminist writers in the 1970s, who wrote to express political and feminist views, were generally antagonistic to the views expressed by Ginzburg and her generation of Italian women authors on the genderless nature of writing.[3] At a conference on women and literature held in Palermo in 1988, however, several Italian contemporary women writers and critics also sought to distance feminism as a political program from literary endeavors. In the published proceedings of this convention one finds mainly familiar topics, such as what women's writing is, how to define women's responsibility as a writer, how to describe women's relationship to the written word, and so on, and the varied answers show that a consensus on any of these topics has not yet been reached.[4] However, despite disagreements, Eleonora Chiavetta notes, in her review of the conference proceedings, abundant calls for a more "professional" and more "literary" style of women's writing in contrast to the overtly autobiographical and political outpourings of the 1970s and early 1980s.[5] Feminist critic and writer Bian-

"Cherchez la femme"

camaria Frabotta discounts theories that a woman has to "write like a woman" and argues that one writes not to know oneself but rather to experience the other: "l'io empirico, quello ben radicato nella psicologia e nella storia, nell'atto dell'opera . . . presto si stanca di se stesso si disgusta dei suoi limiti . . . , anche quelli certificabili all'anagrafe del sesso."[6] Frabotta also challenges the ability of feminist theory, no matter how it emphasizes difference among women, to deal with the solitary act of creativity that constitutes writing: "Anche nella differenza c'è sempre la voce della specie che parla [Even in difference, the voice always speaks for the species]" (147).

At the same conference, writer and feminist critic Maria Rosa Cutrufelli puts the personal quality of women's writing into a historical perspective; what women's writing may have had in common across ages and cultures was that literature was a place for them to talk about sexual difference. If the personal genres of earlier writings were historically determined, however, the present gaze of women writers has expanded to include a wide variety of topics and interests. A good part of contemporary women's literature follows some sort of political choice; therefore, ideology is never absent. Nonetheless, in order to prevent these works from vanishing or being relegated to a simple momentary social or political function, Cutrufelli argues not only for a more literary style of writing but, more important, for a literary method of reading women's works critically. Maria Rosa asks for criteria based on more than empathy and political identification: the method must consist of "an eye trained to pick out the formal characteristics of the text (aesthetics) and one capable of showing how the new themes are reflected in the *structural choices made in the work* [my emphasis]."[7]

The above observations serve as an introduction to our analysis of two recent feminist experiments with the detective novel form in Italy published in La Tartaruga nera, a feminist series launched by the feminist press La Tartaruga to encourage women writers to write mystery and detective fiction. Unlike science fiction, where until recently most readers were male, the detective novel enjoys in Italy an equally divided and relatively high readership among both sexes.[8] In Italy, the successes of Eco and Leonardo Sciascia attest to the ability of the genre to promulgate philosophical ideas, criticize society, and still sell well. And, although the two presses that have launched detective series for women writers still seem to privilege translations of foreign (albeit women) writers of the genre, the entry of women into this realm is a clear trend.[9] Rather than expecting a

Carol Lazzaro-Weis

feminization of the form, however, or a victory of feminist ideology over that of the petit bourgeois or the patriarchy which the form is widely assumed to perpetrate, we will examine how two Italian women writers include feminist themes, motifs, and ideas in their works and exploit generic conventions to do so. The detective novel, a form based on the paradoxical exploitation and imposition of limits and contradictions, has always absorbed ideas by thematizing and contextualizing its own inherent contradictions. The contemporary debate raging at present in Italy concerning the relationship of theories of sexual difference to social justice serves as a fitting backdrop for experimentations with a form that purportedly upholds the democratic ideal of justice and punishes those who fail to do so. The main texts we will discuss are Fiora Cagnoni's *Questione di tempo* (La Tartaruga nera, 1985) and Silvana La Spina's *Morte a Palermo* (La Tartaruga nera, 1987).

Literary and Social Contexts

> *Here were the Universities and the Church of England kissing one another in righteousness and peace, like the angels in Botticelli's nativity. . . . Here without heat, they could discuss their common problem, agreeing pleasantly or pleasantly agreeing to differ. Of the grotesque and ugly devil-shapes sprawling at the foot of the picture these angels had no word to say. What solution could either of them produce, if challenged . . . ? Other bodies would be bolder: the Church of Rome would have its answer, smooth, competent and experienced; the queer, bitter, jarring sects of the New Psychology would have another, ugly, awkward, tentative and applied with a passionate experimentalism. It was entertaining to imagine a Freudian University indissolubly wedded to a Roman Establishment: they would certainly not so harmoniously live together as the Anglican Church and the School of Litterae Humaniores. But it was delightful to believe, if only for an hour, that all human difficulties could be dealt with in this detached and amiable spirit. "The University is a Paradise"—true, but—"then, I saw there was a way to hell even from the gates of Heaven."*
>
> Dorothy Sayers, *Gaudy Night*, 263–64

> *E se nel frattempo le teoriche delle differenza fossero riuscite a metter mano alla costituzione per piegarla verso una cittadinanza differenziata*

per sesso? . . . *Infelice me, biologicamente definita come donna e tuttavia decisa a definirmi sul piano giuridico come semplice cittadino.*
Miriam Mafai, MicroMega, October 1990[10]

Non bastono i diritti e le opportunità. Occorre modificare l'esistenza simbolica e le strutture del linguaggio che hanno codificato come universale una organizzazione umana e sociale in realtà costruita a misura del sesso maschile.[11]
Livia Turco, La repubblica, October 9, 1990 (response to Mafai)

If fictional works are indeed shaped by aesthetic structures that mediate their relationship to reality, we must first outline a few of these structures and discuss how they function in the detective novel. It is not possible nor is it our intention here to resume all the debates over what constitutes a detective novel and how this is different from its many variants.[12] Most critics agree, however, that the detective novel, at least in its popular and purest form, relies on stereotypical figures, a straightforward logical plot development, a contemporary and realistic setting, and, of course, a detective who creates a coherent narrative out of a series of unrelated clues and solves the crime. Since the main action revolves around the resolution of the crime, character psychology and setting, however important, must not overshadow the detective's superior ratiocinative ability.

Most of the above characteristics have been equated with a conservative, bourgeois ideology the detective novel is assumed to represent. Hilfer writes that in the classical detective novel the function of the detective is to guarantee the reader's absolution from any feelings of guilt. The popular detective novel assuages the reader because it neither challenges the possibility of justice and equality for all nor negates the ability of universal logic to overcome justice; rather it punishes those that threaten this potential. The crime novel, in contrast, maneuvers the reader into various forms of complicity that question the universality or possibility of justice (Hilfer, 3–5). Violations of the detective novel's formal characteristics by many authors after World War II drew critical attention to the "metaphysical detective novel," a less reassuring variant that by virtue of its social critique demonstrated the ability of the form to belong to both high and popular culture. According to Michael Holquist, the metaphysical detective novel reversed the detective novel's ideology of "radical rationality," a belief that the mind, given enough time, can understand everything because the relationship between ideas and things is a totally rational one (135–56).

This ideology derives from the bourgeois Enlightenment and its essentially "democratic" belief in the possibility of truth, justice, and equality, a belief the detective, the secularized God figure, and the reader share. Although this description of the form's ideology has been used to buttress explanations for why the detective novel did not take root in those societies (notably Germany and Italy) that lacked a secular democratic Enlightenment tradition, both German and Italian writers have produced their share of the so-called metaphysical detective novels in which the failures of the detectives to solve mysteries or disprove other rational theories called these same principles into question.

In the popular detective novel, the representation of the relationship of society to ratiocinative activity was always problematic. The theoreticians and writers of the form in the 1930s, the so-called golden age of the detective novel, warned that excessive attention to setting would redirect reader interest and sympathies from the crime and its solution to social criticism, as happens in many melodramatic *romanzi d'appendice* that prefigured the classical detective novel form. In order to represent the mind as superior to matter, detective novelists severely limited the latter; indeed, some extreme theoreticians claimed that the only true detective novel would be a purely theoretical puzzle. The sanitized, isolated settings in many traditional detective novels, and the figures of detectives who never left their desk or office to solve the crime, are parodied in Borges's detective, Sandro Parodì, who solves his mysteries from a jail cell.

Nonetheless, many novelists were aware that readers were attracted to the form not only to solve puzzles but to contemplate the contradictions between a theoretical perfect justice for all that was never realized in the text, and the actions and psychology of characters that jeopardized this ideal. Despite different emphases in the detective novel and the crime variant, both restore order through the observance of key conventions. Motives for the crime must be ahistorical ones such as sex, ambition, or greed so that excesses against universal justice can be reduced by the detective's logic to their proper, manageable size. And this literary convention is usually linked to another necessary convention of the detective and crime novel, that of the surprise ending.[13]

The tension between the possibility of an ideal justice and its practice, one of the major potential contradictions in the popular *giallo*, is brought to the fore in Leonardo Sciascia's works; the schism between ratiocinative theory and socially critical practice becomes apparent when Sciascia's detectives easily solve murders but cannot bring anyone to justice in

"Cherchez la femme"

the real world.[14] In *Postscript to the Name of the Rose*, Eco places his novel in the tradition of the crime variant when he writes that the real accomplishment of the *giallo* is to make us see that "we are the guilty party" (81). We, the reader, (criminally) produce the object of study by imposing a certain discourse upon it, by reconstructing the past and our relationship to it according to our interests, prior interpretations and political inclinations (Coletti, 5ff.). In *Il nome della rosa*, Eco sculpts a plot around the demonstration of the process of signification itself. Although William of Baskerville is forced to conclude at the end that the theory on which he based his detection was false, he does solve the mystery with it, thus underlining the usefulness and necessity of such theories for man, the rational being. Since when these theories are allowed to become unquestionable truths they become as oppressive and one-sided as those they claim to overthrow, however, laughter is needed to undo such constructions. Baskerville concludes that the mission of those who love mankind is to "make people laugh at the truth, to make truth laugh, because the only truth lies in learning to free ourselves from insane passion for the truth" (495).

This statement resumes Eco's usage of the popular detective form to get across the philosophical message of postmodernity and demonstrates how semiotics can function as a permanent, radical demystifier of ideologies. In representing his philosophy of how meaning is constructed, Eco does not violate the genre's rules and thus falls victim to its limits as well. Eco's detective from Baskerville displays great erudition in solving the mystery, with the help of a few false theories, but he is powerless to stop other stronger forces.

A precedent for the depiction of deduction as an amusing but irrelevant pastime can be found in the turn-of-the-century detective fiction of Israel Zangwill, Arthur Morrison, E. C. Bentley (*Trent's Last Case*), and G. K. Chesterton, whose works Martin Priestman claims are politically conscious insofar as they are broadly anticapitalist and include socialist overtones. These authors are noted and admired by Eco and Sciascia, especially Chesterton, whose oft-quoted statement equating the criminal with the creative artist and characterizing the detective as his critic appeals to postmodern sensibilities. Priestman's primary argument is that in these works the detective novel form functions as the explanatory, demystifying "other" for many of the period ideas its absorbs, and the "aestheticizing of crime and the corresponding criminalization of the aesthetic" were common structuring themes in the fictional works of the modernist generation of writers of that time, notably Henry James, Joseph Conrad, and Oscar

Wilde (136–50). These preclassic detective novel writers sustain their socially critical position by having their detectives question the truth or usefulness of theories connecting crime to art. Bentley's Trent in *Trent's Last Case* solves a mystery only to find out that theories and logical deductions, however aesthetically pleasing they may be, were incorrect. Ideas and ratiocinative thinking function to train reader and detective in the art of deduction—but since this technique in itself will not "equip us to confront the real problems of life . . . however much we have learnt, this should be for us, as for Trent, the last case" (Priestman, 123).

Eco's helpless theoretical truths are allayed in the film version of his novel by a change in script to show the *menu peuple* rising up against the evil priests, saving Adso's innocent love and effecting a spectacular, melodramatic kind of justice. Teresa de Lauretis agrees that the theory of "radical" semiotics in the detective novel discounts its own radicality, but for different reasons ("Gaudy Rose: Eco and Narcissism," 60–66). De Lauretis argues that, in *Il nome della rosa*, Eco replaces the supposedly moribund word and master theory of the Father with the equally oppressive word of the fathers through endless references to other male texts. The result is the creation of a "homo-sexual" pedagogical link between Adso's adoration for the knowledge of the detective monk and his desire to recuperate and thus salvage the knowledge, vision and power of the (M)aster.[15] Thus, argues de Lauretis, Eco's semiotic logic is not universal but male, and functions to ensure its own survival. Women detective novel writers exhibit a different logic. As an example, de Lauretis refers to Dorothy Sayers's *Gaudy Night*, a text in which the contradiction "constitutive of women as subjects in a social reality instituted in the name of the father, . . . points to the contradiction of the plot itself, the compromise of narrative discourse as it exists historically in that reality" (67).

To be sure, in *Gaudy Night* Sayers deploys the inherent separation of ratiocinative theory and social practice in the detective novel to portray the contradictions and limits of (the theory of) women's emancipation. When Harriet Vane is called in to investigate acts of violence against women in an all-female setting, a women's college in Oxford, the theme of how an intellectual woman can find equality outside of an isolated, single-sexed community is broached immediately. The impossibility of putting the theory of emancipation into practice is mirrored in Harriet Vane's love relationship with Peter Wimsey, whom she is afraid to marry for fear she will lose her autonomous identity. It is precisely these contradictions stemming from female autonomy and women's right to challenge female stereotypical roles

"Cherchez la femme"

that motivate the crime. The criminal in *Gaudy Night* (uncovered by Peter Wimsey's logic and not that of Harriet Vane) is the wife of a male graduate student whose unprofessional academic practices had been uncovered and publicly denounced by a woman scholar, Miss DeVine. DeVine's condemnation ended the plagiarist's academic career, and he committed suicide, leaving his wife, Anna, and his children unprovided for. Anna justifies her revenge on DeVine by arguing that the latter herself committed a crime against all women. As a female, DeVine was expected to uphold woman's traditional social role of supporter of men and family and remain silent. In Sayers's remarkable novel, equality and justice do not exist for the emancipated woman except in that magical moment referred to in the above quote when logic shows us that despite differences we can all think alike. The concrete appearance of female difference on the scene causes trouble in paradise and reveals women to be the gatekeepers of Hell.

The malaise experienced by Sayers's university women and the crimes committed against them elucidate some of the limts and fallacies of the theory of emancipation. The late Italian feminist art critic and philosopher Carla Lonzi had pointed out that as long as the women's movement was based on concepts of emancipation and equality, the movement would essentially inhabit a powerless position nurtured by a rhetoric of victimization and desperate claims for rights from men (*Sputiamo su Hegel*). Not surprisingly, *Don't Think You Have Any Rights* is the title of the recently translated manifesto of the Milan Group, where the theory and political practice of *affidamento*, which posits that a new and empowered female subjectivity can only be thought out and constructed in an all-female environment, is outlined.[16] Lonzi's writings coincided with the general disillusionment of feminists with the Communist party and Marxist philosophy in the 1970s.[17] Lonzi attributes Marxism's inability to transform the female subject to its consistent repression of sexual difference. This repression begins with Hegel who defined feminine essence as a divine principle that presides over the family and the conservation of the species, whereas he charged men with the task of safeguarding the "human" principles of liberty and justice. In real terms, however, writes Lea Melandri, this viewpoint is a theorization and justification of the control men had previously acquired over women, over their sexuality and their autonomous desire. When women enter History, they come in as an economic machine to reproduce the race or as the eternal *Dea madre*, herself a general equivalent of money, the most abstract measure created by patriarchal ideology (*L'infame originaria*, 27).[18]

Carol Lazzaro-Weis

If the feminist theory of sexual difference corrects Marxism's failure to take into account *la differenza sessuale*, its own theorizing is grounded in Marxist materialist analysis. The goal of the practice and theorizing of *la differenza sessuale* is to produce a new female subjectivity, an empowered, responsible subject capable of finding new definitions of justice and liberty that correspond to the materiality of sexual difference. In other words, since the democratic ideals of justice and liberty were constructed to create a parity between men's material existence and desires and the legal rights that protected these elements, it is now time to construct a parity between female desires and liberty and a justice system that corresponds to and protects these desires: "Aprire spazi alla libertà femminile significa fare giustizia," concluded women at an October 1990 meeting of Communist women and feminist theoreticians.[19]

The question of whether or not a *giustizia femminile* is possible or desirable animated a heated newspaper debate in October 1990 that culminated in a public debate ("Eva vs Eva: il femminismo è illiberale?") on October 26 at the Campo Marzio in Rome. In the September issue of *MicroMega*, the well-known and respected Communist women's rights activist and former editor of N*oi*D*onne*, Mariam Mafai, accused her feminist colleagues of becoming even less tolerant and more ideological than their male comrades.[20] Mafai describes separatist feminists seeking to legislate feminine difference as "Lenin's widows" ("*Le vedove di Lenin*"), since he, like they, renounced the illusory nature of equality in democracy. For Mafai, the present effort of Communist feminists to affirm and valorize sexual difference through the incorporation of a special charter for women in the party platform and their suggested laws for reorganizing the workday around women's needs and desires constitute at best a misguided attempt to apply Luce Irigaray's ideological and obscure theories on sexual difference (10); at the very worst, it represents a fanatical regression to Lenin's utopian ideal of a proletarian liberation that feminists repropose in the name of their sex. Mafai takes the more traditionalist stance that she will continue to defend "difference in front of a justice that strives to be as neutral as it can" (11).

Although some women who disagree with Mafai depict her in terms reminiscent of Dorothy Sayers's more exaggeratedly neuter Miss DeVine, "a soldierly woman knowing no personal loyalties, whose sole allegiance was to the fact" (*Gaudy Night*, 22), even supporters of radical theories of sexual difference continue to have questions concerning appropriate ideological framework and methods.[21] According to the feminist philosopher Claudia Mancini, the greatest critical achievement of the theory of sexual difference is that it has replaced themes of oppression, victimization, and inequality in feminist discourse with a powerful and empowering critique of the illusion of neutrality in the concept of equal justice and the homologizing, subjugating, and exclusionary effect of this illusion on women in real life (26).[22] Women must create their own political forms if they are to achieve equality in society, since their desires, needs, and differences have always been excluded from definitions of justice and equality. Others such as Grazia Zuffa charge that some aspects of the theories of sexual difference and the practice of *affidamento* paradoxically undermine the critical and radical force of feminist theory by possibly leaving women unable to recognize moments when they reinforce patriarchal ideology and cooperate with it. Attempts to eliminate the gap between the "theory of what we want to be" and the "practice of what we are" distance women from the fruitful contradictions that emerge from their concrete experience as women (Zuffa, 52).

In response to Eco's proclamation that the real accomplishment of the *giallo* is to make us acknowledge our guilt and complicity, de Lauretis writes: "Who's we, white man?" ("Eco's Gaudy Rose," 68). But if, in her criticism of *Il nome della rosa*, de Lauretis succeeds in exposing Eco's male logic posing as a universal one, something women have no reason to feel guilty about, Zuffa brings up another problem. In *giallo* terms, would an ideal female justice leave us unable to recognize the very historical and social contradictions de Lauretis credits Sayers with bringing to our attention and which cause women to murder?

The Criminal

Fiora Cagnoni's *Questione di tempo* (A question of time) is a detective story about women. The plot bears a certain general resemblance to another one of Sayers's novels recently translated in the Tartaruga nera series, *Strong Poison* (translated as *Veleno mortale*, 1990). In this novel, Sayers begins the love story between Harriet Vane and Peter Wimsey. Lord Wimsey comes to the rescue of Vane when she is accused, in a seemingly open-and-shut case, of killing her boyfriend. In *Questione di tempo*, women save other women: Alice Carta comes to the rescue of her best friend, Elena Noja, who, in an equally hopeless situation, is accused of killing her married lover, Michele, after his body is found on her terrace.

Detective Alice pursues her detective role methodically, interviewing all possible suspects and amassing all the evidence that could prove them innocent or guilty. Alice and Elena travel with a female group upon whom they can count in times of need. All female characters drink whiskey like real men, but cook like real women. They are all stereotypes of a sort, although this in itself is an accepted convention of the *giallo*. Alice spends most of her time interviewing a certain Doctor Cassini, with whom Elena had spent the afternoon of the crime in Florence, and the widow of the deceased, the stereotypical strikingly beautiful, rich woman who is supposedly permanently crippled as the result of an automobile accident. Like Eco and Sciascia, in *Questione di tempo*, Cagnoni critiques a justice system that relies on stereotypical prejudices to find easy solutions that, as Cagnoni shows, victimize women more than men. Elena is presumed guilty and detained in prison after Michele's widow, Magda Saveri, announces that she had known her husband was having an affair with Elena and had demanded that he stop seeing her. Authoritative logic immediately categorizes Elena as the typical outraged other woman seeking revenge.

This situation is reversed when Alice traces to Cassini the disappearance of the raincoat Elena was supposedly wearing when fleeing her apartment after allegedly murdering Michele. Cassini frames his confession in an equally stereotypical situation. Hopelessly in love with the young maid who worked for Michele and his wife, and who was also having an affair with Michele, Cassini claims he detained Elena in Florence and drove to Milan that evening to kill Michele in her apartment. Authorities, familiar with this plot as well, accept it, free Elena, and all is well that ends well.

This is not the real story, though. In the last few pages, Alice visits the beautiful but wicked widow and, in typical ratiocinative fashion, reconstructs the crime, revealing yet another series of clichés and stereotypes. The widow, Magda, taking advantage of Cassini's undying love for her, had involved him and the maid (whom she blackmailed) in her revenge against Elena and Michele. Magda herself, whose paralysis was faked, followed her unfaithful husband to Elena's apartment and killed him. She is now content to continue to manipulate the enamored Cassini, who will take the rap for her. After revealing her theory to the widow, who affirms her narrative, Alice admits she is also content to let Cassini take the blame since she is disgusted by foolish stereotypical men who allow themselves to be ruled by their excessive, romantic love. Alice will not turn the widow in, because she is not the typical detective who seeks absolute truth and assumes that its discovery will ensure justice. Her primary motivation for accepting the case was to free her friend Elena from all suspicion. The story ends with Alice, who was falling in love with the beautiful widow all along, agreeing to spend the night.

The ending in *Questione di tempo* is hardly a reassuring one, but for reasons other than its depiction of the inequities of male justice. Alice's generic deductive speech at the end certainly demonstrates how easy it is to "think like a man," and shows how women can manipulate the same prejudices and stereotypical behavior patterns that subjugate them—such as when the widow provokes her husband's unfaithfulness by faking paralysis. Although Cagnoni has shown throughout how justice is male-oriented, she neutralizes her own critique by representing a world where women (and by extension female justice) would be no different from men and male justice.

This less-than-revolutionary ending is a result of Cagnoni's observance of the *giallo* rules, especially the one demanding a personal motive for the crime so that the ending constitutes a surprise reversal of expectations. To be sure, Elena and Alice are relieved to find that trivial motives such as sex and personal revenge motivated the murder. They had initially suspected that the suspicious disappearance of Saveri's maid, who had befriended Elena, was due to some entanglement with the Red Brigade or drug dealers. Nonetheless, if the denial of historical and social motives in the detective story is essentially what blunts the critical edge of the traditional detective novel, the potentially revolutionary feminist community inhabiting the patriarchal structure in *Questione di tempo* also appears to lack interest in modifying anything. Alice fulfills her generic function of absolving the (female) readers from all guilt by referring to statements from *Non credere di avere dei diritti*, where it is explicitly stated that women owe nothing to men, especially men like Cassini. She also excuses Magda's crime on the grounds that its perfect execution should incite admiration rather than criticism. This latter reason is often given in the traditional detective novel to shift the reader's sympathy away from the victim and social issues, and to glorify the detective's theoretical infallibility (Hilfer, 5–8).

Doubtless one could argue that Cagnoni's observance of the rules is meant to suggest the inability of women to achieve real autonomy in a patriarchal form and the society it represents. In *Questione di tempo* the social irrelevance of the form itself is mentioned: detective Alice Carta says she gave up writing her own detective novel because she finds its ratiocinative tendencies too detached from the problems encountered in real life. In following the genre's rules, however, Cagnoni reinforces a common ideological inference in the detective novel that the problem does not lie in the faulty logic of a universal justice, but rather in the perverse, personal interpretations of it by individuals.

If Cagnoni's detective story shows the homologizing effect of integrating pieces of feminist theory into an established generic structure, Silvana La Spina's Morte a Palermo, published in the same feminist series, exploits the *giallo's* traditional lack of connection between an ideal justice and its practice in a more complex way. In Morte a Palermo, La Spina criticizes Eco in a Sciascian context and, in so doing, more pointedly highlights the dangers inherent in privileging theory over practice. La Spina sets her story in a mysterious Palermo filled with superstition and archaic loyalties. In the first chapter, Professor Costanzo, who was about ready to publish a purportedly revolutionary work on ancient matriarchies in the Palermo area, is murdered. His death is followed by that of his wife, who is for a time a suspect, and finally of her lover, Eugenio Nitti, who was also Costanzo's student and another possible suspect.

Direct and indirect references to Il *nome della rosa* abound throughout. Maps of labyrinths are found near the body of the dead professor, who, like Eco's monk, is found upside down in a large cistern. Besides several discussions on the nature of labyrinths, one of which is taken directly from Eco's Postscript to the Name of the Rose, the blind Argentinean writer Borges is again evoked as a character in the text. Blind poet and writer Bustos Domecq is in Palermo at the time of the murders, which, he immediately notes, follow patterns akin to plots in his detective novels. Finally, for most of the text, it appears that the real criminal is maybe the book of Professor Costanzo, which contains important revelations on Mediterranean Mother Goddess and mysteriously disappears after his death.

Although the pragmatic, down-to-earth detective Santoro has an interest in literature, he distances himself from William of Baskerville when he announces that he has not read Il *nome della rosa* since he prefers to read works when they are no longer in fashion. Unlike Baskerville, Santoro searches for the person responsible for the bizarre murders primarily through the normal investigative channels, while Bustos solves the crime by isolating the mythical plot the criminal is following. Despite their different methods, the two detectives simultaneously discover the real murderer. To find the criminal, Bustos determines that the murders are patterned after the myth of Dedalus and Minos in Sicily: Dedalus had Minos killed by drowning him head first in a cistern. The death of Costanzo's unfaithful wife, who was found hanged in a crypt, was modeled on the figure of Ariadne, who hanged herself either out of remorse for having betrayed her fa-

"Cherchez la femme"

ther Minos by helping Dedalus escape or for having been abandoned by Theseus. Theseus himself was eventually thrown off a cliff by his rival; Eugenio Nitta was killed in the same manner. Finally, Dedalus was an architect and so is the criminal, whose motive is a recognizable one. Out of fear that Costanzo's book on matriarchies would cause archaeologists to demand that a certain area be off-limits for his building project, a well-known architect, De Castro, organized these murders in a parody of the mythical theories outlined in Costanzo's book.

Despite obvious ideological differences with authors like Zangwill, Chesterton, Bentley, and Sciascia, La Spina deploys their method of criticizing the overuse of clever literary theories in detective fiction, where they function to cover up the truth and obstruct the questioning of society's provision of justice, a questioning the form has the capacity to incite. Although Bustos, like Baskerville, solves the mystery through "literary" means, the Argentinean poet is highly critical of De Castro's imitation of his fictional stories to construct his crime: "Questa, architetto, è cattiva letteratura [This, my dear architect, is bad literature]" (*Morte a Palermo*, 128). In the final chapter, detective Santoro, who had arrived in the nick of time to save Bustos, comments that Bustos's interest in the crime was motivated by his desire to avenge himself on the man who had reduced him to the role of a foolish character in a novel (*Morte a Palermo*, 136). Unlike Cagnoni's Alice who dismisses the crime because of its clever nature, La Spina's Santoro and others are irritated by the arrogance of the criminal who constructs the evidence in a way that pushes detection toward "criminal hubris" instead of the discovery of guilt (Priestman, 109). The artful crime committed by De Castro facilitates his capture and serves only temporarily as a cover-up for the real motivation.

Although in *Morte a Palermo* La Spina does not essay a representation of women effecting their own justice, a female-centered critique of the partial nature of so-called democratic justice still operates within the text. In *Morte a Palermo*, the criticism of (male) democratic justice is effected through its contrast to mythical justice, a contrast that, not surprisingly, reveals more similarities than differences. De Castro sets up the murders according to myths that carry with them a theory of archaic justice based on self-interest, unquestionable loyalties, and revenge. "Così giustizia è fatta, non è vero [So this is how justice is done, is it?]," remarks one character to Santoro after they discuss the myths that the criminal is most likely following (*Morte a Palermo*, 123). This type of justice, often associated with primitive matriarchal societies, is what democratic justice supposedly defeats; this is indeed what happens when Santoro exposes the criminal's personal greed and egotistical motivations. The theory of the defeat of matriarchal justice and power by a patriarchal, juridical justice was first advanced in the preceding century by J. Bachofen, who, in his classic *Das Mutterrecht*, read Aeschylus's trilogy, the *Oresteia*, as an allegory of the defeat of matriarchal societies. Feminist theoreticians, notably Luce Irigaray and more recently Adriana Cavarero in *Nonostante Platone*, have extended his theory in their explorations of the appropriation of female sexuality and defeat of female autonomy by the patriarchy. In her review of a recent Italian translation of Bachofen's *Mutterrecht*,[23] Eva Cantarella suggests that, although Italian feminists have traditionally rejected theories glorifying archaic matriarchies and mother goddesses since they, like many French feminist theories on the power of the feminine in writing, reinforced the same stereotypical, antisocial qualities previously deployed to marginalize women, feminists can now reread Bachofen in light of current theories on sexual difference ("Le fortune del matriarcato"). Nonetheless, Cantarella is aware of the dangers of reading Bachofen as a champion of women's rights; in his autobiography Bachofen writes that democracy is not a sign of progress but rather one that barbarity is returning, but he lauds matriarchies by repeating traditional dichotomies where women represent earth and nature and men belong to the realm of light, spirit, and intellect (18).

The *femme fatale* in *Morte a Palermo*, the *Dea madre*, is indeed no more than the abstract, essentially powerless figure described by Melandri and Lonzi as a male construction that men manipulate to further petty rivalries and maintain the status quo. Costanzo's scholarly enemy Professor Lo Giudice, who was one of the suspects in his murder because he had written against Costanzo's book, calls Costanzo's theories on *la gran dea mediterranea* dangerous and regressive; he said that they reflect a pathological tendency to invent an autonomous historical role for Sicily as the cradle of civilization, out of fear of admitting that the Sicilians were only "una grande carovaniera di civiltà altrui [the crossroads of other people's civilizations]" (*Morte a Palermo*, 43). Both theories go unvalidated in the text; neither does the intellectual disagreement of the professors motivate the real crime, although the architect De Castro had unsuccessfully tried to talk Lo Giudice into eliminating Costanzo on these ideological grounds.

La Spina affirms her critique of the inadequacy of a democratic justice that implements the very "feminine" justice it purports to replace through more final ironic allusions to Eco. Costanzo's book, like Aristotle's on laughter in *Il nome della rosa*, disappears at the end. Instead of being lamented as a text that could have changed the course of civilization (or literary criticism), however, its disappearance goes unnoticed; no one, including Costanzo's female student, was really looking for it. The book slides behind a dusty bookcase and finds its place beside a learned but undeciphered and now lost Arabic text. Jesuit priest Don Saverio comments to Santoro that perhaps the work could have shown us how to reread history so that we can understand what we were at one time and why we have become the way we are now. Santoro's response to this statement, which is taken from Eco's *Postscript to the Name of the Rose*, takes a final ironic swipe at Eco's detective: "This we can never know. And I don't need these certainties" (*Morte a Palermo*, 137).

Postscript to the Crimes

Questione di tempo and *Morte a Palermo* show that contemporary feminist authors of detective fiction have a variety of techniques, conventions, and expectations to choose from. Both authors share the feminist commitment to unmask the inadequacies of male justice, many of which are due to the historical, social, and psychological suppression of women, and which deny the ideals to which a universal justice claims to aspire. Form is the key to understanding the main differences between Cagnoni's more consistent and overt use of feminist ideology in a text cast in the traditional detective novel form and La Spina's crime variant where all theories and ideologies are dismissed as entertaining but often dangerously reactionary and certainly always in need of constant questioning. These two novels do not exhaust the possibilities for feminism and the *giallo*, nor do they risk, as Klein fears, destroying the best qualities of each system. The *giallo* as a literary form has long risked extinction due to overdoses of ideology only to come back more popular than before; this popularity is most likely a result of the fact that discussions on the meaning of justice and its possible effects are forever relevant. Clearly, it would be asking a lot to insist the *giallo* solve the question of how justice and equality for women could be achieved, as traditionally these questions are reviewed through the representation of the shortcomings of a theoretical ideal that can only be glimpsed in the contradictory space between theory and practice. But feminist "ideology" is as incapable of killing the form as any other system of thought the *giallo* has absorbed, criticized, portrayed, or rejected in its continuing tradition. Rather, the opposition between the systems is producing more women who are writing their gendered visions and criticisms by asking and answering the supposedly impartial questions the literary genre poses.

Notes

An expanded version of this essay can be found in *From Margins to Mainstream: Feminism and Fictional Modes in Italian Women's Writing, 1968–1990*.

1. "Feminism and Literature," 21. Ginzburg was interviewed by Mary Gordon, "Surviving History," *New York Times Magazine*, March 25, 1990.

2. For example, in her review of a recent Italian translation of Canadian writer Nicole Broussard's work, Maria Rosa Cutrufelli remarks: "It is not a question here of the eternal quest to find out if there exists masculine or feminine qualities in writing. A quest so construed remains ambiguous, even impossible to fulfill unless we banalize the whole thing and start arguing that writing is neutral and writers are androgynes." "Un mondo di parole che parte dal corpo": "Non si tratta dell'eterno quesito se esista o meno una 'qualità femminile' o una 'qualità maschile' della scrittura. Quesito che, così posto, risulta ambiguo e forse d'impossibile soluzione (a meno che non si voglia banalizzare il tutto, come pure spesso si fa, proclamando la neutralità della scrittura e l'androginia dello scrittore)" (6).

3. Sandra Petrignani's interviews of ten Italian women writers born before 1915 (this excluded Ginzburg), *Le signore della scrittura*, began the attempt to remedy this antagonism between the different generations of Italian women writers. See also Marisa Rusconi, "Nuovi percorsi tra esperienza e scrittura," 11–26.

4. *Donne e scrittura*, ed. Daniela Corona. Some writers and critics in this volume persisted in defining autobiography as the type of writing best suited for women. Some continued to claim revolutionary transformational power for the female word while others such as Spanish writer Anna Maria Moix flatly denied this potential: "Un romanzo, una poesia, un concerto per piano, un quadro non hanno mai cambiato il mondo [A novel, a poem, a piano concerto, a picture have never changed the world]" (136). For Moix, feminism may produce feminist masterpieces, but "literature is something else."

5. See Daniela Corona's introduction to *Donne e scrittura*, "Quale genere di scrittura?" These points are also covered in Eleonora Chiavetta's review of *Donne e scrittura*.

6. Frabotta, "L'identità dell'opera e l'io femminile," in Corona, ed., *Donne e scrittura*: "The empirical I firmly rooted in psychology and history, in the act of writing . . . tires of himself and his limits . . . even those certifiable on one's birth certificate such as gender" (144).

7. Maria Rosa Cutrufelli, "Scritture, scrittrici: L'esperienza italiana": "un occhio esercitato a cogliere da una parte le caratteristiche formali del testo, ma dall'altra anche le novità thematiche, e di come poi si rispecchino nelle scelte strutturali dell'opera" (241).

8. Maria Rosa Cutrufelli, "Alla conquista delle lettrici: un nuovo mercato per l'industria editoriale." Cutrufelli notes that narrative is the preferred form of women readers and that detective novels are read by an equal percentage of women and men (33 percent). Cutrufelli published a detective novel, *Complice il dubbio*, in 1992.

9. To date, out of the nineteen titles published by La Tartaruga nera, only three are written by Italian women. Two out of five titles already published by Bariletti (collana Segreto e Mistero) are by Italian women writers but four more titles have been announced for 1991. The two authors to be discussed here published their second detective novels in 1992: Fiora Cagnoni, *Incauto acquisto*, and Silvana La Spina, *L'ultimo treno da Catania*.

10. "And if in the meantime the theoreticians of (sexual) difference succeed in getting their hands on the Constitution and changing it to represent citizens according to sex? Poor me . . . biologically defined as a woman yet determined to define myself as a normal citizen before the law."

11. "Rights and opportunity are not enough. We must modify (both) our existence in the symbolic and the structures of language and thought which have made a social and human organization constructed in the image of the male sex appear to be universal."

12. The bibliography on detective and crime fiction continues to expand exponentially. Important recent works include Martin Priestman, *Detective Fiction and Literature*; Dennis Porter, *The Pursuit of Crime: Art and Ideology in Detective Fiction*; Julien Symons, *Bloody Murder: From the Detective Story to the Crime Novel*; Tony Hilfer, *The Crime Novel: A Deviant Genre*; Stefano Tani, *The Doomed Detective: The Contribution of the Detective Novel to Postmodern American and Italian Fiction*; Peter Alfieri, *Il romanzo poliziesco in Italia*.

13. This convention was later defended by Raymond Chandler, the American writer of the hard-boiled crime novel variant; see Symons, *Bloody Murder*, chaps. 1–3. Hilfer notes that in the crime novel, the reader usually knows who the criminal is and wonders how he will be brought to justice, whereas in the detective novel the action centers on the revelation of the criminal's identity. In both forms the endings should be unexpected (Symons, 3–5).

14. For a more in-depth discussion of this procedure in Sciascia, see Lazzaro-Weis, "The Metaphysical Detective Novel and Sciascia's *Il Contesto*: Parody or Tyranny of a Borrowed Form."

15. "If writing," says de Lauretis, "is an act of love (Eco describes the reproduction of the manuscript as an act of love performed to liberate him from and thus announce the death of certain 'antiche ossessioni'), it is because it works to disavow that death and to allay its threat in the imaginary narrative of male self-creation" ("Gaudy Rose," 64). In this article and elsewhere, de Lauretis attacks deconstructionist theories, especially those of Derrida, Lyotard, and Baudrillard, for their appropriation of the term "feminine" as a revolutionary semiotic category. Their definitions of the feminine, grounded in characteristics such as hysteria, pleasure, fertility, passivity, and jealousy, accord on the one hand a miraculous subversive power to these notions. This eternal feminine, states de Lauretis, called up from the depths of history to liberate the "master-warrior-speaker" from his illusions, represents on the other hand a further marginalization and silencing of real women. For an example of the reading of how this "repressed feminine principle intrudes upon the patriarchal monistic order" and liberates the men from the "repressive tendencies of the patriarchy," see Thomas S. Frentz, "Resurrecting the Feminine in *The Name of the Rose*."

16. For a more detailed account of *affidamento* and the theory of sexual difference in Italy, see Teresa de Lauretis's introduction to this translation, entitled "The Practice of Sexual Difference and Feminist Thought in Italy: An Introductory Essay." See also de Lauretis, "The Essence of the Triangle or Taking Essentialism Seriously: Feminist Theory in Italy, the U.S., and Britain." Journalist Ida Dominijanni, in her review of the first formulation of the principles that would be developed at length in *Non credere di avere dei diritti*, in a special edition of *Sottosopra* entitled "Più donne che uomini," rebuts charges that these theories are not new on the basis of the power they give women to act: "Are the words of this document new? Yes and No. Yes, if we consider where these words are coming from: a 'historical' group of Milanese feminists who have practiced a radical separatism and who have refined it and created a weapon *arma* to intervene in society. Yes, if we consider the tenacity with which they affirm the desire to 'win' on the part of women, the desire to 'stand on their own [in grande] in a world of women,' to translate into their daily actions their desire to be at ease in the world, to get away from the unhappy consciousness that is a result of (emancipationist) feminism" (*Il manifesto*, March 29, 1983).

17. The Communist party avoided using arguments supporting women's autonomous right to decide on issues such as abortion or divorce. For example, the divorce law was presented as a law that would strengthen the family since it would normalize many situations where mothers were living without financial support for their children. The abortion law was

also seen as a way of stabilizing a preexisting situation that threatened the family; since women would abort anyway and in many cases would lose their lives in doing so, the state had a responsibility to protect them and provide them with information on family planning and birth control. In both cases, feminist arguments for women's autonomous right to choose for themselves were shunted aside. See Judith Hellman, *Journeys Among Women: Feminism in Five Italian Cities*, 28–54. In the present debate over the law against sexual violence, feminists demand a law that condemns rape not on moral grounds, but on the premise of the inviolability of a woman's body. In her article attacking feminists and their theory of sexual difference, Miriam Mafai implies that this extremist stance may have hindered the passing of a better law against rape ("Le vedove di Lenin e la deriva femminista"). Turco responded that the real problem was the standard one: parliamentary procedure and the Christian Democrats ("Noi donne ancora deboli").

18. See also Luisa Muraro, "Il segno della differenza sessuale."

19. "Prima la libertà," *Rinascita* 37, October 28, 1990, 44. See also Maria Luisa Boccia, "Il pre-giudizio della democrazia?"

20. Mafai, "Le vedove di Lenin e la deriva femminista." Some angry responses include those of the head of the women's caucus in the Communist party, Livia Turco ("Noi donne ancora deboli"), and Mariella Gramaglia ("Sesso e democrazia"), both published in the same 1990 issue of *La repubblica*.

21. In her introduction to interviews of Communist feminists, Roberta Tatafiore, journalist for *Noi donne* and cofounder of the Centro Culturale Virginia Woolf in Rome, ponders why the theory of sexual difference and female autonomy grew out of the Communist party. Tatafiore qualifies her final reason as *"cattiva* [nasty]": What if, she asks, "'Femminismo/comunismo' è l'incontro escatologico all'ennesima potenza di due totalitarismi che si abbracciano anche se fanno finta di scontrarsi? [What if "feminism/communism are engaged in the final eschatological encounter of two totalitarianisms that are embracing even if they pretend to be fighting one another?]"

22. Both Claudia Mancini and Maria Luisa Boccia refused to speak at the Campo Marzio debate on the grounds that its format reinforced growing prejudices that feminism is *"illiberale."* The question to ask is not if feminism is antidemocratic, but if democracy is antifemale, writes Lidia Menapace in "Seppelliamo il Principe."

23. *Il matriarcato* (Turin: Einaudi, 1988).

Works Cited

Alfieri, Peter. *Il romanzo poliziesco in Italia*. Unpublished dissertation. University of Michigan, Ann Arbor, 1986.

Bachofen, J. *Il matriarcato*. Turin: Einaudi, 1988.

Boccia, Maria Luisa. "Il pre-giudizio della democrazia?" *Rinascita*. Oct. 14, 1990: 28–29.

Cagnoni, Fiora. *Questione di tempo*. Milan: La Tartaruga nera, 1985.

———. *Incauto acquisto*. Milan: La Tartaruga, 1992.

Cantarella, Eva. "Le fortune del matriarcato." *Reti* 3–4 (1988): 17–19.

Cavarero, Adriana, et al., eds. *Diotima: Il pensiero della differenza sessuale*. Milan: La Tartaruga, 1987.

———. *Nonostante Platone: Figure femminili nella filosofia antica*. Rome: Riuniti, 1990.

Chiavetta, Eleonora. "Donne e Scrittura." *LeggereDonna*. July-Aug. 1990: 6–7.

Coletti, Teresa. *Naming the Rose: Eco, Medieval Signs and Modern Theory*. Ithaca: Cornell University Press, 1988.

Corona, Daniela. *Donne e scrittura*. Palermo: La Luna, 1990.

Cutrufelli, Maria Rosa. "Scritture, scrittrici: L'esperienza italiana." In *Donne e Scrittura*, ed. Daniela Corona. Palermo: La Luna, 1990. 237–45.

———. *Complice il dubbio*. Milan: Interno Giallo, 1992.

———. "Alla conquista delle lettrici: un mercato per l'industria editoriale." In *Scritture, Scrittrici*, ed. Maria Rosa Cutrufelli. Milan: Longanesi, 1988. 125–33.
———. "Un mondo di parole che parte dal corpo." *Noi Donne: Legendaria*, June-August 1990, 6.
de Lauretis, Teresa. "Gaudy Rose: Eco and Narcissism." In *Technologies of Gender*. Bloomington: Indiana University Press, 1987. 51–69.
———. "The Practice of Difference: An Introductory Essay." In *Sexual Difference: A Theory of Social Symbolic Practice*. Bloomington: Indiana University Press, 1990.
———. "The Essence of the Triangle, or Taking the Risk of Essentialism Seriously: Feminist Theory in Italy, the U.S., and Britain." *Differences* 1.2 (1990): 3–37.
Dominijanni, Ida. "*Sottosopra* riaccende la discussione." *Il manifesto* (Jan. 21, 1983).
Eco, Umberto. *Il nome della rosa*. Milan: Bompiani, 1980.
———. *Postscript to the Name of the Rose*, trans. William Weaver. New York: Harcourt, Brace, Jovanovich, 1983.
Felski, Rita. *Beyond Feminist Aesthetics: Feminist Literature and Social Change*. Cambridge, Mass.: Harvard University Press, 1989.
Frabotta, Biancamaria. "L'identità dell'io e l'io femminile." In *Donne e Scritture*, ed. Daniela Corona. Palermo: La Luna, 1990. 143–49.
Frentz, Thomas. "Resurrecting the Feminine in *The Name of the Rose*." *Pre/Text* 9.3–4 (1988): 123–45.
Gordon, Mary. "Surviving History." Interview with Natalia Ginzburg. *New York Times Magazine*, March 25, 1990.
Gramaglia, Mariella. "Sesso e democrazia." *La repubblica* (Oct. 9, 1990).
Hellman, Judith. *Journeys Among Women: Feminism in Five Italian Cities*. New York: Oxford University Press, 1987.
Hilfer, Tony. *The Crime Novel: A Deviant Genre*. Austin: University of Texas Press, 1990.
Holquist, Michael. "Whodunit and Other Questions: Metaphysical Detective Stories in Postwar Fiction." *New Literary History* 3 (1971): 135–56.
Klein, Kathleen. *The Women Detective: Gender and Genre*. Urbana: University of Illinois Press, 1988.
La Spina, Silvana. *Morte a Palermo*. Milan: La Tartaruga, 1987.
———. *L'ultimo treno da Catania*. Milan: Bompiani, 1992.
Lazzaro-Weis, Carol. "The Metaphysical Detective Novel and Sciascia's *Il contesto*: Parody or Tyranny of a Borrowed Form?" *Quaderni d'italianistica* 8 (1987): 42–52.
———. "From Margins to Mainstream: Some Perspectives on Women and Literature in Italy in the 1980s." In *Contemporary Italian Women Writers: A Modern Renaissance*, ed. Santo Arico. Amherst: University of Massachusetts Press, 1990.
———. *From Margins to Mainstream: Feminism and Fictional Modes in Italian Women's Writing, 1968–1990*. Philadelphia: University of Pennsylvania Press, 1993.
Lonzi, Carla. *Sputiamo su Hegel: La donna clitoridea e la donna vaginale*. Milan: Rivolta Femminile, 1974.
Mafai, Miriam. "Le vedove di Lenin e la deriva femminista." *MicroMega* 4 (1990): 7–15.
Mancini, Claudia. "Praticare la differenza come categoria politica: Il caso delle donne nel Pci." *Passaggi* 1(1989): 25–32.
Melandri, Lea, ed. *L'infame originaria*. Milan: L'Erba Voglio, 1977.
Menapace, Lidia. "Seppelliamo il Principe." *Rinascita* (Nov. 18, 1990): 38–39.
Muraro, Luisa. "Il segno della differenza sessuale." *Passaggi* 1 (1990): 18–24.
Paris, Sherri. "Riding the Crime Wave." *Women's Review of Books* 7.7 (1989): 8–9.
Petrignani, Sandra. *Le signore della scrittura*. Milan: La Tartaruga, 1984.
Porter, Dennis. *The Pursuit of Crime: Art and Ideology in Detective Fiction*. New Haven: Yale University Press, 1981.

Priestman, Martin. *Detective Fiction and Literature: The Figure on the Carpet*. New York: St. Martins Press, 1991.
Reddy, Maureen. *Sisters in Crime: Feminism and the Crime Novel*. New York: Continuum, 1988.
Rusconi, Marisa. "Nuovi Percorsi tra esperienza e scrittura." In *Scritture: Scrittrici*, ed. Maria Rosa Cutrufelli. Milan: Longanesi, 1988. 11–26.
Sayers, Dorothy. *Gaudy Night*. London: New English Library, 1958.
Sciascia, Leonardo. *Il contesto*. Turin: Einaudi, 1971.
Symons, Julien. *Bloody Murder*. New York: Viking Books, 1985.
Tani, Stefano. *The Doomed Detective: The Contribution of the Detective Novel to Postmodern American and Italian Fiction*. Carbondale: University of Illinois Press, 1984.
Tatafiore, Roberta. *A prova di donna: Interviste sulla svolta del Pci*. Rome: Cooperativa Libera Stampa, 1989.
Turco, Livia. "Noi donne ancora deboli." *La repubblica*, Oct. 9, 1990: 8.
Vendler, Helen. "Feminism and Literature." *New York Review of Books*, May 30, 1990: 19–25.
Zuffa, Grazia. "Tra Libertà e Necessità: A proposito di *Non credere di avere dei diritti*." Reti 1 (1987): 51–53.

Part III
Fashion, Cinema, and Other Orders

Maurizio Viano

Feminism in High Culture, Femininity in Popular Culture
Italy in the Nineties?

The title of this essay suggests an opposition between feminism and femininity. By feminism I mean my understanding of Italian radical feminism, an understanding marred by the fact that perhaps, as suggested by Stephen Heath, "men's relationship to feminism is an impossible one."[1] By femininity here I intend the traditional image of woman as spectacle and seductress, a visual regime and all the duties it entails.[2] However interrelated they are with such a meaning, the psychoanalytical and/or mythical aspects of femininity are *not* implied in my discussion. As I hope to make evident, the opposition between feminism and femininity is only a starting point and by no means reflects the conclusions I wish for my words. The same holds true for the distinction between popular culture and high culture, which, as I use it, is devoid of value judgments: I am merely adopting these two terms for what they commonly describe, although I think that the connotations they carry call for deconstruction.

In fact, what follows is not "an essay": it does not have a clear thesis to prove and, by conventional academic standards, lacks a clear focus. I find rigor and linearity counterproductive. If one's goal is to raise theoretical questions for as large an audience as possible, a well-informed chaos is in my view more fertile and unpredictable in its results. And as the notion of theory is undergoing bouts of growing pains, unpredictability amounts to leaving the door open for a possible visit by the messiah, who, Benjamin reminds us, can come at any moment. As my understanding and practice of theory has been deeply influenced by my readings in feminism, it may be useful for the reader if I spell out what I mean by it. Theory need not be the

Maurizio Viano

esoteric reelaboration of experience by the (un)happy few who think and speak hard enough to be different from the masses. Theory is something that everyone does, at least to some degree. We are in it.

Theory can be characterized as a three-step process. Feeling is the first, where by feeling I intend the complex knot of activities that make up experience: observing, listening, being in a situation or position, having impressions of something. The way in which we look and listen already harbors a theoretical framework, a set of invisible assumptions informing our perceptions. Reordering what has been felt comes next: asking questions, mulling over the "hows," asking oneself why, trying to get out of oneself. Last comes sharing, the act of comparing notes with/in your community. Of course, this last step presupposes a language, a specialized language that fixes what is theory, sets the communicative horizons within which we know that what we are doing is theory. Simply put, we let the kind of language we use influence our ideas on what is theory and what is not.

This essay, then, stems from the need to share some recent feelings of mine. Concurrently, I seek to make theoretical discourse more capable of including subjectivity. Especially in speaking about feminism and femininity, I cannot forget my gendered subjectivity. Eschewing any attempt at objectivity and self-conscious about the lucky fate of being the only male in this anthology, I will say "I" throughout: I, a forty-year-old Italian man stranded in American academia. By situating myself in relation to my object of enquiry and making autobiography pertinent to theoretical discourse, I hope to offer the reader less a presumptuous representation of reality than the reality of a representation. My pendular motion between personal experience and theory aims at valorizing the former and at displacing the latter from its canonical sites and its difficult modes: theory is essential but it must open its horizons and incorporate the speaking subject and his or her experience.

To begin with, then, my impressions. In my last series of trips back to Italy (during the period 1987–93), it seemed to me that feminism was no longer a pervasive force in the way young and not-so-young women organized their individual value systems and lived their lives.[3] The most visible index of this shift appeared in the realm of fashion. In the 1970s, feminism opposed the objectification of women by a male gaze and denounced the self-oppression resulting from internalized patriarchal notions of femininity. A "natural" or unisex look typified young women of the 1970s. An effort was made to redefine femininity in ways that would challenge the dominant regime of visual pleasure. Women did not want to dress for men. In the last few years, however, high heels and black stockings, makeup and laces, have made a grandiose comeback. Today, the look of many Italian women seeks and propounds a femininity at odds with the image of the seventies. My eyes rejoice. Can I stop feeling guilty for some of my fantasies? How am I to situate myself vis-à-vis this recent change? What is the relationship between the fragile rewriting of masculinity that many (some? a few?) of us (males) have more or less willingly undertaken, and the new, unabashed explosion of femininity? These questions are all the more urgent since I have also observed an intensified exploitation of the female body on television (the visual sale of female bodies in some shows has reached levels that North Americans may find hard to believe),[4] in the cinema (the popular success of the *maggiorate* like Serena Grandi),[5] and in national, leading magazines such as L'*Espresso*, *Panorama*, and *Il Mondo*.[6] It thus seemed to me that the conservative backlash experienced in so many other areas of Italian culture had indeed made another victim: along with the comeback of family values, the image of the good *carabiniere* (policen .n), and the good student who does not question the system but rather seeks a career in it, there is a return to a prefeminist image of woman.

Opposite these examples of regression stand the most advanced currents of Italian theoretical thought, respectively postmodernism and radical feminism. An article in the feminist journal *Donnawomanfemme* argues the philosophical adjacency of postmodern philosophy and feminism.[7] And since after the disarray of the left almost every intellectual effort worthy of its name more or less explicitly bespeaks a postmodern sensibility, I felt that feminism had retrenched in high culture; that the positive effects of its long war were visible in some sociolegal recognitions that objectively ameliorated women's status (divorce, abortion, new laws regulating sexual violence and the status of the family, women's access to some positions of power and visibility); and that popular culture was the realm in which the conservative backlash made itself felt. With respect to problems of gender and sexual difference, I concluded, the 1990s would hinge on a basic dichotomy: the citadel of gender awareness on the side of academic cultivation, and the mass of the reprobates—so fascinatingly clad in erotic clothes and ephemeral desires—on the other.

Reordering my feelings, this position struck me as inadequate. On closer observation the dichotomy between what happens in high culture and in popular culture loses its reassuring contours. Even if one excludes the large sector of traditional academics (so obviously nonfeminist) and concentrates on postmodern theorists, high culture as practiced by men is problematic. In fact, feminist discourse is profoundly different from the postmodern theory in whose boundaries it ideally locates itself.

Italian postmodernism is mainly represented by thinkers loosely associated with the group known as *Pensiero debole* (Weak thought), most notably Gianni Vattimo and Umberto Eco.[8] They all operate within the frame of the epistemological uncertainty deriving from the eclipse of reason and foundationalism. As they question the distinction between logos and mythos, reevaluate the local at the expense of the global, and question the totalizing pretensions of Theory, one can say that something good is indeed happening, something that may overlap the thrust of much feminism. Basically, however, their writing is disappointingly oblivious to the real consequences feminism has (or ought to have) in their practice.

I will concentrate here on Vattimo and Eco with the understanding that *mutatis mutandis* my criticism applies to all male academic production of which I am aware. In his latest book, *La società trasparente* (The transparent society), Vattimo argues that postmodernism entails a proliferation of discourses and realities that belie the conventional view of *one* discourse, *one* reality.[9] By this, he implicitly grants feminism a discursive status as well as the privilege of entering the ludic arena of "weak" postmodernity. Vattimo's fashionable eagerness, however, to dismiss the concept of reality is symptomatic of his desire to overlook a basic fact—a reality. Thought becomes weak as a historical consequence of the pressure exerted on it by those who have been officially deprived of it. Differently put, western metaphysics weakens its grip once the other becomes strong and raises her or his voice. The weakening of thought and the decline of strong subjectivity are not magnanimous concessions from enlightened minds. They are, rather, historical necessities.

If we (Italian male intellectuals) genuinely recognized the role played by feminism in the weakening of a centralized theoretical perspective, then we would alter our mode of philosophical investigation accordingly. Instead of overreading Heidegger, we would start reading some of the work produced by contemporary Italian feminism. We would thus familiarize ourselves with the reasoning of the colonized other and stop giving in to what Wanda Tommasi calls *la tentazione del neutro* (the temptation of neuter).[10] The subject of the enunciation in Vattimo's essays is oblivious to the need to consider itself as embodied and en-gendered within historically specific cultural formations. Vattimo keeps asking the philosophical question of "being" and of the fading subject, but he never accounts for the fact that both being and subjectivity take place in a sexed body. As recent feminist theory seeks to demonstrate, our modes of symbolization, our universalizing thought, are based on the effacement of the question of sexual difference and the body. We think being because we do not think gender. The first question we should ask is then "To what extent is my thought overdetermined by my sexed body?"

The same holds true for the question of truth. The absence of truth is the backdrop against which Vattimo's essays move. He advocates a discourse in which truth happens subjectively and aesthetically, as fleeting experience rather than as rational dogma. Very well. But then why not take the recasting of truth's emergence to its logical conclusions? If truth is the passion of a moment, why not say that truth happens first and foremost in the body? It is precisely a plethora of bodily sensations—in our stomachs, throats, groins, and, yes, heads—that gives us the feeling that something is true. The questions that it would then be wise to ask are: "What are the bodily signifiers that engender a feeling of truth? Are they different in men and women?" Feminists, and women in general, have often acknowledged the epistemological value of the body, truth as passion. Vattimo, on the contrary, does not even take the question of the sex of truth into consideration. Not only does he overlook the body in his essays, but he also ignores his own body, his own situation. Although celebrating what is local, Vattimo forgets to account for his own locale, for what Linda Nicholson calls "the politics of location," a male body working in a factory of "universal" knowledge called—by no accident—"university."

The truth is that we (Italian male intellectuals) often pay lip service to feminism only to keep thinking within a conventional framework. For example, in *The Name of the Rose* and elsewhere, Eco gave proof of his awareness of the historical determinants of women's oppression.[11] In his last novel, *Foucault's Pendulum*, there are three women: Lia, who resists the mental machinations of the three male protagonists; Amparo, whose Marxism Eco sees as contradicted by her "trance-and-dance" experience during a Brazilian *candomblé*; and Lorenza/Sofia, who combines both the beauty and the malleability of nature in her own person. Clearly, one could argue that Eco reaffirms the feminine proximity to nature and instincts, to the animal in "us." And, to some extent, there is nothing wrong with this, because proximity to the body is indeed a positive thing for which all men should strive. Our practice, however, often contradicts the implicit sense of our theory. Reading Eco reminds me of Alice Jardine's complaint that we, I mean we "feminist" men, "may have learned a new vocabulary perfectly, but have not paid enough attention to syntax or intonation."[12] Something in the grain of the voice, in our mode of argumentation, reveals our resistance. In chapter 58 of *Foucault's Pendulum*, for example, the narrating protagonist describes a moment of intense terror and, in the effort to find a simile alluding to the horrific nature of his sensations, lists the most revulsive elements that come to mind. As I read the word "menstrual blood" (*mestruo*) thrown in with "dung," "mud," "scum," "coal powder," and "dirt," I regret that Eco never considered an alternate perspective, one from which everything connected with a woman's period may also be a source of pride.[13] Indeed, a sense of historical guilt toward the colonized other would help us proofread our writing and linguistic playing.[14]

As it is, Italian postmodern theory is far from being a good ally to feminism. There is a clear rift between men and feminists in theory.[15] An adequate assessment of Italian feminism exceeds both the scope of the present essay and the limits of my knowledge. Suffice it to say that the work done by Adriana Cavarero, Luisa Muraro, and Rosi Braidotti, to name only a few, is just beginning to ask the questions that a truly politicized postmodernism ought to ask. The body of the subject, the gendering of theory, the sex and gender of truth rank high in the feminist agenda. Whereas male high culture seems to veer toward a relativism that, like capitalism's free market, grants steady expression only to the strongest (those with access to the media), radical feminism opposes noncommittal pluralism and maintains an antagonistic profile. Interestingly, one finds a current within feminist theory (the Diotima group) that suggests the radical alterity of women, aims at sexualizing social relations, and explores the ways and byways in which the female subject can enhance her femininity. While certainly not supportive of the fashionable femininity propounded by the media and the fashion industry, this neoessentialist camp is in a sense treading a parallel path: it is celebrating difference and what makes women women. The pursuit of equality has subsided and difference is sought out, stressed: women do not want to be like us. This desire for difference may regard external appearance as an important area of pleasurable assertion—that is, the refusal to be like men may comprise the reappropriation of fashion and sex appeal, this time as a subject rather than as an object. It is here that feminism may redefine its goals and its stand vis-à-vis types of femininity that have thus far been considered entirely colonized by patriarchy. And it is at this intersection that my theorizing takes the road of popular culture.

There are two basic attitudes within the theories of popular culture, and, interestingly enough, they hinge on whether we (theorists) regard "them" (those who supposedly do not do theory) as either "the masses" or "the people." Alternately, we have the cultural pessimism of those who regard "the masses" as passive subjects constructed by social discourses, and the cultural populism of those who stress, even romanticize, the power that "the people" have to bend, subvert, and appropriate mass-produced texts to their own ends.[16] According to a traditional iconography, feminists would fall into the first category and would agree with Susan Brownmiller's suggestion that today's "renewed interest in femininity," with its "unabashed indulgence in feminine pursuits" is "a deflection of energy and an absorption in fakery" (p. 17). But things are changing; the 1980s have witnessed the phenomenon of "feminine" feminists, that is, women who take pride in being feminine while continuing their practice of self-assertion. This calls for a reconsideration of Brownmiller's rather simplistic judgment and a revision of the value of femininity in popular culture.

The "unabashed indulgence in feminine pursuits" is not always lived passively. Women's exhibitionism does not necessarily imply their subjugation to a controlling male gaze. Kaja Silverman, for example, argues that "the image of a woman in front of the mirror," usually "a familiar metaphor of sexual oppression," relies in fact "upon a much more complex circuit of visual exchange than might at first appear."[17] "Clothing," she argues, "is a necessary condition of subjectivity," and the time spent in the construction of one's subjectivity, the sort of knowledge one gets, are far from being mindless pursuits. Perhaps it is men who have everything to learn from women, and it is men who need to spend more time in front of the mirror and investigate their sartorial subjectivities.

Objectification is not all that takes place when a woman invests time in her appearance. Many Italian women I talked to are aware of the risks of objectification and play with it without feeling that they are obeying a master code. In fact, much of the current interest in a *femme fatale* femininity is pervaded by an ironic distance, a sense of masquerade that may indeed leave room for strong, gender-bending subjectivity. It may be argued that ironic distancing does not prevail in all women; that the subjectivities of most of them are engendered by dominant discourse and its mass-mediated sex texts; that, in short, many women are likely to be victimized by femininity's constraints. A "cultural populist," however, would counterargue that women who devote time and energy to living up to this neofemininity feel they are making a choice and it would be elitist to assume that they really do not know what they are doing. Insofar as it is an activity, femininity provides a sense of identity and it may entail a redefinition of self in the face of social circumstances, as, for example, the battle over the freedom to wear miniskirts in some Italian high schools. When the school principals prohibited wearing them during school hours, miniskirts became symbolic pawns in a struggle between new and old mentalities. Femininity, in other words, can also become something to be flaunted, transgressively. There have been subcultures that have managed to enjoy the pleasure of dressing up without selling out. In the 1970s, there was *la moda fricchettona* (hippie fashion) which glorified the creative use of a politically correct secondhand style. In the 1980s, there was the aggressively sexual femininity of some fringes in the punk subculture—the first to flaunt an uncontrollable use of black fishnet stockings and black leather. However assimilated by mainstream fashion, the perverse beauty of the "black wave" gave a sense of identity to countless youths across national boundaries. New, mutant parameters of appeal were generated; aesthetics was at once glorified and trashed.[18]

The political moralism of the 1970s tended to forget the complex reality of the pleasure principle. Insofar as it is also an art, femininity does not just give pleasure to the (male) spectator. It pleases the artist as well. All the Italian neofeminine women that I know are eager to stress that they pursue a feminine image primarily because of the pleasure *they themselves* derive from looking good: "First and foremost I do it for myself," they say. The Italian situation is of course peculiar because of the cultural emphasis on looking good, on the imperative of *bella figura*. Most typically, Italian women are turned off by what Kaja Silverman, with a splendid euphemism, calls the "sartorial reticence of North American feminism."[19] However excessive, the concern with one's own image opens up avenues of pleasure to a subject who is not passive but has the right to explore them. To be sure, men's pleasure in looking and women's pleasure in being looked at are not politically innocent. But it is important to see the positive elements in this apparatus of scopic pleasures. Fashion may be tyrannical but it forces us to look at ourselves in the mirror and realize that clothing makes the body culturally visible and that in articulating the body it simultaneously articulates the psyche. A concern with one's own look signals the awareness that, whether we like it or not, we are the object of the other's gaze. There is a sense in which the very stuff of social life is this mutual representation: I am a sign for you, you are a sign for me. By glamorizing everyday life, femininity transfigures the boredom in and of a look chosen on the basis of exclusively practical concerns. When the look of people around us is less neutral than it is "out to please," walking and working become (more) pleasurable experiences. The erotization of the social space has its subversive edge, for it challenges the puritanical distinction of work and pleasure, which is to some extent antithetical to feminism in that it tends to regard men as signifiers of the former and women of the latter.

Furthermore, I cannot but welcome the femininity effect on man's image. As testified by the recent explosion of male fashion products, some men are slowly recovering from what J. C. Flugel called the "Great Masculine Renunciation" that took place in the eighteenth century.[20] Sartorial extravagance, up to then a class trait, came to dwell on the divide of gender, so that real masculinity meant a standardized image seemingly above and beyond fashion, an image that is now being subverted by male sex-objectification and by the return of women's gaze.[21]

Finally, a sexist remark often heard in the course of male talk has it that "there are no more ugly women." Strange though it may sound, there is a positive truth behind this statement. At last, looks are being wrenched away from nature and are becoming a cultural fact. It is much less a matter of having the looks than knowing how to have a look. The recent explosion of femininity forces us to become aware of the implications of the distinction between looks and look. The art of finding what suits one's own look—coupled with the ingenuity of an inexhaustible market—has enabled many women (and men) to enhance what they've got. Favored by the postmodern absence of one dominant look, several social groups have access to the knowledge, the time, and the means necessary to incorporate the signifiers of attractiveness into their images, thus deriving pleasure that once was only for aristocrats and stars.

Femininity entails a knowledge and a work in which it is as reasonable to take pride as in the successful accomplishment of all sorts of other tasks. In fact, the reevaluation of the knowledge entailed in the effort to be feminine may help us see through the distinction between frivolous and profound endeavors, between surface and substance. Spending time trying to look good is considered less noble than spending time acquiring bookish cultivation. Such a distinction founds the notions of, respectively, popular and high culture, and may well turn out to be a professional hang-up that we have as intellectuals, a by-product of an ideology that regards the body as transient (and unworthy) and the spirit as immortal.

In sum, not only may a stylized femininity be commensurable with feminism, but it also seems to have an edge over the nonfeminist high culture examined above. For all its vulgarity, popular culture does not forget the body, does not give in to the temptation of the neuter. Whereas Eco and Vattimo roam in the celestial spheres like sexless angels in search of God's grave, the feminine fix in popular culture presupposes an awareness of the body and sexual difference as a major divide. To be sure, we may not be happy with how sexual difference is generally managed in popular culture; we may object to its heterosexism and its dependency on capitalism; but at least it is there, it is not concealed from sight. It's there for everyone to see.

It is now time to look at the negative aspects of rampant femininity as observed in contemporary Italy. Needless to say, an excessive concern with one's image is also a slavery, and a cruel one at that, because it forces women to adopt a regime of censorship and self-control known as the "beauty trap." This argument has been sufficiently explored and documented by feminism for me to indulge in its repetition. Here are six negative theses on the meanings that the current femininity is forced to have by the sociohistorical formation in which it takes place, in a sort of political synchronicity.

1. As it happens, the pursuit of femininity does coincide with an eclipse of radical feminism's social antagonism and signifies the 1980s general acquiescence to the status quo: "Things cannot be changed," so "all you can do is look good." In this respect, femininity as a textually mediated discourse may be seen as complicitous with the duty of being successful, of emerging at all costs, and with the emphasis on the ethos of social competition.

2. Femininity is managed by capitalist industry. This entails the omnipresent bombardment of ads, the circularity of media images, the slow shrinking of alternative spaces and traces and the progressive exclusion of ways of self-valorization from the official channels of communication—in short, the homogenization to one model, which, according to P. P. Pasolini, constitutes the totalitarianism of consumer society. To be sure, the "consciousness industry" does not have the blanket effect theorized by Pasolini and Theodor Adorno, but I cannot help feeling that the current use of femininity by the media goes hand in hand with the attempt to depoliticize the erotic and the gaze.

3. The association of femininity with money is dangerous, for femininity risks becoming a profession. It becomes an investment, a school subject on which authority figures speak, are allowed to speak, are paid to speak.[22] Many Italian men I spoke with maliciously and cynically swore that "things are easy for a good-looking woman provided that she knows how to

manage (*saper gestirsi*) her body." Which is to say, in Nancy Baker's more theoretical assessment, that "beauty often ensures economic benefits far beyond mere survival."[23] Realistically, I am afraid that hoping to change all this is a bit like fighting windmills: a beautiful physical appearance always has paid well, at least in our societies. It's always been like this and always will be. I know. You know. Still, I do not think this is a good reason to endorse and reinforce the cultural stereotypes that enforce the impossibility of change.

4. Femininity in the Italian media is always equated with sexuality, the most powerful selling strategy. This, of course, reinforces the age-old stereotype that petrifies woman as a signifier of sex. Differently put, the new stress on femininity goes hand in hand with the further commodification of sex, the further colonization of all the areas of personal, spiritual, and libidinal life by a capitalist market. To recognize the pleasure in looking good and in looking at good-looking women is one thing; to forego the articulation of such a pleasure with political awareness is quite another. In fact, it is precisely because the look is culturally constructed that it should be a matter of political contention.

5. Italy is not exactly the home of the most liberated man and the current stress on femininity reinforces the country's cultural machismo. The great fascination with the feminine entails a reinforcement of masculine bad habits. By dressing up in sexy clothes women elicit a sexual response that often effaces other avenues of expression and recognition, other modes of communication. In theory, this is men's problem, for they are the ones who ought to change. In practice, however, it is always women who bear the brunt of an irresponsible erotization of the social space.

6. As it happens, the emphasis on femininity has direct consequences for the social construction of masculinity. It represents a parallel strategy in the redefinition of male roles. Most hurtfully, at least for me, the articulation of success and money with femininity goes hand in hand with the social construction of what a successful man is. As much as I enjoy the neofeminine look, something tells me that the surplus femininity will result in a demand for an increased "masculinity." I shall probably be expected to buy a bigger car, to display more of the commonly accepted signifiers of success: I shall have to be "a man when he is a man." As one's concern with the body is increasingly equated to body-building and its soap-operatic ethos, as Armani, Versace, and Co. monopolize an expensive male look, and as the muscles of male pinups become bigger, resistance is becoming harder. What is at stake, then, in neofemininity is also

(what is most important for me) the definition of what the new man shall be. When in March 1988, shortly before International Women's Day, the first issue of the magazine K*ing* came out, I rushed to the newsstand, intrigued by the cover layout: the face of a nice-looking, inoffensive young man, a tall woman carrying a short man in her arms, and, above all, the large caption "ten years of fictions have destroyed his naturalness: from the ashes now rises the LIBERATED MAN." As promptly pointed out by an editorial of N*oi donne* (a nonacademic, feminist monthly from women on the Left) that first issue was more than disappointing: it reeked of old male stereotypes glossed over by a sleek layout and style.[24] The liberation alluded to by the cover turned out to be a freedom from the feminist worries that troubled Italian males during the heat of the 1970s. As suggested by the cover itself, the magazine is out to restore the ideology of nature: "a man when he is a man."[25]

Conclusion in the Form of a Faded Picture from Italian Walls before the 1953 Elections

Try to imagine a heated political atmosphere such as only the Cold War at its peak could give you. Try also to imagine a political campaign conducted with the rough-edged, confrontational spirit of a country that had the largest Communist party in the west. And, finally, try to imagine a nation without television, a nation in which politics have not yet become a mass-mediated spectacle. To be sure, political campaigns were based on speeches and pictures back then as they are now, but the word and the image were mostly separate. There was no way of reproducing speaking images in every corner, in every household. Political speeches took place in the streets, squares, next to churches, outside each party's headquarters. As to the pictures, the only type of image that had the chance to capture people's eyes regardless of their intentions was the political poster. Although it is only with the 1970s that all parties have systematically and meticulously addressed the nation's female constituency, women have been the target of a specifically conceived political propaganda ever since they acquired the right to vote in 1946. Prejudices against women's capacity to make intelligent and independent political decisions were indeed common. From left to right, men thought that women would cast their votes on the basis of their husbands', brothers', or, worse, their neighborhood priests' "knowledgeable suggestions." As a result, posters addressing women were particularly paternalistic and didactic. In these posters, ideology often surfaced raw, in a way that makes us smile. For example, "Madri d'Italia. Il mostro rosso vuole il vostro sangue!" (Italian mothers: The red monster wants your blood!), said a poster of the Democrazia Cristiana (Christian Democrats, hereafter referred to as DC) that portrayed a Soviet soldier snatching a child from a woman's arms.

I do not intend to suggest that posters from the left were not occasionally ludicrous. The "nazional popolari" images of happy women of "the people" were just as ideologically raw as the ones from the DC. Their difference was thus just a matter of political bent. And in 1953, the unbelievable happened: one of the DC's posters was so explicitly couched in the discourse of femininity that the analysis of it becomes a must for anybody picking up its trail. The poster is a four-color drawing. The background is white; a large and tall patch of navy blue takes up the left portion of the poster, a smaller patch of red, the right; a small black rectangle between the two patches contains a caption in white characters. A woman is standing in each patch. I shall call them the woman in blue and the woman in red.

Both women look at the observer. The woman in blue is tall, as tall as the color patch that takes up the entire length of the poster. Obversely, the woman in red is short, one third the height of the woman in blue. The woman in blue is slender, wears a tailored suit with a pleated skirt. A tight belt around her waist makes her figure curvy, albeit in a nonprovocative way. Her left hand, with long painted nails, holds a piece of paper saying *voto* (vote). In sum, she is a "real woman." The woman in red, on the contrary, is short and fat, and appears even more so because of the limited space she is allowed in the poster. She wears a simple dress, her hair is not as neatly styled as the other's, and she has a most unaesthetic double chin. Her left arm is raised; her fist is clenched in a Communist salute. As if this were not enough, there is a hammer and sickle printed on her dress, right above her cleavage. Indeed, the message of the poster was sufficiently clear, but the designers must not have trusted the power of images completely. They felt the need to add a verbal message, to further fix the meaning of the image. The top right corner of the poster says Donna Italiana... (Italian Woman...), and the black rectangle continues the message: *anche la tua femminilità è affidata al tuo voto* (your femininity, too, is entrusted to your vote). To the best of my knowledge, no political advertisement has ever so blatantly said to the voters: ugly women vote for them, feminine women vote for us. Leftist posters were of course coming near to saying this when they alluded to the well-dressed women of the bourgeoisie voting for conservative parties. But they were couching their message within a class discourse: rich versus poor. In this poster, instead, the class factor does not translate into wealth, although that is most certainly implied. Rather, class differences hinge on the issue of femininity. With the pathetic sincerity that characterized ideological struggles in the 1950s, the DC said what no one would normally even think of suggesting in a political campaign: feminine women unite, for there is a bunch of ugly, envious females out there who want to prevent you from enjoying your beauty.

In 1953, there could hardly be any doubt: the discourse of femininity is political. Even the party of the ruling class said so. But things have changed. It is no longer possible to say that femininity is political without raising questions that threaten the very possibility of making such a statement. What does it mean to say that something is political after the advent of postmodernity? Saying that something is political today does not imply blindness to the fact that there is no Truth. Of course there are no ultimate political certainties. Of course there are only partial truths. Not all partial truths receive equal treatment, however. Power's partial truths find a way of becoming, willy-nilly, more influential. It is a struggle of truths, my truth against the truth of those who have interests different from mine. When certainty is gone, only partisanship is possible. My partial truth is that the west is undergoing restructuration in a badly lit tunnel. Multinational capital is slowly subsuming the entire world, and the televised, media image is one of its weapons. This is the terrain of the struggle, a struggle that cannot be fought through old moralisms and dichotomies. The explosion of and in the visual field has generated a need for a photogenic look. Rather than rejecting the narcissistic pleasure it provides as regressive, we ought to consider it as a field for semiotic warfare. Beauty, sex appeal, eroticized look are not inherently bad. The pleasures they provide are genuine. What we need to do is to gain a political control over the pleasure in looking (good). Here, as elsewhere, the motto should not be "just say no" to pleasure and extravagance. Rather, it should be "just say know."

To summarize: although femininity and feminism are not opposite, the particular direction that consumer society imparts to femininity is suspect. I guess then that my position is in favor of a politically aware femininity and masculinity, where the pleasures in one's look and in looking are coupled with a desire to antagonize the status quo. Whereas some looks strive to represent what Pasolini called "a scandalous presence," others are indeed complicitous with dominant ideology, a dominant ideology that is now more elusive than ever, since its workings are obscured by the commonplace rhetorics of the decline of ideologies. Pleasure is there for us to fight for, but, to quote Gayatri Spivak, "we must question what we cannot not want."[26]

Notes

1. The idea that "men's relation to feminism is an impossible one" was voiced by Stephen Heath's "Male Feminism." As attested to by the variety of positions in and reactions to this book, the role of male feminism is far from being ascertained or accepted. Personally, I think that we (men) have a lot to learn from reading feminist theory, that our writing improves once we attempt to incorporate its tenets and that whether or not we (men) may aspire to the label "feminist" is, indeed, secondary.

2. Perhaps more often than its English equivalent, the Italian word *femminilitá* designates the qualities whereby a woman lives up to the patriarchal standards of what a woman "should" look like. Of the eight headings under which Susan Brownmiller's *Femininity* treats the standard signifiers of "a powerful esthetic that is built upon a recognition of powerlessness" (p. 19), five are eminently visual: body, hair, clothes, skin, and movement.

3. This impression was confirmed by articles in the popular press as well as by my random conversations with Italians. As an example of the former, see Emanuela Moroli's "Femminismo ieri e oggi," a good overview of feminism's gains and losses. As to the latter, I can cite a woman from La Libreria delle Donne (Women's Bookstore) in Piazza Farnese, Rome, who told me that the gap between feminists and nonfeminists is widening (June 1990).

4. One good example is *Colpo Grosso* (Strike big), a show that adopts the safe formula of the telequiz in which anybody may win a lot of money, and bends it into a patriarchal, heterosexist extravaganza. The conductor of the show, a fat man, is surrounded by several scantily dressed young women who punctuate the spectacle with stripping and dancing. At some point in the show, the contestant must guess what kind of animal sticker (a rabbit, a cat, a . . .) is hidden under the bra of one of the "girls." After the guess has been made, we see a medium close-up of the girl, who uncovers her breast and reveals whether or not the guess was correct.

5. *Maggiorate* (literally "made bigger") was the term with which Italian film critics in the 1950s indicated actresses such as Pampanini, the early Mangano (the one of *Riso Amaro*, "Bitter rice," 1948), and Loren, because of the size of their breasts. As an aesthetic ideal, the *maggiorate* disappeared from the scene in the 1960s and 1970s. Serena Grandi is a B-movie actress whose body, generously displayed in popular Italian comedies, contributed to the current reevaluation of big breasts for women. If we are to believe national magazines such as *Panorama* and *L'Espresso*, the number of Italian women who turn to silicon soma-technology to enhance the size of their breasts is impressively on the rise.

6. Although sexploitation never really vacated the Italian scene, one needs only to remember L'*Espresso*'s special summer reports, *Le vacanze intelligenti* (Intelligent vacations), which always, I mean always, parades a naked woman on the cover.

7. Jane Flax, "Pensiero postmoderno e relazioni di genere nella teoria femminista." The original English version, "Postmodernism and Gender Relations in Feminist Theory," appeared in *Signs* 12. 4: 621–43. For an outstanding discussion of the interface between feminist theory and postmodernism, see *Feminism/Postmodernism*, ed. Linda J. Nicholson. Jane Flax's article is reprinted there, although Nicholson's introduction and most of the essays are much more cautious about the overlapping of postmodernism and feminism.

8. The anthology-manifesto *Il pensiero debole* contains eleven essays, of which only Vattimo's "Dialectic, Difference, Weak Thought" is available in English. A different collection of essays, mostly by "weak thinkers," has recently appeared in the United States: *Recoding Metaphysics*, ed. Giovanna Borradori. As these anthologies suggest, "weak thinkers" are out to re-

think the possibility of metaphysics, that is, to think again the age-old question of "being." For a sympathetic assessment of Weak Thought, see Borradori, "Italian Weak Thought and Postmodernism," and Peter Carravetta's "Repositioning Interpretive Discourse." For a (male) feminist criticism, see my "Sesso debole, pensiero debole."

9. Gianni Vattimo, La società trasparente. With respect to standard Weak Thought, this book is something of a good surprise in that its language is finally accessible to all and does not dwell on Heidegger's terminology. The silence on gender, however, continues.

10. Wanda Tommasi, "La tentazione del neutro."

11. See, for example, his introduction to Adriana Sartogo, Le donne al muro, where he lucidly enumerates the sexist aspects of the Italian language (69).

12. See Jardine and Smith, eds., Men in Feminism, 56.

13. Interestingly, William Weaver's translation omits the word mestruo: American intellectuals are often more sensitive to gender issues because of the power and visibility feminism has acquired in the sphere of high culture.

14. I think the common view that regards guilt as unequivocally harmful is to be challenged. While often a useless agony over the past or an impediment in the present, a sense of guilt also represents a physical memento against the erasure of the other from the field. Differently put, it is my sense of guilt that prompts me to pay more attention to the needs and demands of the other. As I am writing, one example imposes itself: a sense of historical guilt for what we—western culture—have done to the Islamic world would keep us from exerting too much destructive force in the Middle East.

15. Up until a few years ago, much of recent Italian feminism was missing from the Anglo-American panorama. Things are changing, however. For example, the quintessential Non credere di avere dei diritti, published in 1987 by the Milan Women's Bookstore Collective, has become available through Patricia Cicogna and Teresa de Lauretis, who translated it into English as Sexual Difference. For an informative and accessible history of Italian radical feminism, see Lucia Chiavola Birnbaum, Liberazione della donna. For a discussion (with bibliography) of the most recent developments, see Teresa de Lauretis, "The Essence of the Triangle; or, Taking the Risk of Essentialism Seriously: Feminist Theory in Italy, the U.S., and Britain."

16. An interesting discussion of the two main currents in cultural studies with respect to femininity is to be found in Leslie Roman's and Linda Christian-Smith's introduction to Becoming Feminine: The Politics of Popular Culture, 134, which ends with a large bibliography on the subject. My discussion is largely indebted to this as well as to the first essay in the book, Dorothy Smith's "Femininity as Discourse."

17. Kaja Silverman, "Fragments of a Fashionable Discourse."

18. See Dick Hebdige, Subculture: The Meaning of Style, and Angela McRobbie, ed., Zoot Suits and Secondhand Dresses.

19. Modleski, ed., Studies in Entertainment, 149.

20. J. C. Flugel, The Psychology of Clothes, 117–19.

21. See Sarah Kent, "Corpi d'uomo. Restituire lo sguardo," and The Female Gaze: Women as Viewers of Popular Culture, ed. Lorraine Gamman and Margaret Marshment, especially Jackie Stacey's "Desperately Seeking Difference," on the pleasure that lesbian women derive from looking at other women, and Janet Lee's "Care to Join Me in an Upwardly Mobile Tango?" which argues that the "new woman" is a media concept designed to smuggle in the notion that we have entered the stage of postfeminism.

22. Much to my dismay, I saw a poster in the summer of 1990 in Rome that advertised a "Practical Course to Acquire Femininity, Elegance and Security." Above a perfectly made-up "feminine" face staring at us from the glossy surface of the poster one read: PROFESSIONE DONNA.

23. Nancy Baker, The Beauty Trap, 13.

24. Mariella Gramaglia, "Il re nudo [The king is naked]."
25. A Man When He Is a Man (1982) is a stylistically imaginative documentary by Chilean filmmaker Valeria Sarmiento, who, under the pretense of shooting a film on romanticism, "forced" Costa Rican men to act up and reveal the truth about their machismo.
26. From a talk that she gave at the Boston Public Library on April 28, 1988.

Works Cited

Baker, Janet. *The Beauty Trap*. New York: Franklin Watts, 1984.
Birnbaum, Lucia Chiavola. *Liberazione della donna*. Middletown, Conn.: Wesleyan University Press, 1986.
Borradori, Giovanna, ed. *Recoding Metaphysics*. Evanston, Ill.: Northwestern University Press, 1989.
———. "Italian Weak Thought and Postmodernism." *Social Text* 18 (Winter 1987–88): 39–44.
Brownmiller, Susan. *Femininity*. New York: Fawcett Columbine, 1984.
Carravetta, Peter. "Repositioning Interpretive Discourse." *Differentia* 2 (1988): 83–127.
de Lauretis, Teresa. "The Essence of the Triangle; or, Taking the Risk of Essentialism Seriously: Feminist Theory in Italy, the U.S., and Britain." *Differences* 2 (1989): 1–37.
Flax, Jane. "Pensiero postmoderno e relazioni di genere nella teoria femminista." Trans. Paola Bono. *Donnawomanfemme* 8 (March 1989): 101–19.
Flugel, J. C. *The Psychology of Clothes*. London: Hogarth, 1930.
Gamman, Lorraine, and Margaret Marshment, eds. *The Female Gaze: Women as Viewers of Popular Culture*. Seattle: Real Comet Press, 1989.
Gramaglia, Mariella. "Il re nudo [The king is naked]." *Noi donne* (April 1988): 5.
Heath, Stephen. "Male Feminism." In *Men in Feminism*, ed. Alice Jardine and Paul Smith. New York: Methuen, 1987.
Hebdige, Dick. *Subculture: The Meaning of Style*. London: Methuen, 1979.
Jardine, Alice, and Paul Smith, eds. *Men in Feminism*. New York: Methuen, 1987.
Kent, Sarah. "Corpi d'uomo. Restituire lo sguardo." *Donnawomanfemme* 8 (1989).
Lee, Janet. "Care to Join Me in an Upwardly Mobile Tango?" In *The Female Gaze: Women as Viewers of Popular Culture*, ed. Lorraine Gamman and Margaret Marshment. Seattle: Real Comet Press, 1989. 166–72.
McRobbie, Angela, ed. *Zoot Suits and Secondhand Dresses*. Boston: Unwin Hyman, 1989.
Milan Women's Bookstore Collective. *Non credere di avere dei diritti*. Milan, 1987. Available in English as *Sexual Difference*, trans. Patricia Cicogna and Teresa de Lauretis. Bloomington: Indiana University Press, 1990.
Modleski, Tania, ed. *Studies in Entertainment*. Bloomington: Indiana University Press, 1986.
Moroli, Emanuela. "Femminismo ieri e oggi." *Marie Clare* (March 1989): 111–22.
Nicholson, Linda J., ed. *Feminism/Postmodernism*. London: Routledge, 1990.
Il pensiero debole. Milan: Feltrinelli, 1984.
Roman, Leslie, and Linda Christian-Smith, eds. *Becoming Feminine: The Politics of Popular Culture*. London: Falmer, 1988.
Sartogo, Adriana. *Le donne al muro*. Rome: Savelli, 1978.
Silverman, Kaja. "Fragments of a Fashionable Discourse." In *Studies in Entertainment*, ed. Tania Modleski. Bloomington: Indiana University Press, 1986. 139–52.
Smith, Dorothy. "Femininity as Discourse." In *Becoming Feminine*, ed. Leslie Roman and Linda Christian-Smith. London: Falmer, 1988. 37–59.
Stacey, Jackie. "Desperately Seeking Difference." In *The Female Gaze: Women as Viewers of Popular Culture*, ed. Lorraine Gamman and Margaret Marshment. Seattle: Real Comet Press, 1989. 112–29.

Tommasi, Wanda. "La tentazione del neutro." In Diotima: *Il pensiero della differenza sessuale*. Milan: La Tartaruga, 1987. 81–105.

Vattimo, Gianni. "Dialectic Difference, Weak Thought." *Graduate Faculty Philosophical Journal* 101 (1984): 151–64.

———. *La società trasparente*. Milan: Garzanti, 1989.

Viano, Maurizio. "Sesso debole, pensiero debole." *Annali d'Italianistica* 7 (1989): 394–422.

Beverly Allen

The Novel, the Body, and Giorgio Armani
Rethinking National "Identity" in a Postnational World

LEE: *What do you hate to see in fashion design?*
ARMANI: *Extremism. I hate to see imposed on the human figure a structure that does not belong to it. I've done it myself. My jackets of a few years ago, with the huge shoulders—when I see them now, I ask myself why I did them.*
"Armani," *Mirabella*, July 1990

The thesis I am testing here takes its place within a wide context of recent critiques of and contributions to postmodern discourse. I refer in particular to two of the most well-known postmodern critiques of modern emancipatory and liberatory claims, Jean-François Lyotard's critique of political movements, especially socialism, and Michel Foucault's critique of the human sciences as (to put it excessively simply) universalizing emancipatory discourses that conceal their own potential for oppression.

Recent work by critical thinkers such as John Hinkson and Geoff Sharp in Australia, whose concern is to articulate the possibilities that might remain for a politics of social justice within postmodern constructs of the social, find fault with Lyotard and (to a lesser degree) with Foucault to the extent that the work of those French thinkers fails to recognize the structural differentiation that privileges intellectual culture and distinguishes it from a broader social reality, thereby gifting it with possibilities for initiating social change at the same time that it "constitutes a new order of restraint" (Hinkson, 99) itself.

Further, since both Lyotard and Foucault seem to lack what Hinkson and Sharp call a "theory of extended relations," that is, an adequate theo-

Beverly Allen

rization of the potentially emancipatory role of intellectual production as a social practice, Lyotard's and Foucault's critiques of liberation discourse are, Hinkson maintains, too schematic and "lead to the illusion that postmodernity avoids emancipatory narratives" (Hinkson, 99). In offering a "cultural studies" approach to theorizing cultural productions in their context of social relations, I see the problem of comprehending the extended social relations of intellectual and other cultural production as the wide context of my remarks.

The narrower context is a subsection, so to speak, of this critique. One of the signs of metal fatigue in the high-tension steel of Lyotard's discourse occurs, as Hinkson has it,

> where nineteenth-century emancipatory universals are denounced, while he simultaneously gravitates towards the emancipatory project of postmodern information, which conceals its universalist credentials behind an ideology of heterogeneity. (Hinkson, 99)

Since I share Hinkson's conviction that postmodern society is an expression of a new configuration of the social, I locate the following text in the interstices of contemporary reassessments of the ideologies that notions of universalism and heterogeneity currently negotiate, openly or not so openly.

Finally, the narrowest contexts of what follows are two moments in recent Western cultural production that seem to do the opposite of what Hinkson faults Lyotard for. That is, rather than presenting universals under the banner of heterogeneity, as Lyotard's paean to the information revolution seems to do, they present heterogeneity under the banner of universals. The first of these cultural moments is that of what I call the postnational novel—that is, novels in which a specific national "identity" is indelibly inscribed and yet have had vast international distribution, sales, and readership. The second is the Giorgio Armani fashion collections of the late 1970s and early 1980s—an example of "Italian" design that has also had vast international distribution, sales, and readership. My considerations of these moments in postmodern culture are offered, therefore, as an interrogation of the valence that may be attributed to a sign of heterogeneity, such as national identity, in a universalizing context such as multinational capitalism. They are also offered as rereadings of the "feminine," and of the "feminine" in Italy in particular.

What follows here, then, is an essay written under the sign of distraction, where images of Armani's 1970s fashions recur intermittently as the

The Novel, the Body, and Giorgio Armani

pretext for a series of musings. This series proceeds from a brief presentation of what Armani did in 1975 (and a suggestion that the national identity of his production is highly significant) to a statement of my own subject position inasmuch as it relates to my reading. An exposition of national identity in a postnational context follows, braided with some considerations of the postnational novel.

Armani's fashions are generally read in a universalizing multinational context, where their *aesthetic* properties claim primary attention. The reading I offer, however, based as it is on the more restricted heterogeneous context of the *national* identity of Armani's work, will serve, I hope, to problematize and therefore to elucidate the categories of "universal" and "heterogeneous" that so often trouble those of us who attempt to articulate the extended social relations that characterize our time.

Now let me tell you a story.

In 1975, a surprising woman came walking down the runway at the Milan fashion fair. Calmed with the art of fine tailoring, toned down by the hues of Lombard fogs and Milanese industrial pollution, this new woman hid the sexual signs and reproductive capacities of her body beneath the fabric that hung, in the oh-so-constructed planes of her "masculine" Armani suit, from that suit's most glaring feature: its huge padded shoulders. Almost overnight, this "new" look—actually a quotation of the men's fashion look that had also been applied to women during the 1930s and 1940s—traversed national borders and international oceans, creating a transnational western community of female dressers who presented their sexuality under the sign of the masculine. This Armani look has been so successfully assimilated to notions of appropriate professional dress and its parodies that I find it difficult at times to remember when such apparel as masculine-tailored pantsuits, somberly hued fabrics, berets, fedoras, and even kepis, not to mention padded shoulders, were *not* part of the wardrobe lexicon for middle-class and upper-middle-class women, and for popular culture ironizations, in the west.

But there was a time when all this looked new, or new again. Into European and North American markets dominated by the bourgeois youth revolutions of the 1960s—where miniskirted Barbies and heavy-lidded Twiggies had mingled freely with their braless, diaphanous hippy sisters, all under the banner of body liberation—into these markets Giorgio Armani, a former menswear buyer for the only fashion department store in Italy, La Rinascente, placed this new-looking woman.

Unlike other Italian high-fashion designers—Valentino, Gianfranco Ferré, and the Ferragamos, for example—whose rise to renown was accomplished by aristocratic patronage and by their apprenticeships to long-established Italian tailoring houses such as the Sorelle Fontane in Rome, Giorgio Armani burst on the fashion scene with the marketing savvy of a salesman who knew that the world of fashion had already established itself as a lucrative international industry. With his bold masculine silhouettes, his trademark fine fabrics and exquisite constructed tailoring, Armani soon came to symbolize for an international market the very best in Italian design.

But what does this "new" woman who signaled Armani's accession to his international fashion throne mean? Does she symbolize some sort of culture-transcendent need 1970s women—whoever *they* were—had to assert their "masculinity"? Is she just a designer's whim thrown out to render previous fashions obsolete according to the fickle finger of fashion marketing? Or is there a way to read her appearance differently, as something other than or at least in addition to the manipulation of female gender signs by a powerful male, as something other than or at least in addition to a sign of the cynicism of a profit-mongering industry that chooses as its product the presentation of the human body?

I believe that readings such as those suggested by these questions derive from clichéd interpretations of fashion phenomena in the postindustrial world. Furthermore, even serious attempts to make sense of fashion, such as the lengthy and detailed semiotic analysis Roland Barthes did in 1967, never manage to treat fashion itself seriously. They relegate it, over and over again, to the realm of frivolity, and hence, in Europe since the seventeenth century at least, to the realm of the "feminine" (Wilson, 47–66).

But if I read the new Armani woman of the 1970s as *not* frivolous, as *not* always already relegated to the realm of what does not matter, I find that interpretations such as those I suggested above, and even interpretations that might take into consideration such significant parameters as class, gender, and so-called race, slide all too easily over a frozen lake of essentialism in their tendencies to universalize "woman" and to frivolize and thus to "feminize" fashion. Most important, however, such clichéd readings neglect an aspect of fashion that on the one hand would easily keep essentialist notions at bay and on the other is a prime example of the reordering of identity production in our postmodern era. This aspect, the aspect of Armani's 1970s woman that concerns me here, is not "her"

The Novel, the Body, and Giorgio Armani

traditional function as a sign of great design in an international context but rather the reading that results when I look at this new image in a *national* context, as having, that is, a *national* identity simultaneous to its international one.

Put another way, in looking here at Armani's 1970s women's collections, I am testing the thesis that national "identity" provides a significant context for what dominant discourse in the west may generally represent as international cultural production. Such a national context, while it does not maintain its traditional nineteenth-century power to determine a very great deal about the identity of a given cultural production, nonetheless may well provide the necessary perspective for understanding the contemporary political significance of cultural productions, even those not often considered to have such significance: precisely the case of fashion. I see the specificity of national identity, therefore, as a mark of the heterogeneity of a cultural product within the global context of its multinational distribution. Furthermore, I deem a consideration of cultural specificity imperative in any analysis of gender-producing practices, such as fashion.

Before I go any further, I want to state that my analysis here is deeply engraved by the complicity of my own subject position with both fashion and national identity. I remember very well when Armani's masculine suits first came out, and I still wear the Armani suit I bought on sale at Macy's in the 1970s. I am enthralled by his current collections, which I see as the promise of a world of *luxe, calme, et volupté*, where everyone would get to be very rich and very thin and have nothing but the finest silks and the softest woolens touch their skin, a world where the androgynous implications of my attire would simultaneously insure that I be seen both as a serious intellectual and as a most alluring participant in the ferrously lacy weavings of "desire," a world where desire would be based on a collective recognition of the seriousness of life under postindustrial capitalism and the calm intellect and joyous sensuality with which we all could approach any nuclear-age, AIDS-age difficulty: a kind of idealized Italy, in fact.

At the same time, I cringe at my own recognition that (more than the clothes) the narrative ads instigated by Armani and picked up later in the United States by Calvin Klein, Guess Jeans, and Ralph Lauren, conjure up worlds of metaphysical transcendence and antimaterialist ecstasy (Armani), worlds where racist, classist, and of course sexist rape is normalized and women are all constantly willing objects of sadism (Guess Jeans), worlds where only rich white Europeans or European Americans get to live, and where they play polo and lie around reading leather-bound tomes in surroundings filled with mementos from their latest African safaris (Ralph Lauren).

So I shudder and, for a moment, feel grateful that an Armani wardrobe is clearly beyond the reach of my professorial finances. Slightly politically correct through no fault of my own, and still looking for the rare sale at Macy's, or the next sabbatical in Italy, if the dollar is strong, I am the person who now sets out to analyze Armani's 1970s look as a cultural product.

My subject position is also marked by the configuration of national identities that are braided through my sense of who I am. As a second-generation Swedish American, I have parents—not grandparents or great-grandparents but parents—who "came over on the boat." I am one generation away from being a peasant in the frozen north, one boat trip away from being a village girl gone to clean houses or teach school in Örebrö. I speak a little Swedish, know how to cook some Swedish food, and celebrate holidays like Midsommar and Sankta Lucia, when I wear my traditional costume from the inland province of Dalarna. I know the difference between traditional dress and fashion. Even though I cannot avoid reading the subtitles, I think of Ingmar Bergman's films as reality. I feel Swedish but am not quite that; I feel North American, but that's not the whole picture. All my life, the question of national identity has dogged me, ever since I realized that my parents spoke English with what my friends called an accent and that not everyone went to a church where the sermons were delivered in brimstone Scandinavian.

Alongside the constant questioning of national identity that the immigration experience in my own family has prompted, I have known further subjective ambiguity because I carry out my professional scholarship and teaching under the emblem of other national identities. I am convinced that my choice of scholarly fields is directly related to my sense that national identity is a constructed notion. It has been impossible for me not to problematize this issue when for a number of years now I have found myself in academic situations where I am considered, by students most often, to be some sort of official representative of Italian or French national culture. I certainly have been a professional representative of two national literary canons, a role fraught with contradiction for me not only because I was not "born to" the language of either of them but also because I engage in a constant critique of the very notion of canonical literature, national or otherwise. It is no wonder, then, that sooner or later I would come face to face with the issue of the attention that might best be paid to national identity in

The Novel, the Body, and Giorgio Armani

any interpretation or analysis of cultural production. And now, here I am, trying for some clear thinking in spite of my inevitably messy slate.

To begin, it seems to me that any current notion of national identity—any notion that benefits from previous work done by such thinkers as Raymond Williams and E. P. Thompson, for example—would consider it a kind of linguistic cipher, a signifier that still wanders about in language but that no one would be capable of attaching to any fixed signified or projecting toward any consentually determined referent. At best, perhaps, it provides a kind of generalized sense for a literate dominant and/or middle class of what part of the world a person lives in, what kind of a government and economic system a person lives under, and the sorts of languages and practices a person might use. But it can also easily be a repository of cliché, stereotype, and prejudice. At worst, it can couple with the ideologies of citizenship and become the thing a person is constrained to die for. In any case, national identity is a contextual mark of much contemporary cultural production that is often given less attention than I believe a socially responsible analysis would demand.

Part of the reason for this is that the nation-state is traditionally represented as a natural unit of political action. This fact has been ardently evident recently in the various cross-border interventions, and finally the war, that the United States and its confederates imposed in the Gulf states of the Middle East. But if I uncritically accept the notion of the nation-state as a natural political unit, I neglect the complicity in or opposition to such a politics by groups whose identities do not coincide with that of the nation-state. On the one hand, for example, there are supranational groups such as multinational corporations, the population of people living with AIDS, the ecology movement, the arms market, the women's movement, the African, Jewish, Palestinian, Cambodian, Salvadoran, and other diasporas, ethnic identities in general, groups delineated supranationally by their religious identity, kinship groups, the European Economic Community, tribes, the Chicano land of Aztlán—all of these groups being people with common interests that do not coincide with nation-state configurations.

On the other hand, there are subnational groups based, for example, on ethnic identity, on linguistic community, on so-called minority status vis-à-vis a national image. The fact that some of the subnational identities coincide with some of the supranational identities—I'm thinking of an ethnicity such as Asian American, for example, which also partakes of the supranational notion of "Asian"—emphasizes the degree to which national identity per se is an intermediary construct that does not determine half as much of an individual subjective position now as it might have, say, in eighteenth- or nineteenth-century Europe.

This view of national identity as a median configuration between the highly relevant communities that now operate at supra- or subnational identity levels goes far toward relativizing the notion of national identity in ways that are helpful for studies of public culture. But the most evident instances of the historical relativization of national identity are perhaps the ways in which national identity is culled for purposes of nationalism in postcolonial situations. While modern western imperialism is tightly braided to European nationalism, similar nationalisms have proven to be instrumental in the struggles of postcolonial populations *against* European imperialist colonial rule. Terrific ambiguities derive from these situations. The social formation of subjectivity, for example, is affected by the derivative aspects of national identity in postcolonial situations. Allegiance to a community, moreover, is as complex in such contexts as it is in immigrant communities in, say, the United States. Such ambiguities are amply represented, at least from Frantz Fanon on down through novels such as Tsetse Dangarembga's *Nervous Conditions*. And the terrific confusion of notions of subjectivity and identity that result in contemporary cosmopolitan postcolonial situations are the stuff of which postnational novels, such as Salman Rushdie's *Midnight's Children* and *The Satanic Verses*, are made. Therefore, since national identity is evoked in service both of the European imperialism that colonized continents other than Europe and of the postcolonial anti-imperialist struggles of the peoples of those continents, I understand national identity—even in its function as a kind of political genre, given its representational constraints—as a political entity of chameleon-like qualities, one that in itself bears no specific political coloration.

What it does bear, however, is history—national history, precisely. To state that the notion of national identity is significant because it compels a consideration of the history of the nation-state to which it refers is not as tautological as it may at first appear. The history of a nation-state is the text of its specificity, the specificity under which all subnational identities are subsumed, at least within that chronotope, and from which all supranational identities are excluded. This specificity is a context that provides meanings for cultural production that will go overlooked by observers who fail to take this context into consideration, as I shall show when I return to Armani's "new" woman.

Even a necessarily brief consideration of national identity must note

The Novel, the Body, and Giorgio Armani

its rapidly changing nature. Phenomena and events of recent years have prompted a number of critical thinkers to adopt the term "postnational" to suggest a political geography akin to the aesthetic and social implications of the term "postmodern" (Soysal). The fact that the world population is now globally heading toward, or already living in, a postnational era is clear from the list of supranational and subnational population groups I mentioned above. Postnationality is also clearly implied by currently changing notions of citizenship in the case, for example, of Turkish guest-workers in Germany. Their claims for equitable benefits from the German government while they retain their Turkish citizenship are based not on arguments for their civil rights, which, being civil, would have to be guaranteed by the laws of a state, but on arguments for their human rights, which imply not only a universal community of human beings but also an authority capable of guaranteeing those rights (Soysal). So if I add the case of the Turkish guest-workers in Germany to the list that includes ethnic diasporas, multinational corporations, the ecology movement, the AIDS population, and others I mentioned above, *all of which have political interests not coincident with any given nation-state*, I fill in the picture of the postnational world even more.

In this world, then, national identity has not disappeared. In fact, as I have already implied, it has a dual role. First, it acts as one of the constitutive factors, along with others such as ethnicity, gender, class, languages, age, and what racialized societies call "race," of any subject position. This function of national identity is perhaps nowhere so clear as in postnational novels. These are novels whose plots depend on the clear national identity of their characters and events but whose distribution and readership is multinational. Novels such as Milan Kundera's *The Unbearable Lightness of Being*, for example, or Gabriel García Márquez's *One Hundred Years of Solitude*, have characters and plots that are rationally inconceivable in any cultural context other than their own national one. Simultaneously, like many other postnational novels, they directly interrogate the very notion of the nation-state. Yet their multinational distribution indicates a readership that knows little of what it means to feel oneself Czech or Colombian.

Thus I arrive at the second role of national identity in the postnational world: in addition to being a partially constitutive factor of subject positions, it has a kind of coinage value that belies the deep arbitrariness of the powers that impose it. Unlike a family or tribal identity, which may offer supportive as well as oppressive contexts for a subject, the national identity represented in postnational novels is most often devoid of positive characteristics. Its purpose in these novels is to serve others than the subject herself.

In such novels, national identity reveals itself to be, among other things, a cipher. That is, it functions as a signifier indicating little about the person to whom it applies and much about the power that asserts authority over that person. Moreover, that cipher, national identity, *which indicates the arbitrariness of the power "behind" national identity*, is also a nonpermanent characteristic of the subject, a characteristic that implicitly may be exchanged for someone else's. In this sense, national identity is a kind of contemporary currency: I've got my national identity, you've got yours. What are they worth? What's today's conversion rate? A postnational novel that plays adeptly with this notion of implicit exchange value is Margaret Atwood's *Lady Oracle*, where the Canadian protagonist is constantly taken as a United States citizen during her visits to her favorite country, Italy, where she composes Gothic novels in the English tradition. The protagonist consciously utilizes these identities, and many of the clichés they imply, as she invents a self whose writing, though perhaps a mirror of her being, is never "authentic," not even when it is automatic, or unconscious. Atwood thus represents her protagonist as a multiple subject who tries on national identities the way she might try on dresses. All of them have similar functions; each has its own stylistic peculiarities. And, like dresses, these national identities are all virtually exchangeable.

I find indications of this contemporary, implicitly convertible status of national identity in realms of consumerism other than the postnational novel. For example, the late Raymond Williams noted several years ago that the realities of multinational corporations and international markets undermine notions of national identity. In his 1983 study T*he Year* 2000, for example, he begins a chapter entitled "The Culture of Nations" with this vignette:

> There was this Englishman who worked in the London office of a multinational corporation based in the United States. He drove home one evening in his Japanese car. His wife, who worked in a firm which imported German kitchen equipment, was already at home. Her small Italian car was often quicker through the traffic. After a meal which included New Zealand lamb, Californian carrots, Mexican honey, French cheese and Spanish wine, they settled down to watch a programme on their television set, which had been made in Finland. The programme was a retrospective celebration of the war to recapture the Falkland Islands. As they watched it they felt warmly patriotic, and very proud to be British. (177)

The Novel, the Body, and Giorgio Armani

Williams's major point is that such material realities provide enormous contradictions to old ideas of nationality and yet fail to displace them, in spite of enormous evidence that those old ideas no longer have any traditional referents. Old ideas of national identity persist in strong contradiction to current realities. While such entities as multinational corporations and multinational economic communities have "radically altered the nature of sovereignty," he states, the traditional views of national identity are retained as central, at least by the English couple Williams drops in on for illustration. He continues:

> Our couple may well not have noticed the American aircraft, armed with nuclear weapons, flying high above their house from an English base, or the new heavier lorries on the bypass, whose weight has been determined by an EEC regulation, yet regularly, systematically, these are there. (178)

In 1994, the English couple, though they may still be unwilling to resolve the contradiction of their "warm feelings" of nationalistic patriotism and their material enjoyment of international goods, might have a little more difficulty cranking up that patriotism than they did even seven or eight years ago. Especially if they were to read novels like *The Satanic Verses*, or even journalistic coverage of the death threats resulting from the publication of that novel. Especially if they have seen movies like *The Name of the Rose*, from the postnational novel of the same name which was translated into twelve languages other than the Italian before its second edition in the original. Like Armani's 1970s suits for women, these cultural products, distributed internationally to a multinational market, all problematize the national identities upon which they simultaneously depend. And such tragic recent events as the 1991 war in the Persian Gulf may be seen, in this context, as an attempt on the part of the United States to cull "patriotism" as at least an *international* passion, via its interpolation of "coalition forces," in its own unacknowledged bow to the symbolic realities of what, in fact, is a postnational geopolitical world. By extrapolation, then, the English couple might recognize their own national identity as *their* version of what it is that is so troublesome in these novels and at least be glad, if they are as complacent as they seem to be in Williams's representation, that they don't have to exchange theirs for those others, especially those Middle Eastern ones.

What I would add to Williams's analysis, then, is simply the sense that national identity, in addition to its contradictory and vestigial persistence in a postnational world, has begun to take on the valence of an implicitly convertible coinage, and that an effect of this implicit potential convertibility is to indicate the arbitrary nature of the power that imposes national identity to begin with.

Let me recapitulate. From my own subject position, very much implicated in the matter at hand, I seek to analyze the cultural production which is Giorgio Armani's fashion collections of the late 1970s and early 1980s. My purpose in doing so is first of all to challenge from a feminist perspective the traditional discourse that treats the fashion industry in the west as frivolous, thereby gendering it as "feminine," and second, to interrogate the valence that I might attribute to the national identity of fashion as a cultural production in a postnational context.

As concerns fashion, it seems clear to me that a feminist intervention on the symbolic processes at work in the international discourse of fashion would include a reading that somehow subverts the manner in which that discourse manipulates the finances, images, and finally the bodies of women as well as men. It is precisely the unavoidable emphasis that fashion places on the body, in fact, that affords a possibility for such a subversive reading and an eventual recuperation of fashion as a feminist discourse. In the case of Armani's 1970s collections, this subversive reading insists, first of all, on the way his collections *as fashion*, and more basically *as clothing*, point ceaselessly to the body as the final site of a representational ideology. Second, the blatancy of that ideology, in the case of Armani's 1970s collections for women, is obscured, I believe, by the aestheticizing, *international* discourse of fashion, which read his nostalgia for the 1930s and 1940s as a kind of generic nostalgia for the heyday of another international discourse, the Hollywood film. Therefore, I seek to read his 1970s collections in the context of their *national* identity, to discern what becomes apparent, and quite massively so, in the context of the 1930s and 1940s *in Italy*. Armani's calm 1970s woman suddenly appears as more than an innocent filmic quotation, as I will show later on.

In my readings of postnational novels and of Armani's 1970s women's collections, I see national identity as a median contributory factor in the constitution of subject positions, that is, as a labile category existing somewhere between the sociopolitical groupings that are supranational and those that are subnational. Lest I be accused of belaboring the obvious, let me add that this median position indicates a progressive *lessening of importance* of national identity and the entity of the nation-state in postindustrial multinational capitalism. Therefore, national identity continues in diluted form as, on one hand, still a constitutive factor of subject positions (and consequent possibilities for political activism), and, on the other, an implicit, potentially convertible coinage that indicates the arbitrariness—or the *interestedness*—of the power that imposes it. Finally, I have presented the postnational novel as the cultural product where these two paradoxical postmodern effects of national identity are easily seen: its vestigially constitutive effect with regard to subject positions and its function as a token of potential convertibility in a system of implicit equivalencies. You can see how this second function undermines the first. It weakens the notion of the distinction of national identity, the specificity of national identity, or, to return to my opening context, the particular heterogeneity national identity would seem to guarantee.

Now let me wend my way back to a final look at Armani's Milan runway by elaborating some of my *poetic* reasons for choosing fashion as one of the objects of my investigation of the valence of national identity and the relation between that and "femininity." And since thinking about *poesis* brings me to thinking about poetry, I'll frame my reasons like this: a poem's ideology shimmers clearly in its rhetoric. And often that ideology slips through my reading, especially when I am taken by some lexical brilliance, some phonic remembrance, some rhythmic flip. So I try to pull myself together at regular intervals in order to read beyond my pleasure in the text. I go to this trouble because I have great respect for the power of tropes and because I know that the ideologies they contain all have their final location in my body.[1] Since I am convinced that the final site of ideology is the body, and since I am also convinced that rhetoric is a prime site of ideology, I am prepared to study fashion in its most serious aspect: as the cultural product that always admits, *even if in spite of itself*, that the body is its final referent. Fashion is the cultural production that most blatantly engages the body in a trope: the "look" in fashion is always a disguise, is always a "dressing up as." In fashion, therefore, the body is always troped, similitudinized, metaphorized. But in fashion the body is always also actual, present, physical, biological—the literal condition, rather than simply the effect, of the production of meaning.

Therefore, the discourse of fashion stands in counterdistinction and in opposition to transcendental or post-transcendental discourse that sees the body only as a term of tropes and not as the final site of their ideology. In other words, whatever the specific manifestations of fashion that may be or may seem to be physically oppressive, and whatever the history of its gendering as a "feminine" practice, fashion as cultural production, or fashion as discourse, need not necessarily be an example of disempowered "femininity." Instead, because it blatantly and constantly refuses to let the troping of the human body slip away from the experiential actuality of that body, because it functions under a condition of impossibility whereby no encoding of the body can pass itself off as only "literary" where "literature" pretends to exist in rarefied realms free of contamination with the experiential real, because fashion unites in an inseparable entity rhetoric with its referent, which is always finally the body, my body, I claim fashion as potentially a feminist discourse.

Simultaneously, I hesitate to think in terms of biological essentialism. But I do think of my body's experiential reality as the physical site of my subject position and the basis for cultural action. The body, for me, is what I think through (with Jane Gallop) as I position myself as a subject and as I am positioned as an object by all the determinants that constrain my thought and action. I live my body as my entrance into history. I am therefore quite ready to critique any discourse that traverses my body—as all ideologies finally do—with a certain relief when those discourses, by their very structure at least, draw attention to the effects they have on bodies. This is the beginning of a feminist reading, whether the discourse being read is fashion, or medicine, or pornography, or the law.

It is only by reading a cultural product like Armani's collections in their national identity context as well as in their transnational contexts that I can arrive at some of the political implications of that production. I will insist, therefore, on a third aspect of national identity in this postnational setting, one I mentioned in passing earlier: that is, national identity (for all the paradox of its dual effect) is still the site of a history (for all the problematics *that* raises). Because this is the case, I can therefore read Armani's cultural production as a moment in Italian national history. When I do this, I find an answer to the question Armani poses in my epigraph here: Why did he do it? Or, phrased in a manner that permits me to respond, what is the significant effect of his having done it? So I turn first to the historical context for Armani's new look, and thus begins my final story.

A turning point occurred in 1975 in the political experience of the inhabitants of the Italian peninsula. The extraparliamentary group Lotta Continua disbanded, having succumbed to a ferocious critique of its Leninist politics on the part of feminists and autonomists (partisans of independence from historical left Italian political parties, especially the Italian Communist party). Simultaneously, the Autonomia movement began to gain international acclaim as an inclusionary and oppositional force in a culture

The Novel, the Body, and Giorgio Armani

marked by its varied, but always hierarchical, party system, while the Movimento delle Donne was organizing mass demonstrations for approval of the equal family rights law, which took place in May, and for the legalization of abortion, which would occur three years later. The "hot autumn" of 1969 was fresh in the collective memory, as were the neo-Fascist bombings in Milan's Piazza Fontana. The attempts at state terror of the late 1960s had given way to a wide spectrum of political violence, and the kidnappings and shootings of the Red Brigades and other clandestine groups were rapidly increasing. The middle-class base of young leftist politics in Italy was expanding, via the organization of workers and the homeless, to include the urban proletariat.

Simultaneously, and consequently, a wide swath of the wealthy bourgeoisie was emigrating and investing in agribusiness in the United States, as improved vintages coming out of California's Napa Valley would attest a few years down the road.

In the realm of literature, Italian novelists were scrambling to provide narrative representations of contemporary life. Natalia Ginzburg's early (1973) representation of the "terrorist" as a prodigal son of the bourgeoisie was giving way to the unabashed exercises in othering and demonization evident in Ferdinando Camon's and Carlo Castellanetta's novels of the late 1970s and early 1980s. The ostentatious "avant-garde" experiments of the 1960s, especially those of the Gruppo 63, appeared less and less relevant as their practitioners, notably Umberto Eco, turned to more direct social commentary than such literary experimentation had provided. And Pier Paolo Pasolini, Italy's most prophetic critical voice, having scarred the film screen with what he called his "impossible" film, Salò (a searing indictment of the Fascism inherent in contemporary consumer culture, both in Italy and in white America), was murdered on the beach at Ostia.[2] Not to put too fine a point on it, things were heating up.

Therefore, when Armani set his "new" look upon the runway in Milan, he provided a searing ideological contrast to the sociopolitical reality surrounding that runway. And, since his new look was not new in an originary sense but only in the spirit of *in-ventio*—in the spirit, that is, of bringing a moment of the past into the present, since it was, in postmodern terminology, a nostalgic quotation—I read it as an evocation of the 1930s and the 1940s, the nearest era when the masculine suit adorned the female body.

If I perform this reading in the multinational context in which Armani's cultural production is generally seen, the universalizing discourse of high fashion, I might open fields of signification resonating with the

Beverly Allen

glamor of Hollywood films in the late 1920s and the 1930s. I might conjure the allure of those sirens such as Garbo, Bankhead, or Crawford, whose various negotiations of the implications of masculine attire might lead me to analyze the gender implications of Armani's more recent sexual riddles. This sort of reading, which saw Hollywood's silver screen as the cultural referent of the 1930s and 1940s fashion revival Armani initiated, was a prevalent one in the United States and internationally, in the world of fashion, during the 1970s.

But if I perform a reading of Armani's early cultural production in its *national* context, if I consider it, that is, in its Italian national identity, then I evoke a specific, heterogeneous context, the history of the Italian nation-state. Consequently, then, the referential possibilities narrow. I know that Hollywood films, like other U.S. cultural products, were not easily available referents in the Italy of the 1930s and early 1940s. Italian national history encodes the broad-shouldered suits that characterized Italian fashion of that era, not within the developing international discourse of the cinema, but within the enclosed national discourse of Mussolini's Fascism. Broad-shouldered masculine-tailored suits on women in Italy in the 1970s refer back to broad-shouldered masculine-tailored suits on women and men during the *ventennio nero* (twenty years of Fascism) *before* they refer to the tantalizing androgyny of that era in Hollywood. Italian Fascism is the referent I would miss if I were to read Armani's early collections only in their international and multinational contexts. And this is the referent that signals to me that Fascism was a political response widely perceived as appropriate in the Italy of the recent *anni di piombo*, or "years of lead." The discourse of international fashion, with its cliché of Italian design, thus contains an indicator of a political fact that was determinant during Italian "terrorism" and has remained so ever since: Fascism in Italy, far from disappearing with Mussolini, is alive and well and considered an appropriate response to social unrest.

Armani's interposition of his calm, dusty-colored masculine-tailored woman now appears as a figuration of the order Fascism promised, and still promises, in Italian peninsular politics. In spite of and alongside the feminist potential of a subversive reading of fashion as the constant indicator of the body, and the body as the final site of ideology, this woman is a sign of the continued poles of Italian national politics, a radicalization of the rightist position to match the radicalization Autonomia and the Red Brigades provided on the left. She is the personification of what many of the novels of the era only hint at: a new, Fascist, but always feminine Italia. She is the

The Novel, the Body, and Giorgio Armani

dream girl of the attempted *strage dello stato* (state-sponsored massacre), presented, in fact, as the state itself if we consider as her mascot the stylized eagle logo that still hovers as Armani's active sportswear trademark, providing the most literal quotation of Fascist iconography in Armani's signifying package. And her persistence in the popular culture of fashion, where shoulder pads still rest on Italian women's bodies, may be a mark of the persistence of Fascism in all its banality as a historic pole of Italian political ideologies even in this apparently democratic postmodern decade.

Armani doesn't know why he did it. And he doesn't do it anymore. I have suggested that the national "identity" of his early cultural production provides a clue to the implicit meaning (or better, the effective significance) of what he was doing. And I would close by suggesting further that such a consideration of national "identity" is a sign that not all heterogeneity, not even that of national identity in its vestigial constitutive effect or its implicitly convertible equivalency, is subsumed to universalizing discourse. Instead, it may be something of a toehold, as I propose here, for readings that wish to offer resistance, as mine does, to such discourse because I have learned what I call the lesson of poetry, the lesson fashion reminds me of: rhetoric is never innocent. I can only hope the reading I offer here will encourage those of us who recognize our bodies as the final sites of ideologies of various representations to claim our authority to critique those representations and to keep ourselves free from innocence as well.

Notes

1. For a discussion of the politics of the body in this context, see my "Terrorism, Feminism, Sadism: The Clichéing of Experience in the Brand-Name Novel," and Elaine Scarry, "*The Body in Pain: The Making and Unmaking of the World.*

2. Personal communication to the artist, Giuseppe Zigaina, who is now curator of Pasolini's graphic art and author of *Pasolini e la morte: mito alchimia e semantica del "nulla lucente."* In 1986, Zigaina told me that when Pasolini was preparing to film *Salò* he felt that he would be making a "terrifying" film that no one would want to see, "in order to get to the depths of my desperation," after which he planned to retire to his *torre* in the countryside and spend the rest of his days making drawings.

Bibliography

Allen, Beverly. "One Nation by Terror: Italian National Identity since the *compromesso storico.*" *Italica* 69. 2 (Summer 1992): 161–76.

———. "Qualche appunto sulla crisi dell'*identità* nazionale in letteratura." *Le voci della poesia: Quaderni di cultura letteraria* 1 (July 1992): 70–73.

———. "The Telos, Trope and Topos of Italian Terrorism." *Substance* (Fall 1987): 37–43.

———. "A Terrorism Book Report." *Journal: A Contemporary Art Magazine.* Los Angeles Art Institute (Spring 1987): 8–14.

Beverly Allen

———. "Terrorism, Feminism, Sadism: The Clichéing of Experience in the Brand-Name Novel." *Art and Text.* Sydney (Winter/Summer in northern hemisphere, 1989): 75–80.
Anderson, Benedict. *Imagined Communities: Reflections on the Origin and Spread of Nationalism.* London: Verso, 1983.
Barthes, Roland. *The Fashion System.* New York: Hill and Wang, 1983.
Becker, David G., Jeff Frieden, Sayre P. Schatz, and Richard L. Sklar, eds. *Postimperialism: International Capitalism and Development in the Late Twentieth Century.* Boulder & London: Lynne Rienner, 1987.
Bollati, Giulio. "Identità nazionale: L'Italia s'è persa." *L'Espresso* (Dec. 6, 1987): 110–13.
Bono, Paola, and Sandra Kemp, eds. *Italian Feminist Thought: A Reader.* Cambridge, Mass.: Basil Blackwell, 1991.
Cavaliere, Barbara. "Armani, Giorgio." In Ann Lee Morgan, ed., *Contemporary Designers.* Detroit: Gale Research, 1984. 26–27.
Chatterjee, Partha. *Nationalist Thought and the Colonial World—A Derivative Discourse.* London: Zed Books, 1986.
Derrida, Jacques. "L'altro capo." *Liber* 3 (1990): 11–13.
Fanon, Frantz. *The Wretched of the Earth.* New York: Grove Press, 1963.
Feldblum, Miriam. "The Politicization of Citizenship in French Immigration Politics." Unpublished paper prepared for the seventh International Conference of Europeanists, Washington, D.C., March 1990.
Gallop, Jane. *Thinking Through the Body.* New York: Columbia University Press, 1988.
Kaiser, Susan B. *The Social Psychology of Clothing.* New York: Macmillan, 1985.
Lee, Andrea. Interview with Giorgio Armani. *Mirabella* (July 1990): 76–79.
Maher, Vanessa. "Sewing the Seams of Society: Dressmakers and Seamstresses in Turin Between the Wars." In Jane Fishburne Collier and Sylvia Junko Yanagisako, eds., *Gender and Kinship: Essays toward a Unified Analysis.* Stanford: Stanford University Press, 1987. 132–59.
Quintavalle, Arturo Carlo. "Fashion: The Three Cultures." In Bianchino, Butazzi, Molfino, and Quintavalle, eds., *Italian Fashion*, vol. 1, *The Origins of High Fashion and Knitwear.* Milan: Rizzoli, 1987. 11–56.
Rich, Adrienne. "Notes toward a Politics of Location." In *Blood, Bread, and Poetry.* New York: Norton, 1986. 210–31.
Rosecrance, Richard. *The Rise of the Trading State: Commerce and Conquest in the Modern World.* New York: Basic Books, 1986.
Scarry, Elaine. *The Body in Pain: The Making and Unmaking of the World.* New York: Oxford University Press, 1985.
Said, Edward W. "Narrative, Geography and Interpretation." *New Left Review* 180 (1990): 91–97.
Soja, Edward W. *Postmodern Geographies: The Reassertion of Space in Critical Social Theory.* London and New York: Verso, 1989.
Soysal, Yasemin. "Guestworkers and Citizenship: Old Issues, New Challenges." Unpublished paper presented at the annual meeting of the American Sociological Association, San Francisco, August 1989.
Spivak, Gayatri Chakravorty. *In Other Worlds: Essays in Cultural Politics.* New York: Routledge, 1988.
Williams, Raymond. *The Year 2000.* New York: Pantheon, 1983.
Zigaina, Giuseppe. *Pasolini e la morte: mito alchimia e semantica del "nulla lucente."* Venice: Marsilio Editori, 1987.

Eugenia Paulicelli

Fashion as a Text
Talking about Femininity and Feminism

The revolution cited ancient Rome, just as fashion cites an antiquated dress. Fashion has a scent for what is current, whenever this moves within the thicket of what was once.
                                                            Walter Benjamin

The word "fashion," adapted from the French *façon* and from the Latin *factio*, implies a making, a giving shape or form to something. Moreover, the word "fashion" is related to a particular way or "mode" of making something—hence the French term *mode* and the Italian *moda*. With these etymological premises in mind I would like to consider the fashion text as a process of metonymy within the ongoing act of making, or fashioning.[1]

As *factio*, the fashion text is a complex of signs that we find belonging to two different natures and "grammars": verbal and visual. These two different registers, or codes of language, coexist in the fashion text not only because, as Barthes showed in his study *Système de la mode* (1967), we have a described and/or written fashion (e.g., in fashion magazines), but because fashion as a text implies a distinct awareness of both iconic and verbal signs. This latter is not always a mere description of the former, but is often a separate text.

The relationship between the verbal and the visual within the fashion text is no doubt a complicated one. This relationship is also present in literary texts and obviously in film, advertisements, and in many other verbal/visual media. What I wish to underline here is that in fashion the coexistence of words and images originates a discourse that has particular social and political connotations, and differs in its very form from other discourses of mass communication.

Fashion is a text with an elaborated feature of intertextuality that is easy to see, but to which it is sometimes very difficult to ascribe a meaning. This is mainly why Barthes's study on fashion could be interpreted on two different levels. Barthes's aim is to analyze the written descriptions of the various models in women's fashion magazines. In other words, he is interested in seeing how these models "speak." This example of fashion then becomes both a discourse and an object of discourse for Barthes.

As Ugo Volli has noted in his book *Contro la Moda* (Against fashion, 1989), Barthes's view in *Système de la mode* might be interpreted, on one hand, as a kind of an "extreme logocentric view." On the other hand, Volli remarks that it is difficult to dissent from Barthes if we interpret his study as research on the relationship between a given outfit and the social discourse on and about it, together with the changing value system that chooses a certain outfit as a privileged object of fashion.[2] This suggests that an ideology arises from the relation between certain models and the way they are presented and described. In other words, the fashion system is one of the vehicles that a given society uses to convey and maintain its values and ideology and to decide what is trendy and what is not.

As *mode*, fashion, especially in Italy in the last few years, has become a big industry with a complicated apparatus and a socially hegemonic network (advertising, cinema, television, music, video, and so on). In a way, this industry is a consequence of an ideology that praises the triumph of appearances, and the eager and quick consumption of images. Such a phenomenon represents the condition of a mass society where one celebrates the superficiality of fashion as mere image (*mode*), and where it has become more difficult to criticize a given text or discourse.

What do I mean by this? Reality is an intricate and complex network of "knowledges," fragmented into specialized fields. The more knowledge we acquire, the more segmented and specialized this knowledge becomes. In this process of specialization, we may lose a broader awareness of the mechanisms of a given society. Such a fact also represents a limit to our knowledge. More and more each seems to be interested in his or her particular and individual dimension; we are losing curiosity, and do not explore the different universes that appear to be far from those individual ones. What has become more and more difficult is to employ a *critical* method and attitude toward the "reading" of a text or a given reality. More often, the text is accepted or rejected uncritically according to the current fashionable ideology. Furthermore, we risk idolatry by perceiving "models" as deities. In this, as in ideology, we follow passively the trend of the season. Thus, fashion (as *mode*), with all its enchanting universe of simulations and appearances, represents a text par excellence, but a text that is very complex.

First, fashion as text engenders a chain of texts, situated in synchronicity and diachronicity. This synchronicity is treated by Barthes in the aforementioned study, as he takes into consideration the fashion trends of a year: that is, a complete temporal cycle of fashion.

In addition to this, we can also analyze an outfit in its specific temporal spot (fall 1990, for example) or in relation to different epochs or seasons (the 1960s, 1970s, and so on). Moreover, when we talk about an outfit or a specific detail we refer to, or evoke, an image: it could be a picture in a fashion magazine or a mannequin in a shop window or someone walking in the street.[3] This image inscribes itself in a particular order of images (e.g., within the photographic text) because this image creates other images or subsequent models in an unlimited process. In other words, fashion is a system but it functions as a syntax as well. A real coexistence of the verbal and visual is realized. By "coexistence" I do not mean a correspondence between words and images; the two can sometimes exist independently of each other within the same text. As Bill Nichols says in *Ideology and Image*:

> Words can indeed lie, and they can lie about images as well as anything else. . . . The play between word and image remains a site for disintegration as well as integration. . . . The interplay of codes constituting the image, like those constituting the self-as-subject, forms an ideological arena for ideological contestation. (64)

Both images and words, in this reading, articulate the "weave" of a given text. What is important to my argument in Nichols's quotation is what he calls the "interplay of codes constituting the image" as well as the subject. He raises here other problematic issues regarding images that I would like to discuss in relation to fashion. First, the image in the fashion text represents a site where different languages coexist, and it is for this reason that images are so powerful. They can constitute a discourse in themselves, and also generate a discourse organized and articulated depending on social and political instances.

The English word "look" is associated with fashion, with image and appearance. It happens that having the right "look" for the appropriate circumstance or event is like wearing the right mask or knowing the rules of the (social and political) game. Consequently fashion coincides with the *look* that produces an image. Images trace the trajectories of a game, the game of the gaze, of a narcissistic and kaleidoscopic gaze. The image of woman is generally built up and conceived according to the male gaze, or in order to provoke it, to attract desire.[4] Traditionally, the different (metaphoric) images of women, conveyed by the fashion system, have been produced in order to fulfill men's needs. From ethereal angels to dark ladies, women were not autonomous *subjects* producing a discourse. Rather, they were *objects* of discourse, ideology, and the expectations of a male-dominated society. As a consequence these *objects* have been perceived and considered as *subjects*, as identities with which other women can identify. In doing so one confuses the rules of a game that is political, not neutral.

It is interesting to note in the latest fashion trends that there has been a very strong emphasis on the eroticization of the look; strong, powerful, and sexy bodies recalling Hollywood myths (both female and male) appear in magazine advertisements.[5] Parallel to this trend, other changes have been taking place, some having a theatrical and ironic relation to this image of the healthy, sexy body. We are entering a phase of post-AIDS culture. Let us think of the fall 1992 Calvin Klein ads, Madonna's book *Sex*,[6] or, particularly, the film *Dracula* by Francis Ford Coppola. In this film, set in Victorian England, there are strong allusions to AIDS arranged in a very moralistic frame. A scientist (a blood specialist played by Anthony Hopkins) says, "Syphilis and syphilization have advanced together." Reading between lines such as these in the remake of the Dracula story, we might observe the reposition of the old split between spiritual and sensual love and how an uncontrollable passion with sexual involvement leads to death and damnation. Stark contradictions are created between the overt eroticism of the text juxtaposed with conservative behavior, inhabited by fear of sexual intimacy springing from post-AIDS society.[7]

In the present text the images (or the photographic texts) I have chosen to accompany this essay have to be considered a suggestion and a visual support to my argument (fashion seen as *mode* and as *factio*) and also part of the communicative game we establish with reality. Moreover, in the making of this game it is possible to notice how images (in the streets, on different occasions, and in magazines, advertisements, film, television) might condition our actions (*factio*) and our modes (*mode*) to the point that our actions are accepted because they are "fashionable."

Another source of this complexity is that we live in a technological society where the notion of time has completely changed, and where this notion leads to certain paradoxes in contemporary life. On the one hand, we are asked to maintain a certain "speed" (in careers, personal affairs, and so on) and to act according to its dictates. On the other, we need to be attentive to critical perspectives, yet such analyses require time (a deceleration) that we do not "have" and that in its present accelerated state does not allow for the act of thinking. This paradox also takes place in an academic environment, where people are required *to think*. The continuous multiplication of discourses and information consequent on highly sophisticated technologies fragments knowledge into a number of disciplines and also fragments our experiences of life and our relationships with reality. In these mechanisms several contradictions take place that we experience in our everyday life. This phenomenon requires, in fact, an incredible effort that should enable us to perceive it critically in distinguishing and clarifying our interpretations and choices on personal, social, and political matters; however, when the speed of events is not acknowledged, we often cannot discern our functions as actors and spectators in a reality that produces an enormous number of models to be consumed quickly and to be forgotten afterward. In this way we lose the capacity for criticism and self-criticism, and merely respond to the logic of the "spectacle," of which information itself becomes part.

Barthes criticizes creatively the notion of society-as-spectacle by viewing it from a sociological perspective (e.g., *Mythologies*, 1957). He argues that our age has to be called "the age of writing"—*écriture*—and not, as many intellectuals affirm, one of "image" or spectacle. In the introduction to *Système de la mode*, he maintains that all the objects that constitute our *imaginaire* will continue to depend more and more on "semantics" and not on "images." At the time he wrote *Système de la mode*, of course, his semiotics was very much concerned with signification, as he had previously stated in *Eléments de sémiologie* (1964). Thus in *Système* he states that "linguistics" will eventually become the science of all the "imaginable universes." In arguing this, Barthes subverts the Saussurean order, which states that linguistics derives from semiology—the general science of signs. Barthes suggests that each object or sign does exist—in the actual scene of reality or inscribed in a symbolic order—because it is named. This kind of distinction or separation cannot be maintained in the present context, however, because it does not give us a better understanding of fashion—a very intricate text, which is also a social, political, economic, and cultural phenomenon. In *Système* Barthes intellectualizes fashion, but in previous studies such as *Mythologies*, or in his late studies concerning images, film, and photography, he seemed to possess a fuller conception of the problematic aspects of the image and fashion as a mass phenomenon. In this sense, fashion does not represent "reality," or the reality of the named sign; it is rather a "trace" of sociological reality, or a "taste."

To illustrate this, let us consider one of the so-called new identities that presents a stereotype: the woman manager, or the career woman and her androgynous image. This icon of the androgynous woman has been conceived, represented, and sold by the successful Italian fashion designer Giorgio Armani, especially at the beginning of his career (both in Italy and in the United States).[8] Codes and dictates ruling a given society are continuously subject to change; if it was innovative for women such as George Sand in the nineteenth century to wear a man's suit and smoke a cigar, it is not so today. This androgynous image is one of the dominant images in mass culture today, and consumers attempt to reproduce it by "taking the identity" of the "working girl" models offered by the fashion industry. Such an image is packaged such that consumers can respond to it quickly without critically assessing it. In so doing, the fashion industry conforms to the requirements of modern time, and the fashion of the androgynous working woman becomes a trace of a sociological reality that conforms to the model of the fashion industry.

As a counterexample, note the phenomenon of ultra-"feminine" women, such as Marilyn Monroe or Brigitte Bardot, whose images are legion in fashion magazines and advertisements. The industry packages them as ideals, even as idols. This imagery is promoted with no sense of irony and suggests merely another "model" with which women can identify.[9] All these contradictory phenomenona complicate and articulate the association between ideology and a certain fashion. As stated previously, in the 1960s and 1970s it was very easy to deduce ideology and political orientation from the way people were dressed (remember the famous Eskimo of the "sessanttottino"?).[10] One of the main reasons for feminists in the 1970s to deny their femininity in their look was because they wanted to assert their *equality*, their being on the same intellectual and social level as men. In so doing, the women's aim was to weaken and control the power of the male gaze, or the male symbolic order; by denying their femininity in dress, they would assert their own existence not as sexual or erotic bodies, but as men's intellectual equals. Furthermore, by doing this they also wanted to destroy those social mechanisms that view the female body as a commodity. In the 1970s, feminist movements in Italy as elsewhere claimed that "il personale è politico": "the personal is political." This was an important realization for the feminist movement, because, in so doing,

Fashion as a Text

personal lives, the diverse experiences of women, were discussed and revisited on political grounds and were not confined to the hidden places of private life. Feminists claimed that the first thing that needed to be changed in a male-dominated society were personal relationships between men and women, friends, lovers, and family. They also maintained that the liberation of a woman's sexuality could occur by the acquisition of a new awareness of her own body and erotic drives. Women wanted to undermine male power and its patriarchal values by overcoming the gap in social, economic, and political terms that exists between men and women. There were political reasons for dressing like a man and refusing to wear feminine clothes, even though this kind of attitude did not consider other aspects of the feminine universe. These kinds of features of the *femminista militante*—"militant feminist"—turned out to be after all another prison. In dressing like this, women were responding to another fixed role or stereotype. These women believed that if one was *feminist* one could not be *feminine*, otherwise nobody would take one seriously. One dressed like a man to be considered equal to a man.

But by whom? By men, again, denying that *difference* that primarily comes from the body. The body is an undeniable certainty of existence, and a presence of the self-as-subject in the world. A feminine body occupies a space different, in physical, social, and political terms, from a male one. Who decides, then, the rules and the modes of the game in personal relationships and in society? Who decides which images convey ideological and social and moral/ethical values? Is there any space for personal pleasure and taste? Is there any chance for women not to respond or *to fit* a stereotyped role or image? These, I think, were some of the questions that started to arise as a reaction to the feminist ethics of the 1970s. These problematic questions have led to debates and discussions in many different fields of women's studies in Italy. I am thinking of the formation of a group of women philosophers such as Diotima, as well as other groups of women.[11] In Italy, the present debate involves the commitment of women thinkers who are trying to define "a feminine universe." They are seeking to establish a universe with its own ethics and practice both in society and in personal relationships with other women and men, in order to change its value system and end the rule that reproduces the past and reasserts the status quo. The attempt to define the feminine universe has continued throughout the years, employing different tools in different areas of culture, philosophy, and politics. Simultaneously, an interest in the appearances and look, in an accurate estimate of the meanings of images, has

177

grown among women and in society in general. In the beginning of the 1980s the media talked about "hedonism," which was also promoted by the fashion industry, leading to what is now labeled—especially abroad—the "Italian style."

Italy as a hedonistic country and culture is a cultural icon. One can visualize it just walking down the streets of Italian cities, where a nomadic gaze can enjoy and interpret the playful modes of fashion with its details and trends. In such a reality, it is almost impossible to immediately associate a particular look with a definite political orientation, as one could do in the 1960s and 1970s. A reason for this is that the *structures* in which political ideas are expressed have completely changed. This might also explain why political parties have trouble responding to social changes, and increasingly ignore people's needs, especially those of the younger generation.

Aspects of fashion that were politically meaningful were actually present in various political and feminist groups in the late 1970s. Such group members did not belong to political parties, but they were trying to express their dissatisfaction with certain rigid codes and modes employed by political parties or social institutions (e.g., academia) so as to come to understand their own different needs, and to assert and search for values that strove toward the principle of a "quality of life"—qualità della vita. The presence of such groups required political parties to rethink their modes, as well as their political domains and tenets, to lead toward a transformation of society. One of the dangers in our society, where information becomes a spectacle, where even a war can be a collection of images, is that the media tend to appropriate some feminist or progressive slogans and render them clichés. Consequently their meaning is lost, and the hierarchy and value systems governing a given society never change. The modes and forms shift, but they remain the same in their substance. In this way, the rules governing social values seem to be reaffirmed more and more strongly, instead of being questioned or criticized.

Going back to George Sand, one can see the difference in the way she used her image. In her time, her image served to criticize and shock because it reflected her transgressive life choices. The fact that this image does not shock anymore but has become a model devised by the fashion industry also suggests that the codes governing a text (and a society) are subject to change. Modern criticism must recognize the changes in these codes and shift them according to the nature of a given text.

This also highlights the issue of the identity of the subject, especially the feminine subject, as it relates to the problems of representation and image in fashion. In the current fashion scene we can observe, on the one hand, an aspect of "carnivalization" and, on the other, a constant recurrence of quotations from different ages and epochs: the 1960s, the 1970s, or in some details, in jackets or in hats, the eighteenth century or the Renaissance. This is a typical attribute of the postmodern era. Even the solitary figure of the dandy often recurs, though usually in its more "feminine" form. Both carnivalization and fashion quotation partake of questions of identity, and both refer to the ancient myth of the mask, as Barthes observes. Thus fashion seems to articulate the Sphinx's questions on identity—Who am I? Who are you?—in both tragic and playful ways.

Barthes suggests that fashion represents two aspects of the subject: one of identity—what the image reflects—and another that plays on a notion of identity and responds to an order of "multiplicity." Thus the image suggests a number of different identities, not unlike the ancient myth of the mask, though to Barthes this myth is tragic in the modern context of fashion because it signifies the death of the unified self.

In fact, one side of the self is expressed by the garment, which in Barthesian terms becomes a "sign of the game" and not "the game" itself. From this perspective, fashion is a semantic system in which naming the garment's game means exorcising the "grave side" of the question of identity; for example, playing Marilyn Monroe, Madonna, or Carmen could mean "being" them, but only for one day, only for that one "side." Fashion has a lot to do with fascination, and the desire of the wearer to seduce and enchant through the evocative power of dress and to be seduced by the dress itself. It is interesting to note here the evocative power of dress in literature; I am thinking of Goethe's Werther or Albertine in Proust's *Recherche* as examples, but there are many of them. Werther wished to be buried in the same clothing he wore the first time he met his beloved Liselotte. Clothes, especially their colors, seem to hold the secret, the particular "flavor," of a moment; they become the visible and tangible sign of a moment that would otherwise have been forgotten. Clothing here becomes a writing that expresses the passage of time.

A dress or outfit may evoke an imaginary identity for the wearer. For instance, dressing in a hat like Bogart's or in Peter Falk's "Columbo" raincoat may signify that one wishes to try on an imaginary identity. We can analyze the game a bit more closely, though. On the one hand, this game is not neutral, but in a certain context it has social and ideological connotations because one must conform to the social "rules of the game" in dress.

Eugenia Paulicelli

It is not a game in which women's free and conscious choices are always realized. Rather, the fashion industry sets the mode for fashion—the trends.

Furthermore, the logic of carnivalization that underscores these trends in the fashion industry today is different than it was in the past. First, the fashion industry claims that there are no rules in fashion, that one ought to be free to choose a variety of fashions and trends. One can see this injunction in Moschino's advertisement. After its proclamation "Stop the fashion system," the fashion designer Moschino himself tells us a story, which is more precisely a fable, and like all fables has a moral at the end of it: "La Moda non c'é più, sono rimasti solo la gente ed i vestiti [Fashion does not exist any more, only people and their clothes]." Lately there has been a tendency in publicity and advertisement toward "narrativity," not only identified with the verbal comment on pictures, as this particular ad shows, but also in the photographic text.[12] Ads tell us stories. Are they substituting for the ancient storytellers? This tendency is completely opposite to the logic of quick consumption of images and experiences. The device these texts activate is that of memory, whose principles control the making of a story and, in more general terms, of history. Moschino's ad also presents this kind of interplay between story (fable) and history.[13]

> Stop the fashion system! Moschino and the non-fashion shows. He exalts fashion and denies it, both in the press campaign and fashion-show invitations. Fashion is the dark and sanguinary lady. What about Moschino's fashion show? It is a ballet, among the fog and astonished eyes of the photographers. Certainly Franco Moschino might have enjoyed himself and he succeeded in an enterprise that is not new for him at all: making people talk about him. He also tells us a story, THE STORY, we pass it to you as such. Moschino says so.
>
> ### THE STORY
> Like hundreds of times, the fearful "Fashion" wrapped in its luxury and lugubrious veils, hairstyled and wearing jewels, was training her "victims" in boring classes of style and behavior. Elegant, cold, and self-confident models walked quietly on the carpet of the atelier wearing their uniforms. Meanwhile vicious music surrounded their false gestures. Suddenly some merry goblins appeared. They were playing with a white cloud and at the same time making Fashion vanish together with its victims. The day after at dawn, the world was full of goblins stretching and yawning, so they happily began their dance. Thus they started to get dressed, choosing their clothes with an innocent spontaneity. The clothes they chose were only the ones they really wanted or loved. To tell the truth, there was a great confusion and some of them did not look very nice, but they were glad anyway . . . !

Fashion as a Text

Everybody seemed to be finally very happy about dressing up and playing, and they thought that it would have been very nice to do so every morning. Then a big party was given to celebrate this day of liberty and a great parade of flags started, flying with their wonderful colors.
Fashion does not exist any more, only people and their clothes [emphasis mine].

What kind of meaning does this last statement convey, together with the images and the entire text? It seems very ambiguous. Moschino, one of Italy's top fashion designers, is responsible along with other designers for deciding the look and consequently setting the fashion. So his saying that "fashion does not exist any more" is a contradiction in terms. By negating it, he actually sends us the opposite message. In other words, Moschino, in ironizing the fashion system with all its social events (such as fashion shows), makes such events fashionable. He thus responds perfectly to the system itself. Moreover, he takes part in all the most important events of the fashion world with his particular style and his way of "ironizing" the fashion system but not actually undermining it. Certainly Moschino's clothes are designed for a woman completely different from the one represented by Valentino, for example. Moschino's main difference from classical fashion designers such as Biagiotti or Valentino lies then in this and not in his being outside or on the margin of the fashion system, as his press advertisements state.

Moschino's ad is a clear example of the above-mentioned "carnival" atmosphere in which the ideology of the fashion industry is supported rather than subverted (it thus inverts Bakhtin's "carnivalization"). Moreover, since this "rule" is spread by the mass media it is one to be followed, and thus precludes the sort of freedom and subversion one associates with "carnival." Such a reading of "carnivalization" contributes to the collapse of the unified-self-as-subject (the self in its plenitude), and to the alienation of people in particular historical situations. The constant quotation that characterizes fashion carnivalization constitutes a kind of fluctuating device in this process. In particular situations one can invoke "Marilyn" or the Wildian or D'Annunzian solitary dandy, yet this is an utterance with specific meaning, but a meaning not played out in actual circumstances, a label. This is the kind of game that rules our society because it allows one to be "recognized" by a group of people to whom one wants to be related or by whom one wants to be accepted.

Such recognition seems to be important in an urban, mass, accelerated culture where subjects fear that they can lose their identities (even frag-

Eugenia Paulicelli

STOP THE FASHION SYSTEM!
Ovvero Moschino e le "non-sfilate".

Servizio di Antonella Sabbagh, foto di Alessandro D'Andrea

La esalta e la rinnega, nella campagna stampa, sugli inviti alla sfilata: è la dama nera e sanguinaria, la Moda. La sua sfilata? Un balletto, tra fumi e sguardi attoniti dei fotografi. Sicuramente lui, Franco Moschino, si sarà divertito un mondo ed è riuscito in un'impresa che non gli è affatto nuova: far parlare di sé. Ci racconta anche una storia, LA STORIA, noi ve la passiamo così com'è, parola di MOSCHINO.

Reproduced from Moda In, no. 56 (August-September 1990).

STOP THE FASHION SYSTEM!

LA STORIA

Come tutte le altre volte,
la temibile "Moda", avvolta nei Suoi lussuosi e lugubri veli,
pettinata ed ingioiellata come sempre,
esercitava le Sue "Vittime"
con noiose lezioni di portamento e comportamento;
prima l'una poi l'altra, prima questa poi quella.
Eleganti, fredde e sicure nelle loro uniformi,
scivolavano silenziose sui tappeti dell' "Atelier",
mentre una musica viziosa, sottolineava le loro false movenze...
Ma all'improvviso, degli allegri folletti,
giocando con una nuvola bianca,
come per incanto facevano sparire la Moda e le Sue Vittime...
Il giorno dopo, all'alba,
il mondo era tutto pieno di folletti che pigri si stiracchiavano sbadigliando
e con gioia cominciavano la loro danza,
lentamente accennando a vestirsi,
scegliendo con innocente spontaneità i loro abiti,
solo quelli che volevano loro, solo quelli che amavano.
Per dire proprio la verità,
c'era una grandissima confusione ed alcuni stavano proprio male,
ma erano tutti così contenti...!
Tutti sembravano, finalmente, essere felici di travestirsi e di scherzare,
come sarebbe bello fare ogni mattina.
Venne indetta quindi una grande festa per celebrare questo giorno di libertà
e cominciò subito una grandissima parata di bandiere,
che sventolavano con i loro bellissimi colori.
La Moda non c'é più,
sono rimasti solo la gente ed i vestiti!

Moschino

mented ones) easily. To find examples of this one only has to think about groups that have provided identities to urban youth: "punks," "mods," or "hippies."[14]

Certain outfits, instead of maintaining and reassuring the notion of "wholeness," come together out of different quotations and thus constitute a fragmented text without a preestablished message to communicate. But the idea that one can create a "personal style" is also overdetermined by the corporate fashion designers (note the popularity of the "Units" stores in many exclusive shopping malls in the United States). This kind of text could be related to the Derridean notion of *renvoi* from one signifier to another, thus to the notion of *différance*.

Alternatively, an outfit may not be considered appropriate to the situation, that is, it may not "fit." For instance, it is interesting to observe that the English verb "suit" means "to meet the needs or wishes of, to be convenient for, or also to fit in with." The French word *complet* is clearly related to the idea of wholeness. The very name and its function seem to meet here on the plane of representation. Apparently a "suit" suggests the notion of a certain integrity or wholeness and "plenitude" that may or may not exist, a plenitude that may "mask" a fragmented self.

Quotation, employed in a theatrical and playful manner, also belongs to what one can call the "feminine side" of fashion. This "feminine side" suggests both the tendency to shift identity and gender with a shift in color or pattern, and the coexistence of more than one identity (multiple colors, multiple patterns) at the same time, in the same text. This has led to one of the images mentioned previously: the "androgynous figure."

In sum, there are two distinct tendencies: one suggesting that subjects follow the rules of fashion, and another maintaining that subjects must distance themselves from such rules. The latter element constitutes that which, within any given text, escapes its own rules or any tidy ordering principle. It escapes what Barthes has called *"le sens obvie"* and it overthrows the entropy of imagination and creativity to which the clash of images leads in the society of the spectacle.

Barthes, in the essay "L'Obvie et L'Obtus," offers the critic important theoretical insights for the understanding of fashion. Here he distinguishes the "obvious meaning" of a sign (which responds to the logic of communication or the "simple" act of decoding a message) from its "obtuse meaning." Barthes recovers the mathematical reference of the word "obtuse," which, in his own view, exceeds the "commonsense" or canonical definition of the word. It is something that is not comprehensible (from the Latin *cumprehendere*—to contain), and consequently it does not conform to the rules of a preestablished symbolic order. In this way he also shows that there is an obvious meaning and an "obtuse" in the word itself, and in its use. Barthes relates the obtuse meaning to the notion of *sens supplementaire*, which gives an imaginative openness to the text, and to the notion of sign. Consequently, we can appropriate the *sens supplementaire* within the concept of fashion as *factio* and not as *mode*, and this projects an "openness" for that concept. In this way, fashion as *factio* serves to undermine fashion texts, and can recover Bakhtin's notion of carnivalization. Thus, it may help free the subject from the constraints (the "comprehension") of rules, and perhaps from the tyranny of the fashion system.

The Barthesian view offered here suggests another perspective that needs to be explored in further studies, not only in mass culture but in literary criticism as well. Images as language do not merely reflect the world like a passive mirror; they represent it, or in some cases they "say" or express the very moment of collision between different dimensions. Between language and images a fluctuating passage is established, a passage that creates the textual space the critic is involved in reading.

Reading fashion as a text commits the critic to an activity that is different from mere interpretation, such as decoding a message. The latter suggests an attitude of mere explanation or description which implies that a preestablished truth exists. The critic should not simply discover these presumed hidden truths: the critic must employ critical perspectives that recreate the text. The act of reading in this perspective is not a passive one and it is not so distant from writing or creating a text. In this way a subtle interplay is established between the two acts of reading and writing. In approaching a text one must question the very tools used as mechanisms of transformation. An ultimate interpretation does not exist, since, as noted in the present essay, the fashion text constitutes an example of the mobility of the text itself, and therefore is an example of multiple interpretations.

Fashion criticism in the society of spectacle and information is a theoretical device with its threads, holes, and even trends. Yet in it one can read the changes and multiplicity of a reality with its ghosts, "replicants," androids, and knights, whose silk-armor passes through the urban desert searching for a way to tailor the future.

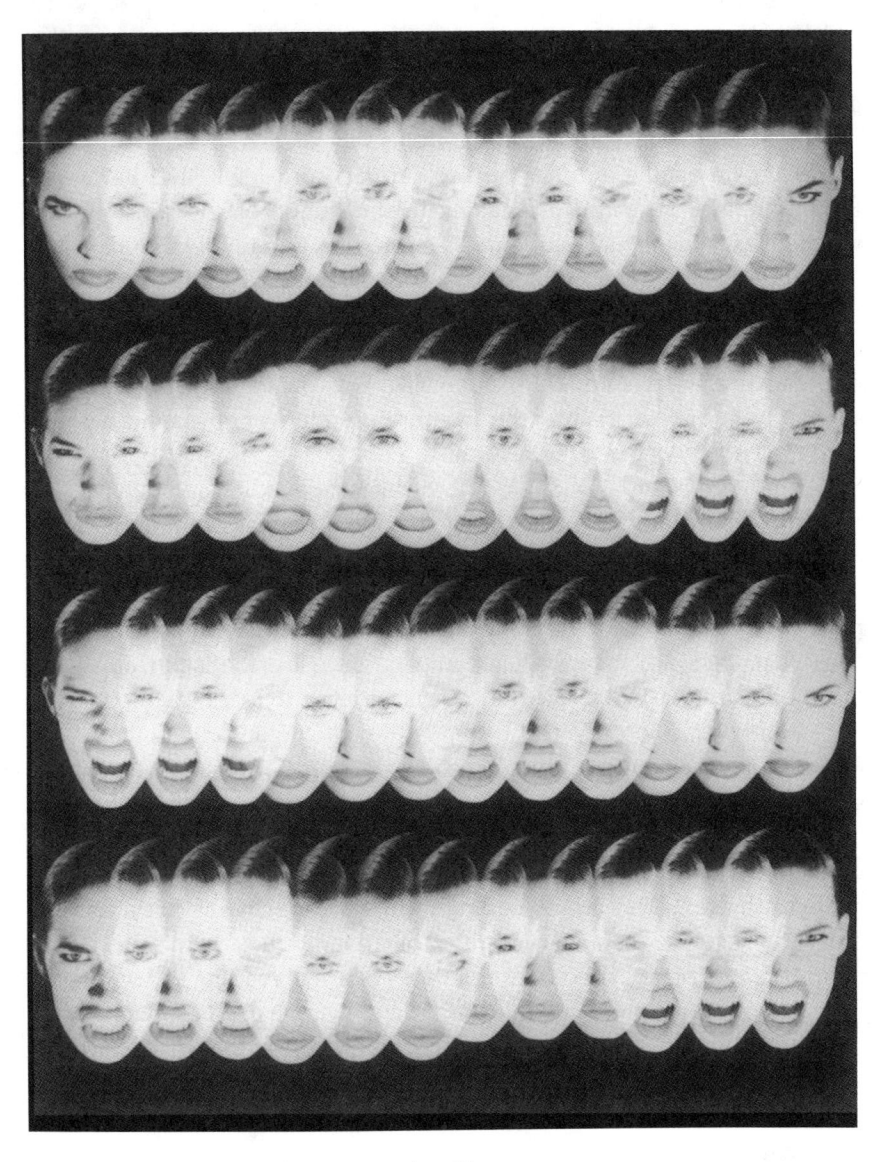

Photograph by Stephane Sednaoui. Reproduced by permission.

Fashion as a Text

Notes 187

I thank Michelle Stein from Moda & Co. for permission to use the Moschino advertisements reproduced in this essay and Stephane Sednaoui for permission to reproduce the photograph that precedes the Notes.

1. In the present essay, I consider the Italian cultural and political landscape, where the structures of feminism differ from those belonging to Anglo-American culture. I bring into my discussion, however, examples belonging to contemporary American culture. The way I discuss certain aspects of my own culture has been affected by my experience of working, teaching, and living in the United States. To what extent the perception of my "italianitá" has changed in the meanwhile is difficult to state and measure. It is very important for me that the two different languages and cultures are continuously involved in a dynamic relationship that generates a diverse openness in the awareness of the words and images I employ to describe and depict Italian phenomena. My discussion, here, will focus especially on the period between the late 1970s and the 1980s to which my generation is closest.

2. See Ugo Volli's study *Contro la moda*, 24.

3. Street fashion certainly deserves a deeper discussion than I can give in this essay. Cities with their different flavors set the scene for this very interesting performance. I have found more daring and transgressive looks in a theater such as the New York City streets than in Italian cities such as Rome or Milan, for example. Perhaps this could be a topic to be developed and analyzed in a future essay. An important source is Walter Benjamin, *Das Passagen-Werk*, published in Italy under the title *Parigi, capitale del XIX secolo*, in which the figure of the *flâneur* is taken into consideration. There is also an essay by Anne Friedberg, "Les Flâneurs du Mal(l): Cinema and the Postmodern Condition," an accurate contribution to the analysis of the topic, which considers the American cultural landscape, especially the malls to which the title of the article ironically alludes.

4. I have simplified my discussion here a little. For a problematization of this discourse see Diane Fuss, "Fashion and the Homospectatorial Look," 713–37.

5. It is interesting to note that Italian weekly magazines such as *Panorama* and *L'Espresso* have almost all males with sexy bodies advertising jeans, perfumes, shoes, clothing, and so on. Women have essentially disappeared in the advertisements in this kind of magazine, but they appear with half-naked bodies on the covers.

6. Camille Paglia avoids the problematization of feminism or, in my opinion, avoids oversimplifying its discourse with relation to sexuality when she affirms in her article on Madonna, "Through her enormous impact on young women around the world, Madonna is the future of feminism," ("Madonna I: Animality and Artifice," in *Sex, Art, and American Culture*, 5). If our future is to respond to and fit the logic of the society of the spectacle, I think Paglia is certainly right.

7. See Frank Rich, "The New Blood Culture—Fantasizing sex and death, America sees its enemy: AIDS. Enter Dracula." *New York Times*, December 6, 1992. The author makes very interesting remarks regarding the film and America's cultural-political landscape: "AIDS, after all, actually does to the bloodstream what Communists and other radicals were once only rumored to do to the nation's water supply. Its undiminished threat has made the connection between sex and death, an eternal nexus of high culture, into a pop fixation, finally filtering down to the vocabulary of commercial images."

8. Armani's most distinctive act was to present a very androgynous woman. His collections celebrated the figure of a woman with clothing and suits that used a male tailor-cut. In the last few years he has modified these aspects, conferring a more "feminine" softness on his collections. Nevertheless, he is still completely different from fashion designers like Fendi, Biagiotti, and Ungaro, who stress the "feminine." It was interesting to note last summer, in an open-air fashion show in Rome in the suggestive Piazza di Spagna, where the stairs became

Eugenia Paulicelli

an unusual *passarella*, that among the various fashion designers' collections for fall-winter 1990–91, Armani's was still recognizable for its extreme simplicity. His models were very different from all the sugar dolls proposed by the other fashion designers for the occasion.

9. One of the fashion suggestions for the 1990s I have found in *Elle* magazine (February 1991) was to be a "Barbie," because "she's always known exactly what to wear." In spring 1991, fashion magazines were showing a strong tendency, in many collections, to revisit the 1960s—in makeup, clothing, accessories, and hair.

10. During the 1968 marches and protests in the Italian cities, some leftist groups were referred to as "Eskimos" because of the winter-green hooded coats they "uniformly" wore.

11. See in this volume the essays by Giovanna Miceli Jeffries and Renate Holub.

12. There are many examples of this; for instance, the ads of Dolce e Gabbana, two other Italian designers, which present scenes inside cafes, or at parties, or other "vernacular" sites.

13. In English the Italian word *storia* means both "story" and "history."

14. Here I am simplifying in giving these examples regarding these groups, which now have and have had, of course, very different natures and roles in the urban and political scene.

Works Cited

Barthes, Roland. *Mythologies*. Paris: Editions du Seuil, 1957.
———. *Eléments de Semiologie*. Paris: Editions du Seuil, 1964.
———. *Système de la Mode*. Paris: Editions du Seuil, 1967.
———. *L'Empire de Signes*. Geneva: Skira, 1970.
———. "L'Obvie et L'obtus." In *L'Obvie et L'Obtus: Essais Critique* III. Paris: Editions du Seuil, 1982.
———. "Le message photographique." In *L'Obvie et L'Obtus*, 1982.
———. *Le Texte et L'Image*. Catalogue, exposition organisée par la Ville de Paris, Pavillon des Arts. May 7– Aug. 3, 1986.
Benjamin, Walter. *Parigi, capitale del XIX secolo*. Turin: Einaudi, 1989.
Burgelin, O. *Moda*. Turin: Enciclopedia Einaudi, 1981.
———. *Abbigliamento*. Turin: Enciclopedia Einaudi, 1981.
Calefato, Patrizia. *Il corpo rivestito*. Bari: Edizioni dal Sud, 1986.
Chambers, Ian. *Urban Rhythms: Pop Music and Popular Culture*. New York: St. Martin's Press, 1985.
Chambers, Ian, and Paolo Prato, eds. *Cultural Studies* 2. 2 (May 1988).
Damisch, Hubert. *Maschera*. Turin: Enciclopedia Einaudi, 1981.
Friedberg, Anne. "Les Flâneurs du Mal(l): Cinema and the Postmodern Condition," PMLA (May 1991).
Fuss, Diane. "Fashion and the Homospectatorial Look." *Critical Inquiry* 18 (Summer 1992).
Kidwell-Brush, Claudia, and Valerie Steele, eds. *Men and Women: Dressing the Part*. Washington, D.C.: Smithsonian Institution Press, 1989.
Longo Di Cristofaro, G., *Immagine Donna-Modelli di donna emergenti nei mezzi di comunicazione di massa*. Rome: Istituto Poligrafico e Zecca dello Stato, 1986.
Lydon, Mary. "Skirting the Issue: Mallarmé, Proust, and Symbolism," *Yale French Studies* 74 (1988).
———. "Hats and Cocktails: Simone de Beauvoir's Heady 'Texts.'" In Elaine Marks, ed., *Critical Essays on Simone de Beauvoir*. Boston: G.K. Hall, 1987.
Mitchell, W. J. Thomas. *Iconology: Image, Text, Ideology*. Chicago: University of Chicago Press, 1986.
Nichols, Bill. *Ideology and Image*. Bloomington: Indiana University Press, 1981.
Paglia, Camille. *Sex, Art, and American Culture*. New York: Vintage Books, 1992.
Poe, Edgar Allan. "The Man of the Crowd." In *The Complete Tales of Mystery and Imagination*. London: Octopus Books, 1981.

Rella, Franco. "The Atopy of the Modern." In Giovanna Borradori, ed., *Recoding Metaphysics: The New Italian Philosophy*. Evanston, Ill.: Northwestern University Press, 1988.
Simon, Donatella. *Moda e sociologia*. Milan: Franco Angeli Libri, 1990.
Volli, Ugo. *Contro la moda*. Milan: Feltrinelli, 1988.
Warmock, Mary. "If you stand on your head, your trousers are above your shirt," *The Listener* (March 7, 1985).

Áine O'Healy

Filming Female "Autobiography"
Maraini, Ferreri, and Piera's Own Story

I have always been very attached to family affections. Very attached, to an almost incredible extent . . . even though I knew that this family was completely in pieces. In my imagination I had to try to stick it back together, as if I were the one who could bind up this thing that was about to collapse, break apart.

Piera degli Esposti, Storia di Piera

As a female coming-of-age film, Storia di Piera (1982)—the cinematic adaptation of Piera degli Esposti's autobiographical reminiscences—belongs to an extremely small subgenre in the repertoire of Italian narrative cinema. This critically neglected film is arguably the most provocative coming-of-age narrative to emerge in Italian cinema in the years immediately following the high point of the neofeminist movement. It prompts a complex set of questions on female subjectivity, the cultural construction of femininity, and women's relationship to creativity, maternity, and discourses of the body. Simultaneously, however, the film's narrative structure problematizes the very representability of the "female story."

Storia di Piera was directed by Marco Ferreri, a controversial outsider among Italian filmmakers, and was based on a script written by Dacia Maraini, Piera degli Esposti, and Ferreri himself. According to the credits in the film's opening sequence, Storia di Piera is adapted from a novel by Piera degli Esposti and Dacia Maraini. This is a rather surprising claim, since the text upon which the film is actually based—a 136-page volume of the same title published by Bompiani in 1980—is not a novel, but the transcript of a conversation between degli Esposti and her friend Maraini, in which degli

Esposti, who was already one of the best-known dramatic actresses in Italian theater, reveals intimate details of her family history in response to Maraini's probing questions. Despite degli Esposti's potential as a "star" presence, the text bears little resemblance to the conventions of celebrity journalism.[1] The actress's often painful reminiscences are interwoven with and frequently interrupted by Maraini's own memories and challenging insights, giving the text a dialectical quality that brings it closer to the discursive practices of feminist encounter groups (*gruppi di autocoscienza*) than to popular journalism or traditional autobiography.

Marco Ferreri's interest in directing a cinematic adaptation of *Storia di Piera* is linked to his ongoing fascination with the bankruptcy of conventional gender arrangements in society. The destructiveness of the heterosexual couple and the problematic influences on early childhood experience within the family system are themes that have appeared repeatedly throughout his work during the past several years. In his other films, however, male subjectivity usually dominates the diegetic exploration of gender issues, and a misogynist bias is often explicit.[2] Although Ferreri's *Storia di Piera* represents many of the events originally described in degli Esposti's dialogue with Maraini and is focalized through the female protagonist's sensibility, it manifests at least as much intertextual resonance with the director's own previous work as with the volume upon which the film is based. Ferreri's distinctive style is so dominant, his thematic preoccupations so recognizable and pervasive, that the issue of enunciation is immediately raised. Whose story is the film version of *Storia di Piera*?

The purpose of my essay is to explore the cluster of issues that emerge in attempting to answer this question. First, I will briefly examine the dialogue between Maraini and degli Esposti, noting convergences with some contemporary discourses within Italian feminism. I will then analyze the adaptation of degli Esposti's memories into a cinematic narrative, taking into account the theoretical writing on the patriarchal bias of narrative structure. As several feminist theorists have pointed out, narrative structure generally functions to reinforce the Oedipal scenario. In her influential essay "Desire in Narrative," Teresa de Lauretis tells how, in traditional narratives, women appear as obstacles that delay the male quest, or as markers of the boundaries through which the hero and his story pass on their way to a destination and the accomplishment of meaning. A simple reversal of the terms of narrative (where the hero is replaced by a heroine) is not enough to subvert this underlying ideological agenda, and usually provides a disguised variation of the same scheme. I am interested in discovering to what extent the film version of *Storia di Piera* could be described as a regressive Oedipal text following the traditional pattern of narrative development, and to what extent this pattern is thrown into disarray by elements that are at least in part a residue of the text upon which the film is purportedly based.

According to the preface to the 1980 volume, Maraini contacted degli Esposti sometime in the late 1970s to discuss the possibility of collaborating on the creation of a project for the stage based on degli Esposti's experiences. The writer recorded their initial conversations on tape as a substitute for note-taking. Eventually, however, Maraini abandoned the idea of writing a stage play and decided to publish their recorded dialogue exactly as transcribed, without editorial reworking or embellishments. The fact that *Storia di Piera* was published by Bompiani, a major commercial publishing house, without changes or revisions (and hence without any overt literary aspirations) is testimony not only to Maraini's position as a well-established though still controversial writer but also to the growing interest in women's issues on the part of the Italian reading public as a direct result of the women's movement.

Personal recollection was originally an integral part of the feminist practice of consciousness raising that came into being in North America in the late 1960s and subsequently became widespread throughout Western Europe. In Italy, women's consciousness-raising groups were often formed spontaneously on the margins of the male-dominated parties and splinter groups of the left in response to what was perceived as a lack of consideration or comprehension of the particular circumstances of women's experience. These groups were generally known as *gruppi di autocoscienza* (self-awareness groups), emphasizing the process of self-awareness and discovery that characterized encounters among women committed to solidarity and self-empowerment, and ultimately to effective political action. In her history of Italian feminist discourses, Luisa Passerini notes that in the early 1970s women's encounter groups were polarized into two different emphases. While some groups stressed an immediate and direct commitment to political activism, others placed greater emphasis on the necessity of self-discovery through *la pratica dell'inconscio*, the process of self-analysis conducted in dialogue with other women. The dialogue recorded in *Storia di Piera* resonates with some of the preoccupations of this particular feminist practice. Although the encounter between Maraini and degli Esposti did not take place within the context of an organized group, it is clearly the product of a specific historical moment—a moment that had perhaps

Filming Female "Autobiography"

already passed by the time the dialogue was adapted to the screen—and is linked intertextually to the discourses of Italian feminism in the late 1970s.[3]

The dialogue between degli Esposti and Maraini begins with the invocation of Piera's mother, Eugenia degli Esposti,[4] whose photograph is shown to Maraini in the initial moments of the conversation, but which the reader never sees. Later in the text, however, Piera makes much of her mother's dark Mediterranean coloring, and of her envious admiration of Eugenia's plump, voluptuous body, which she describes as a total contrast to her own appearance. The first gesture that Piera recalls as she observes her mother's photograph is "that sharp way she had of dragging me by the hand, without affection, like when she pulled my braids" (11). This powerful figure is repeatedly invoked throughout the text, alternately resented and admired, and is linked to recurring discussions of maternity, sexuality, and the body.

Storia di Piera presents a vivid picture of an eccentric family environment, dominated by Piera's energetic and sexually promiscuous mother. Piera's father, Lorenzo degli Esposti—an anti-Fascist activist and later a prominent labor union leader—emerges as a weak but sympathetic figure, affectionately indulgent toward his children, and vaguely tolerant of his wife's infidelities. Although Piera's love for her father is passionate and unquestioning, her feelings for her mother are of a much more complex kind. Eugenia is constructed in her daughter's account as a figure of ambivalent longing, resentment, and loss. The complex, apparently painful interaction between the two is typical of the difficulties of mother-daughter relationships in patriarchal society, as theorized in recent feminist writing.[5] Much of the tension between Piera and her mother is articulated around the role of motherhood as it is socially defined. It is clear that Eugenia herself is ill at ease within this role. Piera complains of the fact that her mother never treated her in a maternal way, but always addressed her as though she were a grown-up, an equal. Another crucial symptom of Eugenia's discomfort with maternal identity is seen in her obsessive terror of pregnancy and her transmission of that fear to her daughter while still a child.

Piera explicitly links her own unwillingness to bear children to this maternally induced obsession, thus indirectly attributing to Eugenia's influence the decision to terminate her nine pregnancies. The fact that abortion is discussed so openly in Storia di Piera is not surprising, since the autonomy of the female body was at the forefront of feminist concern in Italy throughout the 1970s and had led to the implementation of a very liberal abortion law in 1978.[6] What is remarkable in degli Esposti's comments on abortion, however, is her ambivalent, paradoxical feelings about pregnancy itself. She tells of how she repeatedly enjoyed being pregnant, of how this pleasure enabled her to continue with her pregnancies for many weeks, until eventually both her fear of childbirth and her conviction that she could only "give birth to [her]self" motivated her to seek abortion (64). Degli Esposti's disclosures are commented on sympathetically and unjudgmentally by Maraini, who briefly relates her own experience of abortion at a time when this practice was still illegal and dangerous in Italy.

The most extraordinary aspect of Piera degli Esposti's account of her abortions is her suggestion of a link between these abortions and her bouts of life-threatening pulmonary illness. Emphasizing that she had nine of each, she seems to imply that her illnesses, which entailed hospitalizations, operations, and other painful treatments, were somehow psychologically if not physiologically connected to her abortions (65). This implication remains unchallenged by Maraini, who listens empathetically to Piera's long discussion of her illnesses, which were further complicated by incorrect diagnoses and damaging interventions by a series of patronizing or patently inefficient male doctors. Later, Maraini asks Piera why she saw herself as bringing these illnesses upon herself. Degli Esposti's response reinforces the earlier implication that her health problems constituted a form of hysterical symptom, and again she invokes the figure of Eugenia: "Perhaps to punish myself for not being able to save my father from a cruel end, or for having imitated my mother, for having grown up sexually precocious" (85).

The notion of sexual guilt emerges explicitly in Piera degli Esposti's memory, despite her extremely open, unconventional upbringing. Eugenia's pursuit of pleasure and sexual gratification, her total lack of interest in traditional notions of appropriate social behavior, allowed her daughter an extraordinary amount of personal freedom while at the same time causing her confusion and fear, emotions that seem to have led her away from her mother and into a closer alliance with her father. Piera recounts early sexual experiences with male acquaintances of her family, sometimes with her mother's knowledge and complicity. Again, her emotional response to these situations, and particularly to her mother's involvement, remains ambiguous. What emerges with increasing clarity is Piera's strong attachment to Eugenia, a powerful mixture of love, resentment, and protectiveness. "My mother is terrible, and I felt this . . . but I loved her a lot . . . sometimes I hated her, but I desired her so much, I was in love with her" (109).

Piera tells of her mother's manic-depressive cycles, which led to repeated hospitalizations and electroshock treatments. She concedes, however, that she never believed that her mother was really ill, or that her numerous erotic involvements with men and women were merely the symptom of a psychiatric imbalance. Maraini suggests that the mother's electroshock treatments were motivated at least in part by the community's desire to punish a woman whose sexuality refused to be contained within patriarchal limits, and Piera agrees with this insight, adding that Eugenia was widely perceived as a morally dangerous woman (109).

Paradoxically, the experience of growing up with such an iconoclastic female role model seems to have alienated Piera from her own body, heightening her dependency on relationships with men as a way of discovering and asserting her physicality: "I have no relationship with, or no awareness of my body. For this reason I look for my own body in the bodies of men" (126). But for all the blame that is laid at the mother's door, Piera identifies the source of her own dramatic talent in the fact that she had watched her mother survive indignity and brutal medical treatments with her spirit intact. Eugenia had thus provided her with a model for interpreting the great female roles in classical theater (113). According to Piera, her mother had always possessed a certain tragic nobility: "There are few really tragic people who live through terrible things, without a moment of mediocrity or meanness; I understood that my mother was a tragic figure" (15).

In discussing the development of her skills as an actress, degli Esposti openly admits the difficulty of relating to most available female roles: "Female characters are all born of male authors. . . . There is nothing feminine in the theater, there is nothing on the stage that reflects just the way I am as a woman" (113–14). Yet she admits spending a great amount of time trying to fill out a role, trying to infuse it with some meaning and depth rising out of her intuitive experience as a woman. She also describes the difficulties and rejections that she as a self-taught woman had experienced from theatrical institutions when she first attempted to train as an actress. Obviously, these difficulties were long resolved by the time the conversation with Maraini took place, since the Piera degli Esposti whose name appears on the cover of *Storia di Piera* as author and subject was already an established star. The dialogue does not reveal how she accomplished her success within such an entrenched patriarchal institution, or what compromises with male power she was obliged to reach along the way.

Central to Piera's world is the passionately affectionate memory of her now dead father, and of her longstanding desire to "mother" him by protecting him from the powerful presence of Eugenia. Her seductive feelings toward her father during childhood, as well as her resentment and jealousy of his love for Eugenia, are articulated in a manner that appears to correspond with the classical Freudian understanding of the feminine. Yet, as the description of Piera's complicated and deeply felt attachment to her mother testifies, her love for Eugenia was never completely eclipsed by her desire for her father. Rather, she appears to live out the conflicting impulses experienced by a female subject constituted within a patriarchal system by means of an ongoing self-criticism. Her search for a psychosomatic explanation for her recurrent illnesses implies the belief that her body bears the burden of expressing this conflict in a powerful, self-destructive way.

It is hardly surprising that Piera's early feelings about her female identity reveal some ambivalence. She tells Maraini of her childhood wish to be male, to be more like her brother, possessing power "and whatever else his male organ symbolized—freedom perhaps . . ." (40). In the present, however, she sees herself as an androgynous type, a warrior and survivor. In a rather extraordinary sequence, she fantasizes about possessing a penis, but simultaneously feminizes its shape, turning it into something resembling an Easter egg, like the kind of round female breast that appeals to her most (40–41). Her fantasy of appropriating phallic power is tempered by the desire to feminize and domesticate its attributes.

In discussing her own childhood development, Maraini, like degli Esposti, describes a strong attachment to her father and the temporary emotional rejection of her mother. Nevertheless she explicitly criticizes the patriarchal bias of the Oedipus myth, thus rejecting the Oedipus complex as a useful model to describe female sexual development (54). She also rejects the Electra myth as an adequate psychoanalytical model since it similarly fails to resonate with the memories of her own childhood experience. Both women claim to have grown more compassionate and empathetic toward their mothers as they became women themselves, suggesting an eventual, conscious transcendence of internalized patriarchal prejudice toward the mother.[7]

One of the most provocative aspects of *Storia di Piera* is its elliptical and often contradictory quality. Ambivalent themes and unfinished narrative threads remain open and undecided at the dialogue's conclusion. Yet the fact that the persona of Piera degli Esposti, a successful, nationally recognized celebrity, presides over this account as the enunciating subject guarantees some implicit sense of narrative unity and closure.

Filming Female "Autobiography"

In presenting itself as the adaptation of a novel, the film version of *Storia di Piera* deliberately disavows its biographical inspiration, simultaneously suggesting that the character upon which its protagonist is based is an entirely fictional creation. The film's straightforward chronological structure (similar to that of a bildungsroman) smooths out the abrupt leaps back and forth in time that characterize degli Esposti's account, and eliminates the explicit discussion of feminist issues that punctuated the flow of memory in the earlier text. Thus the voice of the "real" adult Piera is absent from the film as enunciating subject, as is also the voice of her sisterly interlocutor, Dacia Maraini, whose contribution provided a dynamic counterpoint in the orchestration of the original text. Partly because of these crucial strategic choices, the film's diegetic development reveals an ambivalent combination of feminist insight and regressive, patriarchal articulations of the feminine.

The film is focalized from Piera's point of view,[8] and is limited to two periods of her life—early adolescence in the first half of the film (where Piera is played by Bettina Gruhn), and early adult life in the second half (where Gruhn is replaced by Isabelle Huppert). The opening sequence—which is entirely the director's invention—stands independent of this scheme, however, and functions as a prologue to the main body of the narrative. This brief opening scene merits special attention, since it distorts the historical context of Piera degli Esposti's birth and raises several important thematic issues.

The film begins in a provincial piazza moments before Piera's birth. The first human figure to emerge into view is an American G.I., seen in the extreme distance. The first words heard in the film are addressed by this anonymous American soldier to a woman standing on the terrace of the apartment where Piera's mother is in labor: "Goodbye, Centomila Lire! Tanti baci a tutti. I'll write when I get back to my country!" The American soldier is never mentioned again throughout the remainder of the film. His presence in the background at the moment of Piera's birth is a deliberate departure from biographical accuracy, since Piera degli Esposti's interview with Dacia Maraini makes clear that she was born years before the Allied landings in Italy. The introduction of the soldier into the film's opening scene immediately achieves several important effects. First, the soldier's greeting to the woman on the balcony, half in Italian and half in English, raises the issue of what Althusser has called *interpellation*, the invocation of an individual as a subject (173). The playful nickname "Centomila Lire" (the only name by which this character is known throughout the film) suggests a price tag, implicitly alluding to what feminist theorists have described as "the traffic in women" (Rubin), a concept that informs traditional patriarchal understandings of the feminine. The American soldier's interpellation of the woman on the terrace is followed moments later by Eugenia's invocation of her newborn baby as "Piera, la mia cocca!" while the other women present comment on the baby's beauty and femininity. The infant is thus immediately incorporated into the ideology of the gender system.

The presence of the soldier in the film's initial scene also obliquely raises the question of Piera's paternity, since no other men are seen or mentioned in the course of the birth sequence. This issue achieves resolution in the next episode, set a dozen years later, when we meet Lorenzo (Marcello Mastroianni), who is apparently the father of the adolescent protagonist. Yet the initial doubt has lingering effect on the film's hermeneutic, where the issue of masculine authority and power is constantly called into question.

The distant figure of the American takes on additional significance in the light of Ferreri's decision to cast Hanna Schygulla in the crucial role of Piera's mother. The presence of the German actress—whose blond northern looks offer a clear contrast to the description of Piera degli Esposti's mother in the published dialogue—is juxtaposed in the opening moments of *Storia di Piera* with the image of the American soldier, creating a powerful intertextual link with the actress's role in Rainer Werner Fassbinder's *The Marriage of Maria Braun* (1978), where Schygulla functioned as an emblem of the problematic postwar alliance between Germany and the United States.[9] As the result of this initial juxtaposition, Hanna Schygulla's presence throughout the remainder of *Storia di Piera* suggests a link between the surface articulation of a domestic drama and the film's largely suppressed historical discourse.

Though Piera is ostensibly the protagonist of the narrative, it is Eugenia who visually dominates at least the first half of the film. This mother-daughter relationship is one of the most complex ever presented in Italian cinema. On the most obvious and accessible level, the film's treatment of the mother-daughter bond offers a fascinating commentary on the function of mimesis in the cultural construction of femininity. Piera learns to be a little woman by watching her mother. Bettina Gruhn, who plays the role of the adolescent Piera, has the undeveloped body of a child, but she is outfitted from the start in odd, womanly clothes—furs, cheap jewelry, and high-heeled sandals—in imitation of her mother's flamboyant and seductive

Filming Female "Autobiography"

mode of dress. By watching Eugenia, the twelve-year-old girl also learns other womanly techniques, such as the art of kissing. In an early scene, Piera emerges in a lace slip and kimono, ready to adjudicate a kissing contest that she organizes for adolescent boys on the terrace of the family apartment. It becomes clear in these episodes that Piera is attempting to construct her feminine identity by adopting the masquerade of womanhood, a skill that is learned by copying—within self-imposed limits—the mother she both despises and adores.

Even as she imitates Eugenia, Piera is obviously ambivalent toward her mother's erotic adventures. While she takes obvious delight in flirting with one of Eugenia's lovers, a local baker, the twelve-year-old Piera voluntarily takes on the task of curtailing her mother's habit of wandering through the streets on a bicycle in pursuit of chance encounters. The daughter thus assumes a pseudo-parental role vis-à-vis her mother, chiding her for her transgressions and insisting that she return home. In her attempts to control Eugenia's sexual adventures, the adolescent Piera takes a stronger position than her father, Lorenzo, who in most instances does not protest against his wife's infidelities. This aspect of Piera's behavior leads to her collusion with the medical discourse, which succeeds in pathologizing Eugenia's sexuality and ultimately in constraining her freedom. Eugenia responds to her young daughter's understanding of home and family with obvious contempt ("Home, what a fantasy!"), and expresses disappointment with Piera's internalization of dominant patriarchal norms of decency ("How moralistic my daughter is!"). In revenge, she mockingly threatens to blind Piera. This startling gesture evokes the blinding of Oedipus in the classical myth, and prepares the spectator for many scenes of triangular jealousy between Eugenia, Piera, and Lorenzo.

Oedipal issues—explicit but not dominant in the autobiographical account upon which the film was based—achieve an overwhelming prominence within the film's narrative economy. It is not only the daughter who vies with her mother for the father's love; Eugenia herself is driven to a jealous rage by the knowledge of Piera's affectionate collusion with Lorenzo. The first scene of triangular jealousy is played out in the public square in the course of a workers' demonstration. Discovering Piera involved in a private conversation with her father, Eugenia angrily accuses them of sexual intimacy. As the exchange escalates, it assumes an exaggerated, theatrical quality, suggesting a scenario that the three participants are driven to replay, without much reflection or conviction. (In fact, Eugenia's rage is instantly transformed into gentle solicitude when Lorenzo turns his attention to the violence of the labor dispute.) It is precisely this depiction of Oedipal jealousy as a learned performance that gives Ferreri's treatment of the family romance a subversive, self-reflexive edge.

In many respects, however, the film's articulation of the tensions between Piera, Eugenia, and Lorenzo conforms with traditional psychoanalytic accounts of the construction of the female subject, and particularly with the identification of femininity as castration or lack. Furthermore, the difficulty imputed by Lacan to the entry of the female subject into the symbolic order is represented in the fact that both Piera and Eugenia seem grounded primarily in the imaginary or prelinguistic stage of development, relying largely on visual or tactile communication.[10] In contrast, Lorenzo is explicitly associated with the symbolic, with the world of books, politics, and history.

Though Oedipal competitiveness dominates many of the transactions between mother and daughter, the film also foregrounds the daughter's affectionate, even erotic absorption with Eugenia, suggesting a longing for closeness with the lost, pre-Oedipal maternal body. In their moments of intimacy, Piera and Eugenia do not communicate with words, but nuzzle each other while uttering playful, growling noises, similar to animal sounds. The episode where Piera, suddenly stricken by an unnamed illness, begins a sexual relationship with another woman provides a further clue to her suppressed erotic yearning for Eugenia. This brief lesbian relationship (initiated at the moment when Piera begins to nurse frantically at her friend's breast) is imaged specifically as a recuperation of the nurturing, pre-Oedipal mother. It functions as a rite of passage, empowering the protagonist to recover from her illness and to move ahead in the pursuit of a professional acting career.

Nevertheless, the film emphatically "normalizes" the protagonist's sexuality soon after this lesbian interlude, not only in the scene where Piera abruptly discards her female lover but also in the sequence where she claims to avenge her father's memory by seducing Eugenia's young lover Massimo. The reinscription of heterosexuality and the Oedipal agenda is clearly overdetermined, and receives its most forceful expression in a scene between Piera and the dying Lorenzo, which makes explicit the erotic potential of the relationship between father and daughter. This encounter takes place in a bleak hospital setting where Lorenzo has been confined because of his deteriorating health. Piera, who has by now achieved celebrity as an actress, is hailed by her father as his "masterpiece" (*capolavoro*), echoing his interpellation from an earlier scene in the film and reinstating his claim as Piera's master and creator. Later, in the hospital yard, Lorenzo begs his daughter to let him see her thighs. After a moment's hesitation, she obliges, removing her trousers. He looks, and then remarks sadly: "Eugenia's were more beautiful." In a spontaneous gesture of jealous rage, Piera then exposes her genitals, angrily demanding: "Is hers any better?" The gesture, shown in medium closeup, vividly inscribes the sight of female "castration," usually concealed and disavowed in cinematic representation, into the film's articulation of the Oedipal agenda. Lorenzo's reply to Piera's question, however, immediately juxtaposes female "lack" with the complementary specter of male castration: "I could never satisfy her. . . . I would make love to her for hours, but she was never satisfied."

The film's insistence on the theme of castration is one of the most noteworthy modifications of the treatment of Oedipal issues in the original autobiographical text. Lorenzo's admission to Piera of his sexual inadequacy and its source (i.e., the "voracious" Eugenia) echoes a confession made in an earlier scene in the film: "The 'Bandiera rossa' [the Communist Party] has forced me to retire, and Eugenia is taking my life away from me." Shortly after Lorenzo's death, Eugenia's culpability is implicitly invoked in Piera's terse "explanation" of Lorenzo's demise: "My father died for love." Displaced onto the castrated and castrating figure of Eugenia is the responsibility for all the father's failures—from his decline as a leftist labor leader to his premature death. Though the father is seen as a sad, weak figure, his presence within the film's narrative economy is accorded a definite tragic dignity. Lorenzo's sexual inadequacy is associated metonymically with the decline of the Italian intellectual left (suggested on the soundtrack with the recurrent refrain from the popular Communist song "Bandiera rossa"). This connection is particularly interesting in the light of the American associations that have, in contrast, attached themselves to the desiring, "consuming" figure of Eugenia (set in motion by the presence of the G.I. in the opening scene, and reinforced in scenes where Eugenia is seen dressing up in garish, cast-off American wigs and clothing, while on the soundtrack "American" music is repeatedly heard). Piera's Oedipal trajectory is thus implicitly linked to the discourse of European history in the postwar decades, especially Italy's entry into consumerism and international capitalism.

The film's ambivalent articulation of Oedipal themes is played out on many different levels. Visually, the narrative vacillates between assertion and disavowal of female power. Piera, as protagonist, is frequently inscribed at the source of the camera's subjective gaze, departing from the model of dominant cinema practice in Italy and elsewhere, where male characters usually mediate the relay of looks between the characters on the screen and the viewers in the cinema audience.[11] Since Piera is largely in control of the gaze, her subjectivity complicates the construction of the other characters in the film, especially the figure of her mother, Eugenia. In a number of instances, Piera's gaze romanticizes her mother's thirst for sexual freedom. As Eugenia rides around the town square on her bicycle, her skirts billowing behind her and the sunlight in her hair, her movement is associated visually with the flight of birds. On another occasion, during Piera's voyeuristic contemplation of her mother's erotic activity, Eugenia's *jouissance* is linked to the pounding of the ocean waves. Nevertheless, the scenes that romanticize Eugenia's libidinal energy alternate ineluctably with episodes depicting her humiliation and punishment. Thus we see her struck by her husband, kicked by her lover, hospitalized against her will, submitted to electroshock treatment, and finally locked up in solitary isolation where her hair is shorn almost to the scalp. Since all of these incidents are mediated through the gaze of the daughter, Piera's look is often aligned sadistically with the punishing agency of patriarchal institutions. The daughter's voyeurism seems to place her in a position of control, a control that is acknowledged within the narrative when the psychiatrist gives the twelve-year-old Piera a whistle, and entrusts her with the task of tracking down her mother and bringing her in for hospitalization. Nevertheless, within the same narrative sequence, Piera's voyeurism is also punished when the same psychiatrist forces her to witness Eugenia's electroshock treatment, on the pretext that it will teach the girl a lesson.

The lesson that Piera learns is, of course, central to the direction that her story takes. It is the patriarchal lesson of what femininity ought to be. Piera thus learns to channel her own delight in narcissistic self-display into a form condoned by dominant societal norms, that of a theatrical career. In the film's penultimate sequence we see Piera perform as Medea before an audience of hundreds. The sequence foregrounds Piera's acquisition of adult femininity and the fulfillment of her theatrical ambitions.

Piera's elaborate jewelry, headdress, and makeup in this scene offer a sharp contrast with her more modest appearance throughout the rest of the film. The representation of Piera's maturation as a woman—and of the consolidation of that maturity in an acting career—is thus explicitly linked with masquerade, evoking the Lacanian concept of femininity as a mask construed to disavow nonidentity.[12] Despite her obvious success, Piera is

Filming Female "Autobiography"

still associated with lack, and still excluded from the realm of the symbolic. Her access to discourse is mediated through the classic texts she recites at each performance. Piera's choice of a career in professional acting as it is constructed in the film can be read both as a ritual assumption of the mask of womanliness and as her ultimate transformation into the ornament, the "masterpiece" of her father's heart's desire.[13] Yet despite these signs of complicity with the masculine system of woman, the scene also offers a hint of Piera's nonconformity. Encoded into her performance of Medea—a woman who killed her children to defy patriarchal rule—is a possible allusion to Piera's rejection of the traditional feminine role of motherhood.

It is significant that Piera's fetishization as a performer is juxtaposed with the scene of Eugenia's ultimate disfiguration. In a rather brutal economy of justice, the spectacle of the daughter's success is immediately followed by a scene in which the mother's hair is forcibly cut by a hospital orderly with Piera's full complicity. Some catharsis is provided, however, in the next and final scene, where mother and daughter strip bare on the seashore and embrace at the water's edge. It is with a long shot of this maternal embrace that the film ends. Visually, this is a powerful moment, suggesting a resolution of the women's hostility toward each other and acknowledging the daughter's desire for oneness with the mother, a desire that her social upbringing has trained her to suppress.

This concluding image seems to offer a departure from conventional female coming-of-age stories, where narrative resolution tends to coincide with the heroine's fulfillment within the embrace of heterosexual romance. Yet even as the film's final scene affirms the power of the nurturing connection between the adult protagonist and her mother, it simultaneously undercuts that image with the words spoken on the soundtrack, reminding us that the true hero of Piera's tale cannot be far away. Just as the women begin to embrace, Eugenia tells her daughter that she can feel Lorenzo's presence all around them. Piera replies with the hope that her father is indeed watching, since almost everything that he wanted for her has by now been fulfilled. Piera's words subvert the visual impact of the women's intimacy, by anchoring its intensity to the triangular edifice of the family romance, thus reinscribing the figure of the father not only as transcendental spectator, but as prophet and foreteller of the daughter's own story. Roland Barthes's observation on the nature of narrative pleasure seems particularly pertinent in the light of this concluding scene: "The pleasure of the text is . . . an Oedipal pleasure (to denude, to know, to learn the origin and the end), if it is true that every narrative (every unveiling of the truth) is a staging of the (absent, hidden, or hypostatized) father" (*The Pleasure of the Text*, 10).

The crucial concluding scene is symptomatic of the vacillations and ambiguities that recur throughout Ferreri's restaging of Piera's story. What makes the film compelling, however, is that these ambiguities remain accessible within the film's narrative texture and diegetic development, neither fully suppressed nor fully resolved. While it might be claimed that the film version of *Storia di Piera* offers yet another masculine view of the dark continent of femininity, the film nevertheless draws attention in a highly conspicuous and self-conscious way to its own gaps and its own lack of ultimate authority. In contrast to the generally seamless web of mainstream cinematic narrative in Europe and elsewhere, *Storia di Piera* opens up a welcome space for feminist reflection, simply by leaving the spectator with the knowledge that this story is surely not "the whole story."

Notes

All citations from Italian sources have been translated by the author of this essay.

1. This is not to deny the fact that *Storia di Piera* enjoyed considerable commercial success due to Piera degli Esposti's fame and the frankness of her self-disclosure.

2. *Ciao maschio* (1976) is the most provocative of Ferreri's films in this regard. The film's opening sequence depicts the "rape" of the male protagonist by a group of enraged feminists. For an analysis of Ferreri's work from *L'ultima donna* to *Ciao maschio*, see my 1990 essay, "Gender and Ideology in the Films of Marco Ferreri."

3. Bono and Kemp describe the practice of "autocoscienza" as "a process of the discovery and (re-)construction of the self, both the self of the individual women and a collective sense of self: the search for the subject-woman" (9).

4. Eugenia and Lorenzo degli Esposti, Piera's parents, are not referred to by their first names in the published text, although these names are used frequently in the film version. For the sake of clarity I have decided to use the names throughout this essay.

5. In "Mothers, Displacement, and Language in the Autobiographies of Nathalie Sarraute and Christa Wolf," Bella Brodzki has thus summarized the difficulties of the daughter's position within patriarchy: "To be exiled from the maternal continent is to be forever subjected to the rules of a foreign economy for which one also serves as the medium of exchange" (244). Adriana Cavarero's recent volume *Nonostante Platone* theorizes the exile of daughters from the maternal realm through a feminist rereading of the Demeter myth.

6. According to Birnbaum, "The feminist theme that came to be the most important in the 1970s was 'the right of a woman to her own body is the capstone of her liberation'" (104).

7. Dacia Maraini and Piera degli Esposti both offer contributions to Mori's anthology of essays written by well-known Italian women on their mothers (56–66; 122–31). These essays provide more detailed portraits of the two mothers than the powerful though fragmentary impressions that emerge in *Storia di Piera*.

8. In discussing the film version of *Storia di Piera* I will refer to the film's protagonist as Piera. Obviously, I am referring to the character constructed by the film, as distinct from Piera degli Esposti, enunciating subject in the dialogue with Maraini.

9. For a succinct analysis of the intersection of gender and political ideology in Fassbinder's film, see Haralovich, "The Sexual Politics of *The Marriage of Maria Braun*."

Filming Female "Autobiography"

10. In "The Mirror Stage," Lacan uses the term "imaginary" to describe the pre-Oedipal identification of the infant with its mirror image, an identification guaranteed by the gaze of the mother holding the child in front of the mirror. At this point of development the child has neither gender nor language. The mirror phase initiates the process where the child will eventually acquire gendered subjectivity and a relationship to the symbolic order, that is, the order of language and social processes. Male anatomy has a role in determining female and male access to the symbolic. As in Freudian psychoanalysis, and despite his own claims to the contrary, Lacan makes an anatomically based elision between the phallus and the penis which implies the necessary organization of desire and sexuality. Women, lacking the penis/phallus as the primary signifier, have no access to the Lacanian symbolic, except in relation to men. In recent years, some feminist theorists have been working toward the delineation of a female symbolic order (an impossible concept for Lacan) as a way of theorizing women's access to language. Luisa Muraro's L'*ordine simbolico della madre* is one of the most interesting explorations in this direction to date.

11. Psychoanalysis has enabled feminists to articulate a critique of vision as sexually biased. Within Freud's description of human development it is the act of looking that leads to the infantile discovery of sexual difference and that establishes the penis/phallus as the primary signifier of sexual identity and difference. In 1975, Laura Mulvey's important essay "Visual Pleasure and Narrative Cinema" argued that in classical Hollywood cinema the camera, conceptualized as the instrument of a male character's subjective gaze, controls and limits the spectator's eye to what is fundamentally a male field of vision, thus radically affecting the manner in which female characters are represented on the screen.

12. The notion of femininity as masquerade, first theorized by Joan Riviere, was subsequently elaborated by Jacques Lacan: "Paradoxical as this formulation may seem, I would say that it is in order to be the phallus, that is to say, the signifier of the desire of the Other, that the woman will reject an essential part of her femininity, notably all its attributes through masquerade. It is for what she is not that she expects to be desired as well as loved" (Lacan, 1982, 86).

13. Piera's choice of vocation also brings to mind a remark in Nietzsche's *The Gay Science*: "Reflect on the whole history of women: do they not have to be first of all and above all else actresses. . . . Woman is so artistic" (cited in Heath, 51).

Works Cited

Althusser, Louis. "Ideology and the Ideological State Apparatuses." In *Lenin and Philosophy and Other Essays*. New York: Monthly Review Press, 1971. 127–86.
Barthes, Roland. *The Pleasure of the Text*. Trans. Richard Miller. New York: Hill and Wang, 1975.
Birnbaum, Lucia Chiavola. *Liberazione della donna: Feminism in Italy*. Middletown, Conn.: Wesleyan University Press, 1986.
Bono, Paola, and Sandra Kemp, eds. *Italian Feminist Thought: A Reader*. Oxford: Blackwell, 1991.
Brodzki, Bella. "Mothers, Displacement, and Language in the Autobiographies of Nathalie Sarraute and Christa Wolf." In *Life/Lines: Theorizing Women's Autobiography*, ed. Bella Brodzki and Celeste Schenck. Ithaca: Cornell University Press, 1988. 243–59.
Cavarero, Adriana. *Nonostante Platone: Figure femminili nella filosofia antica*. Rome: Riuniti, 1990.
degli Esposti, Piera, and Dacia Maraini. *Storia di Piera*. Milan: Bompiani, 1980.
de Lauretis, Teresa. "Desire in Narrative." In *Alice Doesn't: Feminism, Semiotics, Cinema*. Bloomington: Indiana University Press, 1984.
Haralovich, Mary Beth. "The Sexual Politics of *The Marriage of Maria Braun*." *Wide Angle* 12.1 (1990): 7–16.
Heath, Stephen. "Joan Riviere and the Masquerade." In *Formations of Fantasy*, ed. Victor Burgin, James Donald, and Cora Kaplan. London and New York: Methuen, 1986. 45–61.

Áine O'Healy

Lacan, Jacques. "The Meaning of the Phallus." In *Feminine Sexuality: Jacques Lacan and the école freudienne*, ed. Juliet Mitchell and Jacqueline Rose. New York: Norton, 1982.
———. "The Mirror Stage." In *Ecrits: A Selection*, trans. Alan Sheridan. London: Tavistock, 1977.
Mori, Anna Maria. *Nel segno della madre*. Rome: Frassinelli, 1992.
Mulvey, Laura. "Visual Pleasure and Narrative Cinema," *Screen* 16.3 (1975): 6–18.
Muraro, Luisa. *L'ordine simbolico della madre*. Rome: Riuniti, 1992.
O'Healy, Áine. "Gender and Ideology in the Films of Marco Ferreri." *Romance Languages Annual* 2 (1990): 258–63.
Passerini, Luisa. *Storie di donne e femministe*. Florence: Rosenberg and Sellier, 1992.
Rubin, Gayle. "The Traffic in Women: Notes on the 'Political Economy' of Sex." In *Toward an Anthropology of Women*, ed. Rayna R. Reiter. New York: Monthly Review Press, 1975. 157–210.

Part IV
Toward a Transcultural Dialogue

Serena Anderlini-D'Onofrio

I Don't Know What You Mean by "Italian Feminist Thought." Is Anything Like That Possible?

Can Italian feminist women think? To try and answer the question one would have to know what "Italian," "feminist," and "woman" mean. But to determine whether or not the question is relevant, one would simply have to decide whether or not a feminist needs to think. Given the deep metaphysical-ity in which the problematic terms of my question are imbricated, I will sidestep the first question and answer the second: a feminist needs to think to resist commodification of action, learning, and position. An Italian feminist needs to think fast these days because the forces of commodification are acting quickly against her newly obtained right to be a thinking subject.

The logic of the marketplace of ideas constructs me as the "proper" person to present this new "feminist thought," based on my qualifications as a foreign national acculturated in Italy, and as a new immigrant reacculturated in the United States. But I must caution that, owing to the experience that these qualifications carry with them, I will not simply share in the ownership of this now translated, and therefore marketable, feminist property (Milan Women's Bookstore Collective, 1990; Bono and Kemp, 1991, 1993). Instead I will argue to persuade the reader that understanding this thought does not simply mean figuring out what new item is on the menu. I assume this role of presenter and therefore participant in the commodification, but I must present myself in turn as a person whose personal history, including decisions at very intimate levels, is related to the conceptual articulations this thought contains.

The immigrant wave in which my process of re-acculturation is inscribed is perhaps the first to contain a substantial contingent of female immigrants whose decisions to relocate are independent of males in their immediate or extended families.[1] This ability to decide positions female immigrants in the traditionally masculine role of providers exposed to the perils of reacculturation, with their origins in a homeland that also contains their families and affections. This posture presumes an already formed feminist consciousness. For me, a new immigrant imported as an intellectual laborer into the system of higher education, this formation of consciousness prior to immigration is exemplified by the project that brought me to the United States: studying the work of women writers for the theater. This project is twice marked by feminism: theater is an artisan and participatory form of popular culture, a site of direct intervention in the democratic process; on this site the contributions women offered in thought —that is, the words in which their presence as thinkers was expressed— are observable.

My choice of project postulates two political assumptions that in the situatedness of U.S. feminism are untenable: first, that women can write words in plays even when they do not sign them; second, that there is thought in a dramatic text. The first assumption implies that literary property is sometimes a plagiarism, a "theft" in the Marxian sense marked by signatures denoting undue appropriations; the second problematizes a central interest-group agreement of the U.S. university: that U.S. popular culture is entertainment and therefore devoid of thought altogether.

The technology of postmodernity enables bicultural people to retain their formations. But as a presenter of Italian feminist thought in translation I speak to Americans in their language. One must concede me the liberty of postulating that the economy of discourse of American English is negatively marked by the Cold War: consent is built around the notion that capitalism and socialism are competitive, not allied, forces; and "communism" is a dirty word, not a legitimate system of belief with a substantial dose of patriotism to its credit, as it is in the economy of discourse in which Italian feminism developed.[2] I can show that this foreign feminism is indeed feminist. But I must be trusted as a guide who enters a foreign territory in which the negative marks of Cold War ideology are reversed. In the economy of discourse in which Italian feminist thought developed, "communism" and "socialism" are legitimate ideologies, and profit and socialization are allied forces necessary for development. Owing to this reversal, my use of American English to convey the social consciousness in which Italian feminist thought developed may sound "a bit foreign."

Is Anything Like That Possible?

The historical situation in which Italian feminist thought was produced is that of periphery: while Italians learn English when they go to school and watch American movies on TV, they are physically closer to the sites of real socialism, the areas in which communism is (or was) a system (not a fantasy), than they are, say, to New York, Los Angeles, or Rio. Therefore, Italian feminists were distant from the centers where the cultural products they consumed were produced.

This meant that if one was a political activist on the left before the Prague Spring and Dubček, the reality of communism seemed too gloomy and opaque to coincide with the utopia the legitimate belief system imaged. In this phase (which I like to call dichotomous or schizophrenic) if you were in the culture of dissent, in your room you would listen to Beatles songs whose lyrics were in a language you did not speak, while in the party cell you would be lectured in Italian on how to make the new party line from the Kremlin digestible to the membership.

The beginnings of the thought process that Italian feminism started are in this phase. Carla Lonzi's reflection on women's political equality in the liberal-capitalist democratic state was articulated in this period (Boccia, 1990; Bono and Kemp, 1991, 36–61). It was prompted by a comparison of the Anglo-American suffrage movement (and the partial enfranchisement it obtained in the World War I period) to movements for national independence developed in French and British colonies in Asia and Africa. Political enfranchisement (as national independence) produced the expectation that its beneficiaries would perform as if their energies had not been depleted by their long exploitation. On the contrary, Carla Lonzi argued that in the period of convalescence from this abuse it was hypocritical to expect that, all of a sudden, women would do well (Lonzi, 1970). Italian women were in a dichotomous situation: liberatory impulses were associated with media culture, which was Anglo-American, but spaces of growth and development for women were in the organisms of the left, the opponents of the cultural and political hegemony exerted from Washington. Lonzi's analysis helped them to understand and control their situation.

In Italy, the modern feminist culture that produced original thinkers and philosophers developed in the Cold War era, when the Jewish holocaust of central Europe and the nuclear holocaust of Japan had already marked the civil and social consciousness of postmodernity. Carla Lonzi, one of these philosophers, preceded Adriana Cavarero, whose work is more clearly placed in the cultural context of the 1970s.[3] The writers and thinkers of this feminist culture based in Italy operated in a cultural landscape in which social interaction and cultural production were regulated by the overarching system of the Cold War. This was also true of the landscape in which American feminists of the "second wave" operated. In the Italian works, however, this landscape is viewed from a different angle. Some definition of this angle helps in comparing the situatedness of Italian-American women to the situatedness of Italian women in the Cold War order.

In this world order, Italy was a passive member of the defense system of NATO, while the United States was a superpower in control of nuclear warheads and weapons. Geographically, Italy was at the periphery of the area defined as "west." But, owing to the absence of former Italian colonies in the New World, it was a country with a very limited postcolonial legacy.[4] The United States was the center of power in "the west," and it was, at least culturally and linguistically, a British filiation. Italy had a national language of its own that was used in the publishing industry and in education. But Italian had this official role only in the small area constituted by the Italian nation-state. The United States used the language of its former colonizer, Britain, for these purposes. This was an international language used in numerous systems of education, in modern science, computer technology, and the largest modern publishing industry. In Italy the teaching of the English language became a chief focus of the public education system when it became apparent that it had replaced French as the language learned by an international cultural elite. In the United States learning Italian was not a priority, even for persons with a special interest in this area, such as Italian American women. Owing to the system of power that the Cold War order set in place, and to the absence of an Italian colonial legacy, Italian feminists and American feminists of Italian descent worked in isolation from one another because they expressed themselves in two different linguistic codes. This situation remained unchanged until some of the writings by Italian feminists became available in English translation.

In Italy, modern feminism became a political force when its work helped to pass the Italian laws for divorce and abortion, both of which were approved in the 1970s (Ufficio Stampa, 1981; Seroni, 1977; Cecchini and Lapasini, 1977). In the United States feminism had been a political force since the suffrage era. In this situation, it was possible for Italian feminist thinkers and philosophers who used the Italian language to read and learn from American, French, and British feminists. Many educated Italian women read English and French. Furthermore, the Italian book industry relied heavily on the sale of translations.[5] These European and North Ameri-

Is Anything Like That Possible?

can feminists whose work Italian feminists read did not know Italian, however, and could not read their counterparts, as their works were not yet available in translation. Consequently, Italian feminists remained unheard in the international arena of modern feminist discourse until translations of their writings into English began in the late 1980s. Three volumes of translated Italian feminist writings are now available: one is a volume authored by a feminist collective; the other two are anthologies (Milan Women's Bookstore Collective, 1990; Bono and Kemp, 1991, 1993).The title of the second anthology, *The Lonely Mirror*, alludes to this difficult and isolated situation.[6]

The portion of the Anglophone world that is interested in intellectual debate began to learn about Italian feminist thought through this recent work of translation. But the larger part of this population still imagines Italian women based on the stereotypical representations that the media offers—for example, the Italian American female characters of the Hollywood film industry. There are partial exceptions: in Spike Lee's *Jungle Fever*, an Italian American woman is represented as educated and independent—a far cry from the mothers and sisters of gangsters in typical Italian American movies like *The Godfather*. Lee's Italian American female is not the protagonist, but she has a leading role. She also displays a sexual, racial, and social consciousness that would be atypical for a representation of an Anglo-American female: she is capable of treating a racially diverse person as an equal. The interracial relationship in which she engages transgresses the social order, not simply her family's Italian American culture. Even so, when this relation dissolves, she is still willing to take physical abuse from her male relatives in the closet of her Italian home.[7] This representation indicates that the culture in which it functions, the United States, still constructs Italian women as dependent on their male relatives and unable to reverse the family roles that determine the oppressions related to gender.

Given these representations, and considering the linguistic isolation of Italian feminist writers and Italy's position at an embattled junction between the first and the second "worlds," it takes a big stretch of the imagination to believe that in the 1970s the women's movement in Italy was one of the most intense in the world; that it produced a vast amount of works in the areas of theory, pedagogy, and social and political thought (Cavarero, 1990; Collettivo, 1987; Piussi, 1987; Franco, 1987; Seroni, 1977; Cecchini and Lapasini, 1977); and that it beat the politics of the Roman Catholic Church twice, thereby granting the civil rights of consensual divorce and legal and subsidized abortion to the population.

All this happened in the context of the national culture that hosted it and made it possible. In the Cold War order, Italy was a cultural arena with linguistic independence, but this arena was situated at a strategic point near the border where the first and the second world met: the Iron Curtain. The defeat of Fascism helped to valorize ideological pluralism and cultural diversity, but the goals of democracy and economic well-being to which these values pointed had long been deferred—first by European domination and later by Fascism. The two superpowers of the Cold War established two areas of ideological influence. Italy was at the junction of these areas, where the two conflicting ideologies met. Consequently, many Italians felt that the pressure of this conflict often directed the course of Italian politics. But through the defeat of Fascism some important lessons had been learned. One such lesson was that being "number one" was less important than being an articulate and pluralistic democracy. Another was that capitalism and socialism are not irreconcilable forces, but two complementary systems that cannot really function independently.[8] From the angle Italian feminists had on the cultural landscape in which they operated, the two superpowers that claimed to be opposite looked a lot more similar than they were willing to admit. They appeared especially similar as they focused on controlling the cultural and political configuration of the Cold War order itself. The cultural arena in which these feminists operated seemed a powerless one in the face of these larger forces, but owing to its ideologic pluralism and linguistic independence it was in fact a safe place to develop a strong and independent feminist consciousness.

This historical situatedness is the background against which most Italian feminist writers and thinkers worked. In their thought, Italy's passive role in NATO and its strategic position in the Cold War order were givens that could not be changed. But their thought was expressed in a language that, by its own logic, resisted this subordination. So, while one would expect an identification with the female "masters" of this order—with modern Anglophone feminists such as Margaret Fuller and Margaret Sanger, for example, whose pioneer work in the areas of equality and birth control many Italian women knew—the cultural production of Italian feminism warrants that this identification happened in indirect and mediated ways. It happened, for example, through a praxis of interpreting French feminist works against the grain of the influential interpretations of these works later produced by academic American feminists.

The early works of Luce Irigaray were influential in the American cultural arena. But in the United States they were constructed as essentialist

Is Anything Like That Possible?

(Moi, 1985; Stanton, 1986). This was a way to represent these works as less progressive than the works of American feminists. But this representation expresses the modes of thought encoded in the English language; for example, it expresses the values of a liberalism focused on a universalized, masculine individual self (Violi, 1986).[9] Many Italian feminists identify Irigaray as a source of inspiration, but they read her works against the grain of the interpretations of American feminists. In the logic of their thought, as expressed in the Italian language, the "essentialism" these interpretations allege is the historical-materialist base of Irigaray's philosophy.[10] This logic is possible because of the role of grammatical gender in Italian. The masculine subject is not universal but only one of two possible subjects, the male and the female.[11] This resistance of language and logic to the interpretive modes of an Anglophone feminism, and to the values that it expresses through the English language, is the common base of the work of two otherwise different thinkers (to whom I will return later), Lonzi and Cavarero.

The second phase of the Cold War era in which post-holocaust feminist thought developed in Italy is one that, with a term borrowed from African American linguist Selase Williams, I would call "diunital" (Williams, 1992).[12] The Italian left affirmed its independence from Moscow after the Prague Spring. At this time the left turned to the teachings of Antonio Gramsci. In arenas not penetrated by the industrial revolution, a proletarian class of industrial workers structurally oppositional to the capitalist bourgeoisie was not in place. Marxian theory had not anticipated a situation in which social consciousness would grow in this kind of arena. Stalin's way of handling the traditionalism of small landowners (or *kulaki*) was to persecute them for their backwardness and eventually to kill them off. But Gramsci was persecuted by a totalizing ideology: he was a political prisoner of the Fascist regime and wrote from his prison cell. Gramsci proposed a "third way" in the oppositional logic between capitalism and socialism that the failure of the Soviet experiment prompted: his project was to educate traditionalist masses in the concepts and political analyses socialism proposed, forming organic intellectuals in the process. So the political institutions of the left were sites of this educational process, toward which innovative cultural forces gravitated.[13]

In the diunital phase, Gramsci's teachings served to articulate dissent from the Soviet regime. Dissent from what was now perceived as a totalizing doctrine helped to gather consent for the largest communist party in a democracy, the PCI, a party that, in a field of more than a dozen, gathered

Serena Anderlini-D'Onofrio

about one-third of the popular vote (Seroni, 1977; Negri, 1990). The thought of the Milan Women's Bookstore Collective and of other philosophy groups such as Diotima in Verona developed in this diunital phase, articulating in significant ways a discourse of women on women in postmodern democracies.

These groups developed in a culture of dissent in which historical materialism was taken for granted. Culturalism was the accepted norm, not the innovative exception marked against essentialism and religious fundamentalism. Therefore, to focus on women's autonomy of thought and philosophic independence, it was possible to develop what Gayatri Spivak was later to call a "strategic essentialism." In other words, as Teresa de Lauretis put it in one of her works on feminism in Italy, it was possible to "take the risk of essentialism seriously," without seriously questioning the culturalism, materialism, and dialecticism of the economy of discourse in which this risk was taken (de Lauretis, 1989).

In 1990 the first book of Italian feminism appeared in the United States: *Sexual Difference*, by the Milan Women's Bookstore Collective. It is authored by a group of feminist women active in an urban, collectively managed noninstitutional cultural center, the Women's Bookstore of Milan. Their feminist consciousness formed in the struggles for divorce and abortion in the 1970s, and in those for compensation of homemaking services and antirape legislation in the 1980s (Bono and Kemp, 1991, 211–59, 260–72, 273–83; Seroni, 1977; Ufficio Stampa, 1981; Cecchini and Lapasini, 1977). The publication of this book gave a feminist like me, a young militant in some of these struggles, a lot to think about.

In the process of transference between a relatively small and compact cultural arena, the Italian publishing industry, and the much more wide-ranging and diversified American-English publishing industry, the title of the book was transformed. *Non credere di avere dei diritti!* (Don't presume that you have any rights!) translates Simone Weil's disillusionment with the capability of liberal capitalism to grant women the rights it promises, enjoining the listener to accept that personal rights in the postmodern state are "degree zero." The more sexually appetizing title *Sexual Difference* echoes the famous misogynist French saying *vive la différence*, from which Derridean *différance* is a takeoff. The hook markets the product, turning up a female version of the stereotype of the Italian Latin lover. But does it get the message across that Italian feminism is also theoretical? Does it sug-

Is Anything Like That Possible?

gest that it is analytic of the situatedness of women in late capitalist nation-states?

The chief theoretical concept the book explains—entrustment—denotes a commitment of Italian feminism to invest in other women as mentees, colleagues, collaborators, allies, and friends (Milan Women's Bookstore Collective, 1990, 108–23; Campari and Canzano, 1985; Dominijanni, 1987). Entrustment is a primary relationship in which eros turns into learning, in a sort of Freudian sublimation. The juridical meaning of the word *affidamento* denotes the right to parental custody of a child, a minor, or a disabled person (Garzanti, 1987, 4). In this right, the Italian system privileges females. If it is correct to postulate that, in the system of rights of a postmodern nation-state, "you [woman] don't have any rights," then it is wise for a woman to think that pledging allegiance to a woman more powerful than herself can be beneficial. Entrustment can give the less powerful woman the freedom-granting protection the system of rights does not offer. This is the political logic in which the concept of entrustment is inscribed. But the concept also functions in a psychological dimension, signified in the maternalism to which the word alludes in the original culture. As Ida Dominijanni, one of the group's spokeswomen, puts it, the reflection on the practice of entrustment helps to "bring into focus what blocks women's access to the symbolic and, tied with this, the problem of an unresolved relationship with the mother" (Dominijanni, 1987, 133). This reflection also points to the transgressiveness of this practice: entrustment is Oedipal, maternal, and also latently lesbian-incestuous.

Entrustment is Oedipal in the sense that it denotes a relation of unequals like the relation of a mentor and, to coin a word, a "mentee," or a child and a parent. This relation implies an imbalance of power and a degree of dependency. Entrustment is maternal in the sense that the mentor and the mentee are both female, therefore the mentor is a *magistra*—a "master," yes, but one of the female gender, who has lost the attributes of masculinity that a male mentor has. In this capacity of protector, the *magistra* functions as a symbolic female parent. Finally, entrustment is latently lesbian and incestuous. The relation that it denotes is not sexual, in the sense that the two women implicated in it are not a socially acknowledged or committed couple. Nevertheless, the relation itself denotes a desire between women that is latently incestuous. The mentee seeks protection in the mentor. This denotes a secret desire of the mentee to go back to the protected space of the mother's womb, in a sexual manner. The mentor sees a semblance of her younger self in the mentee. This relation denotes a secret desire of the mentor to establish a relation of erotic love with the mentee, in which the mentee functions as a youthful object of pleasure.[14] Therefore, the desire between women that the relation of entrustment expresses is a lesbian desire that is also latently incestuous. The original title of the book justifies the transgressiveness that this desire represents: perhaps relations of entrustment do not comply with the system of rights that we have, but if the system of rights cannot be trusted then it does not have to be respected. Therefore, the book's title cautions: "Don't presume that you have any rights" under the system at hand. Why is the transgressiveness of the concept of entrustment elided in the transference to U.S. culture?

The organ of the discipline of women's studies, the *Women's Review of Books*, reviewed *Sexual Difference* in June 1991 (Lister, 1991). The title of the review, "Feminism alla milanese," plays with the fame styles of Italian cuisine have in English-speaking cultures owing to the traditional occupations of Italian immigrants in the restaurant industry. It also alludes, of course, to the meat recipe associated with the geographic location of the collective: the *cotoletta alla milanese*, a breaded and deep-fried veal cutlet. So the gift Anglo-American feminism offered to the newly groomed Italian feminism was a place in the marketplace of U.S. feminist cultural industry, but it also confirmed the stereotype that Italians are good cooks even when feminism gets into them. The question, of course, remains: Can Italian feminists also think well?

I kept being disturbed by the title of the review: this image of a breaded and deep-fried feminism kept popping up in my head. Two gifts from male mentors became associated with it: a collection of aprons and a lecture on Dante, forming two anecdotes of my acculturation. In my young adulthood, like the Italian woman of Spike Lee's film *Jungle Fever*, I ran the house of my male relatives. My dad took international trips and brought me a different apron from each country he visited. These folkloric, characteristic, and often quite pretty cooking implements enriched the store of homemaking objects I had been accumulating. I had a nice collection! But these gifts did not make me happy. I wondered why. A few years later I explained that, even though the aprons were multicultural and diverse, they invariably made me feel like a good cook, and in my acculturation, that of an Italian female growing up during the Cold War, this was incompatible with being a thinking person.

The stereotypes related to nationality and gender conspired to construct the category of "good cook" as a stigma for an Italian female with literary and intellectual aspirations. In the culture of the Italian left, the sub-

Is Anything Like That Possible?

ject of class struggle was constructed as masculine. This subject strove for better conditions of employment, as the political theories of this culture enjoined. But in a socialist logic, the chief difference between a salaried worker and a slave is that the worker's salary is the basis of a relative economic independence. This independence enables the struggle in which salaried workers as a class engage. The work of female cooks and homemakers was, and still is, unpaid. This unpaid work was an embarrassment to a national culture of the left, which had constructed the subject of class struggle as male and was not willing to examine new and continuing forms of bondage hosted by the postmodern landscape.

Partly to assuage this embarrassment, the culture developed a rhetoric in which the concept of a "good cook" was antithetic to the concept of a "good revolutionary." The Brechtian categories of "culinary" and "epic" theater were used to represent this oppositional logic. The adjective "culinary" denoted a theater based on traditional and reliable conventions. "Epic" theater did away with tradition, thereby inciting and producing social change (Willett, 1964). When the culture of the left chose to focus on demanding better conditions of employment for salaried workers rather than on demanding social services and salaries for homemakers, it imposed a passive role on working-class females, whose chief area of production still was this unpaid work. The rhetoric opposing the "culinary" to the "epic" essentialized the qualities of good cooks: they mediated conflicts with their culinary rhetoric, and passed on useful traditions, but they could not be good revolutionaries, precisely because their "culinary" virtues were not "epic." The cultural stereotype of a "good [female] cook" (*una buona cuoca*) constructed wives, mothers, and other female relatives of the masculine protagonists of the struggle for better conditions of employment, as persons who chose a passive role in this struggle. The stereotype helped to divert attention from the hypothesis that this passive role might have been chosen for them. This was problematic for a female who was appreciated for her meals and recipes and, precisely because she was a female operating in an order dominated by men, learned from her experience that mediation was more effective in achieving positive and lasting change than aggressiveness.

In the culture of the United States, Italian immigrants had not succeeded in imposing their language and mode of thought, but had instead learned and assimilated the language and mode of thought of the Anglophone dominators. Very often this had happened at the expense of the language and mode of thought with which they came. Nevertheless, there was a mode of expression in which these immigrants had succeeded in imposing their language: the cuisine that good Italian cooks used in the restaurant industry. This cuisine might have expressed the wisdom that these cooks' ancestors had learned in the many centuries during which Italy was invaded and oppressed by foreign dominators. Nevertheless, in the Anglophone culture of the United States, Italians were appreciated for their cooking, not for their philosophy. Writers, thinkers, and intellectuals rarely had Italian names. Most Anglophone consumers that adored Italian recipes did not bother to ask Italian cooks if they were also good thinkers and intellectuals. When I became an immigrant to the United States, I was automatically inserted in the relatively intellectual culture of an American university. Nevertheless, with my notably Italian name, I was not perceived as a serious thinker and intellectual as long as, in these intellectual circles, it was known that I also cooked well.

The second anecdote of my acculturation refers to the situation that I just mentioned. As an expatriate suspended between two cultures, I also received stereotyping gifts that referred to the culinary rhetoric that denied my intellectual aspirations. But in this situation of immigrant academic laborer, I threw the stereotyping gift back in the giver's face. As a graduate teaching assistant, I taught the Italian language. One year the professor who conducted the course was my future dissertation director. In our textbook, the reading on cuisine focused on spaghetti, the one on literature on Dante, his favorite author. When we made class plans he innocently proposed, "I teach the literature and you teach the cuisine . . ." I turned around and repeated his words with an ironic intonation: "I the cuisine and you the literature, uh-huh?" This foreign-Italian, yet familiar-Italian, feminist wanted to think! He replied something like, "Oh, no, no, no, what did I say . . . *you* do the literature, and I do the cuisine, I am a very good cook because I am Italian, didn't you know?" As I remember, that year he taught spaghetti and I taught his favorite author. Of course I did not teach my favorite author, who would have been a female, because there were no female authors in that text.

These gifts are not, as Derrida would perhaps suggest, "poisons."[15] They are anecdotes, and I offer them as invitations to ponder the following question: Why would the Anglo-American feminist book industry do to Italian feminism what my male mentors did to me? A suggested follow-up question is: How can Italian feminist thinkers talk back?

* * *

Is Anything Like That Possible?

In the diunital phase of Italian history of the Cold War era, the democratic administration established the two civil rights of divorce and abortion (in 1974 and 1978). In the 1970s the Pope campaigned to repeal these rights, violating the separation of church and state that the democratic constitution established when, at the end of World War II, the totalizing regime of Fascism crumbled. Women's vote came with the armistice, when the democratic parties returned. The male leadership of the left felt that women's political opinion was controlled through the process of Catholic confession, and therefore constructed this concession as a strategy to confirm the position of Italy with respect to the Iron Curtain. So in Europe, there was a notion of Italian women as one of the most bigoted and afraid national female groups. In the 1970s, conservative forces expected the Pope's campaigns to be effective, because they overestimated this constructed backwardness. As a young militant in the campaigns to keep the divorce and abortion laws in place, I am proud to report that both papal attempts failed.[16]

Italian feminist thought is a theoretical reflection validated by pragmatic effectiveness. As women's groups helped in the struggle to keep the rights in place, they conquered social spaces in which their thought developed: the *centri culturali delle donne* (or women's cultural centers), often located in abandoned buildings women restored and activated (Bono and Kemp, 1991, 1–23, 139–47). Based in the Gramscian lesson, Italian feminist thought validates experience as an important epistemic method. Gramsci suggested that the Soviet revolution failed because the Bolsheviks did not have the experience of being peasants, not because the analyses socialism offered were incorrect. So Italian feminist thinkers agreed that being-woman helped one to understand what being-women means better than being-men.

The groups from which thinking proceeds, the Gruppo Transizione in Naples, the Movimento Femminista Romano, the Gruppo Diotima in Verona, the Libreria delle Donne in Milan, are diverse in cultural legacies, backgrounds, and concerns (Bono and Kemp, 1991, 62–81, 109–38, 181–85; Diotima, 1987, 175–84). But all work in self-managed spaces and include women in various professions: schoolteachers, university professors, lawyers, politicians, writers, students, homemakers, and so on. At the cost of generalizing questions needing more detailed attention, I want to suggest that this situatedness produces three characteristics worth observing and learning from:

First, their feminism has academics in it (many writers and thinkers do teach at the universities), but is not an academically produced feminism. Its exclusion from the official repositories of knowledge offers a literal and concrete answer to Woolf's rhetorical question, "Is it better to be locked in or to be locked out of the Oxbridge library walls?" This exclusion, many theorists argue, is partly coerced and partly self-determined, because a realist feminism articulates itself in the double militancy of educational system and independent cultural center.

Second, postmodern culture fabricates bipolar opposites such as socialism and capitalism, homo- and heterosexual identities, culturalism and essentialism, and multiculturalism and Eurocentrism. Academic discourse analyzes these opposites, but when debate paralyzes action a realist feminism, as Linda Alcoff has suggested, seeks the Gramscian "third way" (Alcoff, 1988). The double militancy in and out of universities turns academics in working-class intellectuals engaged in nonacademic discursive practices outside the library walls. It helps to articulate a feminism with women, not a feminism perpetuating culturally constructed diversifications.

Third, Italian feminism understands sexual preference as a question of experience, not of identity. The decisions not to split groups over the question of sexual preference that this understanding has made possible enables interlocutions between women in same-sex and opposite-sex love relations. As the introduction to *Sexual Difference* explains, many Italian feminist groups have adopted the convention that sexual experience is what gay and straight women talk about when they speak of their pleasures, not an "identity" writers, public speakers, and theorists are expected to affix to their works (Milan Women's Bookstore Collective, 1990).[17] This convention makes personal sexual history opaque. But precisely because it does not presume that a purely lesbian or a purely heterosexual identity is possible, this convention enables theoretical articulations of the connectedness of sexual and maternal eros in the subject-hood in which women are situated. These articulations are the suppressed of Anglo-American feminism.

Three notions the theory-praxis of Italian feminism has articulated enable reflection on the political dilemmas the present situatedness of U.S. women presents.

First, liberal ideology has a limited power to repair the damages oppression effects. But certain groups of women have heavier legacies of oppression. The notion of equality Carla Lonzi articulated is defined as a "juridical principle" denoting "what is offered as legal rights to colonized people [and] what is imposed on them as culture" (Lonzi, 1970, 41). From the way in which the official history of the women's movement configures

Is Anything Like That Possible?

itself, it would seem that liberal feminist women's movements in Anglo-American cultures position themselves in the forefront of the struggles, with French movements following by one length. All the other movements are reduced to spectators or passive students watching the teachers deliver their lectures, with nothing to teach or offer in turn. Lonzi critiques a concept of equality that serves to confer on the dominant ideology the power to blame historically oppressed persons for their own oppression. It is a departure for a reflection on how specific legacies of oppression that some groups of women carry in feminism crystallize and perpetuate themselves.

Second, the notion of entrustment denotes a relation of two women divided by class, age, or acculturation. One person functions as a guide or a mentor, someone the student can call "one like herself."[18] The recognition of similar sexed embodiments and erotic mechanisms enables the development of the mentee-woman's potential for cultural agency and expression.

Entrustment has been attacked as "medieval," based as it is in a relational mode functioning on subordination and supremacy like the relation of a lord to a vassal.[19] Yet my sense is that postmodern relational modes implicate people in highly institutionalized relations in which hierarchies can be teased but not transgressed. Entrustment does not institute the power structures in which women's relations develop; it recognizes their presence and reclaims women's power to inhabit them with other women like themselves.

The theory-praxis of entrustment positions itself as realist thought: hopeful enough to hold that theorizing the functioning of power structures from the perspective of women's situatedness is a good investment, and disillusioned enough to hold that infiltrating power structures and eroding the ideology they encode from within is as effective a strategy against oppression as one can take.

Third, the notion of "concrete essentials" denotes the organic asymmetry of women's and men's sexed bodies. As Adriana Cavarero of Diotima in Verona explains, the symbolic order of the Occident erases symbols of female sexedness, leaving women without symbolic placement in the system of acculturation. In a culture in which notions of social medicine prevail, and as long as transsexual operations are the exception, for women, being-women is a reality they cannot change. This reality is a "concrete essential" because "for each of us who was born a woman, this is always something given, something *which is so* and could not be otherwise" (Cavarero, 1988, 180). Based on this notion Cavarero articulates a position on women's right to partly self-manage their reproductive organs. The subtlety of this position is worth reporting in detail.

In *Nonostante Platone* (Despite Plato, in the process of being translated) Cavarero explains that, in the logic of the modern democratic state, women in social contracts controlling the contents of their reproductive organs are not juridical subjects in the proper sense. A partly developed fetus is a subject-to-be contained in the mother, who is a subject of right in the modern nation-state. In the logic of separation of mother and fetus, the mother is a "stronger subject" and the fetus a "weaker subject." The rights of the weaker subject are those the social contract of a democratic modern state must protect. But, as Cavarero explains, the problem of applying this logic to the organic asymmetry of human sexedness is that, as long as men do not get pregnant, it suggests that "of course, as a citizen, a woman is supposed to be a full juridical subject, but as a pregnant person, she is the container of the unborn child," and therefore object, not subject, of right. A social contract denying the civil right of abortion in reality denies the power of maternity, ascribing to women responsibilities of subjects of right (to respect the law and to preserve life), but treating parts of their bodies organically connected to their persons (their internal genitals) as objects of the rights of subjects-to-be. As Cavarero puts it, "Neither her womb nor what is happening belongs to [the pregnant woman], so that the decision to generate or not is not hers."[20]

The accepted norm that the father is the name giver exemplifies the elision of the power of maternity the unresolved juridical status of pregnant women produces. Cavarero emphasizes women's right to know "what happens" in their bodies as male persons do. Inscribing reproductive choice in a social contract like the constitution of a modern state is the beginning of cultural acceptance of the power of maternity and of symbolization of women's eros. The semiotic system of naming indicating the father as the "real" parent leaves daughters without symbolic placement in the system of acculturation, leading women to conflate their eros with response to phallic penetration. It stops them from learning that their eros is different from men's eros because they have different body parts, such as clitoris, vagina, labia and vaginal walls, uterus, breasts, in which erotic mechanisms are situated.

Cavarero's "concrete essentials" turn the logocentrism of the Cartesian cogito inside out. They suggest that essence is concrete, not abstract. In other words, in her vision, "I am-woman therefore I think-as-a-woman" makes more sense than the abstract and generic "I think therefore I am." In a complex and multilayered society, female bodies are culturally constructed. But in Cavarero's view being-women is the concrete essential of inhabiting bodies equipped with sexual and reproductive apparatuses in which desires for other bodies reside. This concrete essential validates women's experience as a method to understand women's situatedness.

Before I can conclude on what seems to me conceptually relevant in the content of Italian feminist thought, I feel I must offer not simply a positional preface explaining how I situate myself with respect to this new thought coming up in the marketplace, but also an account of how my personal history is affected by and inscribed in this thought. When I think of the experience of transcontinental immigration to the United States I sometimes think of the experience of transsexualism as possibly the most appropriate term of comparison. In the experience of immigration as a single female laborer of the intellect with a "foreign" feminist consciousness, there is a preoperational and a postoperational phase. The moment of the operation corresponds to the moment of acceptance as a resident alien. Reacculturation is in some ways a normalization, or, as the INS calls it, a "naturalization."

Sandy Stone explains that sexual dysphoria, the medical syndrome with which transsexuals are diagnosed, is cured when the transsexual person is surgically transformed into a person of the other sex and therefore becomes "normal" according to the bipolar logic of the system of acculturation (Stone, 1990). The preoperational phase, between the diagnosis and the operation, is denoted by acceptance of the rules by which gender is defined at the site of acculturation, even though some preoperational transsexuals make interventions in the system by wearing, say, blue jeans and T-shirts, claiming that this is transsexual because persons of the opposite sex also do it. The postoperational phase is one in which the political consciousness of the "normalized" person grows out of the awareness of being part of a unique experience of having, at different moments, been embodied as a person of either gender. The experience of the transcultural person is not so different. The period of probation during which the immigrant person is subject to scrutiny to verify his or her acceptability in the system of reacculturation is often a period of silence and passive acceptance of the new norms. After juridical acceptance there is a phase of consciousness in which the reacculturated person becomes aware of the power of knowing by experience two different worlds.

But in the social conventions of U.S. culture in postmodernity the experience of transformation is suppressed, and does not fit into social conversation. Just as a male-to-female postoperational transsexual will not be heard at a social gathering conversing about "when she was a little boy," so a naturalized "American" will not speak of "when she was a little Italian person." So the story of transcultural/transsexual transformation that does not get narrated becomes material for books, talks, or therapy.

In the U.S. cultural landscape images referring to foreign postmodern cultural situations are absent: there are no dubbed foreign films in conventional distribution channels, no foreign shows on mainstream broadcast U.S. television, and scarcely any foreign news in the media. A person who, when interpellated by a sentence like "You have an accent, where are you from?" plainly answers "I am Italian, I am from Rome" will see a wall grow between herself and the interlocutor. She will think, "Oh god, this person must be seeing the Godfather, Al Capone, Little Italy, Mafia, Mussolini, spaghetti, and so on. How can I explain that I am not that?"

The offense that these associations give the foreign person will silence her. The non-foreign person might be desperately trying to find a decent question to continue the conversation, but in most cases the dichotomous logic that opposes multiculturalism and Eurocentrism will stand in the way. The foreign person is from what an ironic Britishism Americans inherited with the English language calls "the Continent." The U.S. national will perceive her as a living example of the concept of Eurocentrism. The single female immigrant of Italian origin will see herself as someone who has dangerously turned her back on the continent of her origin, because, owing to various historical legacies, this "Continent" constructed Italian women as backward and never truly respected them anyway. The non-foreign person will not know what to say, and will end the conversation. So the foreign person, as soon as she acquires a passing accent and interactive mode, will pass for an American and forget to explain what her previous life was like.

For me speaking of Italian feminism is like telling the story of "when I was a little Italian girl." It is not something I do frequently in my social life in the United States. Whatever is suppressed in social conversation and becomes material for books, talks, and therapy becomes, indeed, the site of performance, and my "performance" on Italian feminist thought is no exception. Italian feminism was nurtured in a cultural landscape in which Fascism was associated with the idea of a univocal identity producing a totalizing system of subjectification. Owing to this rootedness in a culture that now rejects univocal identities, no matter how oppressed or disenfranchised they might be, this thought helps differently positioned U.S. femi-

Is Anything Like That Possible?

nists find terms for a discourse of coalition against common enemies, such as economic backlash and the new forms of commodification it produces. Italian feminist concepts such as the concept of equality as neocolonial "independence," the concept of entrustment as a privileged woman-to-woman relation that may or may not be sexual, and the concept of being equipped with certain sexual and reproductive organs as the concrete essential of being-women are useful transcultural articulations. They indicate possible "third ways" in the oppositional logic on which the dichotomies of heterosexual and lesbian identities, culturalism and essentialism, multiculturalism and Eurocentrism, and liberalism and socialism are based.

Notes

1. Braidotti, "United States of Europe or United Colors of Benetton?" 117–18. For the concept of postmodern feminists, or "women of ideas," as "migrants," "nomads," and "exiles," I refer to this source.

2. From the end of World War II to the mid-1980s, in Italian culture "Fascist," not "Communist," was considered an unpatriotic political orientation (even though neo-Fascists existed in Italy, as everywhere else). This is quite contrary to American culture, where "Communist" still connotes affiliation with the enemy (even though the former Soviet Union has now dissolved). Many Italian partisans who helped to defeat Fascism at the end of World War II were Communists. Also, members of the Communist Party (PCI) participated in the writing of the new Italian Constitution, in 1947 (*Grande Dizionario Garzanti*, 379). In the 1994 elections, a party that reclaims the Fascist legacy has emerged under the leadership of Gianfranco Fini, and along with other conservative formations. In the period of preparation for these elections, Fini visited a major cultural site of anti-Fascist consciousness, the Fosse Ardeatine (Ardeatine Graves), near Rome. This is the burial place of the victims of a wartime Nazi slaughter perpetrated in retaliation for a partisan ambush in which some German soldiers were killed. The press interpreted Fini's act as a way to create a patriotic image for a party that at least in part successfully claims the Fascist legacy as its own.

3. Carla Lonzi and Adriana Cavarero were born in the 1940s. (For Lonzi I do not have a specific year, but I have indications that she was born during or shortly after the end of World War II; see Boccia, *L'io in rivolta*, 42). Cavarero was born in 1947 (Cavarero, *Nonostante Platone*, backflap). Lonzi died prematurely in 1982 (Boccia, *L'io in rivolta*, 189). Cavarero is writing a new book in Verona. Lonzi can be characterized as a "pioneer" of Italian feminism. She founded one of the first collectives, Rivolta Femminile, in 1970. She also lived a dramatic life. The contradictions of this life reflect the contradictions in which Italian feminism developed (Boccia, *L'io in rivolta*, passim). Cavarero came to feminism more serenely, via her work as a scholar of the classics and her role in the feminist philosophy collective, Diotima. (See also Cavarero, *Nonostante Platone*, and Diotima, *Il pensiero della differenza sessuale*.)

4. This absence of a linguistic and juridical postcolonial legacy separates Italians who live abroad from many other Europeans of my generation. This mark of separation refers to an absence of what might be called the "colonizer's complex": a sense of guilt and shame held by European baby boomers who travel and live abroad in the face of the disastrous legacies of their ancestors' colonizations. I have frequented North European emigrés in the United States, and I am familiar in very intimate ways with the psychological consequences of postcoloniality that they experience with respect to the political situations of countries such as Algeria, South Africa, India, and so on. But the first time that I experienced a "colonizer's com-

plex" was when international political attention focused on the Somalian situation. Somalia was an Italian colony. A bizarre linguistic legacy of this colonization is that the university system of Somalia functions in Italian, while the elementary and intermediate systems of education function in Somali and English, respectively. For me, a person who has at some point identified as a European expatriate, "Somalia" drove the point home that no one was innocent of the negative legacies of colonization.

5. Braidotti, *Patterns of Dissonance*, 261. Braidotti observes that the "speed with which Irigaray's texts are published in Italian" is "almost simultaneous" with their publication in French, while "*Speculum* [an important Irigaraian text] took ten years to appear in English." This is just one of the numerous examples of how the heavy reliance on translation of the Italian book industry helps Italian women readers to have timely access to important texts.

6. On North European and American influences in Italian feminism (and its inability to be heard abroad) see "Introduction: Coming from the South" (Bono and Kemp, *Italian Feminist Thought*, 2–29).

7. For this point, I am indebted to a paper by Pasquale Verdicchio. See Verdicchio, "Spike Lee's Guineas."

8. The complementarity of capitalism and socialism may be said to be the basis of the most original political concept the Italian Communist party produced in the aftermath of the events of 1968, the Historic Compromise (*compromesso storico*). According to this concept, after the events of 1968, it was no longer realistic to think of socialism alone or in a pure state. Socialism had to be thought of in the context of a market economy and a capitalistic development. (See Hellman, *Italian Communism in Transition*, 30–33 and passim.)

9. Anglophile anthropology assumes that grammatical gender is a sign of primitivism, a "useless category" which is eliminated as language becomes more scientific and objective (Sapir, *Language*; Lyons, *Introduction to Theoretical Linguistics*). In English grammatical gender only applies to personal pronouns, which denote persons or animals. This is called "natural gender" because it does not apply to things or concepts. But if modern women are supposed to be like men, what is "natural" about natural gender? The construct of "natural gender" seems to me an ethnocentric way of reading the difference between English and Romance languages, in which nouns, adjectives, articles, and pronouns are either masculine or feminine. Natural gender constructs English as "superior" to some of the languages from which it derives, Italian and French. Even though linguists have resolved this issue by attributing the absence of grammatical gender in English to its composite nature, the idea that grammatical gender is just a cumbersome complication is deeply rooted in the minds of many otherwise well-educated monolingual Americans. An interesting new way to look at gender in language has been proposed by Patrizia Violi. She establishes a continuum between cultures in which women still use language differently (or have a different language) and cultures in which all speakers use grammatical gender. Far from being "primitive," these cultures help to understand how a subjectivity in the feminine (that cannot be reduced to a copy of the falsely neutral male subject) can structure itself (Violi, *L'infinito singolare*, 39–69 and passim).

10. Any interpretation that charges Irigaray with essentialism is at least reductive. Biology and organicity are implicated in culture, not outside of it. To ignore this is more "essentialist" than it is to face it. A historical-materialist analysis of the social utility of the female body is the necessary step to move beyond orthodox Marxism and its failure to analyze women's reproductive and household work. Italian feminism has opened the debate on this question (Bono and Kemp, *Italian Feminist Thought*, 26–269).

11. Linguistic gender is a central category of signification in French and Italian. But in Italian this category has a concrete quality that it does not have in French. In Italian grammatical gender affects oral and written language. In French it often affects written language only. For example, the feminine Italian word *amata* is recognizable from the masculine word *amato*

Is Anything Like That Possible?

from its ending vocalic sound *a*. In French, the words *aimée* and *aimé* are spelled differently but sound alike. This oral quality of Italian gender makes the category more concrete because children learn about it long before they start to write. In the consciousness of native speakers of Italian, this concrete quality of grammatical gender may be said to substantially undermine the presumed universality of the masculine subject at a very early age. For native speakers of French, on the contrary, grammatical gender is an abstract category of which they become aware when they make the transition between oral and written language. Therefore, it may be said that the illusion of a unified, masculine subject remains alive for a longer time. I have been able to verify this hypothesis in teaching these two languages to adults. Students of French whose native language is Italian are less likely to make agreement errors between nouns and adjectives than are students of French whose native language is French. In my view, this is because the former automatically transfer their oral sense of linguistic gender to French, and do not have to learn it as an abstract grammatical category.

12. The concept was presented in a paper Selase Williams delivered at UCLA in 1992 and was further explained in the discussions that followed this event. See Williams, "Developing an Afrocentric Discipline."

13. I am making a generalization about the distinctiveness of the Italian left, and its major (though not unrivaled) political representative, the Italian Communist party. This party hosted and represented a wide range of positions, and the successive leaderships of Gramsci, Togliatti, and Berlinguer had very different directions. Nevertheless, this communist party had a distinctive character with respect to other communist parties, for example, the French and the Soviet: its constant aspiration to win the people's consent by persuasion and democratic process. This distinctiveness has been attributed to the situatedness of the PCI in relation to the "Catholic Question." The Vatican is in Italy's capital, Rome, and Catholicism is still the religion of the Italian state. In this situatedness, a communist party must act as a model of pluralism and democracy or else it falls prey to those who claim that communism is "evil" and leads to the "fire of hell." As a consequence, the PCI was strongly committed to being an accepting and available (if sometimes unsophisticated) source of political and social education for cadres, youth, and sympathizers (Hellman, *Italian Communism in Transition*, 190 and passim). In the wake of the dissolution of the so-called evil empire, the PCI renamed itself Democratic Party of the Left (PDS or Partito Democratico della Sinistra). In preparation for the political elections of 1994, it negotiated an alliance with other progressive forces, which did not obtain a majority of the vote.

14. These relations may be compared to the relations between women that developed in the female communities called *thiasoi*, one of which is known to us owing to the poems of Sappho. These relationships were between women of different age groups, and their purpose was educational. Nevertheless, it would be reductive to see these relationships as "copies" of the more famous pederastic relationships of men and boys in Athens. For a full treatment of this subject, see Cantarella, *Bisexuality in the Ancient World*, 78–86.

15. I refer generically to Heidegger's *Gift* (the German noun means gift and poison) on which Derrida speculates in his works (Derrida, *Heidegger et la Question de l'Esprit*).

16. In the Italian system, a popular referendum can repeal, not approve, laws and amendments. To obtain a referendum on a particular law, 500,000 Italian citizens must sign a petition to the government. In 1974 a referendum to repeal a recently approved divorce law was lost. Between 1971 and 1978 the Congress and Senate developed an abortion law. In 1976 there were general elections. Socialists and Communists, the two chief parties of the left, supported abortion. This was a chief selling point of the campaign. I was an activist, and I was, so to speak, happily married. I was also visibly pregnant. I worked really well as a political statement that abortion was optional, not mandatory, and that not all pro-choice persons wanted to "kill babies."

Serena Anderlini-D'Onofrio

17. In the introduction to *Sexual Difference*, de Lauretis discusses this convention, and the positions individual members of the Milan collective have taken on it, extensively (15–19). De Lauretis sees the convention as a way of accepting a rhetoric of passing that co-opts lesbians in the dominant sex/gender system. But this view accepts the culturally constructed notion that gay and straight sexuality are incompatible and mutually exclusive. As a woman who identifies as bisexual, I disagree. Another convention for women who participate in projects that have a lesbian focus is that of identifying by their first name only as participants in these projects. For example, the proceedings of the "V Convegno Nazionale Lesbico" were published by a collective author composed of women identified only by their first names (Anna, Claudia, et al., *Da desiderio a desiderio*).

18. In the *Poetics*, Aristotle speaks of Oedipus as "someone like ourselves" and "the man like ourselves." This likeness produces the emotions of pity and fear. It is through this likeness that the students learn. But the students to whom Aristotle explains this are male. Do female students have someone they can call "one like themselves"? Entrustment explains why a pedagogy that does not teach about women is not really a pedagogy that wants women to learn (Aristotle, *Poetics*, 57).

19. As Nadia Fusini commented on a report on entrustment by Silvia Vegetti Finzi, another feminist group member: "Entrustment . . . introduc[es] an almost medieval-knightly code of behavior, as between a lord and a vassal, or mystic and religious, as between a master and a slave" (Fusini, "Commento alla relazione de Silvia Vegetti Finzi"). Cf. Boscagli, "Unaccompanied Ladies," 133–34.

20. "Suggerendo che la donna è sì, in quanto cittadina, un pieno soggetto di diritto, epperò, in quanto gravida, è contenitore del nascituro. Insomma il suo ventre non le appartiene, né le appartiene ciò che in esso sta avvenendo, cosicchè lei non può decidere della generazione" (78).

Works Cited

Alcoff, Linda. "Cultural Feminism Versus Post-Structuralism: The Identity Crisis in Feminist Theory." *Signs* 13.3 (1988).

Anna, Claudia, Franca, Gabriella, Giovanna, Liana, Lore, Moira, Nerina, Nicoletta, Rosetta, Serena, Giovanna, eds. *Da desiderio a desiderio: donne, sessualità e progettualità lesbica*. Florence: L'Amandorla, 1989. The book contains the proceedings of the V Convegno Nazionale Lesbico (Fifth National Lesbian Convention), Dec. 5–7, 1987. The convention was hosted by the Centro Convegni CGIL dell' Impruneta near Florence, a major study and convention center of the political parties and unions of the left. This hospitality is worth noting inasmuch as it represents the pluralism of these organizations.

Aristotle. *Poetics*, trans. James Hutton. New York: Norton, 1982.

Boccia, Maria Luisa. *L'io in rivolta: pensiero e vissuto di Carla Lonzi*. Milan: La Tartaruga, 1990.

Bono, Paola, and Sandra Kemp, eds. *Italian Feminist Thought: A Reader*. Oxford: Blackwell, 1991.

———. *The Lonely Mirror: Italian Perspectives on Feminist Theory*. London: Routledge, 1993.

Boscagli, Maurizia. "Unaccompanied Ladies." *Differences* 2.3 (1990): 122–35.

Braidotti, Rosi. "United States of Europe or United Colors of Benetton?" *Differences* 2.3 (Fall 1990): 109–21.

———. *Patterns of Dissonance*. London: Routledge, 1991.

Campari, M. Grazia, Rosaria Canzano, Lia Cigarini, Sciana Loaldi, Laura Roseo, and Claudia Shanmah. "Entrustment Enters the Palace." In *Italian Feminist Thought*, ed. Bono and Kemp, 1991. (First published in Italian in 1985.)

Cantarella, Eva. *Bisexuality in the Ancient World*, trans. Cormac O'Cuilleanàin. New Haven: Yale University Press, 1992. (First published in Italian in 1988 as *Secondo Natura* [According to nature]. Rome: Riuniti.)

Is Anything Like That Possible?

Cavarero, Adriana. "L'elaborazione filosofica della differenza sessuale." In *La ricerca delle donne*, ed. Marcuzzo and Rossi-Doria.
———. *Nonostante Platone: Figure femminili nella filosofia antica*. Rome: Editori Riuniti, 1990.
Cavarero, Adriana, et al., eds. *Diotima: Il pensiero della differenza sessuale*. Milan: La Tartaruga, 1987.
Cecchini, Anna di Fausta, Gabriella Lapasini, Mara Valli, and Luciana Viviani, eds. *Sesso amaro: Trentamila donne rispondono su maternità, sessualità e aborto*. Rome: Editori Riuniti, 1977. This is a survey of women's perceptions of sexuality, maternity, and abortion based on testimonials.
Collettivo della libreria delle donne di Milano. *Non credere di avere dei diritti: La generazione della libertà femminile nell'idea e nelle vicende di un gruppo di donne*. Turin: Rosenberg & Sellier, 1987.
de Lauretis, Teresa. "The Essence of the Triangle, or Taking the Risk of Essentialism Seriously: Feminist Theory in Italy, the U.S., and Britain." *Differences* 1.3 (1989): 3–37.
Derrida, Jacques. *Heidegger et la Question de l'Ésprit*. Paris: Galilée, 1987.
Dominijanni, Ida. "Radicality and Asceticism." In *Italian Feminist Thought*, ed. Bono and Kemp, 1991. (First published in Italian in 1987.)
Fiocchetto, Rosanna. *L'amante celeste: La distruzione scientifica della lesbica*. Florence: Estro, 1987. This book is a synoptic history of lesbian sexuality, life, and persecution in Italy. It is the most dependable source until a forthcoming history (by Rina Macrelli) is available.
Franco, Elvia. "L'affidamento nel rapporto pedagogico." In *Diotima: Il pensiero della differenza sessuale*. See Diotima, 1990.
Fusini, Nadia. "Commento alla relazione di Silvia Vegetti Finzi." In *La ricerca delle donne*, ed. Marcuzzo and Rossi-Doria, 1988.
Garzanti. *Grande dizionario Garzanti della lingua italiana*. Milan, 1987.
Hellman, Stephen. *Italian Communism in Transition*. New York: Oxford University Press, 1988.
Lister, Maureen. "Feminism alla milanese." *Women's Review of Books* 8.9 (June 1991): 26.
Lonzi, Carla. "Let's Spit on Hegel." In *Italian Feminist Thought*, ed. Bono and Kemp, 1991. (The article was first published in Italian in 1970, as *Sputiamo su Hegel*, *La donna clitoridea e la donna vaginale*.)
Lyons, John. *Introduction to Theoretical Linguistics*. London: Cambridge University Press, 1968.
Marcuzzo, Maria Cristina, and Anna Rossi-Doria, eds. *La ricerca delle donne: Studi femministi in Italia*. Turin: Rosenberg & Sellier, 1988.
Milan Women's Bookstore Collective. *Sexual Difference: A Theory of Social-Symbolic Practice*. Bloomington: Indiana University Press, 1990.
Moi, Toril. *Sexual/Textual Politics*. London: Methuen, 1985.
Negri, Magda, and Alberta Pasquero. "La differenza sessuale nel PCI." *Il Ponte* 46.12 (Dec. 1990): 19–33.
Piussi, Anna Maria. "Visibilità/significatività del femminile e logos della pedagogia." In *Diotima: Il pensiero della differenza sessuale* (115–52). See Diotima, 1990.
Sapir, Edward. *Language: An Introduction to the Study of Speech*. New York: Harcourt Brace & World, 1921.
Seroni, Adriana. *La questione femminile in Italia*. Rome: Editori Riuniti, 1977.
Stanton, Domna. "Difference on Trial: A Critique of the Maternal Metaphor in Cixous, Irigaray, and Kristeva." In *The Poetics of Gender*, ed. Nancy K. Miller. New York: Columbia University Press, 1986.
Stone, Sandy. *Body Guards*. New York: Routledge, 1990.
Ufficio Stampa del Gruppo Comunista del Senato. *Perchè i comunisti invitano a votare NO ai due referendum sull' aborto*. Rome, 1981.
Verdicchio, Pasquale. "Spike Lee's Guineas." Paper presented at Café Cinema, San Diego, March 12, 1993.

Violi, Patrizia. L'*infinito singolare: considerazioni sulla differenza sessuale nel linguaggio*. Verona: Essedue, 1988. This book analyzes sexual difference in Italian language and linguistics.

Willett, John (trans.) *Brecht on Theater*. New York: Hill & Wang, 1964.

Williams, Selase. "Developing an Afrocentric Discipline: Intellectual, Cultural and Political Issues." Paper presented at the conference "Multiple Tongues," University of California, Los Angeles, Jan. 31, 1992.

Renate Holub

Between the United States and Italy
Critical Reflections on Diotima's Feminist/Feminine Ethics

Die Sittlichkeit ist
die Idee der Freiheit
    Hegel

L'uguale che non ammette
differenze non lascia
spazio alla mediazione
    Adriana Cavarero

. . . il faut que le monde
des femmes réalise ensemble
un ordre éthique
    Luce Irigaray

Doubling the Paradox

Since the mideighties, groups of women philosophers have emerged on the Italian cultural landscape.[1] From Naples to Milan and from Rome to Verona, women engage in critical encounters with the western philosophical traditions. In Naples, they tend to organize themselves around the journal *Transizione*. In Rome, the Casa Virginia Woolf, a cultural center of and for women, renowned since the beginnings of the women's movement in Italy, is the preferred point of reference. In Milan, the important meeting ground is the Women's Bookstore of Milan, as historically credentialed as the Casa Virginia Woolf. In Verona, the community of women philosophers meets at the university. They call themselves "Diotima," and what they genuinely postulate is, in the geometrical traces of Luce Irigaray, a philosophy of liberatory practices based on the concept of sexual difference.[2] The purpose

233

of my argument is to comment on Diotima's discourse and the function this discourse from another world might play in the context of our feminist cultures here in the United States. I would like to state from the outset that the two major concepts promoted by Diotima—a philosophy of liberational practices and a notion of sexual difference on which that philosophy is based—do lend themselves to a critical analysis of contemporary U.S. feminist practices. For whereas the latter concept, sexual difference, has received sustained attention throughout the history of second-wave feminism, the former has not. So it is in reference to this former concept of a feminist/feminine ethics that I will conclude my argument in this article, and it is in reference to the latter concept, sexual difference, that I will begin it.

That Italian feminist theorists would conceptualize the notion of sexual difference does not command at first sight, and from this side of the ocean, more than ordinary attention. After all, here in the United States, we have been, *nolens volens*, amply treated to that concept in the form of essentialism. Indeed, sexual difference *qua* essentialism has become a household term of U.S. feminist theory. Ever since the early 1970s, many an exciting debate on the advantages and disadvantages of sexual difference and its politics has kept feminist, feminine, and female discourse going.[3] With the publication in English of the work of Hélène Cixous, Luce Irigaray, and Julia Kristeva, this discourse, always potentially more theoretically than practically oriented, turned into an even more prolific academic enterprise. Due to the self-imposed social isolationism of large parts of the U.S. academic intelligentsia, however, this discourse could become central in the academy and remain marginal to society at large. So from behind the apparently irreducible fronts of essentialism, non-essentialism, and anti-essentialism alike, we have been instructed by the mandarines of the feminist establishment what the essential cause of women's oppression is. For some theorists our sex, different from the opposite sex, is the sexual difference that accounts for all inequities between men and women. For others it is not nature but culture that should be held accountable for differently structuring the world of the two different sexes in terms of ubiquitous inequities. So whether we should ground our liberational struggle on a foundational principle that affirms or denies essential difference has become the foremost controversy of second-wave feminist theory in the United States. Equally controversial is what seems to some an inexorable paradox: How can we pursue social, political, economic, and cultural equality for women by insisting on the irreducible fact of sexual difference, a concept that always potentially establishes a vertical system of hierarchies between the two differentiated terms, thereby hauling one sex, the entire world of women, onto a pedestal of moral, epistemological, and ontological superiority?[4] And conversely, how can we pursue equality for women by insisting not on the existence of a foundational sexual difference, but on the existence of the genderization of culture, society, language, and philosophy? The concept of gender potentially establishes an all-pervasive power system within which both sexes ultimately fall victim, whether in a differentiated or undifferentiated fashion, to the machinations of engendered constructions. Should our feminist strategy pursue the effacement of difference or its generation? Is difference good or bad, biological, social, or historical? Is it a weakness or a strength? Should we forfeit a notion of sexual difference on the grounds that all people, men and women, are not essentially different from each other, but merely culturally constructed as different? Can these constructions of masculinity and femininity be undone? Or should we maintain the notion of sexual difference, of femininity, on the grounds that men and women are not equal but essentially different from one another, a difference that, due to the powers ultimately inscribed in feminine sexuality, purportedly harbors enormous advantages for women? Should one seek out the subversive powers of the unessential positionality of a feminine unconscious, with Julia Kristeva? Or should one uncover the creative powers of an essentially feminine unconscious with Luce Irigaray and Hélène Cixous, since such powers have been marginalized, silenced, by the symbolic all-pervasiveness of the law of the father?[5] Or should one, with Mary Daly and Adrienne Rich, embrace a view that values our physicality as a powerful resource, rather than a weakness?[6] Should we divide the world into a feminine good and a masculine evil? Or should we proceed differently, not theorize exclusively universalist questions of feminine sexuality and the body but rather questions of the body in social, cultural, political, and economic spaces, whereby the differences in women's oppression, namely their ethnic, class and religious differentials, come to the fore?[7]

These are some of the questions that have informed the discourse on essentialism over the last few decades. What should also be mentioned are debates on the notion of subjectivity, on the construction of the subject, and on the possibility of a feminine unconscious present, as Jung thought, in all human beings, and not only in women. There were also feminist discussions on the possibility of an undifferentiated infant sexuality, and thus a sexually undifferentiated experience of the unconscious, as Juliett Mitchell and Jacqueline Rose pursued. In addition, feminists debated the issue of human agency in relation to subjectivity, identity, and positionality. Many of these issues were generated in the contest between the modern and postmodern faculties.[8] What is interesting is that in spite of this publication explosion on the issue of sexual difference in the United States, there has been very little discussion of differences that have little to do with sex. I am referring to differences enacted among women. Indeed, there is a specter that haunts the feminist landscape here: the specter of power struggles among women. Most feminist theory dispenses with the most basic protocols of feminist ethics by not addressing relations of power among women. As a result, feminist theory has run into a paradox: a lack of ethics marks the upshot of a discourse originally constructed on nonnegotiable ethics. I don't recall feminisms ever stating that the oppression of women by men is a good thing.

The discourses on essentialism often attempt (perhaps in order to follow critical trends) to present themselves as ontological and epistemological. So the voices that feel compelled to raise the issue of the superiority of essentialism at every occasion simultaneously imply the inferiority of all those positions that seem to espouse non-essentialist or anti-essentialist points of view. Surely the term moral, as old-fashioned and theoretically unsophisticated as it is, activating images of eighteenth-century imperatives or twentieth-century liberal thought, is not easily deployable under these circumstances, particularly in the context of the many current discursive practices that adhere to the orthodox party line of antihumanist, anti-Enlightenment, and anticommunicative ontological dogmatics. Yet as long as the essentialist/anti-essentialist debacles continue, in which one party claims to espouse a better view than the other and in which one claims superior political efficacy in the struggle for women's liberation, we are, whether we like it or not, dealing with rather traditional issues of morality and ethics. A discourse on feminist/feminine ontology does not, all wishful thinking to the contrary, *ipso facto* replace or displace a discourse on ethics. If anything, it misplaces it. If the discourse on sexual difference has lost some of its ground, it is not because it has slowed its profuse discursive assembly line. It is rather because it has to share its ground with the paradox of a lack of feminist ethics. This has not gone unnoticed in the feminist community.

Many women these days value not what is being said for or against essentialism, but rather what is being done. Therefore, the important question is not what those women who speak for or against the superiority of essentialism say but rather what they do—their decisions and their actions concerning other women, in the practices of their everyday lives. Perhaps more political than the written and published is that which appears nonpublic, but which privately manifests itself in the practices of everyday life. The private is, as ever, eminently political. It is hardly a secret that the 1980s ushered in an unprecedented shift in the morality of neofeminism, something that has led to what I call the poverty of critical feminism. Many parts of the academy did not hesitate to refuse their share in this booming business carried out at the expense of the ideals of the feminist movements. From eagerly trading women's studies, fought for by generations of feminists, for gender studies to refusing to reflect on the agendas that turn gender studies into accomplices of a degendered status quo, and from consenting to the seizure of the feminist banner by a series of men thoroughly illiterate in feminist cultures to contributing to the seizure of power by a series of "feminist" women thoroughly illiterate in matters of feminist solidarity, large parts of the academy have given distinct proof of their immense ability to adjust uncritically, in theory and practice, to the general winds that blow. Those winds blew strongly in the direction of abandoning the materiality of everyday life in favor of an ideality called "theory." And those winds blew perhaps strongest not only in suppressing a critique of the often unsettling political practices in the everyday life of so-called feminists, but also in dogmatically resisting any form of self-critique. Indeed, what is striking about the predominant essentialist/anti-essentialist rhetoric is its immense lack of self-reflection, the absence of a concept of the politicality of the practices of everyday life, the nonexistence of a sense of accountability for what happens or does not happen among, next to, for and against women.[9] In the predominant feminist discourse, the jubilant celebration of the multiplicitous politicality of feminist theory goes hand in hand—a rather pathetic union—with a dogmatic repression of any self-critique of practices among women. As in a traditional patriarchal setup, the language of power attempts to contain, censor, and even silence the experiential knowledge of those women whose bodies have been marked by promoters of monitored silence.

Resistance to that union arrives from many quarters. Younger women, with visions relatively unimpaired by the multiple layers of essentialist/anti-essentialist theoretical squabbles, astutely observe the interested silencing of power-laden conflicts between powerful and powerless women, and draw their conclusions. For some this means, for better or for worse, to go post—if not even anti—feminist. This is hardly a gain for the movements at large. Other women reflect upon the sometimes unsolicited support they can get from women without established feminist credentials. Others still activate, on their terms, concepts and experiences that played a central part among many women at the beginning of the movements: they contribute to a construction of feminist solidarity at their place of work or study. Moreover, they continue with critical examination of the effects of patriarchal power structures on women and their relations with other women, an examination that has become more difficult to pursue in the 1980s due to the lip service paid to feminism, or rather to the feminine. Furthermore, many of these women are dedicated—in the face of the patriarchy and dynastic male privilege badly hidden behind the mask of "interest in questions of femininity"—to the construction of feminist cultures, to solidarity among women who stand for effacing women's oppression in particular and effacing the oppression of other social groups in general. In short, they adhere to a political philosophy, they have a concept of political practice, a notion of feminist ethics. They cultivate this notion in the interstices and at the margins of the official feminist culture and, as of late, with the help of electronic technology. Other women continue to do what they have done for a while: they keep raising uneasy questions, as Barbara Christian does, questions that address the marginalization or exoticization of nonwhite women, in any event their condescending treatment, by the white and middle-class feminist establishment.[10] In this vein, bell hooks adds new dynamics and new ways of seeing to our coming to terms with the poverty of feminism. Of the many feminist publications opportunely dedicated to the "feminist/feminine track," bell hooks's writings are in contrast striking in their effort to preserve measures of critical thinking, and above all of self-critique.[11] Indeed, it seems to me that it is not from the centers of feminist power but from the margins that notions of genuine solidarity are evoked, that a critique of women's actions in the practices of everyday life is voiced, and, above all, that the concept of self-critique, so conspicuously and unconscionably absent from predominant feminist discourse, is reactivated as a powerful tool for the advancement of liberational ways of thinking and willing. It is not from the centers but from the margins, I think, that feminist discourse can regain strength and energy, renew an agenda of community, while simultaneously listening to the powerful insights of new, perhaps younger, but not necessarily less experienced voices. Not from the centers but from the margins can feminism activate some of the powers, moral and otherwise, it lost in the spectacular display of the doubling of the feminist paradox in the 1980s.

Predicaments of the Cultural Business

Perhaps it is appropriate here, when talking about margins and centers, to mention that Italian feminism and feminist theory has lived its own marginal existence, next to big-time feminist theory, in the United States. For those more or less initiated in the cultural exchange business between Europe and the United States, however, the marginalization of Italian feminism rings no particular bell. Italian cultural goods in general have not been distributed in a fashion in any way comparable to the heavy imports from France and Germany. Indeed, rumor has it that the world historical spirit of theory prefers to settle on German and French grounds, avoiding whenever possible any contamination with cultural configurations that lie at the edge of the Heideggerian antihumanist rejection of Cartesian subjectivisms and Kantian imperatives. It does not take much to conclude that a culture such as Italy's, which has produced centuries of many different humanisms, and in particular a philosopher such as Giambattista Vico, would have the conceptual resources to problematize facile forms of current thinking.[12] Italian imports might offer alternatives or differentiated forms of different notions in the context of the global cultural business. That Italian cultural goods, including feminisms, are indeed not easily marketed on the North American continent is a phenomenon for which there is no simple explanation. Until recently, Italian departments in the U.S. academy were notoriously keeping what seemed to many a deliberately low profile on most campuses, resisting, with their insistence on self-imposed ghettoization, isolation, and monodisciplinarity, the general trends toward interdisciplinarity and cross-culturization. While Italian culture produced highly fascinating events throughout the 1960s and 1970s, the cultural workers on this side of the ocean, who by profession and training would have been the logical selectors of Italian goods, played it safe. With a few exceptions, they stayed within the literary canons of an outdated tradition constructed by a handful of Italian intellectuals—De Sanctis, Croce—who, however brilliant, responded with their canonization schemes to cultural problems of their time, and not of ours. There is reason to believe, however, that the marginal status of Italian studies is related not only to the somewhat curious adherence to outdated disciplinary models but also to the social status of Italian American ethnicity in this country. The marginalization of things Italian is possibly as much a "colonial" imposition as it is self-imposed. With recent developments in the area of ethnic self-awareness and consciousness raising, both coercion and consent to the status quo could become increasingly nonviable in the context of Italian studies.[13] Whether these developments will enhance the imports of modernized Italian goods remains largely to be seen. Business is usually done by two parties, and cultural business is no exception. If cultural workers on this side of the ocean were slow in distributing relevant material, it must also be noted that cultural workers in Italy were reluctant, on their own account, in actively marketing their goods as well. So the apparently uneven competition among European cultural politics, visible in a particularly heavy flow from Germany and France, does not tell the whole story, since Italy does belong, after all, to the most powerful nations in terms of its economic and technological affairs, passing Great Britain with its G.N.P.[14] Judging from the relatively small number of Italian foundations and cultural institutes substantially encouraging research on Italian affairs, there is indeed little reason to believe that superior economic resources necessarily lead to an increase in cultural influence. Whether intellectuals in Italy will reassess their reluctance to sell their goods on the North American market—a reluctance hidden behind a mixed facade of professed anti-Americanism and self-congratulatory provincialism—is an open-ended question. And, of course, this reluctance can be viewed as something altogether different: as a deliberate move to resist hegemonic homogenizations, a desire to stay at the margins and to observe and comment from there, unencumbered by the frenzy of ever more swiftly alternating theoretical models. As heirs to a great theorist, Antonio Gramsci, who attended to the subversive powers inscribed in marginal positions, Italian intellectuals might after all not be all that impervious to such an ideology. If my discussion of Diotima's concept of "sexual difference" helps to stimulate a discourse on this side of the ocean on questions of power-laden relations among women, then the importance of marginality in its relation to change would surely be affirmed. Yet this is not the foremost item on my agenda. More important to me is a discussion of practices among women, and the political philosophies of Diotima are a suitable point of departure for addressing such practices. To these I will now turn.

Diotima's Heritage

There are many ways of telling the story of Diotima, this community of philosophers from the Northern Italian city of Verona that has chosen to name itself after an ancient woman philosopher, Diotima of Mantineia. One could tell the story in the context of feminist groups in Italy in general. In this case, the modalities of Diotima's political strategies are easily written off as something they share with most other feminist communities in Italy in the context of second-wave feminism. They make sure to choose for themselves a value-laden name, as the very first women's groups had done, such as Gruppo Demau and Rivolta Femminile.[15] And, as with many of the Italian women's groups in pursuit of a nonnegotiably democratic political agenda, an agenda that can speak to the needs of women from many if not all walks of life, Diotima too has an eye to a constituency that includes more than simply academic women. Moreover, with their insistence on a set of foundational assumptions in philosophical discourse, such as sexual difference and a social-symbolic practice, the women of Diotima again reflect the penchant of Italian feminists to focus on a set of foundational concepts. In addition, their resistance to dispensing with the protocols of meticulous argument, to dispensing with hermeneutic tact and decorum when dealing with regarded and unregarded texts alike, I also see as a trademark of many Italian feminist productions.[16] Although Diotima busily trades its commercial shares on the philosophical market, it would be simplifying matters very grossly if one were to presume that only Diotima, as a group that treats philosophical matters, is talented when it comes to dealing with Western philosophy as an object of knowledge. Many Italian feminist individuals and collectives alike have, in intelligent disregard of the arbitrary demarcations of their originary disciplines, rendered intensely problematic many a text of the guarded Western philosophical tradition. Carla Lonzi, unofficial spokeswoman of Rivolta Femminile, comes to mind with her *Sputiamo su Hegel*, and so does Mariarosa Dalla Costa, whose analysis of the unpaid labor of the housewife brilliantly revised Marx's analysis of the political economy of capitalism.[17] There are other examples: Adele Cambria's formidable critiques of Marx and of Gramsci, and many of the intermittent articles by Rossana Rossanda.[18] Furthermore, Diotima's aligning herself with a feminist center, in this case with the historically credentialed Women's Bookstore of Milan, and perhaps Diotima's functioning as the Northern Italian think tank of the differentiated rank and file of that bookstore, as the theoretical avant-garde of a practically oriented movement, is also not new in the context of the history of Italian feminism. Many Italian feminists have managed—in spite of a pervasive cultural trend toward rampant individualism, in spite of the historical force of an antifeminist counterrevolution—not only to sustain notions of the importance of socially differentiated collectives but also to insist on the liberational powers that potentially arise from a dialectical relation between practices and

Renate Holub

theories. If Diotima does not depart from the usual path of Italian feminisms, however, the space it inhabits on this path, I will argue, is unusual nonetheless. And perhaps it is by pointing to an up-to-now unregarded detail that the specificity of Diotima's role, and the way in which Diotima self-consciously understands her role in the context of Italian second-wave feminism, can come to the fore. What I am referring to is the very name this group has chosen for itself: "Diotima." We first encounter the name Diotima, and the woman who is known under that name, in the history of Western thought, in Plato's *Symposium*.

This is to say, we do not encounter Diotima in Plato's *Symposium* the way in which we encounter the participants at the symposium, a "working banquet" taking place in Agathon's house. Socrates, Phaedrus, Pausanias, and Alcibiabes, and Aristodemus, Aristophanes, and Eryximachus, and perhaps a few more—a group of men who have come together to eat, drink, and talk about love, while simultaneously staking out for themselves new possibilities for and of passion and love. There are no women present in the salon in which this seminar takes place, though some women must be present in adjacent chambers: the servants and the flute-girls, and perhaps, who knows, Agathon's wife. There are many interconnected threads to this narrative told by Plato, yet the main storyline seems to go something like this. According to Plato, Aristodemus, who apparently participated in the seminar, told Appolodorus about what Socrates had to say about love at the symposium. After a series of proposals put forth by the various participants concerning the nature of love, at some point during the night Socrates took the floor and offered to tell a tale he had heard from a woman, Diotima of Mantineia, "a woman wise in this [love] and in many other kinds of knowledge," who was Socrates' "instructress in the art of love."[19] So according to Plato's account of Appolodorus's account of Aristodemus's account of Socrates' account of Diotima's account of love, love is not something you have but something you want, a great spirit, a *daimon*, an intermediary between the divine and the human, an interpreter between gods and humankind. Diotima goes on in this narrative to describe love as the mediator who spans the chasm dividing the divine from the human, as in love all is bound together. Moreover, love brings about the passage of nonbeing into being, a force that impregnates soul and body, that generates creation, knowledge, poetry, making, immortality, as well as eternity.

In the context of Plato's *Symposium*, Diotima is the authoritative text from which Socrates mediates, as he seizes the floor, the various proposals put forth in this nocturnal seminar as to the nature, function, and possibilities of love. Indeed, Diotima's notion of love incorporates aspects of and in some ways dialectically mediates the various positions put forth at the symposium. It incorporates Phaedrus's notion of the relation between love, life, and death. It includes Pausanias's contention that there are two kinds of love. It also speaks to Erychimachus, who maintains that two kinds of love are necessary. In addition, it contains elements from Aristophanes' proposition concerning the androgynous elements in love. And finally, it also includes the attributes Agathon enlists in his praise of love. In this sense, by way of her proposition on love Diotima practices what she herself had to say about the way love generates and effects ideal and material change, guaranteeing not only the continuity of being but also the immortality of knowledge—material and ideal eternity at once. Love impregnates the body as well as the soul, unites that which is known with that which is yet to be generated, and it is in the generation of the new that some of the old is recollected and mediated. The lines from paragraph 208 of the *Symposium* read like this:

> For what is implied in the word "recollection"
> but the departure of knowledge, which is ever being
> forgotten, and is renewed and preserved by recollection,
> and appears to be the same although it is new according
> to the law of succession by which all mortal things are
> preserved, not absolutely the same, but by substitution,
> the old worn-out mortality leaving another new and
> similar existence behind unlike the divine,
> which is always the same and not another?[20]

Socrates' or Plato's Diotima practices or performs mediation in her presentation on love. She also deploys concepts that bring into metaphoric play the foundationally transformatory and mediating powers of love, combining stasis with motion, nonbeing with coming into being, noncreation with creating, nonknowing with processes of knowing. Her thought activates an imagistic horizon that knows of desires for the infinite, for poetry (in the sense of *poein*, making), for creativity, for immortality. It is also a horizon that, in its metaphoric choice not of contracting circularity but of extending teleology, evokes a human drive or desire for the divine, the endless, the unbound, for perfect nonconstrainedness, and perhaps for pure or absolute freedom.

It is surely a fortuitous choice Verona's community of women philosophers has made in appropriating Plato's Diotima for their purposes. This choice is not merely nominal but spiritual and symbolic as well. Plato's Diotima is a positive figure who constructs, mediates, generates, creates.[21] Many of these key metaphoric attributes of Plato's Diotima reemerge in or are part of Diotima's program: not the dismantling or deconstruction of what there is, but the generation of nonbeing into being; not questioning the possibility of subjecthood and identity, but generating a feminine subject and a feminine identity that as of yet has not been; not the interrogating of how the language and culture of patriarchal or phallogocentric power works and what it does, but the generation of a language, of a culture, of a conceptuality of and for women, of a social-symbolic practice among women that has not yet been. When Diotima specifies, however, that the generation of a social-symbolic practice is a nonnegotiable dialectical mediation along a specified phenomenological trajectory that transforms a bound and unfree consciousness into a subject of feminine freedom, then it brings another philosophical tradition of credentialed standing into play, namely that of Hegel. With this, Diotima does not so much abandon Plato in favor of Hegel as she mediates between these two. In a motion that doubly advantages the feminist cause, Diotima mediates between those elements in Plato's Diotima and in Hegel's *Phenomenology* (as well as in Hegel's *Philosophy of Right*) which are most propitious for developing the generation of an authentic feminine subject and absolute feminine freedom. Yet this modern incarnation of the mediating powers of Plato's Diotima operates in other ways, and more important ones: Diotima attempts to mediate between women, not only, as it turns out, in terms of the various factions and theories making up the geography of Italian feminism but also between the practices of actual, living women. That mediation, based on a theory of social-symbolic practice founded on sexual difference, presupposes not identities but differences among women, not indifferentiation but differentiation when it comes to status, power, functions, abilities, possibilities, and so forth. It is to that mediation and the potential of that mediation that I will now turn.

Between Plato and Hegel: Diotima's Ethical Order

Some of the cardinal questions of Diotima, as recorded in their many publications, read like this: How can woman become a subject? How can she love herself, if indeed her effective situation is to be in exile, and to love others, her children, a man, the house?[22] How can woman become a subject if the symbolic, the linguistic, the conceptual within which she moves is not of her own making? How can she be a subject if she is the negated other of the theory of the subject of Western phallocratic discourse? How can woman be a subject if she lives in perennial alienation, alienated from herself and from others? These questions are surely reminiscent of Luce Irigaray's rigorous interrogation of the place and function of woman in Western constructions of the symbolic, as she has worked it out in her famous *Speculum* (1974) or *This Sex Which Is Not One* (1977), as well as in *Ethique de la différence sexuelle* (1984). Diotima has decidedly turned to Irigaray for a good deal of inspiration. They have also added a problematic that goes well beyond Irigaray.[23] Here I refer to the distinct style many of the philosophers of the Diotima collective have chosen to adopt. That style, by following traditional logics of causality, syntax, and diction, reflects their reluctance to dispense with the protocols of realist philosophical writing. It also probably reflects their reluctance to dispense with the protocols of traditional rhetoric. If Diotima's goal is to reach with their theoretical model the largest number of women possible from all walks of life, indeed to write a major philosophical narrative of and for women, then their decision to not emulate Irigaray's experimental prose but to pursue a straightforward, comprehensible, and realistic step-by-step style, as unimaginative as that might seem to postmodern minds, was surely well taken. Yet it is not only in rhetorical wisdom, in pragmatics when it comes to style, that Diotima goes beyond Irigaray. Equally pragmatic is their cardinal precept that an ethical order of and for women must be conceptually presented in orderly fashion. An ethics that speaks of a realization of desires and needs in the private as well as the public realm, in civil as well as in political society, one that celebrates the coming into being of woman as subject—that ethics cannot be presented *only* as an abstract model. Rather, the path to that stage of realization of feminine freedom must be staked out in some imaginable fashion, not simply as a promise but in concrete steps and motions. So while Diotima appropriates Irigaray's questions, in particular as Irigaray discusses the question of feminine freedom in her lecture "L'amour du même, l'amour de l'autre," Diotima simultaneously transcends Irigaray. With Irigaray, and not the least less apodictically, this group of women philosophers maintains that a feminine ethical order is necessary and states why. "Il faut qu'un symbolisme soit crée entre femmes pour que l'amour entre elles puisse avoir lieu," writes Irigaray.[24] The creation of a feminine order "acquisisce una sua necessità storica [becomes a historical necessity]," writes one of the philosophers of Diotima.[25]

Yet Diotima not only believes in the categorical necessity of a feminine order. "Non si esce da un pensiero semplicemente pensando di uscirne, almeno finche quel pensiero dell'uscita si struttura sulle medesime categorie del pensiero dal quale vuole uscire."[26] One cannot escape the logic of an order simply by wanting to escape it, writes Adriana Cavarero. What one needs is a set of new categories, capable of structuring differently the logics of an order that attempts to be new. So when, beyond Irigaray, Diotima ventures to indicate how that new ethical order can come about, they work hard to invent new categories commensurate with that new order. Among these are "the mediating category of women resembling each other, or of being similar to one another" (*"categoria mediatrice del somigliarsi"*) and the "originary duality or originary double nature of feminine being" (*"duale originario"*), not an ontic but a socio-ontological category that determines the double alterity of woman's existence, which woman can turn into a decidedly feminist political advantage via the practice of "the act of entrusting herself," of the *affidamento*.[27]

But let me reproduce Diotima's reasoning and logic within which these extraordinary concepts find their propitious sphere of operation. It goes something like this: How can woman be a subject if she identifies, fuses with her origins, the mother, given that that mother, as benevolent as she might be, or as benevolently as she might have sedimented herself in and with the primary narcissism of the unconscious, has always already been excluded from the symbolic, from language, from culture, from self-realization, from sociality and community, has always been the "other" of the patriarchal discourse? How can woman gain presence in and access to reality by identifying with an absence in that reality? Instead, asks Diotima, why not have recourse to a different relation with and to the mother, a relation that stresses difference, distantiation, and differentiation, rather than identity and fusion? A relation of fusion of difference and differentiation between symbolic mothers and daughters creates powerful conditions for new and liberatory possibilities. By seeing themselves not as the same as but different from the other woman, who is the "other" of the male discourse, but also as similar to the other woman, women approach the possibility of their own ethical order. Recognizing not identity but similarity, similarity that respects the differences between women, makes woman, as differentiable similarity, into the Other (capitalized). That Other can activate the potential that exists somewhere in women in spite of and because of their differentiation, be it social, economic, psychological, volitional, and so on. It is then not by being the other of phallocratic culture, but by being

Between the United States and Italy

the other/Other, by living and recognizing this double alterity and the potential inscribed in this state, that a feminine ethics can be constructed. An awareness of double alterity becomes the quid pro quo of a feminine ethics, a mediating category that moves woman from nonbeing into being, from nonsubjecthood to subjecthood, from nonfreedom to freedom.

Diotima's relation to Irigaray is characterized by a continuous play of theoretical separation and reunion. The Diotima collective seems to both separate itself from and return to Irigaray, or rather to Irigaray's interest in Hegel, when they explicate and substantiate the liberatory process from nonfreedom to freedom.[28] The concept at issue is what we might call the backbone of Diotima's ethical paradigm, the notion of *affidamento*. It is a critical appropriation, indeed a transformation, of the motions of Hegel's master/slave dialectic, on the one hand. Yet it is also an appropriation of the far-reaching political and social dimensions of Hegel's notion of ethicality, on the other hand. So while Irigaray, with her many studies of philosophical texts, has charted the way for Diotima when it comes to critical readings and appropriations of classical philosophical texts, Diotima charts her own way for new readings and appropriations of similar texts. What again emerges is Diotima's extraordinary practical, pragmatic sense. The point is not, so it seems, to reread the world, as is seen in Diotima's adaptation of the eleventh thesis on Feuerbach, but to change it.[29] Thus the trajectory toward feminine freedom, as outlined by Diotima in the traces of their understanding of Hegel's political project, looks something like this: by identifying with other women, as women have done almost throughout the beginnings of second-wave feminism, woman reenacted a symbolic fusion with the mother. It was a consciousness that existed in itself, in an undifferentiated fashion with respect to other women, not in sexual difference, and therefore without possibilities of movement toward higher stages of consciousness, liberation, and freedom. The result was a community of women, together as women yet separate and isolated from sociality at large. Therefore, women lived largely, in spite of the feminist movement, at the margins of sociality, and they were not in the position of substantially affecting it. Through the practice of *affidamento*, however, women can activate a liberatory project that is individual and collective at the same time. How does this work? A woman, perhaps a younger woman of less experience and of less social and political prestige, privilege, and power, entrusts herself to another woman, who is perhaps but not necessarily older, and who has more prestige, more power, and more status. In this process of *affidamento* the age-old relation between mother and daughter is symbolically activated, a relation that is unequal in that the mother has an emotional, physical, and psychological advantage over the daughter. The mother will then use her power to mediate between the outside world and the daughter, between the patriarchal and phallocratic law of the father and the realm of the daughter that is devoid of a specifically feminine symbolic, a language, a conceptuality, and an ethics. In the act of mediation, that which exists among women in spite of and because of their differences, that which is latent and similar in women precisely because they live a sexual difference, perhaps the remnants or traces of metaphorics of an ancient, buried, and forgotten imaginary, rises to the surface and becomes powerfully activated, and the potentialities of a feminine subject begin to spark: a feminine language, culture, and symbolic can be created, particularly as this project does not and cannot remain a private matter between a few individuals, between two women. Since these two women are always already social beings, living in political and civil societies, that project takes on collective dimensions. Indeed, women then mediate between their needs and the reality principle of phallocratic society, not in order to adjust their needs—their desire for a language, a symbolic, a culture of their own—to that principle, but in order to adjust that principle to their desires. This progression toward a realization of feminine needs and desires, toward the unearthing of the remnants of an ancient feminine imaginary as well as toward the birthing of a feminine symbolic, is made possible, it seems, by the nature of that interaction between women, by the process of *affidamento*.

Crucial for the practice and the process of *affidamento* is the act of recognition, an act that changes one state of consciousness into another, an act by which consciousness leaps forward, both quantitatively and qualitatively. In the act of recognition, a consciousness recognizes that it is not identical to but different from other consciousnesses, specifically from that of the other woman. Its possibility for freedom is contingent on engaging with the other—a differentiated consciousness—in an act of distantiation that recognizes and, most important, affirms and accepts the power differential between women. The two women of differential power engage with one another, not perhaps in a life-and-death struggle as in Hegel's master/slave dialectic, but in an act of dialectic nonetheless. One woman, by entrusting herself to another woman in recognition of the differential that exists between the two, mediates her social alienation resulting from engagements that seek identification and fusion. Simultaneously, by accepting the gift of *affidamento*, by acknowledging, recognizing, and affirming the distantiated trust of another woman, the more powerful woman must account for and is held accountable for her mediation between the outside world, the phallocratic symbolic orders, and the yet nonexistent world of feminine symbolics. Although it seems that it is the less powerful woman who gains and the more powerful woman who loses in that encounter, the dialectics of the *affidamento* make both women winners in their struggle. For it is not by being-for-herself, by being a simple consciousness, but by being self-consciousness, by being-for-herself-in-herself, that the feminist spirit reaches its liberatory goal. That goal is achieved when woman wants to be not only for herself (stage one) but recognizes and desires to be being-in-and-for-the-other in a differentiable way, a stage where, by being-for-and-in-the-other, both women are potentially unfree and dependent. The unfree, bound, and isolated consciousness of stage one moves to the bound and semifree consciousness of stage two, and from there it can move onto the more liberated realm of stage three, a stage where consciousness can be in-and-for-itself, a free consciousness, that is both simple and complex, identical with but also different from the other. Both women move toward that stage, although they set out from different points of departure. By engaging with the daughter in the dialectic of the *affidamento*, the more powerful woman experiences a moment of reversal: in being held accountable by the other woman, she lives in momentary bondage. By desiring that accountability and by actually being accountable for the other woman, the more powerful woman both converts her own bondage to a nonbondage and simultaneously works to break the less powerful woman's bondage in the phallocratic world. Conversely, by engaging with the mother, the less powerful woman transforms her double alterity, her bondage to the phallocratic world and to the world of the mother. She turns her condition of double bondage, of being oppressed by the patriarchal order of men and women alike, into an advantage by recognizing the power of double alterity. The images that ensue are as elegant and beautiful as those of a mathematical equation: mothers and daughters, by potentiating the numbered roots of their imaginary, squarely unleash infinitesimal symbolic powers.

It should become clear from the conceptual imagery deployed in the process of *affidamento* that Diotima operates, whether expressly stated or not, with the dialectical process of Hegel's *Phenomenology*, in particular as it worked out in the sections on dependence and independence of self-consciousness.[30] Indeed, Diotima appropriates not only a version of the master/slave dialectic but also parts of Hegel's ambitious political project as it is worked out in his *Philosophy of Right*.[31] In both cases Diotima adjusts Hegel to her own purposes, as she uses those aspects of the Hegelian system that are propitious for her program of a feminist/feminine ethics. For instance, the struggle of the consciousness for self-realization and freedom is, in Hegel's design, presented not only in its individual, epistemological, and ontological dimension but in its collective dimension as well, in the realm of practical philosophy, political philosophy, of philosophy of right, and ethics. This is precisely what Diotima, albeit perhaps inadvertently, adopts—namely, the collective, the social, and political dimensions of Hegel's agenda, his preoccupation with civil society. I think it is important to stress this factor, for it explains Diotima's position on a variety of recent issues as they have come up in Italian culture and politics, such as the controversies surrounding the struggle for a law against sexual violence. I will get to some of these problems as I conclude my article. Let me say here that the practice of *affidamento*, enacted and possibly mostly enactable between two individual women, is also an experiment with Hegel's notion of ethicality or *Sittlichkeit*. In this sense, Diotima hopes that the concept of *affidamento* is capable of laying the grounds for a language and a symbolic, indeed for an entire culture of and for women, a world of a political and civil society aiming toward the realization of feminine freedom. It is in the individual and collective power inscribed in the concept of *affidamento*, in its ethicality, that the extraordinary political ambitions of Diotima come to the fore, theoretically staked out without in the least dispensing with the rigor of philosophical protocol. What also comes to the fore are Diotima's extraordinarily theoretical and philosophical ambitions. In her desire to create a new major philosophical narrative, Diotima not only appropriates entire provinces of Hegel's philosophical empire, but rearranges that territory to suit her own purposes. Surely, one might be quick to point out that a feminist project dealing with the Hegelian system would have little choice but to adjust Hegel to feminist sensibilities, given his deplorable record when it comes to women. For one, the master/slave dialectic, emphasizing the singularity of the slave's consciousness, is easily homologizable to another kind of singularity and individuality of consciousness as it appears in Hegel's text: that of woman. Related to the individuality rather than the universality of consciousness, in Hegel's discussion of the ethical world, the world of governments, citizens, laws, and orders, men represent the universal individual in that they, devoid of natural determinacy, create the world of human law, of community, of sociality. Women, on the other hand, as generators of life, as the embodiments of family and thus of religious community, represent the particular individual and divine law. Women take part in universal individuality, as wives of citizens, but only indirectly. As such they do not represent universal individuality but only particular individuality. Their activities, in their nonuniversality, are inconsequential for sociality, ethicality, and community. It is only as sister to brother, so Hegel presumes, that a woman comes close perhaps to assuming an authentic, socially unalienated existence. Indeed, as sister, as woman, the feminine has a premonition (A*hnung*), albeit not a consciousness and no possibilities of realizing for herself, the universality of ethicality. The lines from Hegel's *Phenomenology* read thus:

> An unmixed intransitive form of relationship, however, holds between brother and sister. They are the same blood, which, however, in them has entered into a condition of stable equilibrium. They therefore stand in no such natural relation as husband and wife, they do not desire one another; nor have they given to one another, nor received from one another, this independence of individual being; they are free individualities with respect to each other. The feminine element, therefore, in the form of the sister, premonizes and foreshadows most completely the nature of ethical life (*sittliches Wesen*). She does not become conscious of it, and does not actualize it, because the law of the family is her inherent implicit inward nature, which does not lie open to the daylight of consciousness, but remains inner feeling and the divine element exempt from actuality.[32]

So given Hegel's prejudiced position on the role and function of woman in society and history, and her ultimately insignificant status in his paradigm of ethicality, it should come as no surprise, one might think, that Diotima adjusted and corrected Hegel for their own purposes. However, since there is much more ammunition than the few quotes and explanations provided above that could be brought into play concerning Hegel's prejudiced view of women, Diotima's project assumes much broader dimensions.[33] Working from Hegelian premises, however transformed, means first and foremost staying within a framework that views human beings as the makers of their own societies and communities.[34] In Diotima's project, women can create their own sociality, their laws, their symbolics, not by mediating between what exists and what they want, mediating between the law of the father and the desire for feminine freedom in such a way that they have to adjust their desires to what there is. In some ways, women have always done that. Rather, in Diotima's project, women are the creators of their own world of freedom by activating that desire for feminine freedom that in an incipient stage is perhaps already there, as Hegel suspected, and of which the Diotima of ancient times spoke.[35] This activation can take place when women meet not on equal but on unequal grounds, mutually recognize and address that inequality in power in the process of the *affidamento*, and by doing so engage not in overcoming that unequal power relation among women, but in beginning to mediate and negotiate together, in solidarity, as different women, the unequal power relations between the world of men and of women. In that sense, in the belief in the self-creation and the perfectibility of freedom, Diotima seems indeed to evoke the ancient teachings of Plato's Diotima: a mediator who creates, by mediating, an idea—perhaps more—of freedom.

Toward a Feminist Pragmatics

Diotima's project is, then, a highly ambitious one. Similar to Luce Irigaray, the women of Diotima are out to depart from the logocentric order of western metaphysics. They would like to set the philosophical record straight, as they depart from it, and they would like to think a philosophy, and an ethics, in their own image and liking. Because of the extraordinary philosophical and political scope of their projects, and the attention they have commanded thus far both in Italy and Germany, Diotima has been the object of critique from all kinds of corners. For instance, Diotima has been critiqued for its notion of the subject, a notion that, unencumbered by the psycholinguistic discourses that call into question the unity and the identity of the subject, speaks of human agency, responsibility, and communicative ethics.[36] In addition, Diotima has been critiqued for not taking into account the lesbian issue when talking about sexual difference.[37] Furthermore, Diotima, next to its rank-and-file, the Milan Women's Bookstore Collective, has been at the center of the struggles over the law on sexual violence that have split the women's community in Italy for almost a decade by now.[38] Rather than supporting a law that would establish mandatory prosecution, a letter circulated by the Women's Bookstore envisioned a law that would support voluntary prosecution. This was considered commensurate with expressions of women's self-determination.[39] These are but three of many critiques that point to the controversial nature of Diotima's program, to its political, philosophical, and ethical dimensions. What could also be added is a critique of the self-understanding, the self-consciousness of Diotima with respect to the women's movement in Italy. In a publication that traces the genealogy of second-wave feminism in Italy, there is some indication that the positions of Diotima and the Milan Women's Bookstore Collective are viewed as historical necessity.[40] The images evoked in that history of Italian second-wave feminism replay a version of Hegel's phenomenology of the mind, whereby the consciousness of Italian feminism has developed in a three-act drama. In the first act, feminism is at the stage of merely being-in-itself, then it proceeds to a stage of being-in-and-for-the-other. In its opposition or antithesis to the stage of merely being-in-itself, this second act has mediated the liberatory process of the consciousness of Italian feminism in such a way that the third act, dealing with a consciousness of being-in-and-for-itself, of a realized and free self-consciousness, represents the realization of feminine self-determination and freedom. In this presentation of the historical trajectory of the feminist consciousness, the social-symbolic practice of *affidamento*, attempting to overcome relations of power among women, is not an arbitrary but a necessary and historical point of arrival. As in Hegel's *Phenomenology*, or at least as in some interpretations of Hegel's presentation of the march of the spirit based on the relation of the Preface to the main chapters of the work, where the path of consciousness toward self-consciousness, from bondage to freedom, was always already latent in phase one of the phenomenological motion, this description of the trajectory of Italian feminism depicts the self-consciousness of Italian feminism, which it reaches via the social-symbolic practice of the *affidamento*, always already inscribed in the first motions of the feminist consciousness of Italian second-wave feminism.[41] In their emphasis on sexual difference, the quid pro quo of the *affidamento*, or so this publication claims, early feminist groups such as Demau and Rivolta Femminile had a premonition of the stages Italian feminism had to experience necessarily and historically in order to begin to realize authentic feminist freedom. These stages included a historically necessary recognition of the power differential inscribed in the relations among women. In this scenario, the spirit of Italian feminism wanted to address power relations among women, and indeed had no choice but to do so. Therefore, the social-symbolic practice of *affidamento*, based on sexual difference, is as much a result as it is a cause of Italian feminism. As in Hegel's rigorous phenomenological system, there was for Italian feminism no other way.

Such a master narrative, where the practice of *affidamento* between two individual women seems the all-too-perfect micro-model of the macro-trajectory of Italian second-wave feminism tout court, is both fascinating and intriguing in its geometricity, but it leaves little room for that which is not reducible to its splendid mathematical rigor. This critique too, however, requires the protocols of meticulous argument, in this case a response that does not simplify matters when it comes to specificities and differences in national cultures—but this is not the place to pursue such argument. More important, it seems to me, is the candor with which Italian feminists have dealt with the uneasy problem of relations of power among women, and the pragmatic suggestions they offer—all elegantly abstracting Hegelianizations to the contrary—regarding that problem. In both areas, in how and what they do, Diotima's messages and the messages of all those women whom they represent are indispensable, so it seems to me, for a rigorous, sustained discussion of power relations among women. Whether Diotima's style and its message are useful for the international women's community in general and for the U.S. women's community in particular is an open-ended question, simply because cultural predicaments do figure in the way we address problems and in the kinds of problems we address. Yet perhaps we can learn from the pragmatics of Diotima's way of being: not silencing what there is, but speaking it; not only speaking feminist theory but performing liberatory practices among women; and, ultimately, mediating rather than entrenching oppositions, essentialist or anti-essentialist alike. In my view, these pragmatics, in which women actively attempt to be accountable to and for each other, represent a feminist future in the making.[42]

Notes

1. For information in English on the Italian women's movement I refer to Lucia Chiavola Birnbaum, *Liberazione della donna: Feminism in Italy*; Judith A. Hellman, *Journeys Among Italian Women: Feminism in Five Italian Cities*; Zygmunt G. Baranski, and Shirley W. Vinall, eds., *Women and Italy: Essays on Gender, Culture, and History*. See also Renate Holub, "Towards a New Rationality: Notes on Feminism and Current Discursive Practices in Italy," "For the Record: The Non-Language of Italian Feminist Philosophy," "The Politics of 'Diotima'," "Weak Thought and Strong Ethics: The 'Postmodern' and Feminist Theory in Italy," and "Diotima: A Western Universalist Feminist in a Multicultural World." The most complete bibliography to date is in Paola Bono and Sandra Kemp, eds., *Italian Feminist Thought: A Reader*. See also their *The Lonely Mirror: Italian Perspectives on Feminist Theory*. *Italica* 65 (1988) and *Annali d'Italianistica* 7 (1989) are issues dedicated to feminist matters.

2. Almost all of Luce Irigaray's publications have been translated into Italian. The translator is Luisa Muraro, one of the most important philosophers of Diotima and a member of the Milan Women's Bookstore Collective. Muraro is also the author of a wonderful study of medieval feminists: *Guglielma e Maifreda: Storia di una eresia femminista*. A first review in English of this volume has appeared in *Differentia* 6 (1990). Her *L'ordine simbolico della madre* is from 1991.

3. Linda Alcoff's "Cultural Feminism versus Post-Structuralism: The Identity Crisis in Feminist Theory" is a solid piece on that debate in the context of the humanities. Since then, this concept has also gained currency in the social sciences, in particular in political theory. It usually appears as "difference" next to the concept of "equality."

4. For a reexamination of the important debates in Western feminism see Juliet Mitchell and Ann Oakley, *What Is Feminism: A Re-Examination.* The term "paradox" was used by Myra Jehlen, "Archimedes and the Paradox of Feminist Criticism." It was also used, though in a much different context, by Irigaray with respect to Kant in her *Speculum of the Other Woman*, pp. 203–14.

5. Elaine Marks and Isabelle de Courtivron, eds., *New French Feminisms*, is still a good primary source for these theorists. A coherent reading of Kristeva, Cixous, and Irigaray is found in Toril Moi, *Sexual/Textual Politics.*

6. Mary Daly, *Gyn/Ecology*, and Adrienne Rich, *Of Woman Born: Motherhood as Experience and Institution*, both pursue a view of essentialism that celebrates the capacities of woman's body in its epistemological and spiritual dimensions. An entirely new body of thought on this issue has been developing under the notion of "ethics of care."

7. In her "Cultural Feminism and Poststructuralism," Linda Alcoff speaks of "cultural feminism" when discussing positions of essentialism, in that many feminists involved have emphasized the cultural potential, the epistemological and spiritual dimensions, of the essence of women—their femininity. Conversely, Alcoff cites women's voices who dissent from "cultural feminism" and from assumptions of essentialism, considering these positions as eminently "white feminist." Among these she mentions in particular women from minority groups, such as Cherríe Moraga, Barbara Smith, Audre Lourde, and bell hooks.

8. Juliet Mitchell and Jacqueline Rose, in *Feminine Sexuality: Jacques Lacan and the école freudienne*, have written powerful introductions to the issue of an undifferentiated infant sexuality. The problems inherent in the relation of subjectivity, identity, and agency are at the center of many postcolonial debates. See the excellent *Remaking History*, where the relation of "first-world" discourse to "third-world" discourse is evoked. I have discussed some of these problems in *Antonio Gramsci: Beyond Marxism and Postmodernism*, in particular on pp. 151–90, where I focus on "Gramsci's Intellectual in the Age of Information Technology."

9. What should be mentioned here is an exception to this rule, namely, Valerie Miner and Helen E. Longino, eds., *Competition: A Feminist Taboo?*, which does address issues of power among women.

10. See Barbara Christian's well-known "The Race for Theory," in *Gender and Theory: Dialogues on Feminist Criticism.*

11. I would like to thank my friend Nancie Caraway for introducing me to the work of bell hooks, especially *Talking Back: Thinking Feminist/Thinking Black, Yearning: Race, Gender, and Cultural Politics*, and *Ain't I a Woman: Black Women and Feminism.*

12. For a discussion of the humanism/antihumanism debate in the context of Italian culture see Renate Holub, "Critical Il/literacy: Humanism, Heidegger, Anti-Humanism," and *Anti-Humanism* (forthcoming).

13. Much work in a new direction is well under way. Pioneers of a new direction in Italian Studies are, among others, the circle around Fred Gardaphe and Anthony Tamburri in the Chicago Midwest Area (focusing on Italian American ethnicity issues), the journal *Differentia*, edited by Peter Carravetta, in New York (focusing on Italian philosophical culture), and the group around Lucia Birnbaum in the San Francisco Area, in particular the IRAS project at the Center for German and European Studies (focusing on social science, feminist, and historical issues.)

14. The German and French ministries for foreign affairs generally spend larger amounts for cultural affairs in the United States than the Italian Ministry for Foreign Affairs. Germany's recent selection of Harvard/MIT, Georgetown University, and the University of California System as "Centers for Excellence," accompanied by an endowment check of 15 million marks that gets channeled into the "Centers for European Studies" of each of these institutions, is a case in point. A comparative study of the "politics of cultural politics" that would

Renate Holub

take into account the economic status and foreign affairs policy (or the lack of it) of the countries involved would yield fascinating results.

15. There are many histories of Italian feminism that have been published in Italy over the last twenty years. I recommend Anna Rita Calabrò and Laura Grasso, eds., *Dal Movimento Femminista al Femminismo Diffuso*; Ginevra Conti Odorisio, *Storia dell'idea femminista in Italia*; Yasmine Ergas, *Nelle Maglie della Politica: Femminismo, istituzioni e politiche sociali nell'Italia degli anni '70*; Biancamaria Frabotta, ed., *La politica del femminismo* (1973–76); Manuela Fraire, *Teorie del femminismo*; Adriana Seroni, *La questione femminile in Italia*; and Rosalba Spagnoletti, ed., *I movimenti femministi in Italia*.

16. I am at present revising my book manuscript, *The Feminist Paradigm in Italy*, which focuses on the structure of knowledge production of Italian neofeminism from a sociological, philosophical, and historical point of view.

17. Carla Lonzi, *Sputiamo su Hegel: La donna clitoridea e la donna vaginale*. This fascinating volume is vaunted as, in its most recent edition, "a classic of most 'radical' feminism"! Mariarosa Dalla Costa, *Potere femminile e sovversione sociale*.

18. Adele Cambria, *In Principio Era Marx: Rilettura femminista della vita e dell'opera del fondatore del socialismo scientifico*; Adele Cambria, *Amore Come Rivoluzione*; Rossana Rossanda, *Anche per me: Donna, persona, memoria dal 1973 al 1986*, and her *Le altre: Conversazioni sulle parole della politica*.

19. Plato, *Symposium*, p. 327.

20. Ibid., pp. 301–49, paragraph 208.

21. That positivity is called into question by Luce Irigaray's essay on Diotima, "L'amour sorcier. Lecture de Platon. *Le Banquet*, 'Discours de Diotime,'" in *Ethique de la différence sexuelle*, pp. 27–41. This essay has appeared in English in a special issue, ed. Nancy Fraser and Sandra Bartky, on "French Feminist Philosophy" of *Hypatia*: Luce Irigaray, "Sorcerer Love: A Reading of Plato's Symposium, Diotima's Speech," *Hypatia* 3.3 (Winter 1989): 33–44, where it was introduced by Eleanor H. Kuykendall: "Introduction to 'Sorcerer Love' by Luce Irigaray." In the same issue, see a rebuttal to Irigaray's reading of Diotima by Andrea Nye, "The Hidden Host: Irigaray and Diotima at Plato's Symposium." For an assessment of Plato's feminism, see Gregory Vlastos, "Was Plato a Feminist?"

22. Franca Bimbi, Laura Grasso, Maria Zancan, Gruppo di filosofia Diotima, *Il Filo di Arianna: Letture della differenza sessuale*; and Adriana Cavarero, Cristiana Fischer, Elvia Franco, Giannina Longobardi, Veronica Mariaux, Luisa Muraro, Anna Maria Piussi, Wanda Tommasi, Anita Sanvitto, Betty Zamarchi, Chiara Zamboni, Gloria Zanardo, Diotima: *Il pensiero della differenza sessuale*. Diotima, *Mettere al mondo il mondo: Oggetto e oggettività alla luce della differenza sessuale*, and *Il cielo stellato dentro di noi: L'ordine simbolico della madre*.

23. There is no doubt that the work of Luce Irigaray plays an important role in the work of Diotima. See Renate Holub, "Irigaray in Italy." Paper presented at the UC-Santa Barbara Conference on Italian Feminism, May 1992.

24. Luce Irigaray, *Ethique de la différence sexuelle*, p. 103.

25. See Giannina Longobardi, "Donne e Potere," in *Il pensiero della differenza sessuale*, p. 110.

26. See Adriana Cavarero, "Per una teoria della differenza sessuale," in *Il pensiero della differenza sessuale*, p. 64.

27. See Giannina Longobardi, "Donne e Potere," pp. 107–11, and Adriana Cavarero, "Per una teoria della differenza sessuale," pp. 43–81.

28. Irigaray's encounters with Hegel go back to her *Speculum, de l'autre femme* (English edition *Speculum of the Other Woman*), where she takes Hegel up, on the basis of meticulous readings of the Hegelian text, on several accounts, in particular with respect to his assessment of male and female sexual organs as mentioned in his philosophy of nature, as well as with re-

spect to the famous passages in both the *Phenomenology* and in his *Philosophy of Right* concerning the possibilities and limits of women in sociality and community.

29. I refer to Marx's well-known theses on Feuerbach: "The Philosophers have only *interpreted* the world, in various ways; the point, however, is to *change* it." Karl Marx, "Ludwig Feuerbach and the End of Classical German Philosophy." Quote cited on p. 406.

30. See G. W. F. Hegel, T*he Phenomenology of Mind*, pp. 228–40.

31. See *Hegel's Philosophy of Right*, trans. and ed. T. M. Knox, pp. 105–22 on "Ethical Life"; and T*he Phenomenology of Mind*, trans. J. B. Baillie, pp. 462–505 on "The Ethical Order."

32. See *Phenomenology*, on "The Ethical Order," pp. 475–76.

33. See the addition to par. 166 of Hegel's *Philosophy of Right*, p. 263 of T. M. Knox, trans., *Hegel's Philosophy of Right*. I will quote from the German edition, where, from my point of view, the prejudice toward woman comes much more powerfully to the fore than in English: "Frauen können wohl gebildet sein, aber für die höheren Wissenschaften, die Philosophie und für gewisse Produktionen der Kunst, die ein Allgemeines fordern, sind sie nicht gemacht. Frauen können Einfälle, Geschmack, Zierlichkeit haben, aber das Ideale haben sie nicht. Der Unterschied zwischen Mann und Frau ist der des Tieres und der Pflanze: das Tier entspricht mehr dem Charakter des Mannes, die Pflanze mehr dem der Frau, denn sie ist mehr ruhiges Entfalten, das die unbestimmtere Einigkeit der Empfindung zu seinem Principe enthält" (p. 166 in G. W. F. Hegel, *Grundlinien der Philosophie des Rechts*, intro. and ed. G. J. P. J. Bolland). It is well known that Marx wrote a commentary on Hegel's *Philosophy of Right*. Hegel's text is divided into three major parts: Abstract Right, Morality, and Ethical Life. The section on "Ethical Life" is again subdivided into three parts. Marx does comment on the "Ethical Life," the third part of Hegel's philosophy of right, yet he does not concern himself with the family and civil society, although these two issues take up a considerable part of part 3. An outstanding critique of Hegel on the issue of femininity is the essay by Rosa Schena, "Die Fraulichkeit: Sulla 'cattiva coscienza' del sistema hegeliano," in Rossana De Gennaro, Silvia La Piana, Laura Marchetti and Rosa Schena, *Metafore per una filosofia della carezza: Dal femminino immaginato all'immaginazione femminile*, pp. 30–74.

34. There is a long Italian tradition of viewing Hegel from such a liberatory point of view, a point of view that stresses human rather than divine orders. Francesco De Sanctis, for instance, a progressive thinker of the mid to late nineteenth century, translated Hegel while in Bourbon prisons, in defiance of his monarchic persecutors. That people are capable of making their own history is, of course, the key concept of the extraordinary philosopher Giambattista Vico.

35. See the quote from the *Phenomenology* reproduced above, n. 32, where Hegel speaks of a premonition (A*hnung*) sedimented in the feminine. With reference to the ancient Diotima see the pages above at the beginning of the section "Diotima's Heritage," in particular the discussion of Diotima's notion of love as a *daimon*, a human activity that relates the human and the divine in the act of creation, which can also be viewed as an enactment of freedom.

36. A beautiful critique of Diotima's concept of subject and subjectivity has been proposed by Rosi Braidotti in *La ricerca delle donne*, pp. 188–203. See also Renate Holub, "Diotima: A Western Universalist Feminist in a Multicultural World," presented at the Diotima-Seminar in Verona in October 1992, in *Iride*, and Holub, "Italian Difference Theory," in *Rewriting the Canon*, ed. Maria Marotti (forthcoming).

37. See Teresa de Lauretis, "The Essence of the Triangle, or Taking the Risk of Essentialism Seriously: Feminist Theory in Italy, the U.S., and Britain," as well as her introduction to the Milan Women's Bookstore Collective, *Sexual Difference: A Theory of Social-Symbolic Practice*, pp. 1–21, in particular her response to Luisa Muraro's letter, p. 18.

38. See Elisabetta Addis, "Women's Liberation and the Law on Sexual Violence: The Italian Feminist Debate," *Socialist Review* 19.4 (1989): 114–15.

39. Ibid., p. 115.

40. Librerie delle donne di Milano, *Non credere di avere dei diritti: La generazione della libertà femminile nell'idea e nelle vicende di un gruppo di donne*; this book has recently appeared in English. See n. 37.

41. For a discussion of the relation of the Preface to the body of the phenomenology and the theoretical implications of that relation for both Hegelian and Marxist understandings of history, see Jean Hyppolite, *Studies on Marx and Hegel*, trans. and ed. John O'Neill (New York and London: Basic Books, 1969), original French ed. 1955; and his *Genesis and Structure of Hegel's Phenomenology of the Spirit*, trans. Samuel Cherniak and John Heckman (Evanston, Ill.: Northwestern University Press, 1974), original French ed. 1946. See also Alexandre Kojève, *Introduction to the Reading of Hegel: Lectures on the Phenomenology of the Spirit* (Ithaca and London: Cornell University Press, 1969), original French ed. 1947.

42. As these pages go to press, I should mention some titles of Diotima philosophers that have appeared since the writing of this essay: Adriana Cavarero, *Nonostante Platone: Figure femminili nella filosofia antica*; and Wanda Tommasi, *Simone Weil: Segni, Idoli e Simboli*. The latter publication is paradigmatic of the current direction many Diotima philosophers pursue: to focus on women philosophers in their attempt to construct a new world for women.

Works Cited

Addis, Elisabetta. "Women's Liberation and the Law on Sexual Violence: The Italian Feminist Debate." *Socialist Review* 19.4 (1989): 114–15.

Alcoff, Linda. "Cultural Feminism versus Post-Structuralism: The Identity Crisis in Feminist Theory." In *Feminist Theory in Practice and Process*, ed. Micheline R. Malson, Jean F. O'Barr, Sarah Westphal-Wihl, and Mary Wyer. Chicago and London: The University of Chicago Press, 1989. 295–327.

Baranski, Zygmunt G., and Shirley W. Vinall. *Women and Italy: Essays on Gender, Culture, and History*. New York: St. Martin's Press, 1991.

Bimbi, Franca, Laura Grasso, Maria Zancan, Gruppo di filosofia Diotima. *Il Filo di Arianna: Letture della differenza sessuale*. Rome: Cooperativa Utopia, 1987.

Birnbaum, Lucia Chiavola. *Liberazione della donna: Feminism in Italy*. Middletown, Conn.: Wesleyan University Press, 1986.

Bono, Paola, and Sandra Kemp, eds. *Italian Feminist Thought: A Reader*. Oxford: Basil Blackwell, 1991.

Braidotti, Rosi. "Commento alla relazione di Adriana Cavarero." In *La ricerca delle donne*, ed. Maria Cristina Marcuzzo and Anna Rossi-Doria. Turin: Rosenberg & Sellier, 1987. 188–203.

Calabrò, Anna Rita, and Laura Grasso, eds. *Dal Movimento Femminista al Femminismo Diffuso*. Milan: Franco Angeli, 1985.

Cambria, Adele. *In Principio Era Marx: Rilettura femminista della vita e dell'opera del fondatore del socialismo scientifico*. Milan: Sugar Edizioni, 1978.

———. *Amore Come Rivoluzione*. Milan: Sugar Edizioni, 1976.

Cavarero, Adriana. *Nonostante Platone: Figure femminili nella filosofia antica*. Rome: Editori Riuniti, 1991.

Cavarero, Adriana, Cristiana Fischer, Elvia Franco, Giannina Longobardi, Veronica Mariaux, Luisa Muraro, Anna Maria Piussi, Wanda Tommasi, Anita Sanvitto, Betty Zamarchi, Chiara Zamboni, Gloria Zanardo. DIOTIMA: *Il pensiero della differenza sessuale*. Milan: La Tartaruga, 1987.

Christian, Barbara. "The Race for Theory." In Linda Kauffman, ed., *Gender and Theory: Dialogues on Feminist Criticism*. Oxford: Basil Blackwell, 1989. 225–38.

Conti-Odorisio, Ginevra. *Storia dell'idea femminista in Italia*. Turin: Eri, 1980.

Dalla Costa, Mariarosa, and Selma James. *The Power of Women and the Subversion of the Community.* London: Falling Wall Press, 1972 (third ed. 1975).
Daly, Mary. *Gyn/Ecology.* Boston: Beacon Press, 1978.
De Gennaro, Rossana, Silvia La Piana, Laura Marchetti, and Rosa Schena. *Metafore per una filosofia della carezza: Dal femminino immaginato all'immaginazione femminile.* Preface by Maria Solimini. Brindisi: Schena Editore, 1986.
de Lauretis, Teresa. "The Essence of the Triangle, or Taking the Risk of Essentialism Seriously: Feminist Theory in Italy, the U.S., and Britain." *Differences* 1 (1989): 3–38.
Diotima. *Mettere al mondo il mondo: Oggetto e oggettività alla luce della differenza sessuale.* Milan: La Tartaruga, 1990.
———. *Il cielo stellato dentro di noi: L'ordine simbolico della madre.* Milan: La Tartaruga, 1992.
Ergas, Yasmine. *Nelle Maglie della Politica: Femminismo, istituzioni e politiche sociali nell'Italia degli anni '70.* Milan: Franco Angeli, 1986.
Frabotta, Biancamaria, ed. *La politica del femminismo (1973–76).* Rome: Savelli, 1976.
Fraire, Manuela. *Teorie del femminismo.* Milan: Edizioni Gulliver, 1978.
Hegel, G. W. F. *Grundlinien der Philosophie des Rechts,* ed. G. J. P. J. Bolland. Leiden: A.H. Adriani, 1902.
———. *The Phenomenology of Mind,* trans. and intro. J. B. Baillie. 2d ed. London: George Allen & Unwin, 1910. New York: Humanities Press, 1977.
———. *Hegel's Philosophy of Right,* trans. and ed. T. M. Knox. Oxford: Clarendon Press, 1952.
Hellman, Judith A. *Journeys Among Italian Women: Feminism in Five Italian Cities.* Oxford and New York: Oxford University Press, 1987.
Holub, Renate. *Anti-Humanism.* Lincoln: University of Nebraska Press, 1995.
———. *Antonio Gramsci: Beyond Marxism and Postmodernism.* London: Routledge, 1992.
———. "Critical Il/literacy: Humanism, Heidegger, Anti-Humanism," *Differentia* 3.4 (1989): 73–90.
———. "For the Record: The Non-Language of Italian Feminist Philosophy," *Romance Language Annual* 1 (1990): 133–40.
———. "The Politics of 'Diotima'," *Differentia* 6 (1990): 161–73.
———. "Towards a New Rationality: Notes on Feminism and Current Discursive Practices in Italy," *Discourse* 4 (1981–82): 89–107.
———. "Weak Thought and Strong Ethics: The 'Postmodern' and Feminist Theory in Italy." *Annali d'Italianistica* 9 (1991): 124–41.
hooks, bell. *Ain't I a Woman: Black Women and Feminism.* Boston: South End Press, 1981.
———. *Talking Back: Thinking Feminist/Thinking Black.* Boston: South End Press, 1989.
———. *Yearning: Race, Gender, and Cultural Politics.* Boston: South End Press, 1990.
Hyppolite, Jean. *Studies on Marx and Hegel,* trans. and ed. John O'Neill. New York and London: Basic Books, 1969.
Irigaray, Luce. "L'amour sorcier. Lecture de Platon. *Le Banquet,* 'Discours de Diotime.'" In *Ethique de la différence sexuelle.* Paris: Les Editions de Minuit, 1984. 27–41.
———. *Speculum, de l'autre femme.* Paris: Les Editions de Minuit, 1974. Trans. as *Speculum Of The Other Woman.* trans. Gillian C. Gill. Ithaca, N.Y.: Cornell University Press, 1985.
Jehlen, Myra. "Archimedes and the Paradox of Feminist Criticism." In Nannerl O. Keohane, Michelle Z. Rosaldo, and Barbara C. Gelpi, eds., *Feminist Theory: A Critique of Ideology.* Chicago: The University of Chicago Press, 1981. 189–217.
Kemp, Sandra, and Paola Bono. *The Lonely Mirror: Italian Perspectives on Feminist Theory.* London: Routledge, 1993.
Knox, T. M., ed. *Hegel's Philosophy of Right.* Oxford: Clarendon Press, 1952.
Kojève, Alexandre. *Introduction to the Reading of Hegel: Lectures on the Phenomenology of the Spirit,* as-

sist. Raymond Queneau, ed. Allan Bloom, trans. James H. Nichols, Jr. Ithaca and London: Cornell University Press, 1969. Original French ed. 1947.

Kruger, Barbara, and Phil Mariani, eds. *Remaking History*. Seattle: Bay Press, 1989.

Libreria delle donne di Milano. *Non credere di avere dei diritti: La generazione della libertà femminile nell'idea e nelle vicende di un gruppo di donne*. Turin: Rosenberg & Sellier, 1987.

Lonzi, Carla. *Sputiamo su Hegel: La donna clitoridea e la donna vaginale*. Milan: Gammalibri, 1982. Original ed., Milan: Rivolta Femminile, 1974.

Marks, Elaine, and Isabelle de Courtivron, eds. *New French Feminism*. New York: Schocken Books, 1980.

Marx, Karl. "Ludwig Feuerbach and the End of Classical German Philosophy." In Karl Marx and Frederick Engels, *Selected Works in Two Volumes*, vol. II. Moscow: Foreign Languages Publishing House, 1962. 360–406.

Milan Women Bookstore Collective. *Sexual Difference: A Theory of Social-Symbolic Practice*, trans. Patrizia Cigogna and Teresa de Lauretis. Bloomington: Indiana University Press, 1990.

Miner, Valerie, and Helen E. Longino, eds. *Competition: A Feminist Taboo?* Foreword by Nell Irvin Painter. New York: The Feminist Press at the City University of New York, 1987.

Mitchell, Juliet, and Ann Oakley. *What Is Feminism: A Re-Examination*. New York: Pantheon, 1986.

Mitchell, Juliet, and Jacqueline Rose. *Feminine Sexuality: Jacques Lacan and the école freudienne*. New York: Norton and Pantheon, 1985.

Moi, Toril. *Sexual/Textual Politics*. London and New York: Methuen, 1985.

Muraro, Luisa. *Guglielma e Maifreda: Storia di una eresia femminista*. Milan: La Tartaruga, 1985.

———. *L'ordine simbolico della madre*. Rome: Editori Riuniti, 1991.

Nye, Andrea. "The Hidden Host: Irigaray and Diotima at Plato's Symposium," *Hypatia* 3.3 (Winter 1989): 45–61.

Plato. *Symposium*. In *The Dialogues of Plato*, trans. B. Jowett, introduction by Raphael Demos. 2 vols. New York: Random House, 1937.

Rossanda, Rossana. *Anche per me: Donna, persona, memoria dal 1973 al 1986*. Milan: Feltrinelli, 1987.

———. *Le altre: Conversazioni sulle parole della politica*. Milan: Feltrinelli, 1989.

Seroni, Adriana. *La questione femminile in Italia*, ed. Enzo Rava. Rome: Editori Riuniti, 1977.

Spagnoletti, Rosalba, ed. *I movimenti femministi in Italia*. Rome: Savelli, 1976.

Tommasi, Wanda. *Simone Weil: Segni, Idoli e Simboli*. Milan: Franco Angeli, 1993.

Vlastos, Gregory. "Was Plato a Feminist," in *Times Literary Supplement*, March 17–23, 1989.

Contributors

Beverly Allen is the author of *Andrea Zanzotto: The Language of Beauty's Apprentice*, editor of *Pier Paolo Pasolini: The Poetics of Heresy*, and coeditor of *The Defiant Muse: Italian Feminist Poetry from the Middle Ages to the Present* and the forthcoming *Designing Italy: "Italy" in Europe, Africa, Asia, and the Americas*. Her recent work concerns the cultural constitution of national identity in contemporary literature in Italy and the social text of recent Italian political violence. A prizewinning translator of contemporary Italian poetry, Allen also writes for Il *Giorno* and Il *Manifesto*. She teaches at Syracuse University, where she is associate professor of French, Italian, comparative literature, and women's studies and director of the Humanities Doctoral Program.

Serena Anderlini-D'Onofrio is a writer, teacher, scholar, and critic who writes chiefly on women and their works. She has published in *Feminist Issues, Diacritics, Leggere Donna, Theater*, the *Journal of American Theater and Drama*, and the *Journal of Dramatic Theory and Criticism*. Her new articles are on women mentoring women and on representations of women's bisexuality in theater and film. Serena has taught modern drama for three years and is developing her own theoretical study of modern plays by female writers. She is also cotranslating the work of Italian feminist philosopher Adriana Cavarero. Serena lives in Cardiff, a small town near San Diego, with her dog, Eliot.

Lucia Chiavola Birnbaum is a feminist cultural historian and Affiliated Scholar of the Institute for Research on Women and Gender of Stanford University. She is the author of *Liberazione della donna: Feminism in Italy* (1986, 1988) and *Black Madonnas: feminism, religion, and politics in Italy* (1993).

Contributors

Renate Holub is the author of *Antonio Gramsci: Beyond Marxism and Postmodernism* (London: Routledge, 1992), *Anti-Humanism* (forthcoming), and *The Feminist Paradigm in Italy* (forthcoming). She is currently working on a communicative action theory ("differential pragmatics") that attempts to facilitate communication between differently traditioned groups by relying on Habermas, feminist theory, and Gramscian theory.

Giovanna Miceli Jeffries is an Italian- and U.S.-educated scholar in contemporary Italian literature and culture. She is the author of *Lo scrittore, il lavoro e la letteratura: Italo Svevo* (Work and literature: The case of Italo Svevo, 1989), and of numerous studies on contemporary Italian writers. Her current research is on the presence of food and recipes in women's writings across cultures. She is an Honorary Fellow at the Women's Studies Research Center of the University of Wisconsin, Madison.

Carol Lazzaro-Weis is a professor of Romance languages and chair of the Department of Foreign Languages at Southern University. She is the author of *Confused Epiphanies: L'abbé Prévost and the Romance Tradition* (1991), *From Margins to Mainstream: Feminism and Fictional Modes in Italian Women's Writing, 1968–1990* (1993), and numerous articles on Italian and French literature.

Maria Marotti is the author of *The Duplicating Imagination: Twain and the Twain Papers* (1990) and the editor of a collection of essays on American autobiography published in Italy. She is on the faculty in the Department of French and Italian at the University of California, Santa Barbara. She is now editing a forthcoming collection of essays entitled *The Revision of the Canon: Italian Women Writers from the Renaissance to the Present*.

Áine O'Healy is associate professor of Italian and director of the European Studies Program at Loyola Marymount University in Los Angeles. Her research interests are focused mainly on the exploration of contemporary Italian literature and cinema from the perspective of feminist theory. Her recent publications include articles on Fellini, Ferreri, Wertmüller, and Antonioni. She is currently preparing a study of the discourses of gender and sexuality in Italian cinema, and a critique of the production of Italy's new female directors.

Graziella Parati is an assistant professor at Dartmouth College. Her articles deal with twentieth-century women writers and women's autobiographical texts. She also writes on contemporary African Italian literature and on Italophone studies.

Eugenia Paulicelli is assistant professor of Italian at Queens College, City University of New York. She has written on Italian and American literary semiotics, and on Italian and English literature. She is co-editor of *Lo spreco dei significanti: L'Eros, le Morie, le Scritture* (1983). Her articles have appeared in *Carte Semiotiche*, *Differentia*, *Romance Language Annual*, and *Voices in Italian Americana*. Currently she is working on a book manuscript tentatively titled *Itinerari di scritture tra parola e immagine* (Pathways of writing between word and image).

Robin Pickering-Iazzi is associate professor of Italian at the University of Wisconsin, Milwaukee. Coauthor of the cultural reader *In Terza Pagina*, she has recently published *Unspeakable Women: Selected Short Stories Written by Italian Women during Fascism* (1993). She is currently editing a volume of essays entitled *Mothers of Invention: Critical Studies on Women in Italian Culture and Society during Fascism*, and is working on a book-length study of gender, genre, and self-representation in women's literature of the 1920s and 1930s.

Maurizio Viano teaches in the Department of Italian Studies at Wellesley College. He is the author of *A Certain Realism: Making Use of Pasolini's Film Theory and Practice* (1993) and is one of the translators, with Michael Ryan and Harry Cleaver, of Antonio Negri's *Marx Beyond Marx* (1991). He is currently writing on Italian, Italian American, and American cinema.

Index

abortion, 193–94, 212–13, 216, 221, 224, 229n; in Fascist era, 32. See also law
acculturation, 209, 218, 220, 223–25. See also culture(s)
Adam, Eve, and the Serpent (Pagels), 3
affidamento (entrustment), 246, 247–49, 252–53; critique of, xv, 121; disparity between women, xiv; practice of, xiii–xiv, 87, 119–21; as practice of care, 102; and women's responsibility, 103. See also entrustment
Africa, 221
AIDS, 159
Alcoff, Linda, 222
Aleramo, Sibilla, 24, 34, 67–68, 70
Algeria, 227n
Alice Doesn't (de Lauretis), 20
Alone of All Her Sex (Warner), 3
Althenopis (Ramondino), 80
American(s), 210–11, 226, 228; naturalized, 226
Anglo-Americans. See feminism; feminists
Anglophone. See English language; feminism; feminists
Apuleius, 4
Aristotle, 229, 230n
Armani, Giorgio, fashion of, 156; androgyny of, 176, 187; as cultural production, 166–69; and Fascism, 168–69; and Hollywood silver screen, 168; and national identity, 155, 167–68; 1970s collection, 154, 157
Athens, 229n
autobiography: ambiguity in, 66; female as distinct from male, 65; female identity in, 66; as genre, distinct from novel, 65; in Italian women writers, 67; matrilineage and patrilineage in, 67; matrilineal theme in, 78–80; omissions in, 76–77; as pact, 74; relational, 75–77; resistance to patriarchy in, 66; subversive potential of, 66
Azione Nonviolenta (Italian nonviolence movement), 7

Bachofen, J., 126
Backlash (Faludi), xxii
Bandiera rossa, 201
Barthes, Roland, 171–72, 175, 179, 184, 203–4
Bassnett, Susan, xxii
Beatles, 211
Beauty Myth, The (Wolf), xxiii
Becoming Feminine: The Politics of Popular Culture (Roman and Christian-Smith eds.), 150n
behavior, human, xxii
Bellah, Robert, 5
Berlinguer, Enrico, 229n
Beyond Feminist Aesthetics (Felski), 111
Biasin, Gian-Paolo, 100–101
bildungsroman, 69
Bimbi, Franca, 10
Birnbaum Chiavola, Lucia, xxii
black madonna(s): depictions of, 5–6, 7–8; and difference, xvii; and heretic movements, 7–8; in Italian American women's writings, 12–13; and Italian peasant Communism, 5; and liberation theology, 4; and patriarchy, 9; sites of in Italy, 4–11; in

265

Index

Song of Songs, 4, 6, 7; and subversive movements, 9; veneration and worship of, 4, 7–8, 9; in women's culture, 14; and women's resistance to patriarchy, 8
Black Madonnas (Chiavola Birnbaum), 3–10
Blum, Cinzia, 57
Boccia, Maria Luisa, 211
body, human: as site of ideology, 165–67, 177
Body in Pain, The (Scarry), 169
Bolsheviks, 221
Bono, Paola, 209, 211, 213, 216, 221, 228n
Boscagli, Maurizia, 230n
Braidotti, Rosi, 227n
Brechtian categories, 219
Brownmiller, Susan, 149n

Cagnoni, Fiora, 121–24
Cambria, Adele, 241
Campari, M. Grazia, 217
Cantarella, Eva, 126, 229n
Canzano, Rosaria, 217
capitalism, 210, 214–15, 222
Capone, Al, 226
caring and nurturing in women: defining woman's morality, 92–93; as essentialist, 104; ethics of, 98, 104; as female/feminine culture, 74, 77; as knowledge, 92; in looks, 97; in personal health, 102; politics of, 104; practices of, 92, 97–98; in self-caring, 93; sociology of, 101–2; strategies of, 94; in women's thinking, 93
Cartesian cogito, 224
Casa Virginia Woolf, 233
Casella, Angela, 88–89
Casalinghitudine (Sereni), 91, 96, 98, 100–101
castration: fear of, in Futurist interpretation, 50, 51, 54. *See also* Oedipal themes
Catholicism, 229; doctrine on women, 3
Cavarero, Adriana, 106n, 204, 211, 213, 223–25, 227n, 233, 246
Cecchini, Anna di Fausta, 212, 216
centri culturali delle donne (women's cultural centers), 221
Chambers, Iain, 31
Chesterton, G. K., 117
Chodorow, Nancy, xxiii, 90, 105n
Cialente, Fausta, 77–80, 83
clothing: and femininity, 72; genderization of, 143; and sartorial extravagance, 143; and subjectivity, 141. *See also* fashion
Cold War, 210, 215, 218, 221
Come si seducono le donne (Marinetti), 44–52, 55
Communism, 210–11
Communists, 227n; Italian Communist Party (PCI), 215, 227n, 228n, 229n; Ufficio Stampa del Gruppo Comunista del Senato, 212, 216
concrete essentials, 223–25, 227
Contemporary Italian Women Writers in Italy (Aricò, ed.), xxii
Contro la moda (Volli), 172
critical feminism: feminist accountability, 237, 249; feminist solidarity, 238; poverty of, 237–38
cuisine. *See* Italian cuisine
cultural practices: forms of, xi; as popular culture, xi; in women's gendered roles, 92
cultural productions: multinational markets, 163; and national identities, 163
Cultural Writings (Gramsci), 35
culturalism, 216, 222, 227
Culture of Consent, The (De Grazia), 39n
culture(s), 220, 222, 228n; academic/intellectual, 220; Anglo-American, 223; of dissent, 211, 216; English-speaking, 218; feminist, 211; Italian, 214, 217, 228; Italian-American, 213; of the Italian left, 218–19; media, 211; popular, 210; postmodern, 222; U.S., 210, 213, 218–20, 225
Cutrufelli, Maria Rosa, 113

Da desiderio a desiderio (Anna, Claudia, et al.), 230n
Dalla Costa, Mariarosa, 240
Dante, 218
de Certeau, Michel, 20–21
De Grazia, Victoria, 16, 39n
de Lauretis, Teresa, xiv, 20, 118, 121, 191, 216, 230n
de Vries Guido, Rachel, 12
death impulse, in Freud, 18
degli Espositi, Piera, 190–204
Democrazia Cristiana (Christian Democrats; DC), 147–48
Derrida, Jacques, 220, 229n
Derridean différance, 216
"Desire in Narrative" (de Lauretis), 191

detective novel: conventions of, 114–16; crime novel compared to, 115–18; and deduction, 117–18; female archetypes in, 110–11, 120, 126; and feminism, 109–11; *Morte a Palermo* as, 124–27; and narrative authority in women writers, 110; Oedipal myth in, 111; and postmodernism, 115–17; *Questione di tempo* as, 121–24; theme of justice in, 109, 115, 116–17, 120–23, 125–26; uses in mythology of, 124–25
di Prima, Diane, 13
difference (sexual). See sexual difference
differential power, 248
Diotima: Il pensiero della differenza sessuale (Cavarero et al.), xxii
Diotima (collective), xiii–xvi, 221, 223, 227n, 233, 240, 245; ethical system of, xv; style of, 245; thought of, 87. See also sexual difference
disparity between women. See *affidamento*
divorce, 213, 221, 224, 229n. See also Italian laws
Dominijanni, Ida, 217, 229n
Donna: Women in Italian Culture (Testaferri, ed.), xxii
La donna delinquente, la prostituta e la donna normale (Lambroso and Ferrero), 25
La donna "nera" (Macciocchi), 17–18
Donnawomanfemme, 137
Donne e scrittura (Corona, ed.)
double alterity, 247, 249
dressing up, 97; and identity, 142
Dubček, Alexander, 211

Eco, Umberto, 31, 117–18, 139
education, 210, 212, 215, 227, 229n
Electra complex, 196
English language, 211–13, 215, 218, 226, 228n; translation, 212–13
entrustment, 217, 223, 230n. See also *affidamento*
equality, 214; as neocolonial independence, 211, 222–23, 227
eros, 217; maternal, 222; women's, 224
Esquivel, Laura, 100
essentialism, 215–16; anti-essentialism, 234–36; discourses, 235; strategic, 216, 222, 228n
essentials. See concrete essentials

Family Sayings (Ginzburg), 74–76
Fanon, Frantz, 160
Fascism, 214, 215, 227n; and consent, 16–17, 20; and fashion, 168; and femininity, 17–19, 21–23, 25, 28, 32, 38; and feminism, 29, 33; and motherhood, 19, 22, 26, 29–30, 33, 37–38
fashion, 31–32, 156; and advertisement, 157, 180–81; androgyny of, 176; and the body, 177; carnivalization of, 179, 181; as codified text, 173; consumption industry of, 172; and cultural productions, 157, 165; definition and etymology of, 171; erotization of the look in, 174; essentialist reading of, 156; fascination of, 179; and the fashion industry control over, 180–81; and feminine/feminist polarization, 176; as feminist discourse, 164, 166; and feminist equality, 176–77; gender-producing practices in, 157; and ideology, 165, 172, 176, 178; as images and words, 173; and the militant feminist, 177; and national identity, 156–64; and objectification of women, 174; postmodern identity in, 179; as quotation, 167, 179, 181, 184; and social code, 176; and street fashion, 187; and subject identity, 179. See also body; Fascism
Fassbinder, Rainer Werner, 198
Felski, Rita, 104, 111
female: culture, 80; desire, 71, 75–76; Futurist definition of, distinction from woman, 43; as opposed to femininity, 67; as subject, 196, 200
female body, 32; care of, 93, 101–2; disease in, 53–54; diseased womb in Futurist interpretation, 53–54; in female autobiography, 81; Futurist cure of, 55; maternal, 200; site of difference, 177; spaces of, 177
Female Gaze: Women as Viewers of Popular Culture, The (Gamman and Marshment, eds.), 150n
feminine/feminist ethics, 234, 238; concept of freedom in, 245, 247, 251, 253; concept of mediation in, 244, 246, 248; concept of recognition in, 248
Femininity (Brownmiller), 149n
femininity/feminine: appearance of, 97; as art, 142; as beauty trap, 144; and capitalism, 144; clichés of, 95; and commodifica-

Index

tion of sex, 145; as cultural productions, xii; as defined by the church, 10; definitions of, xii; 66–67; effects on masculinity, 145; in emancipatory practices, 142; fashion glamorization of, 142; Freudian understanding of, 196; Futurists Constructions and definitions of, 44, 46–48, 58; in homemaking practices, 96; ideological construction of, xii, 198; in Italian political propaganda, 147–48; Lacanian concept of, 202; as language, 74; as masquerade, 199, 202, 205n; and money, 144; 48; in mothers, 72; and national identity, relation with, 165; patriarchal articulations of, 197; performing, xii; in personality and relational modes, 105n; as pleasure factor, 142, 148; polarization with feminism, 135; as political discourse, 147; in popular culture, 141; readings of in deconstructionist theories, 129; as resistance to patriarchy, 66, 76; as survival mechanisms, 76; as transgressive, 142; as valorization of difference, 102. See also caring and nurturing

feminism, 210, 223; Anglophone, 214–15; and Communism in Italy, 130; critical, 237–38, 249; as decentralizing force, 138; deep-fried or "alla milanese," 218; and emancipation, 119; and feminist accountability, 237, 249; French, 66; gendering theory of, 140; impact on men, xv; heretical, 76; historic femininity, difference with, 10; Italian, 210–16, 221–22, 225–26; and literature, 111–13; and poverty, 237–38; revision of, 66; and solidarity, 238. See also critical feminism

Feminism and Psychoanalitic Theory (Chodorow), 90

feminism, Italian, xii, 140, 191; and nonviolent revolution, 10

Feminism/Postmodernism (Nicholson; ed.), 149n

feminist aesthetics, 111

feminist pragmatics, 252

feminist theory (Italian). See sexual difference

feminist thought, 209–10, 213, 215; Italian, 210–16, 221–22, 225–26. See also philosophy; sexual difference

feminists: American, 212, 214–15; British, 212; European, 212; French, 212, 214, 223

femme fatale: in detective novel, 110–11
Ferreri, Marco, 190–93
Fillia (Colombo, Luigi), 43, 57
Fiorenza, Elisabeth S., 4
food (cooking), 98–102; across cultures, 100; as caring practice, 99; descriptions of, 99; and feminism, 100; and literature, 99–100; preparation of, 98; sociology of, 101–2

La forza degli italiani, xxii, 88
Foucault, Michel, 153–54
Foucault's-Pendulum (Eco), 139–40
Frabotta, Biancamaria, 113
Franco, Elvia, 213
French language, 212, 228–29n
Freud, Sigmund, 18, 27
Freudian sublimation, 217
Fuller, Margaret, 214
Fusini, Nadia, 230n
Futurism: and man's superiority, 47; and the *Problema femminile*, 44
Futurist women, 45, 58; resistance of to Futurist gendered identity, 45, 48, 49–50, 58n

Gaudy Night (Sayers), 114, 118–19
gaze, cinematic, 202
gender, 213, 218, 225, 228–29n, 230n; in detective novel, 110, 128; differences of and psychological development, 90; female, 217; grammatical, 215, 228–29n; ideology of, 197; linguistic, 228–29n; in literature (writing), 111–14; natural, 228n
giallo. See detective novel
Gift (Heidegger), 229n
Gillan, Maria, 11
Gilligan, Carol, 92–93, 95,
Gimbutas, Marija, 3
Ginzburg, Natalia, 74–76, 167
goddess: ancient culture of in Italy, 5; civilization of, 3–4; in Hebrew and Christian scriptures, 4; in Italian American women's writings, 12; in Italian folk stories, 6; as nurturing mother, 4
Godfather, The (film), 213; character, 226
Golden Ass (Apuleius), 4
Gramsci, Antonio, 16, 34–36, 215, 221, 229n
Gravenites, Diana, 12
gruppi di autocoscienza, 191–92
Gruppo Demau, 241, 253

Index

Gruppo Transizione, 221
Guglielminetti, Amalia, 26

Heat-Moon, William Least, 100
Heath, Stephen, 135
hedonism: in fashion, 178; in Italian culture, 178
Hegel, G. W. F., 233, 241, 247, 248, 252; concept of ethicality, 247, 250
Heidegger, Martin, 229n
Hellman, Stephen, 228n, 229n
Hinkson, John, 153–54
Hirsch, Marianne, 83
Hollywood, Calif., 213
holocaust: Jewish, 211; of Japan, 211
Holub, Renate, xxii
home/homemaking: control over, 101; as empowerment, 97; gendered operativity in, 101; relationship with woman, 96, 106n; rhythms of daily practices in, 106n; rituals of, 101; and roots, 106n; and self-preservation, 101; site of separateness, 97; as site of women's history, 107n; and women's creativity, 97; and woman's identity, 107n; and women's lives, 106n
How Fascism Ruled Women (De Grazia), 39n
hysteria, 54

I sapori della modernità (Biasin), 101
ideology, 210, 215, 222–23
Ideology and Image (Nichols), 173
immigrant(s), 225; female, 209–10, 220, 226; Italian 218–220, 226; new, 209–10, 220
In a Different Voice (Gilligan), 92–93
In Memory of Her (Fiorenza), 4
incestuous desire, 217–18
India, 227n
interpellation, 197–98
Irigaray, Luce, 214–15, 228n, 233–34, 245, 247, 252
Iron Curtain, 214, 221
irredentismo, 77–78
Italia futurista, 45–46
Italian cuisine, 218–20
Italian design: in fashion, 156
Italian Feminist Thought (Bono and Kemp, eds.), xxiin
Italian language, 212, 214–15, 220, 228n, 229n
Italian laws, 224, 229; on abortion, 211, 213, 221, 229n; on divorce, 211, 213, 221, 229n

Italian mothers, images and stereotypes of, 88
Italian Studies, 239–40
Italian style, 178
Italian-American. *See* culture(s); women

Jungle Fever (film), 213, 218

Kemp, Sandra,
King, 146
Klein, Kathleen, 109
Kremlin, 211

La Spina, Silvana, 124–27
Lacan, Jacques, 205n
Lady Oracle (Atwood), 162
language, 211, 214, 219–220, 228n, 229n; American English, 210, 212, 214–15, 220; English, 212–13, 215, 226; of translation, 210, 212–13, 228n. *See also* English, French, and Italian language
Language of the Goddess (Gimbutas), 3–4
Lapasini, Gabriella, 212, 216
law, 217, 222, 224–25; on sexual violence, in Italy, 130, 252. *See also* Italian laws
Lee, Spike, 213
Lejeune, Philippe, 74
lesbian: desire, 217–18; identity, 222, 227, 229n, 230n, 231n
Leto, Denise, 11
Levi, Carlo, 5
liberation discourse: critique of, 154
Libreria delle donne di Milano, 221. *See also* Milan Women's Bookstore Collective
Life/Lines: Theorizing Women's Autobiography (Brodzki and Schenck, eds.), 84
Lister, Maureen, 217
Little Italy, 226
Lonzi, Carla, 119, 211, 215, 222–23, 227n, 241
look(s). *See* fashion
Los Angeles, Calif., 211
La lupa (Verga), 5
Lyons, John, 228n
Lyotard, Jean-François, 153–54

Macchello, Lorraine, 12
Macciocchi, M. Antonietta, xxii, 17–20, 39n
Mafai, Miriam, xv, 120
Mafia, 226
male feminists, 139–40, 150

269

Index

Man When He Is a Man, A (Sarmiento), 151n
Manicomio primavera (Sereni), 91, 94–95
Manzini, Gianna, 24, 34, 38, 71–74
Mapping the Moral Domain (Gilligan), 95
Maraini, Dacia, 107n, 190–94, 196–97, 204n
Maria (mother of Christ), and femininity, 10
Marinetti, F. T., 26–27, 30, 43–57
Marini, Shara, 50
Marriage of Maria Braun, The, 198
Marxism, and sexual difference, 119–20, 228n
masculinity, social construction of, 145
maternal model, rejection of in women's writings, 68
maternity, power of, 224
matriarchy, 80–81; control over daughters in, 81; in the detective novel, 125–26; fear of in Fascism, 30; operating in patriarchy, 80
matrilineal history, 78
Men in Feminism (Jardine and Smith, eds.), 150n
mental illness/madness, in mothers, 69
mentor(s), 217–18, 220, 223
metaphysical detective novel, 115–16
Midnight's Children (Rushdie), 160
Milan Women's Bookstore Collective, 209, 213, 216–17, 222
Moi, Toril, 215
Mondello, Elisabetta, 16, 21–23
Morte a Palermo (La Spina), 124–27
Moschino, Franco, 180–81
Moscow, 215
mother(s), 213, 217, 219, 224. See also maternity
Mother/Daughter Plot, The (Hirsch), 83
mother-daughter relationships, 193
motherhood/mothering: and autistic children, 94–98; and biology, 90; desentimentalization of, 94; as experience, 68; as gendered role, 91; as institution, 69; rejection of, 193, 203. See also caring and nurturing
Movimento Femminista Romano, 221
multiculturalism, 222, 226–27
Mulvey, Laura, 205n
Muraro, Luisa, 84, 205n, 253n
Mussolini, Benito, 19, 24, 30, 226
Das Mutterrecht (Bachofen), 126
Mythologies (Barthes), 175

Name of the Rose, The/Il nome della rosa (Eco), 117–18, 139–40
Naples, 80
narrative: cinematic, 204; Oedipal, 191, 204
national identity(ies): contradictions and persistence of, 162–63; and cultural productions, 159; and the immigrant experience, 158; and national history, 160; and postcolonialism, 160; and postnational novel, 160; in postnational world, 160–61; and subject position, 158
NATO, 212, 214
Negri, Ada, 24, 34, 36–37
Negri, Magda, 216
neofemininity, 141
Nervous Condition (Dangaremba), 160
New Feminist Criticism, The (Showalter), 84
New York, N.Y., 211
Nichols, Bill, 173
Nicholson, Linda, 149n
Nietzsche, Friedrich, 53, 205n
Il nome della rosa. See The Name of the Rose
Non credere di avere dei diritti! (Collettivo), xiv, 216
Nonostante Platone (Cavarero), xxii, 106n, 204, 224
Nozzoli, Anna, 57n

Oedipal: entrustment, 217; jealousy, 200; pleasure, 203; themes, 200
Oedipus, 229n
Oedipus complex, 196; myth, 196, 199
One Hundred Years of Solitude (García Márquez), 161
L'ordine simbolico della madre (Muraro), xxii, 84, 205n

Pagels, Elaine, 3
La pantera siamo noi (Capitello, ed.), 10–14
Paris, Sherri, 109
particular individuality, 251
Pasolini, Pier Paolo, 167
Passerini, Luisa, 16, 31–32
Patchett Tramontana, Frances, 11
paternal model: attraction to in women's writings, 68, 70; rejection of, 78
patriarchy: founded in religion, 10; women's participation in, 80
PCI (Italian Communist Party), xiv. See also Communism

Penelope, 106n
Il pensiero debole (Vattimo, ed.), 58n, 149
Pensiero debole, and Italian postmodernism, 138
Persephone, 5
Phenomenology (Hegel), 244, 249, 253
philosophy, 215–16, 220, 227. See also feminist thought
Philosophy of Right (Hegel), 244, 250
Pickering-Iazzi, Robin, 39n
Pieces of Song (di Prima), 13
Piussi, Annamaria, 213
Pleasure of the Text, The (Barthes), 204
Poetics of Women's Autobiography, A (Smith), 83
politics, 214; in 1970s Italy,166–67; pertaining to politics, 211–13, 215, 217, 219, 221, 225, 227, 228n, 229n, 230n. See also socialism
Pope, the, 221
popular culture: and conservative backlash, 137; interpretation of, 140–41
postmodernism, 153–54; in Pensiero debole, 138
postnational novel: forms of, 161; and postcolonial identities, 160; representation of national identities in, 161–62
postnationality: definitions of, 161; and postmodern, 161
Practices of Everyday Life, The (de Certeau), 20
Prague Spring, 211, 215
PrairyErth (Heat–Moon), 100
prophetess, prechristian, 7

Le quattro ragazze Wieselberger (Cialente), 77
Questione di tempo (Cagnoni), 121–24

Ramondino, Fabrizia, 80–82
Re, Lucia, 58n
recipes: as gendered form of discourse, 107n; literality of, 99; reproducibility of, 106n. See also food (cooking)
Reddy, Maureen, 109
Reproduction of Mothering, The (Chodorow), 90
rights, 209, 216–18; civil, 213; of divorce and abortion, 221, 224, 229n; legal, 222; subject of, 224
Rio de Janeiro, 211
Ritratto in piedi (Manzini), 71–72, 74
Rivolta femminile, 241, 253
Robert, Enif, 46–47, 52–56

Roman Catholic Church, 213
Romano, Rose, 12
Rome, 226
Rosà, Rosa, 47–50
Rossanda, Rossana, xv, 241

Sanger, Margaret, 214
Sapir, Edward, 228n
Sappho, 229n
Sassafras, Cypress & Indigo (Shange), 100
Satanic Verses, The (Rushdie), 160
Sayers, Dorothy, 114, 118
Scarry, Elaine, 169
Sciascia, Leonardo, 116
seduction of women: in Futurist interpretation, 46; in Futurist writings, 45
Sereni, Clara, 90–96, 98–99, 102–4
Seroni, Adriana, 212–13, 216
sex, 213, 216–17, 222, 225, 227, 230n; bisexual, 230n; and female sexedness, 223–24; homo- and heterosexual, 222; sexed bodies, 223; sexual preference, 222; and transsexualism, 223, 225–26. See also eros
Sex, Art, and American Culture (Paglia), xxii, 187
Sexual Difference (Collettivo), xxii, 216, 218, 222, 230n
sexual difference, theory of in Italian feminist thought, xii–xiv, 119–21, 140, 233, 241, 247, 252; critique of, xv, 120; and female justice, 120–21; in love relationship with man, xvi; separatism, xv; in symbolization, xiv
sexual violence. See law
sexuality, female, 193–204; in the mother, 73, 193–95
sexualization, of voting process (in Italy), xv
Seyla, Benhabib, 93
Shange, Ntozake, 100
Sharp, Geoff, 153
Showalter, Elaine, 67
Silverman, Kaja, 141–42
situadedness, 210–12, 214, 217, 221–23, 225
Smith, Sidonie, 83
social-symbolic practice, 241, 244, 249, 253
socialism, 210–11, 214–15, 219, 221–22, 227, 228n, 229n
La società trasparente (Vattimo), 44, 138
Socrates, 242
Somalia, 228n
Song of Songs, 6

Index

South Africa, 227n
Soviet Union, 227n; regime, 215
Soysal, Yasemin, 161
spaghetti, 220, 226
Speculum of the Other Woman (Irigaray), 228n
Spivak, Gayatri, 216
Sposa e madre esemplare (Meldini), 25
Sputiamo su Hegel (Lonzi), 119
Stalin, Joseph, 215
Stanton, Domna, 215
Stone, Sandy, 225
Storia di Piera (film), 190–204
Students of *novanta*: demands of, 9–10; revolt of, 9
Sulla soglia (Manzini), 71, 73
Symposium (Plato), 241–43; mediation in, 243
Système de la mode (Barthes), 171–72, 175

Tabù e coscienza (Nozzoli), 57n
Technologies of Gender (de Lauretis), 20
theory, definition of, 136
Togliatti, Palmiro, 229n
Transizione, 233
Trieste, 77

Ufficio Stampa. *See* Communists
Unbearable Lightness of Being, The (Kundera), 161
United States, 209–10, 212–14, 217–20, 222, 224–26, 227n
universal individuality, 251
Unspeakable Women (Pickering-Iazzi), 39n

Vattimo, Gianni, 44, 138–39
Vegetti Finzi, Silvia, 230n
Vendler, Helen, 111–12
Un ventre di donna (Marinetti and Robert), 49, 52, 55–56
Verdicchio, Pasquale, 228n
Verga, Giovanni, 5
Verona, 223
Violi, Patrizia, 215, 228n
"Visual Pleasure and Narrative Cinema" (Mulvey), 205n
Volli, Ugo, 172

Warner, Marina, 3
Weil, Simone, 216
Willet, John, 219
Williams, Raymond, 162–63
Williams, Selase, 215, 229n
Woman, A (Aleramo), 67–68, 70
woman/women, 209, 213, 216–17, 219, 221, 222–25, 227, 228n, 229n; androgyny of, 49, 68–69; centrality of in Italian culture, 5; and cultural centers, 221; definition of, in Futurism, 43; and eros, 224; in Futurist manifestos, 43; gay and straight, 222; and groups, 221; Italian, 218, 221, 223–24, 227; Italian American, 212; and love relationship with man, xvi; as modeled on Futurist male, 48–49; moral judgment, 93; morality and psychological development, 92; multiple roles in, 4; peaceful values of, 7; and political equality, 211; political irresponsibility, 103; pregnant, 224; and relations, 223; silence of, 72–73; vernacular culture of, 8; victimization, politics of, 103; and vote, 221; U.S., 222; and women's movement, 222, 213, and women's studies, 218
woman-mother, in Italian culture, 88–89; images of, in Fascist ideology, 17–20, 26–27, 32, 34, 37
Women and Italy (Baranski, ed.), xxii
women writers, 210; in Fascist era, and the daily press, 34–39
Women's Bookstore of Milan, 233, 241, 252–53
women's press, in Fascist era, 20–24
Women's Review of Books, 218
Woolf, Virginia, 222
World War I, 211
World War II, 227n

Year 2000, The (Williams), 162

Zuffa, Grazia, 121